EVALUATION AND MANAGEMENT OF EATING DISORDERS

ANOREXIA, BULIMIA, AND OBESITY

EVALUATION AND MANAGEMENT OF EATING DISORDERS

ANOREXIA, BULIMIA, AND OBESITY

Edited by

Kristine L. Clark, MS, RD
La Crosse Exercise and Health Program

Richard B. Parr, EdD
Central Michigan University

William P. Castelli, MD
Framingham Heart Study

Life Enhancement Publications
Champaign, Illinois

RJ
399
.C6
E93
1988

Library of Congress Cataloging-in-Publication Data

Evaluation and management of eating disorders.

(La Crosse exercise and health series)
Includes bibliographies.
1. Obesity in children.   2. Eating disorders in
children.   3. Children—Nutrition.   4. Exercise for
children.   I. Clark, Kristine L., 1953-   .
II. Parr, Richard B.   III. Castelli, William P.
IV. Series. [DNLM: 1. Anorexia Nervosa—in adolescence.
2. Anorexia Nervosa—in infancy & childhood.   3. Appetite
Disorders—in adolescence.   4. Appetite Disorders—in
infancy & childhood.   5. Obesity—in adolescence.
6. Obesity—in infancy & childhood.   WS 130 E92]
RJ399.C6E93   1988   616.85'2   87-26195
ISBN 0-87322-911-8

Developmental Editor: Sue Wilmoth, PhD
Production Director: Ernie Noa
Assistant Production Director: Lezli Harris
Copy Editor: Peter Nelson
Assistant Editor: Julie Anderson
Typesetter: Sandra Meier
Text Design: Keith Blomberg
Text Layout: Denise Peters
Printed By: Braun-Brumfield

ISSN: 0894-4261
ISBN: 0-87322-911-8

Copyright © 1988 by Kristine L. Clark, Richard B. Parr, and William P. Castelli

All rights reserved. Except for use in a review, the reproduction or utilization
of this work in any form or by any electronic, mechanical, or other means, now
known or hereafter invented, including xerography, photocopying and record-
ing, and in any information retrieval system, is forbidden without the written
permission of the publisher.

Printed in the United States of America

10 9 8 7 6 5 4 3 2 1

Life Enhancement Publications
A Division of Human Kinetics Publishers, Inc.
Box 5076, Champaign, IL 61820
1-800-342-5457
1-800-334-3665 (in Illinois)

1668271 3

Contributors

Mary E. Allen, MS, OTR   Associate Director of Occupational Therapy, University of Wisconsin Hospital, Madison, Wisonsin

Kristine Larson Clark, MS, RD   Unit Director, Nutrition Services, College of Health, Physical Education and Recreation, University of Wisconsin, La Crosse, Wisconsin

Barry A. Franklin, PhD   Division of Cardiovascular Disease, William Beaumont Hospital, Royal Oak, Michigan

John P. Foreyt, PhD   Department of Medicine, Baylor College of Medicine, Houston, Texas

Sharon W. Foster, PhD   Clinical Instructor, Department of Pediatrics, Staff Psychologist, General Pediatrics and Teenage Clinic, University of Wisconsin, Madison, Wisconsin

Gordon M. Giles, BA, DipCOT, OTR   Clinical Director, Transitions Recovery Program, Berkeley, California

G. Ken Goodrick, PhD   Department of Medicine, Baylor University College of Medicine, Houston, Texas

Judith Bograd Gordon, PhD   Coordinator, Masters Program in Gerontology, University of New Haven, West Haven, Connecticut. Lecturer, Department of Psychiatry and Mid-Career Fellow, Bush Center of Child Development and Social Policy, Yale University, New Haven, Connecticut

Ann C. Grandjean, MS, RD, EdD   Instructor, Sports Medicine Program, Orthopedic Surgery and Rehabilitation Department, University of Nebraska Medical Center. Associate Director, Swanson Center for Nutrition, Inc., Omaha, Nebraska

Joan Hornak, EdD   Associate Professor, Counseling Center, Central Michigan University, Mt. Pleasant, Michigan

Craig Johnson, PhD   Associate Professor of Psychiatry, Co-Director of Eating Disorders Program, Northwestern University Medical School, Chicago, Illinois

Christin Lewis, PhD   Research Associate, Eating Disorders Program, Northwestern University Medical School, Chicago, Illinois

Betty Lucas, MPH, RD   Nutritionist, Child Development Mental Retardation Center, University of Washington, Seattle, Washington

M. Joan Mallick, RN, PhD

Janet H. McClintock, MS, MSN   Clinical Nurse Specialist, University of Wisconsin Hospital, Madison, Wisconsin

Elizabeth S. Ohlrich, MD   Co-Director, Eating Disorders Program, University of Wisconsin Hospital and Clinics; Department of Pediatrics, University of Wisconsin Medical School, Madison, Wisconsin

Richard B. Parr, EdD   Department of Health Education, Central Michigan University, Mt. Pleasant, Michigan

Judith Reinke, MPH, RD, MSSW   Family Counselor and Crisis Intervention Case Manager, Briarpatch, Madison, Wisconsin

Ellyn Satter, RD, MS, MSSW   Department of Psychiatry, Jackson Clinic, Madison, Wisconsin

Stacey Steinberg, BA   Research Associate, Eating Disorders Program, Northwestern University Medical School, Chicago, Illinois

John N. Stephenson, MD   Co-Director, Eating Disorders Program, University of Wisconsin Hospital and Clinics; Department of Pediatrics, University of Wisconsin Medical School

Alice L. Tobias, EdD, RD   Director of Program in Dietetics, Food, and Nutrition, Department of Health Services, Herbert H. Lehman College, CUNY

Contents

Series Preface

On behalf of the chapter authors and editors and Human Kinetics Publishers, it is my pleasure to welcome you to this book. *Evaluation and Management of Eating Disorders: Anorexia, Bulimia, and Obesity* is one of a collection of eight books of the La Crosse Exercise and Health Series, offered by Life Enhancement Publications of Human Kinetics Publishers. The series is an outgrowth of various topics of the annual symposiums of the La Crosse Exercise and Health Program of the University of Wisconsin-La Crosse. Offered by the program's Educational Services Unit, these symposiums are directed to professionals in athletic training and rehabilitation, cardiac rehabilitation, corporate and hospital-based fitness and wellness programs, nutrition, and sports medicine. The individual editors of each book in the series were initially responsible for developing the topics and presenters for that specific symposium.

We intend for these books to provide readers with both theoretical and practical information specific to their fields of interest. Symposium topics and speakers, and consequently chapter authors, have been chosen to provide "hands-on" information to assist practitioners. The symposiums and the resulting books are intended to truly assist you in the everyday practice of your profession. Cognitive knowledge applied in both theory and practice to daily problems and concerns is the ultimate goal of the La Crosse symposiums and book series. It is truly the hope of the symposium presenters and chapter authors, of the book editors, and of myself that each reader finds the information provided appropriately serves their daily professional needs.

On behalf of the chapter authors and book editors, I thank Human Kinetics Publishers of Champaign, Illinois, for its involvement as the La Crosse Series publisher. Over the past 10 years Human Kinetics has become a leading publisher in the field of health and physical fitness, and we are pleased and appreciative for its commitment to this book series.

Philip K. Wilson, EdD
Series Editor

Preface

Researchers, clinicians, and the general public are deeply concerned about obesity's complex and often subtle relationship to disease. As researchers, we question our methods and findings; as clinicians, we doubt our ability to treat obesity effectively. Perhaps the best introduction to this book, then, is a review of the historical context of research into obesity and disease.

Obesity's role in disease has long been researched in American medicine. In early epidemiological studies, such as the Framingham study (Ashley & Kannel, 1974), as people gained weight, the incidence of malignancy increased for a host of risk factors. Gordon and Kannel (1976) showed that the greater an individual's weight per inch of height, the greater the risk for cardiovascular disease, especially coronary heart disease and stroke.

As a result of such findings, researchers focused on multivariate analyses of risk factors for cardiovascular disease (e.g., high cholesterol level, high blood pressure, high or low glucose level, high uric acid level) and obesity's relationship to these factors. They concluded that the changes that obesity produced in these risk factors explained the relationship between obesity and cardiovascular disease.

Many at this time thought that if an individual became obese but exhibited no changes in risk factors, he or she would not be at any greater risk for cardiovascular disease than before the weight gain. Such individuals became known as "obesity-per-se" people (few who gain weight, however, fall into this category).

As researchers followed the obesity-per-se persons of the Framingham study, a new dimension emerged. Helen Hubert (Hubert, Feinleib, McNamara, & Castelli, 1983) demonstrated with 26-year follow-up data that obesity became an independent risk factor on multivariate analysis for both morbidity and mortality after 8 years in men and 14 years in women.

Again, the research focus changed. Investigators conducted total death studies from the Framingham data (Andres, 1980), not tracing pathological mechanisms to death, but rather pooling all deaths. No discrimination was made according to cause of death, but certain researchers did correlate death and obesity. When they did this using the nondiscriminatory Framingham data, they discovered a U-shaped curve: Thin people were found to be dying earlier, too. Many concluded that skinny people were "dropping like flies," and the Metropolitan Life Insurance Company even raised its ideal-weight standards (1983).

Intrigued by this U-shaped curve, Garrison and Castelli (1985) examined the data and causes of deaths, focusing on the two ends of the curve. He found that for obese people, the most frequent cause of death was cardiovascular disease, whereas for thin people it was cancer.

Garrison and Castelli (1985) also noted that nonsmoking men who exceed the 1959 Metropolitan ideal-weight figures (Metropolitan, 1959) by more than 10% are 4 times more likely to die over a 30-year span than nonsmoking men of ideal weight. Men 20% over ideal weight will die at 5 times the rate of men at ideal weight. Garrison and Castelli further observed that male smokers at ideal weight will die at 9 times the rate of male nonsmokers at ideal weight; and correlatively, that male smokers 10% or 20% over the 1959 Metropolitan ideal-weight figures will die at rates 10 and 11 times, respectively, those of nonsmokers.

Clearly, combined with smoking or not, obesity is a considerable risk factor. The conclusion seems so simple. Yet students of obesity must realize that the implications of the Garrison and Castelli study are anything but simple. The campaign for a slim America has left its casualties. If the therapy of choice for obesity is weight loss, then we must recognize its side effects. Some—anorexia and bulimia—are symptomatically obvious. Others are subtler: Who knows the toll of a lost sense of self-esteem or well-being?

Should we continue to promote a therapy that places the price of losing weight out of some people's reach? I hope we who study and treat obesity will soon find a solution to the problem of promoting normal weight without diminishing self-worth. *Evaluation and Management of Eating Disorders: Anorexia, Bulimia, and Obesity* can help us all become more sensitive to the physiological and psychological benefits and costs of weight loss.

William P. Castelli

References

Andres, R. (1980). Effect of obesity on total mortality. *International Journal of Obesity*, **4**, 381-386.

Ashley, E.W., & Kannel, W.B. (1974). Relation of weight change to changes in atheogenic traits: The Framingham study. *Journal of Chronic Diseases*, **27**, 103-114.

Garrison, R.J., & Castelli, W.P. (1985). Weight and thirty-year mortality of men in the Framingham Study. *Annals of Internal Medicine*, **103**, 1006-1009.

Gordon, T., & Kannel, W.B. (1976). Obesity and cardiovascular disease: The Framingham study. *Clinics in Endocrinology and Metabolism*, **5**, 367-375.

Hubert, H.B., Feinleib, M., McNamara, P.M., & Castelli, W.P. (1983). Obesity as an independent risk factor for cardiovascular disease: A 26-year follow-up of participants in the Framingham heart study. *Circulation*, **67**, 968-977.

Metropolitan Life Insurance Company. (1959). New weight standards for men and women. *Stat. Bull. Metrop. Life Insur. Co.*, **40**, 1-4.

Metropolitan Life Insurance Company. (1983). *1983 Metropolitan height and weight tables for men and women*. New York.

Part I

Social Environment: The Family

Obesity is a multidimensional disorder requiring dieting, exercise, and behavioral modification as primary modes of intervention. Family patterns of exercise and eating play significant roles in the etiology and management of obesity in children. This section discusses the role of the family in establishing psychosocial patterns that lead to childhood obesity.

1

Chapter 1

Feeding in the Family Context

Ellyn Satter

Eating is always bound up with family relationships, especially the mother-child relationship. The health worker who intervenes with feeding must be aware that interventions can have a major, and sometimes unpredictable, impact on the feeding relationship. Conversely, the way the family functions determines how it institutes the interventions of a health worker.

Because eating is such a sensitive barometer of emotional state and parent-child interaction (Ainsworth & Bell, 1969), psychosocial distortions often first become apparent in the form of eating/feeding problems. A disruption in eating is a difficulty that can be seen and named when underlying feelings and interactions are more difficult to isolate and recognize.

We health workers cannot always be expected to change the way an individual reacts or a family operates. However, in helping families, we must do all we can to be sure our interventions are realistic and their impact positive (or, at worst, neutral) for each family. We should also accumulate enough information and have enough sensitivity to recognize distorted situations and to encourage families to seek further help when necessary.

With these goals in mind, this paper will first describe the interactions and implications of the feeding relationship. Secondly, it will sketch out in more detail the family context in which the interactions take place. Finally, it will briefly outline (and delimit) the health worker's role in intervening with feeding and, thereby, with the feeding relationship overall.

The Feeding Relationship

The feeding relationship is the complex of interactions that take place between parent and child as they engage in food selection, ingestion, and regulation behaviors. Successful feeding demands a caretaker who trusts and depends on information coming from the child about timing, amount, preference, pacing, and eating capability (Ainsworth & Bell, 1969; Brody, 1956). Feeding is successful when the parent attends to the child's rhythms and signals of hunger and satiety, works to calm him, and develops mechanisms of feeding that are effective with the child's particular emotional makeup and feeding skills and limitations (Satter, 1984).

The Broader Significance of the Feeding Relationship

In the positive feeding relationship, mother and child develop synchrony: they get to know each other, and are successful with each other. The child learns some important lessons from the mother-child interaction. He gains awareness of what he is feeling, knowledge that he is capable of conveying what he wants, and trust that someone will be willing to provide for those wants (Bruch, 1973; Palazzoli, 1978).

On the other hand, if the caretaker is consistently inaccurate or domineering about feeding, parent and child develop an asynchronous relationship: they are out of rhythm with each other and, therefore, are unsuccessful. This is to the detriment of both. The parent is confronted with a dissatisfied or overly passive baby. The child grows up confused and anxious about his needs, because his wants are seldom accurately identified and gratified and often conflict with what his mother seems to want to give him. As a consequence, he gains little in a sense of effectiveness: he feels that what he gets is independent of anything coming from him.

Social and emotional learning is especially powerful with feeding. Parent and child spend much of their time together in the first year with feeding. Feeding is the most concrete demonstration to the child during that early time of his parent's attitudes toward him and expectations of him.

The things health workers teach about feeding and growth can have a major impact on the feeding relationship. Health workers who dictate amounts of formula, feeding schedules, and slavish adherence to growth charts can interfere with a parent's ability to tune in on her infant's signals. Depending on the predisposition of the parent, this can be more or less disruptive. The healthy parent will evaluate and eventually discard advice that interferes with her ability to mother. The domineering parent will use the advice to reinforce her already overcontrolling method of operating. The neglectful parent is unlikely to be affected by advice of any kind.

The Child's Increase in Initiative

Bruch (1973) and Palazzoli (1978) have underscored the importance of the parent's role in helping the child distinguish his body cues. They speculate that an infant is aware only of positive and negative sensations. He cannot at first distinguish either their source or solution. It is up to the sensitive caretaker to sort it out for him in a reasonably consistent fashion by identifying the child's problem and offering the appropriate solution. Without fairly accurate responses from the parent, the child does not gain self-awareness and remains confused about sensations.

As a child grows, he increases in self-knowledge and initiative. Positive, helpful feeding practices support a child's developmental tasks at any age. In infancy the child's task is to develop trust. During this stage, the parent is appropriately supportive and accepting of the child's demands and applies herself to satisfying those demands.

During the toddler phase, the child becomes oppositional as he seeks limits from his parents. These limits, and his contrariness, allow him to experience himself as a separate person. Appropriate parenting during this time demands the ability to set reasonable limits—to give the child autonomy and support, but also to be clear that there are boundaries. Parents who can accept a child's aggression and initiative help him to avoid later psychosocial disorders, especially in the realm of eating (Palazzoli, 1978).

During the preschool and early school-age years, the child becomes cooperative, having established a firm sense of himself. Feeding continues to provide structure as he grows in skills, in ability to participate in the feeding process, and in sense of self. It isn't until the adolescent phase that the feeding relationship is again put to the test, as the adolescent pushes for more autonomy at the same time that he seeks reasonable and supportive limits from his parents.

Nutrition and the Feeding Relationship

Optimal nutrition depends on the development of a positive relationship between parent and child. Children eat best when parents recognize and respond appropriately to their needs.

Slow-Growing and "At-Risk" Children.   Based on their observations with failure-to-thrive children, Pollitt and Wirtz (1981) surmised that maternal behaviors during feeding have an impact on the child's ability to ingest food and on his subsequent weight gain. Mothers, they observed, worked against a smooth feeding with such activities as frequently taking the nipple from the infant's mouth, continuously rotating or moving the nipple, and grooming the baby's body. Babies of mothers who were too active ate less than babies of mothers who provided a more smooth, continuous feeding.

Wright, Fawcett, and Crow (1980) have found that mothers tend to be more active in feeding infants of low birthweight. The greater the mother's response, the less the small infant consumes, possibly because the activities are time consuming and the baby runs out of energy. Certain behaviors indicate that some mothers ignore infant behavior in feeding, such as pushing the nipple into the baby's mouth even when he is looking the other way or has his mouth closed.

It appears that feeding practices and responsiveness to infant cues are factors in failure to thrive. It has been hypothesized that neglected institutionalized infants fail to do well because of some psychologically induced deficit in absorption or metabolism (Bruenlin, Desai, Stone, & Swilley, 1983). The hypothesis assumes they eat enough but simply cannot metabolize their food appropriately. However, Whitten, Pettit, and Fischhoff (1969) found poor food intake to be a mediating factor. Caretakers failed to take time with infants to interpret their satiety cues and to be sure they had finished feeding.

Ainsworth and Bell (1969) have found that certain behaviors are likely to produce underfed, underweight infants. A parent who underfeeds terminates feeding at pauses, rather than giving the baby time to finish the feeding. Also, such a parent interprets the baby's fussiness as satiety, rather than soothing fussiness and going on with the feeding.

Field (1977) has found that feeders tend to be more active with both premature and postmature babies. She has surmised that the "at risk" designation, and parental perception of it, acts as a stimulus to parents to increase their attempts to promote food intake. Pressure tactics include jiggling the nipple (and the baby) and forcing the nipple into the baby's mouth. Although Field did not monitor food intake, the reports above indicate that pressuring an at-risk infant to increase food intake, and thus growth, is a tactic that can backfire.

Older Children.   The parent-child relationship appears to have an effect on the food intake of older children as well. Kinter, Boss, and Johnson (1981) found poorer quality diets in dysfunctional families—families that had too much control, unresolved conflict, organization, and cohesiveness. In some earlier studies, Hinton, Chadderdon, Eppright, and Wolins (1962), found that the diets of teenage girls decreased in quality as family interference and criticism related to eating increased.

The Influence of Parent-Child Interactions

A child who is consistently frustrated or thwarted in feeding or who has food forced upon him when he doesn't want it comes to associate hunger not with pleasurable anticipation, but with anxiety. If a parent consistently overlooks, ignores, or overrules cues coming from the child, the child does not learn to experience, interpret, and trust his own reality. He does not know or respect his own signals of food regulation and learns to regulate feeding based on the interaction with his parent. Eventually he becomes embarrassed at his needs.

Bruch (1973) observed the anorexic and morbidly obese children of domineering and oversolicitous parents and has commented that it seems that to them, their ability to regulate the amount they eat lay outside of them. This ability to regulate can be so displaced as to cause the child to over- or undereat.

Undereating. A previous section described interactions that can decrease food intake or interfere with nutritional quality of the diet. A parent can be so insensitive to a child's feeding cues that he doesn't get enough to eat. This insensitivity can take the form of being overbearing. The mother who complains that her child "simply won't eat unless he is forced" is revealing a great deal about her own need to dominate and her child's need to defend himself against her pressure. There must be considerable intensity on both sides to overshadow a child's need for food. At times that pressure will cause the child to overeat. At other times the child will fight back, and the struggle can be vehement enough that it appears to interfere with food intake and growth.

Overeating. The parent-child interaction can be a factor in a child's overeating as well. Some mothers treat too broad a spectrum of cues and signals as indicating hunger. Other mothers simply overstuff their babies with the intent of making them sleep a long time, thus demanding little attention (Ainsworth & Bell, 1969).

In either case, the pressure to overeat must be considerable and continuous to overwhelm a child's food regulation abilities. Children have the capability of compensating for fluctuations and errors in food intake. If they are overfed one time, they can simply spit up, wait longer to get hungry for the next feeding, or eat less the next feeding or the next day.

Birch, Marlin, Kramer, and Peyer (1981) have observed that too-fat children receive less appropriate attention from their mothers in the feeding situation. Obese children, as opposed to normal-weight children, are more demanding of their mothers' attention, the mothers are less responsive to their overtures, and the mothers use less appropriate interventions to keep them on task with their eating.

Mellin (1982) has said that a pattern of overeating reactive to emotional distress and subsequent weight gain is predominant among obese adolescents.

One can hypothesize that social and emotional neediness becomes translated to physical hunger in obese children. This is a hypothesis that is supported only by circumstantial evidence: Disruptions in food regulation are well-documented correlates of emotional disequilibrium (American Psychiatric Association, 1980); adults misuse food as a way of coping with stress or escaping conflict.

In actuality, however, it may be that there is a more concrete connection between poor parenting and a child's failure to regulate body weight. The overindulged child may get food instead of limits. The neglected child may get attention only during feeding. The scapegoated child may have so many negative feelings that they overwhelm his feeding cues.

Some parents withhold food from their children in an attempt to keep them slim. This is a tactic that can backfire. Restrained eating and habitual, virtually constant dieting appear to help set up the pattern of using food to cope. Compared with "normal" eaters, people of all weights who are chronic dieters tend to overeat, rather than undereat, in response to stress and to be more susceptible to external cues in regulating their eating (Herman & Polivy, 1979). If a child has been raised with restrained feeding, he is likely to continue these patterns and may also show periods of pronounced weight gain throughout life (Bruch, 1973).

Parental Concern About Obesity.   Parents today are concerned about overfeeding and producing too-fat children. Some are so concerned, in fact, that they withhold food from children or become fearful of totally gratifying their hunger.

This concern is potentiated when parents are anxious or ambivalent about their own eating. Obese women who are chronic dieters prefer thin babies and are concerned about preventing obesity in their children. They are more likely to use external cues, such as time and quantity, for regulating feeding. They also tend to overinterpret hunger in their babies (they feed, rather than looking for other causes of fussiness), but spend less time feeding (Wooley & Wooley, 1979). Thus, their children are frustrated twice: once when they are induced to eat when they don't really want to, and again when they are made to stop before they are completely satisfied. The pressure that obese parents get from health workers to prevent obesity in their children probably simply gets passed on to the children in the form of increased pressure on the child's eating.

Feeding as a Mirror of the Relationship

The type of interaction displayed in the feeding situation is typical of the parent-child relationship overall. Birch et al. (1981) have found that feeding interactions between child and mother are very similar to play interactions. Ainsworth and Bell (1969) have found that mothers who allowed their babies to actively participate in feeding scored higher on variables of the quality of maternal care—realistic perception of the baby, delight in the baby, acceptance of the baby, appropriateness of the interaction, amount of physical contact, and effectiveness of response to crying.

Ainsworth and Bell (1969) have observed infant attachment behavior at 12 months in the same mother-baby pairs they had observed at 3 months. Appropriate attachment behaviors at 12 months include expressing a clear preference for, and attraction to, the mother; ability to explore in a strange situation and to use the mother as a secure base for explorations; and discomfort at separation from the mother. Babies of high-scoring and supportively feeding mothers show a greater number of appropriate attachment behaviors.

Intervening in the Feeding Relationship

The health worker can inadvertently put considerable pressure on the feeding relationship in the course of offering nutrition or feeding advice. The parent may interpret inquiries about the pattern of eating as pressure to get the baby on a schedule. Educating the parent about nutrition may induce her to use pressure tactics to get her child to eat his vegetables, for instance. Presenting tactics of childhood obesity prevention to the obese mother may increase her ambivalence about feeding and encourage her to try to withhold food from her child.

It is essential that any interventions with childhood feedings be made with an awareness of the overall impact on the feeding relationship. Parents should be taught to be sensitive to a child's feeding cues, to avoid trying to regulate quantity, and to provide a positive feeding environment (Satter, 1983).

Family Context

The feeding relationship, to be fully understood, must be put in the context of the overall family interaction. The way families operate has a major impact on feeding. Much of the work with adolescent eating in the family context has been done with anorexia nervosa. Some study has concerned obesity, bulimia, and bulimic syndrome.[1]

Observations indicate that certain types of family organization characterize the eating-disordered family. Minuchin (Minuchin et al., 1975; Minuchin, Rosman, & Baker, 1978) has said these characteristics include overprotectiveness, enmeshment, rigidity, lack of conflict resolution,

---

[1]A major difficulty in the study of eating disorders is the variety of terminology used to describe clinical entities. In this article, bulimia is defined as gorging, or overeating compulsively on food. Bulimic syndrome includes the component of purging, which can include vomiting, laxative abuse, starvation, and exhausting exercise.

involvement of the child in diffusing parental conflict, and overconcern with physical well-being or eating.

Bruch (1973) has commented on the "intense involvement" of her obese patients with their families. Both she and Palazzoli (1978) have observed high levels of unresolved conflict in parents of eating-disordered patients.

Anderson (cited in Shiner, 1980) reviewed data on 50 families over a 4-year period. His data indicate that 60% of families fit Minuchin's descriptions of rigidity and enmeshment. Twenty percent of the families displayed the opposite extremes—disengagement, chaos, and disorganization—and 20% of the families were classified as "normal."

Strober (1981) contrasted anorexic patients who had bulimic syndrome to those who did not and has noted that the family environments of the former feature significantly greater conflict and negativity, less cohesion, and less structure than those of the latter. Kinter et al. (1981) have found poor food intake to be correlated with some of the other sorts of dysfunctional family patterns: excessive control, conflict, organization, and cohesion.

Protection, Enmeshment, and Rigidity

The overprotective family carries to the extreme its responsibilities of control, guidance, and nurturance, limiting the child's risk-taking, exploration, and eventual sense of mastery and autonomy. The chaotic family, on the other hand, doesn't protect enough and is so disorganized that any new information has little impact on the general chaos (Olson, Sprenkle, & Russell, 1979).

The enmeshed family closes itself off to outside influences and becomes overinvolved with its own family members. Each has little privacy and is intolerant of allowing a family member to go off with friends (or bring friends in), make his own decisions, or develop interests separate from those of the rest of the family. At the opposite extreme, members of a disengaged family have little to do with each other, and parents don't know or even seem to care what other family members are doing.

The overprotective, enmeshed family becomes rigid. Because they isolate themselves, pressure for social and physical growth is ignored or suppressed, and the family remains the same. In contrast, in the normal family, the adolescent becomes increasingly interested in spending time with friends. This interest is supported, or at least tolerated, by parents. Along with peer involvement comes pressure for more freedom: later hours, boy-girl parties, R-rated movies. The rigid family discourages or devalues these inclinations. The normal family allows freedom to increase slowly as the child demonstrates responsibility and reasonably good judgment. The disorganized, chaotic family simply cuts loose of all controls.

Family Dynamics

Olson et al. (1979) have said that the family characteristic of cohesion exists on a continuum, as illustrated below:

Disengaged ___⌐___ Normal ___⌐___ Enmeshed

Adaptability within a family follows a similar pattern:

Chaotic ___⌐___ Normal ___⌐___ Rigid

Only a very indistinct dividing line separates one type of family from another. The normal family provides a range of structure and organization but has built into it the ability to protect its members and provide for their needs, while at the same time being able itself to change.

It is enormously difficult for the families that are either extremely adaptable or cohesive to change. Change often comes about catastrophically, under the pressure of some major family crisis. A more productive way to allow change is to move the family more toward normal ranges. This requires family therapy.

Olson et al. (1979) have arranged the two continuums at right angles:

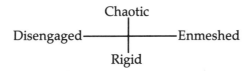

Families are assigned values in both ranges; thus, a family can be chaotic and disengaged, or chaotic and enmeshed, for instance. Families toward the center are the more normal families.

Child's Involvement in Parental Conflict

To discuss the final two characteristics—lack of conflict resolution and the child's involvement in parental conflict resolution—we have to talk about causes. Why would parents continue in a rigid, repetitive, unproductive approach to parenting? Why can't they see their child failing to develop appropriately and becoming socially isolated?

Parents often are preoccupied with their own emotional struggles and are involved in unresolved, and even unacknowledged, conflict with one another (Palazzoli, 1978). Each has unexpressed feelings about the other, their situation, and their relationship. Both preserve the relationship at all costs and, further, preserve the image of the ideal relationship. Feelings that cannot be expressed directly must be expressed indirectly. The child becomes involved as a confidant or as a butt of parental frustration.

Both the feeding relationship and the overall family context are based on the personal characteristics of parents. A parent's compulsiveness, rigidity, or dependency is reflected in the couple relationship, relationships with children, and overall family interaction.

Family Preoccupation With Eating

Family preoccupation with eating is often, but not always, attached to dieting and maintaining a slender physique. One woman with bulimic syndrome of 12 years duration has told of growing up in a family of nine children—step siblings, half siblings and full siblings. Parents were competitive about each other's children and stingy with feeding. Although there was plenty to eat, children were given "a look" if they took "too much" casserole or "too many" slices of bread.

Parental stinginess with food was typical of other interactions: Her parents were rigid and depriving. Because she was so strongly ruled at home, the patient didn't develop any intrinsic controls. When she left home, she lost all her guidance. To try to provide for herself, she imposed the same stinginess on herself as her parents had imposed; she began dieting and maintained herself for several years in the anorexic range.

The Identified Patient

It is axiomatic in family dynamics theory that a "problem child" reflects a disturbance in the family as a whole. A child's behavior is a very sensitive indicator of the parent-child relationship and of family emotional health (Satir, 1967).

A disturbance in a family is based on disruptions in the parental interaction. Most typically, the parents are in conflict with one another and lack the ability either to admit that the conflict exists or to resolve it. Because the parents can't deal with each other, they use excessive preoccupation with their children as a way of diverting attention from each other (Minuchin et al., 1978; Satir, 1967; Haley, 1963).

Typically, one child is seen as being the problem, or the *identified patient*. The identified patient might be chosen because of unlucky timing, poor health, a temperament that conflicts with that of the parent, unattractiveness, a nervous system that makes him difficult for the parent to cuddle and comfort, or other reasons.

The Family Secret

In disturbed families there is a family secret, family conflict or emotional dissatisfaction that "can't" be named or resolved. Generally, this is a variation on the theme of parental conflict, which is in turn based on parental emotional limitations (Haley, 1963; Minuchin et al., 1978; Satir, 1967). For instance, a young asthmatic patient who was growing poorly appeared to be reacting to enormous parental pressure on his eating. The parents seemed unable to decrease their control and preoccupation with his eating, even though they were coached in appropriate approaches to feeding and were encouraged to adopt a more relaxed attitude.

The mother denied that there was any significant family stress. However, on further examination it emerged that she was working at a job she disliked in order to pay for the father's chronically failing business attempts, the parents worked different shifts and rarely saw each other, and the father was gone every weekend to compete in costly sporting tournaments. Despite all evidence to the contrary, the mother insisted that their relationship was good and that they were cooperating well in raising the children. She was unwilling to confront the situation with her husband and attempt to get it resolved. Meanwhile, she was displacing her anxiety onto her son.

This was a family that was organized in a way that they couldn't change, even for the welfare of their son. Intervening with feeding in this situation was largely nonproductive; the parents were unable to let go of their intense preoccupation with it. They were equally unable to deal with their relationship.

Implications

Education about nutrition and feeding can have a major impact on the feeding relationship and overall family interaction. Conversely, the emotional and social climate of the family has a major impact on feeding. Family dynamics are powerful enough, and at times can be distorted enough, to negate any changes attempted with feeding. What's worse, interventions can be misused by the family in making a child an identified patient and increasing the negative pressure on him.

The health worker intervening in feeding has to know enough about family dynamics to be supportive and not disruptive. He or she must also be able to recognize situations that are so distorted that changes are impossible. In such cases, she should refer the family to a therapist who can help them modify the way they interact.

Summary

The feeding relationship concretely provides for the psychosocial development of the child. A positive feeding relationship helps ensure good nutritional status, as well as appropriate food regulation. Pressure on feeding can be disruptive for the entire relationship.

Patterns of family interaction have a major influence on feeding. A balance in the family functions of cohesion, adaptibility, and protectiveness and the ability to resolve conflict are necessary for optimal support of the feeding relationship. Feeding problems in families outside the range of normal can likely be corrected only after psychotherapeutic intervention.

References

Ainsworth, M.D.S., & Bell, S.M. (1969). Some contemporary patterns of mother-infant interaction in the feeding situation. In A. Ambrose (Ed.), *Stimulation in early infancy* (pp. 133-170). New York: Academic Press.

American Psychiatric Association. (1980). *Diagnostic and statistical manual of mental disorders* (3rd ed.). Washington, DC: Author.

Birch, L.L., Marlin, D.W., Kramer, L., & Peyer, C. (1981). Mother-child interaction patterns and the degree of fatness in children. *Journal of Nutrition Education*, **13**, 17-21.

Brody, S. (1956). Patterns of behavior in feeding. In *Patterns of mothering: Maternal influence during infancy* (pp. 286-321). New York: International Universities Press.

Bruch, H. (1973). *Eating disorders: Obesity, anorexia nervosa and the person within*. New York: Basic Books.

Bruenlin, D.C., Desai, V.J., Stone, M.E., & Swilley, J.A. (1983). Failure-to-thrive with no organic etiology: A critical review of the literature. *The International Journal of Eating Disorders*, **2**(3), 25-49.

Field, T. (1977). Maternal stimulation during infant feeding. *Developmental Psychology*, **13**, 539-540.

Haley, J. (1963). *Strategies of psychotherapy*. New York: Grune & Stratton.

Herman, C.P., & Polivy, J. (1980). Restrained eating. In A.J. Stunkard (Ed.), *Obesity*. Philadelphia: W.B. Saunders.

Hinton, M.A., Chadderdon, H., Eppright, E., & Wolins, L. (1962). Influences on girls' eating behavior. *Journal of Home Economics*, **54**, 842-846.

Kinter, M., Boss, P.G., & Johnson, N. (1981). The relationship between dysfunctional family environments and family member food intake. *Journal of Marriage and the Family*, **43**(3), 633-641.

Mellin, L. (1982). *Evidence of reactive obesity in adolescent females*. Paper presented at annual meeting of the Society for Adolescent Medicine, New York.

Minuchin, S., Baker, L., Rosman, B.L., Liebman, D., Milman, L., & Todd, T.C. (1975). A conceptual model of psychosomatic illness in children: Family organization and family therapy. *Archives of General Psychiatry*, **32**, 1031-1038.

Minuchin, S., Rosman, B.L., & Baker, L. (1978). *Psychosomatic families. Anorexia nervosa in context.* Cambridge: Harvard University Press.

Olson, D.H., Sprenkle, D.H., & Russell, C.S. (1979). Circumplex model of marital and family systems: I. Cohesion and adaptibility dimensions, family types, and clinical applications. *Family Process,* **18,** 3-28.

Palazzoli, M.S. (1978). *Self-starvation: From individual to family therapy in the treatment of anorexia nervosa.* New York: Aronson.

Politt, E., & Wirtz, S. (1981). Mother-infant feeding interaction and weight gain in the first month of life. *Journal of the American Dietetic Association,* **78,** 596-601.

Satir, V. (1967). *Conjoint family therapy.* Palo Alto: Science and Behavior Books.

Satter, E.M. (1983). *Child of mine: Feeding with love and good sense.* Palo Alto: Bull Publishing.

Satter, E.M. (1984). Developmental guidelines for feeding infants and young children. *Food and Nutrition News, National Livestock and Meat Board,* **56**(4), 21-26.

Shiner, G. (1980). Anorexia nervosa studies at several centers. *Research Resources Reporter,* **4**(5), 1-11.

Strober, M. (1981). The significance of bulimia in juvenile anorexia nervosa: An exploration of possible etiologic factors. *International Journal of Eating Disorders,* **1,** 28-43.

Whitten, C.F., Pettit, M.G., & Fischhoff, J. (1969). Evidence that growth failure from maternal deprivation is secondary to undereating. *Journal of the American Medical Association,* **209,** 1675-1682.

Wooley, S.C., & Wooley, O.W. (1979). Obesity and women: I. A closer look at the facts. *Women's Studies International Quarterly,* **2,** 69-79.

Wright, P., Fawcett, J., & Crow, R. (1980). The development of differences in the feeding behavior of bottle and breast fed human infants from birth to two months. *Behavioural Processes,* **5,** 1-20.

Chapter 2

Family Patterns and Their Relationship to Obesity

Betty Lucas

Obesity is a multidimensional disorder, making it particularly resistant to treatment. The family milieu has impact on the overweight child, and, conversely, the overweight status of the child has impact on the family. This chapter will explore the various influences of the family in the development of obesity, as well as the family's role in management programs.

Obesity as a Problem in Children

The incidence of obesity in the pediatric population is probably in the range of 5-25% (Dietz, 1983; Dietz & Gortmaker, 1984; Weil, 1977). Numerous factors determine this incidence, including age (infancy to adolescence), sex, socioeconomic group, ethnic group, geographical location, and method of measuring obesity (weight and height for age, triceps fatfold percentage, weight for height index, etc.). The longer a child has been obese, the less likely it is that the problem will spontaneously resolve.

Debate has occurred for decades regarding the etiology of obesity, most of it centered around nature versus nurture concepts. Currently there is support for the inheritability of overweight, as well as for the various metabolic adaptations that make some individuals more efficient at utilizing food energy, thus gaining excess weight (Dietz, 1983). It is known that fat parents have more fat children than thin or normal weight parents, but similar trends have also been demonstrated in adoptive and foster families (Foch & McClearn, 1984; Garn & Clark, 1976). Both genetics and environmental factors no doubt determine overweight; fatness is familial, although it may not always be genetic.

Increased health risk is an assumed consequence of obesity, but this has been documented primarily in adults. There is little evidence of greater morbidity in obese children, and an association may not exist at all (Mallick, 1983). In general, the psychosocial consequences of obesity have a greater impact on the child than any health risks.

Today's culture focuses on thinness as the desired look, and we are constantly bombarded by this through the mass media, often resulting in a preoccupation with weight control. Young people also absorb this message, and they see the significant adults in their lives showing dissatisfaction with their bodies or constantly dieting. There is a normal "bodily overconcern" which is a typical part of adolescent development, but recently this preoccupation seems to be intensifying, even in younger children. A recent report has documented short stature and delayed puberty in children 9-17 years of age who restrict their diets due to "fear of fatness" (Pugliese et al., 1983). One may speculate on the significance of a trend in which body size and shape are so integral to self-worth and -acceptance.

The Influence of Family Patterns

The family plays a significant role in a child's development and behavior. Even though there is greater influence from peers and the broader world as children grow to, and through, adolescence, the family remains the base. For the child who is obese, the family has great impact both on the development and subsequent management of the overweight condition. The primary areas of influence are (a) growth patterns, (b) eating and food-related behaviors, (c) physical activity, and (d) family functioning.

Growth Patterns

Physical growth is the result of genes, nutrition, and time. Attainment of one's genetic potential can be affected by malnutrition, illness/disease, or socioemotional factors, with the end effect on growth dependent on the timing, severity, and duration of the insult.

Body type (ectomorph, mesomorph, endomorph) is inherited (Sheldon, Stevens, & Tucker, 1940); we have all heard comments such as "He's built just like his dad." Although individuals are most often seen as combinations of more than one type, body composition is predetermined, rather than being externally controlled. For instance, persons with high ectomorphy cannot be highly-muscled or heavy, and those with endomorphic characteristics naturally lay down more body fat and are more at risk for obesity.

A common growth pattern seen in many overweight children is that they are tall for their age. This has been observed in clinical practice. One researcher has raised the question of whether the tall, big child is at increased risk for obesity, or whether overnutrition in the early years results in increased height (Forbes, 1977). Obese children and adolescents may also have other characteristics in common, such as early maturation, advanced bone age, early menarche, and increased lean body mass (Forbes, 1976). Not all obese children have these advanced growth patterns, however. Characteristics such as these probably have a genetic/metabolic basis and can help predict vulnerable individuals. More importantly, there needs to be acceptance by families and the larger community for a wide variability in size, shape, and growth patterns in children.

Eating Patterns

The feeding relationship, beginning in infancy, has been discussed in depth earlier. From the start, the family shapes the child's food attitudes and behaviors, both openly and subtly. Gradually, the child observes and integrates into his being some sense of the following:

• The importance of food and mealtimes
• Liked and disliked foods (mine, my parents', my siblings')
• Particular foods that are "treat" foods, special occasion foods
• Foods used for nonnutritive reasons (reward, sadness, anxiety, comfort, etc.)

The family's lifestyle also determines eating patterns that can lead to overweight. Irregular or erratic mealtimes may make it difficult for a child to maintain a good balance between hunger and satiety. Unlimited snacking or easy access to food between meals can promote excess intake. Frequent meals eaten outside the home may contribute excess calories.

Some reports have documented that obese children eat more rapidly and consume more food than average weight children (Birch et al., 1981; Drabman et al., 1979). In addition, interactions between obese children and their mothers at mealtimes have been shown to be less frequent and less positive than interactions between normal weight children and their mothers (Drabman et al., 1979; Olson, Pringle, & Schoenwetter, 1976). Not answered by these observations is the question of whether these differences are a result or a cause of overweight. It certainly seems plausible that mothers might react differently to an obese child in a mealtime situation.

Other findings have shown a relationship between a family's interaction and members' nutrition (Hertzler & Vaughan, 1979; Kintner, Boss, & Johnson, 1981). Kintner and co-workers have found that families with high levels of conflict, control, and organization had poorer diets (Kintner et al., 1981). This suggests a significant relationship between the dysfunctional environment of a family and overall poor dietary intake. Children from these families may be predisposed to such eating disorder as obesity and anorexia nervosa.

One cannot assume that all overweight children consume excess energy or that eating habits and food patterns are the primary bases for the development of obesity. Studies have shown that obese children and adolescents have energy intakes similar to, or less than, normal weight individuals (Corbin & Fletcher, 1968; Johnson, Burke, & Mayer, 1956; Stefanic, Heald, & Mayer, 1959). Some children no doubt eat more for periods of time, and excessive weight gain is a result. However, once attained, this increased fatness often can be maintained by a modest energy intake. Thus, we cannot equate overweight with continual overeating in children.

Activity Patterns

There is current support for the idea that decreased energy expenditure is as significant a factor in obesity as is excess energy intake. Some experts have suggested that obesity is a disease of inactivity. Data in this century have shown gradually decreasing energy intake, while at the same time the incidence of overweight and obesity has increased (Stern, 1984).

It is not clear whether inactivity is a cause or result of obesity. Obese adults are generally less active than normal-weight adults, but the evidence is not as clear-cut with children. Classic studies using motion picture samples of adolescent girls at a summer camp, as well as the infant movement study of Rose and Mayer, have shown that the obese were less active than the nonobese (Bullen, Reed, & Mayer, 1964; Rose & Mayer, 1968). Corbin and Fletcher (1968) have demonstrated that obese fifth-grade students are less active than their nonobese peers, the difference being greatest in games of low organization and free play. Other reports using objective measures have not shown a significant difference in the activity level of obese and nonobese (Brownell & Stunkard, 1980). A recent study has compared the energy expenditure of four obese boys with their normal-weight brothers, using oxygen consumption and measurements obtained in a laboratory. The somewhat decreased activity of the obese boys was more than compensated for by the increased energy expenditure required by their greater mass, so that they actually expended more energy than the normal-weight controls (Waxman & Stunkard, 1980).

The obvious reason for promoting increased activity in overweight children is to have the energy expenditure equal or exceed the energy intake. An additional benefit is that a higher level of activity may increase the metabolic rate and thus add to the energy deficit. This increased metabolism from activity could then counteract the decreased metabolism that occurs when people decrease their energy intake, or "diet" (Stern,

1984). Although this theory is controversial, and the extent of the benefit unknown, future work may provide more specific information that can be used in obesity intervention.

Obese children demonstrate a wide variability in activity, and this has been observed in clinical experience. Here again, the family's attitudes and lifestyle are critical in developing the child's level of physical activity. What kind of models are the parents? Adults who spend most of their leisure time watching television, reading, or spectator sports are setting a stage for children's sedentary activity. On the other hand, parents who walk, bicycle, hike, swim, or jog influence their children to engage in these activities.

Due to the familial nature of obesity, however, the parents of many overweight children are themselves overweight and thus are less likely to be physically active. In addition, many youngsters are likely to experience awkwardness, embarrassment, and humiliation with their activity attempts.

Family Functioning

The quality of family interaction is a major factor in both the development and management of obesity. Inconsistency and lack of stability within a family are associated with a poorer outcome in weight management attempts (Hertzler, 1981). Many health professionals dealing with eating disorders, however, do not consider or adequately deal with family functioning in their programs. Yet, without including the family interaction in assessment and therapy, a case can end up in the "unsuccessful" category, with child, family, and professional all feeling frustration and failure.

The quality of family functioning runs along a spectrum of very good functioning to severe dysfunction. There is some evidence that increasing severity of obesity is associated with increasing family dysfunction (Bowers, Falkner, & Michel, 1979) (see Figure 1). The structure of some families may be so rigid and overcontrolled that the children or adolescents cannot make normal developmental progress. These individuals usually are not allowed much responsibility or decision-making. Other dysfunctional families may manifest disorganization with few or inconsistent limits, lack of routine in daily activities, and crisis-oriented approaches to problems. Children in such families may take on a parental or peer role at times.

The obese child in a dysfunctional family may become a focus or "project," with the result that he or she diffuses the basic underlying conflict and maintains the family's status quo. Many of these interaction patterns are similar to the characteristics that Minuchin uses to describe the dysfunction seen in families in which a child has a psychosomatic illness. These include (a) enmeshment, referring to an extreme form of

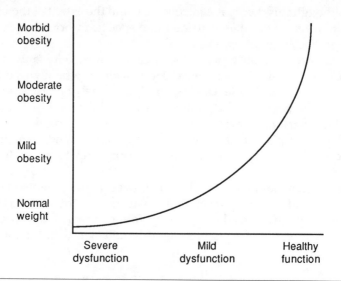

Figure 1. Relationship between family functioning and degree of obesity. *Note*. From "Obesity in Children: An Ecological Approach" by J.E. Bowers, B. Falkner, and S. Michel, 1979, *Journal of Continuing Education in Nursing*, 10(4), p. 44. Copyright 1979. Reprinted with permission.

proximity and intensity in the family's interactions; (b) overprotectiveness; (c) rigidity; (d) lack of conflict resolution; and (e) the role of the child's symptom in regulating the family system (Minuchin, Rosman, & Baker, 1978).

In many unhealthy families, the child's overweight is merely a symptom of the family's poor functioning. Given the continual stressful situation, the child uses food and eating in response to a myriad of feelings (anger, loneliness, frustration, isolation, depression, anxiety, powerlessness) and as a way to seek comfort or gain control. Most individuals react to stress by either eating or not eating; these children respond with eating and weight gain. This has been seen in many clinical cases. One boy initially gained weight after being immobilized in a cast for hip surgery. Following his recovery, however, weight gain continued to increase, a result of severe marital discord and family disruption. Another boy came from a rigid, controlling family where guilt and manipulation were used liberally. When asked whether people eat other than for hunger, his emphatic reply was, "Yes, revenge!"

Predicting Prognosis and Outcome

The success rate of obesity treatment is dismal, be it for adult or child (Coates & Thoreson, 1978). Some experts question whether obesity should be treated at all (Mallick, 1983; Wooley & Wooley, 1984). More recently there has been an interest in, and appreciation of, a more comprehensive approach encompassing changes in eating and activity patterns, behavioral therapy, counseling techniques, school involvement, and family support (Brownell & Kaye, 1982; Brownell & Stunkard, 1980; Coates & Thoreson, 1978). Yet, it continues to be difficult to predict which program will work best for which individual.

Considering each of the various factors determining overweight in children—genetic predisposition, family functioning, energy intake, and activity level—may help in establishing a prognosis and reasonable program goals. Table 1 puts these factors in a visual context. Genetic predisposition (the child either does or does not have a metabolic tendency towards overweight) is not variable; family functioning, energy intake, and activity level are variable and can be controlled or altered.

Table 1 Overweight Children and Family Patterns

Genetic Predisposition	Family functioning		Energy intake		Activity level	
	Good	Poor	Normal	Excessive	Normal	Low
No metabolic tendency	1	–	1	–	1	–
	2	–	2	–	–	2
	3	–	–	3	3	–
	4	–	–	4	–	4
	–	9	9	–	9	–
	–	10	10	–	–	10
	–	11	–	11	11	–
	–	12	–	12	–	12
Metabolic tendency	5	–	5	–	5	–
	6	–	6	–	–	6
	7	–	–	7	7	–
	8	–	–	8	–	8
	–	13	13	–	13	–
	–	14	14	–	–	14
	–	15	–	15	15	–
	–	16	–	16	–	16

Note: Numbers 1 and 9 are normal-weight children. 1 represents good prognosis (easy to change) at one end of the scale; 16 represents poor prognosis (difficult to change) at the other end. Developed by L.K. Mahan and B.L. Lucas, 1984, Child Development Mental Retardation Center, University of Washington, Seattle.

Basically, the lower the the number, the better the prognosis; the higher the number, the worse the prognosis. Children with no metabolic tendency and good family functioning are the easiest to change and have the best prognoses. Many of these, in fact, will never be seen by the health professional or will require only minimal intervention. Children with a genetic tendency to be obese coupled with poor family functioning have the poorest prognoses. With these families, counseling and/or family therapy may need to be the initial step. Specific goals for behavior or weight changes should be very conservative and in slowly progressing stages. Long-term success will be dependent on improved family interaction.

An Assessment and Intervention Model

A weight management clinic for pre-adolescents (5-11 years of age) has existed for several years at the Child Development and Mental Retardation Center at the University of Washington. The clinic team currently consists of a nutritionist and two nurses with expertise in child development, parent-child interaction, and family therapy. Consultation from pediatricians and other disciplines is available as needed. Approximately one quarter of the patients have developmental disabilities. It is required that the entire family—everyone in the household—be willing to be involved. This stipulation has been found to be a useful screening tool.

The assessment for a new patient includes six components. A *history of the child's growth* and development of obesity is obtained, in addition to the incidence of obesity in immediate and extended family members. *Anthropometric data* are taken, including height, weight, upper arm circumference, and triceps fatfold. *Food records* from the entire family show individual as well as family eating patterns and help establish a baseline. The *family assessment* looks at overall family interaction and identifies areas of dysfunction and/or conflict. The *fitness test* assesses the child's strength, endurance, flexibility, and cardiovascular fitness. During the *child interview*, areas assessed are self-image, motivation, locus of control, and perceptions regarding his or her weight and changes to be made.

Although the intervention program is individualized for each patient and family, some common components are included in every program. First of all, family involvement and support are critical; otherwise, both child and professional are powerless.

As part of a comprehensive program, the following aspects are included in ongoing sessions:

- Nutrition information and education. This includes hands-on activities to learn about energy balance, portion sizes, snack choices, label reading, a healthy diet, caloric comparisons of foods, etc. The child and family identify food behaviors to alter, and make contracts for changes.

- Planning and support for physical activity. In many, but not all cases, these children have low energy expenditure, so it is appropriate to increase output. The professional helps the child and family consider options that are reasonable, practical, and enjoyable. Adding the constraints of time, money, and safety makes this area a challenge, especially since some of the families are also not active. Care needs to be taken so that physical activity does not become negative or a punishment for the child. Goals should be reasonable and attainable. For some children, an initial step may be involvement in a social group or hobby.

- Strategies using behavioral rationale. Changes in both food and activity are incorporated into a contingency approach. Children often contract for changes with their parents, the latter providing some reward in 1 to 2 weeks. The professional's role is to keep the goals of the contract attainable (not ''I won't eat any snacks for 2 weeks''), yet in the right direction, and to assure that the family follows through. An individual's progress is noted by changes incorporated into daily living, rather than weight loss.

- Counseling. In some cases, family therapy is recommended before, or concurrent with, the weight management program. Families who are not willing to deal with the basic problem do not usually continue in the clinic. For others, counseling for families is included as part of the program. Issues covered are general parenting difficulties, limit-setting, conflict resolution, and increasing communication between family members. Efforts are also made to help improve the child's self-esteem.

Because expected improvement is slow and gradual, the clinic emphasizes a long-term commitment. A year is usually the goal, although sessions are less frequent after the first few months. Some families discontinue when faced with the underlying problem(s) that they refuse to deal with; others mutually agree with the team to terminate when there is lack of progress for similar reasons.

What about the success rate? This is difficult to determine, and is dependent on which measure of success is used. Obviously, it is inappropriate to equate success with weight loss; yet, most reports use this as a measure. Other parameters (social and emotional) are difficult to measure. In general, however, it seems that improvement or success can be determined by how far the child or family progresses toward the goals of intervention: (a) decreasing the weight/height index, achieving slow weight gain or weight maintenance; (b) altering eating behavior to a more normal pattern, decreasing nonnutritive uses of food; (c) promoting increased physical activity and fitness; (d) increasing the child's self-esteem and body image; and (e) receiving appropriate family support.

Conclusion

In summary, family patterns play a significant role in the etiology and treatment of obesity in children. Some youngsters are genetically and/or metabolically more vulnerable to becoming obese. Early identification of these children and preventive measures (promoting healthy eating habits and an active lifestyle) may make their future brighter, but may not necessarily make them normal weight. Health professionals need to lead the way in setting realistic, rather than idealistic, goals for these individuals.

Good family functioning and support are essential for any permanent changes and long-term progress. Without at least some positive movement in this direction, specific program implementation can be an exercise in futility and frustration.

As helping professionals, we must be aware of these various interrelating factors and avoid being overaggressive or unrealistic in our treatment. Caution needs to be taken to prevent weight gain-loss cycles or eating behaviors that may lead to long-term eating disorders. Although a conservative approach with modest goals may not be exciting, it may be the safest and wisest. A recent statement by the Academy of Pediatrics supports this idea (Committee on Nutrition, 1981).

Finally, in our zeal for healthier, more fit persons, we should not reinforce the exaggerated media focus on slimness in our society, which is intolerant of overweight. Rather, there needs to be support for a broader acceptance of body size and shape, especially concerning the vulnerable child. Children and adolescents, overweight or not, need to know that they are lovable, strong, smart, and competent just as they are.

References

Birch, L.L., Marlin, O.W., Kramer, L., & Peyer, C. (1981). Mother-child interaction patterns and the degree of fatness in children. *Journal of Nutrition Education, 13,* 17.

Bowers, J.E., Falkner, B., & Michel, S. (1979). Obesity in children: An ecological approach. *Journal of Continuing Education for Nursing, 10,* 40.

Brownell, K.D., & Kaye, F.S. (1982). A school-based behavior modification, nutrition education, and physical activity program for obese children. *American Journal of Clinical Nutrition, 35,* 277.

Brownell, K.D., & Stunkard, A.J. (1980). Behavioral treatment for obese children and adolescents. In A.J. Stunkard (Ed.), *Obesity* (pp. 415-437). Philadelphia: W.B. Saunders.

Bullen, B.A., Reed, R.B., & Mayer, J. (1964). Relative importance of inactivity and overeating in the energy balance of obese and nonobese adolescent girls appraised by motion picture sampling. *American Journal of Clinical Nutrition, 14,* 211.

Coates, T.J., & Thoresen, C.E. (1978). Treating obesity in children and adolescents: A review. *American Journal of Public Health, 68,* 143.

Committee on Nutrition, American Academy of Pediatrics. (1981). Nutritional aspects of obesity in infancy and childhood. *Pediatrics, 68,* 880.

Corbin, C.B., & Fletcher, P. (1968). Diet and physical activity patterns of obese and nonobese elementary school children. *Research Quarterly, 39,* 922.

Dietz, W.H. (1983). Childhood obesity: Susceptibility, cause, and management. *Journal of Pediatrics, 103,* 676.

Dietz, W.H., & Gortmaker, S.L. (1984). Factors within the physical environment associated with childhood obesity. *American Journal of Clinical Nutrition, 39,* 619.

Drabman, R.S., Cordua, G.D., Hammer, D., Jarvie, G.J., & Horton, W. (1979). Developmental trends in eating rates of normal and overweight preschool children. *Child Development, 50,* 211.

Foch, T.T., & McClearn, G.E. (1984). Genetics, body weight, and obesity. In A.J. Stunkard (Ed.), *Obesity* (pp. 48-71). Philadelphia: W.B. Saunders.

Forbes, G.B. (1976). Lean body mass and fat in children. *Acta Pediatric Scandinavica, 65,* 279.

Forbes, G.B. (1977). Nutrition and growth. *Journal of Pediatrics, 91,* 40.

Garn, S.M., & Clark, D.C. (1976). Trends in fatness and the origin of obesity. *Journal of Pediatrics, 57,* 443.

Hertzler, A.A. (1981). Obesity-impact of the family. *Journal of the American Dietetic Association, 79,* 525.

Hertzler, A.A., & Vaughan, C.E. (1979). The relationship of family structure and interaction to nutrition. *Journal of the American Dietetic Association, 74,* 23.

Johnson, M.L., Burke, B.S., & Mayer, J. (1956). Relative importance of inactivity and overeating in the energy balance of obese high school girls. *American Journal of Clinical Nutrition, 4,* 37.

Kintner, M., Boss, P.G., & Johnson, N. (1981). The relationship between dysfunctional family environments and family member food intake. *Journal of Marriage and Family, 43,* 633.

Mallick, M.J. (1983). Health hazards of obesity and weight control in children: A review of the literature. *American Journal of Public Health, 73,* 78.

Minuchin, S., Rosman, B.L., & Baker, L. (1978). *Psychosomatic families. Anorexia nervosa in context.* Cambridge, MA: Harvard University Press.

Olson, C.M., Pringle, D.J., & Schoenwetter, C.D. (1976). Parent-child interaction: Its relation to growth and weight. *Journal of Nutrition Education, 8,* 67.

Pugliese, M.T., Lifshitz, F., Grad, G., Fort, P., & Marks-Katz, M. (1983). Fear of obesity. A cause of short stature and delayed puberty. *New England Journal of Medicine, 309,* 513.

Rose, H.E., & Mayer, J. (1968). Activity, calorie intake, fat storage, and the energy balance of infants. *Pediatrics, 41,* 18.

Sheldon, W., Stevens, S.S., & Tucker, W.B. (1940). *The varieties of human physique.* New York: Harper Brothers.

Stefanic, P.A., Heald, F.P., & Mayer, J. (1959). Caloric intake in relation to energy output of obese and nonobese adolescent boys. *American Journal of Clinical Nutrition, 7,* 55.

Stern, J.S. (1984). Is obesity a disease of inactivity? In A.J. Stunkard & E. Stellar (Eds.), *Eating and its disorders* (pp. 131-139). New York: Raven Press.

Waxman, M., & Stunkard, A.J. (1980). Calorie intake and expenditure of obese boys. *Journal of Pediatrics, 96,* 187.

Weil, W.B. (1977). Current controversies in childhood obesity. *Journal of Pediatrics, 91,* 175.

Wooley, S.C., & Wooley, O.W. (1984). Should obesity be treated at all? In A.J. Stunkard & E. Stellar (Eds.), *Eating and its disorders* (pp. 185-192). New York: Raven Press.

Part II

Children
and Adolescents

Obesity is a significant problem among children and adolescents. The primary approach to its management revolves around prevention, rather than intervention. This section discusses social and psychological implications of obesity. The risk to normal growth patterns associated with calorie deprivation is also discussed.

Chapter 3

Changing Concepts of Childhood and Adolescent Obesity

Judith Bograd Gordon
Alice L. Tobias

At first I was merely plump; in the earliest snapshots in my mother's album I was a healthy baby, not much heftier than most. . . . The photos went on in an orderly series; though I didn't exactly become rounder, I failed to lose what is referred to as baby fat. When I reached the age of six, the pictures stopped abruptly. This must have been when my mother gave up on me, for it was she who used to take them; perhaps she no longer wanted my growth recorded. She had decided I would not do. (Atwood, 1976, p. 42)

Tales of childhood such as this turn our attention to the meaning of weight in the lives of children. As the social theorist Schutz (1964) has reminded us, we can approach the world of everyday life in a variety of ways. We can look at people's actions by use of concepts we as objective observers develop and use, or we can try to see the world from the point of view of the subject. The study of eating behavior, similar to the study of any social action, requires us to take account of the need to link our objective ways of giving meaning to weight with the subjective meanings given by people under study.

Children labeled obese, as we all know, do not have an easy time (Cahnman, 1968). The linking of what Schutz (1964) has called the subjective and objective frames of reference is particularly important when children are concerned. Growing up is not easy, as Carroll brilliantly illustrated in describing the experiences of Alice in Wonderland; children who grow while struggling with weight often find the world "curiouser and curiouser" as adults try to shape children's bodies and lives. How sad it is

31

for a child to grow dreading each new pound. Surely, the pain observed in childhood and adolescent obesity clinics requires us to pay close attention to the repercussions of the alternative meanings given to body size.

The study of the life histories of people who weighed more than a specified "normal" weight as children provides us with much information about the sociology of suffering (Gordon, 1977). Feminists were among the first to give voice to the pain of those who feel damned in a society that judges human beings on the basis of their bodies' thin appearance. Fat became a feminist issue in reaction to the standards of slim feminine beauty held out by the fashion and entertainment industry (Obrach, 1978 and 1982). Both sexes suffer when lovability is linked to thinness. Increasingly, men, as well as women, wage lifetime battles against the weight of their bodies; often this battle is initiated in childhood.

In previous papers, we have urged researchers and clinicians to closely examine the psychosocial consequences of the assumption that at each age there are standard body weights, specified by the height/weight tables or growth curves, that everyone must maintain (Tobias and Gordon, 1980; Gordon and Tobias, 1984). An inflexible application of these standards can have even more greatly negative ramifications during childhood and adolescence, as our young grapple with cultural values shaped by adult members of society who fear obesity and pay intense attention to weight. Observers of our cultural preoccupation with weight have used different words to describe it. Bruch, for example, has called it a "fetish" (1973); Chernin, an "obsession" (1981). Allon (1981) has referred to the "mania for slimness" and has applied concepts such as "stigma" and "spoiled identity" to analyze the actions of the people she studied who organized their lives around losing weight.

Natalie Allon's (1980) extensive bibliographical work done in the late 1970s demonstrates that for over 30 years, a growing number of social scientists and health care professionals have urged a humane approach to body size. As other papers delivered at this conference indicate, objections have long been raised about the unnecessary suffering being experienced by people who have been taught to believe the body must be shaped in one standard form and who act on that belief, ignoring sociocultural variations or genetic givens. The conclusion of Bennett and Gurin's (1982) book, *The Dieter's Dilemma*, again expressed the hope that "those who have become obsessed with weight" can be helped to accept themselves "if the cultural attitude toward fatness changes" (p. 283). Why has the obsession with weight persisted for so many years, despite the continuing humane injunctions found in the literature?

In order to understand why certain ideas are applied and others are rejected, we must turn our attention to what Schutz (1964) has called the "social distribution of knowledge" and study the ways in which the knowledge of experts becomes connected with the knowledge used by ordinary people. The social processes by which knowledge about obesity is approved, distributed, and used can be studied by looking at the meanings given to eating, weight control, and weight loss both by professionals and by people in the everyday world. To begin, we have mapped out some of the ways in which knowledge about the meanings, prevention, and management of obesity has been distributed and used (Gordon & Tobias, 1984). Ongoing attention to this process is needed to generate the kind of multidisciplinary research that is necessary to develop humane intervention strategies that effectively link what we know and what we do not know to the eating behavior of children and adolescents.

The Social Distribution of Knowledge

Starting with the study of religious beliefs and political ideologies, the sociology of knowledge has investigated who knows what, why, and how. People derive knowledge in a variety of ways (Schutz, 1964). Like other knowledge, knowledge about the desirability of body size reflects the biographical and sociocultural situations into which one is born. Fat, like beauty, is defined first in the eyes of the beholder, and then of the self; for by communicating cultural attitudes about the meaning of such shapes, people teach children to judge their bodies' shapes.

The process by which body image is formed is complex indeed. Societies and groups have a variety of sources that influence meaning transmitted to the young. For instance, the meaning given to female shape throughout history has been influenced by many factors, including politics and economics. In America not all groups share the same evaluation of body size. The media, advertising agencies, fashion designers, manufacturers, and retailers play a powerful role in influencing perception of desirable body sizes and shapes. If, as Henry (1965) has argued, we strive to exhibit the prestige symbols of our culture, the obsession with weight can be studied by examining the connections between advertisements and behavior. Indeed, the poor, who lack the money to conspicuously consume fashions and dress according to the dictates of designers, also do not always value a slim body (Allon, 1973). Yet, not all the variation is explained by economics alone.

In a culture as technologically and medically oriented as this one, the knowledge of ordinary people is influenced by the knowledge of experts. In the case of obesity, overweight has become defined as a medical problem, and health care professionals lay claim to be the recognized experts on body weight. Children also learn to give meaning to their shapes by use of ideas that are communicated by a variety of specialists, such as pediatricians and school nurses; these meanings may or may not be accepted by their parents and peers. Knowledge about obesity, like all other knowledge, therefore reflects the complicated processes by which meanings are communicated from one generation to another, from one group to another, and from experts to ordinary people.

Experts, too, receive knowledge from the groups to which they belong. The content of science reflects the social interactions of scientists and practitioners (Cooley, 1918; Barber & Hirsh, 1962). Each group, as Schutz (1964) has put it, has its own "domains of relevance" that it uses to make sense of the world. These are not necessarily shared by others interested in the same phenomenon, but belong to different specialty groups. For example, when we address groups of physicians, nurses, and nutritionists, we find that although sociological concepts such as "stigma" have begun to wend their way into their vocabulary, many still do not see the relevance of sociological theory and research for clinical practice and therefore do not utilize such work in shaping their own activities. However, Millman (1980), a sociologist, has oversimplified the medical approach to obesity by taking it for granted that obesity has "lately come to be viewed by the medical profession as an incurable disease" (p. 89) and cited only one book by a nutritionist (published in 1968). Exhibits catering to exercise specialists, such as aerobic staircases, are not found at sociology or nutrition meetings. Most importantly, each group has its own professional journals in which findings are published. We, like others, presented some previously published work at this conference. We know that many in this audience do not customarily read the *Marriage and Family Review*, and many do not customarily read all the journals in which some of the other speakers have published their work. Indeed, the exciting collection of papers in these proceedings, delivered by specialists who do not routinely interact with each other, manifests the very process that must concern us, because none of us can use knowledge to which we're not exposed.

The only knowledge that is routinely used is the knowledge about obesity that has been socially approved and communicated by the groups to which we belong. The definition of the key concept "obesity" in itself carries with it sociological consequences and illustrates the impact of the varying social distribution of knowledge upon the lives of everyday people.

The Key Concept: Obesity

In order to test hypotheses, obtain valid and reliable measurements, and apply findings in treatment, it is very necessary for scientists and practitioners to share a precise definition of the concepts used in research designs. This is a period of time in which the scientific definition of obesity has become one of the problems at hand, for specialists in a variety of disciplines have become aware that the "clinical definitions and understanding of . . . etiology, diagnosis, and treatment remain blurred and undefined" (Paige, 1982).

The lack of conceptual clarity is reflected in research as well. As Allon (1980) has found, reviews of the literature on obesity are complicated because researchers have not always operationally defined the term in the same manner. Some, for example, never specify the weight of the people they study and simply accept the self-definition of obesity presented by women who attend weight-control groups because they have identified themselves as "obese" (Laslet & Warren, 1975). Others have distinguished between overweight (weight in excess of average) and obesity (excessive fatness) (Anderson, Dibble, Turkki, Mitchell, & Rynbergen, 1982). However, these studies have been handicapped by the fact that not all overweight indicates "excess fatness." Athletic girls, for example, may weigh more than average, but should not be considered obese on the basis of weight alone. Therefore, others have tried to use more objective measures, such as calibrating the amount of fat under the skin. Yet, unless everyone measures obesity this way, studies cannot be easily compared or replicated—and everyone does not.

One commonly accepted manner of proceeding has been to operationally define the concept *obesity* by use of standards found on height/weight charts developed by insurance companies, distributed by health care professionals (Jesse, 1982), and also made available to people via popular magazines, newspaper articles, and even the now-antique "penny scales." One pediatrician, for example, put on a reducing diet any child who was 10% over the weight specified on the chart for that age and height; a child whose weight was 20% over the norm had the word *obese* stamped on the medical record, and the mother was called in for a conference, in which she was asked to review the family's life situation and eating behavior, in order to identify the "emotional factors" that might have been contributing to the child's obesity.

However, this way of dealing with obesity has proven to be neither valid nor reliable, because the height/weight charts themselves fluctuate over time (Gordon & Tobias, 1984; Weigley, 1984). A person might be put on a reducing diet in one era; yet, in another era the very same person at the very same weight might be congratulated upon his or her ability to maintain the desired weight. For example, in 1940, the ideal weight for a woman of 50 who was 5 feet 3 inches was set at 141 pounds (Rose, 1940). These tables were modified over the next 40 years: age variations were eliminated, and the charts were revised to take account of body frame variation. The new charts postulate that adults should maintain the same weight throughout their lifetime, once they achieve full growth in height around age 20; this weight is assumed to vary according to whether the person has a small, medium, or large frame. However, as yet there is no commonly accepted criterion for precisely estimating each person's frame size. A 50-year-old, 5'3'' woman somehow must determine whether or not she has a small, medium, or large frame. In 1976, if she weighed 136 and decided she had a small frame, she found herself overweight and even labeled obese, because the desired weight was 105-113 (Metropolitan Life Insurance Company, 1960). In 1979, the tables were again revised (Bennett and Gurin, 1982). The same woman now finds that the new tables have raised the desired weight for a woman with a small frame to 111-124. If she is wrong and in fact has a medium frame, her ideal weight ranges from 121-135. On the basis of a revision by a group of actuaries, she has become far less overweight than she was the night before! Indeed, Bennett and Gurin have estimated that when these new tables finally become public knowledge, 16 million Americans would find that they no longer have to worry about excessive weight, because they weigh what is now desired. Recent research suggests that this revision is incomplete, for the ideal weight has again been found to vary with age (Andres, 1983), so we may return to the ideas Rose presented in 1940.

If the standards fluctuate so, how should obesity be defined? Many struggle with this dilemma, and to date no satisfactory answer has been found. How then do we resolve this dilemma? Some fall back upon an operational definition stating that "in a social context, the obese state is clearly observable and requires no sophisticated measurements. It simply refers to a surplus of body fat, while overweight implies excess body weight in relation to height" (Paige, 1982).

Such a solution may free us from the need to define obesity, but it forces us to seriously consider the social context (Tobias & Gordon, 1980; Hertzler & Owen, 1984)—and that context varies. For example, the women at the gym whom Chernin interviewed felt that anyone whose stomach "bulged" was too fat (1981). Allon found that during her study of group dieting, some upper-middle-class Jewish women looked her "up and down, . . . some becoming so bold as to suggest that she should really come to the groups to try to lose some weight herself, not just to carry out academic research." However, in the lower-middle-class Italian groups, women expressed concern that she was "too skinny and should take care of herself" (personal communication, 1977). As we know, the social contexts of families vary, and a child who is tormented by a family obsessed with diet and weight may weigh the same amount as another who lives in a home in which her weight is not an issue (Sussman, 1956).

From the point of view of a sociologist, the social context requires as sophisticated measurement as other variables, particularly if it is that context which is used to define obesity operationally. The need for a multidisciplinary approach to obesity grows out of the fact that both the eating behavior of human beings and the value attached to specific body shapes take place in a social environment; this must be taken into account in attempting to understand the etiology and management of weight gain and loss.

The Etiology of Obesity and Thomas's Theories

The revision of the Metropolitan Life Insurance Tables in 1983 was based on data on longevity and the actual distribution of weight that suggested previous desired weights were too low. This revision indicates that we live in a time in which scientific theories about the causes and consequences of overweight are also changing because new research has challenged past interpretations of the correlations between weight, disease, and mortality (Bennett and Gurin, 1982). Yet, ordinary people are still being instructed by physicians to lose weight in order to stay well (Bennett and Gurin). Data, after all, is only as significant as interpretations make it to be. As Thomas noted years ago, if people define situations as real, they are real in their consequences. Whether or not overweight is caused by overeating and in itself leads to disease and death, if people believe this to be true, this belief is true in its consequences.

The prevailing concepts and hypotheses of any specific time period affect how scientists design research investigations and how clinicians manage their patients. Let us therefore look at some of the most recent concepts and theories about the etiology of obesity.

Obesity is a complex phenomenon, and currently it is insufficiently understood. Many factors have been shown to be involved in the development of obesity. Although it is recognized that the belief the obese are fat because they overeat is clearly inadequate, a great deal more needs to be learned about the way in which specific physiological, psychological, sociological, economic, and political factors exert their effects. At present our understanding is often too limited to identify and describe the factors involved in the development and maintenance of obesity in given individuals.

The two components in weight are energy intake and energy expenditure; an abnormality in either can lead to obesity. In the late 1960s and early 1970s many investigators believed that hyperphagia was the primary cause of obesity. Schacter's externality theory, formulated during this time, portrays obese people eating principally in response to environmental cues (the sight or smell of food), rather than internal physiological stimuli (for example, visceral hunger sensations).

More recently, Schacter's externality theory has come under scrutiny and has been reassessed. Rodin, for example, has concluded that the initial externality theory has relevance, but in its initial formulation was too simplistic. She states that being highly responsive to external cues does not necessarily imply an inability to perceive and respond to internal physiological signals (Rodin, 1980).

Alternative theories have been formulated to account for the eating behavior of the obese, and some have gained acceptance by the many investigators and clinicians working in the field. One popular theory postulates that food intake is regulated to maintain a biologically preferred level of fat stores, known as the set point. Food intake is regulated at the set point (of adipose cell size) through a feedback mechanism (Nisbett, 1973). The hypothalamus and some substance produced by fat or dissolved in fat that serves as a sensor to measure energy storage are probably part of this feedback mechanism (Hervey, 1971).

The set point theory may have significance for obese people who have difficulty in reducing or in maintaining a reduced weight. Presumably, dieters who are below their set point sustain this state of deprivation because they habitually restrain their eating. However, they also run the risk of counterregulatory eating responses aimed at restoring their fat mass to its preferred level.

Data from many studies indicate that dieters in laboratory settings are unable to regulate their food intake in response to external cues. Researchers report that dieters usually consume more after a preload snack than after consuming nothing. Herman and Mack believe that this pattern can be explained by their restraint eating theory. Key elements of the externality theory and set point theory are merged in their concepts about restraint eating. These investigators assume that there are persons at and below their set point among normal weight and obese populations. They hypothesize that normal-weight and obese persons who are below their set point inhibit their eating tendencies. They argue that such persons become disinhibited after consuming a preload snack and exhibit latent externality in response to food cues (Herman & Mack, 1975). This research is suggestive but must be confirmed in the real world in which dieters customarily eat.

In attempts to define the determinants of human obesity, researchers formerly concentrated mainly on factors that influence energy intake and food behavior. More recently, research has begun to link the efficiency with which energy is expended and stored to leanness and obesity. A considerable amount of controversy now exists concerning the possibility that excess energy can be dissipated in the form of heat.

A number of investigators suggest that mechanisms exist for maintenance of a stable weight despite differences in energy intake. These investigators differentiate between the metabolically active fat, known as brown adipose tissue, and more quiescent fat. They believe that brown adipose tissue may have an important role in determining energy expenditure (Sims, 1976). Brown adipose tissue may serve to dissipate excess energy, in addition to its function of maintaining body temperature

(Himms-Hagen, 1982). It is hypofunctional in genetically obese animals, but its significance to obesity in animals and humans is currently unknown.

It also has been suggested that biochemical reactions in tissues other than brown adipose tissue may play a role in determining the energy available for storage as fat. The metabolic efficiency of tissues may vary with the rate of sodium and potassium transmission between cells. (Deluise, Blackburn, & Flier, 1980) and with the ability of cells to dissipate heat via futile cycles (Newsholme, 1982). This body of research has not been confirmed but represents some alternative possibilities that can be useful in explaining differences in body weight.

At this point in time, therefore, the clinician has a real dilemma in designing protocol for the assessment and management of the obese, for changing theories challenge past practices. Alternative biomedical hypotheses about the etiology of obesity do have different impact upon prescriptions for dieting; these differences directly affect children's eating behavior in everyday life. Such sociological differences are becoming more evident as scientific theories change and reinforce the recognition that the prevention and treatment of obesity have been generally unsatisfactory because the etiology and pathogenesis are inadequately defined. Current research therefore challenges past dieting practices by calling into question the findings on which such diets are based.

Developing Concepts of Developing Bodies

Not only are the theories of the etiology of obesity changing, but there are also new challenges to taken-for-granted ways of thinking about the body's growth and development. For instance, following Foucalt, medical sociologists are giving renewed attention to the ways in which health care professionals shape the knowledge used to evaluate and analyze one's physical being. Studies are being conducted on the ways in which the body is given meaning in different societies, at different points in historical time, and by different groups within these societies (Armstrong, 1980). These studies of the changing ways in which the human body is socially construed identify the interesting variations between societies and groups within the same society who see the same body but describe and manipulate it in different ways. Such studies have direct bearing upon the changing ways in which people see, describe, and react to obese bodies.

People's understanding of the changing bodies of children is, of course, also linked to their concept of the child—and that concept, too, is continually being redefined. For instance, in America it was not until the 1930s that medical supervision of healthy babies and nutrition education in schools developed. These programs took over 30 years to be initiated and grew out of the child welfare movement, which popularized the finding that children were not only small adults. As Frank summed it up in 1933, "The importance accorded to the child as a child is behind all child welfare programs" (p. 751).

Attention to infant and child nutrition, as well as other child welfare programs, was based on the "gradual acceptance of the principle of variability among children and a giving up of the belief that children are essentially alike and should be treated alike. The willingness to recognize individual differences in all aspects of the child is bringing far-reaching modifications in child nuture (Frank, 1933, p. 752). It was this assumption that gave rise to both clinics and school programs in which nutritionists, psychologists, pediatricians, sociologists, and teachers worked together to accentuate the individual differences between children and to create special educational programs to deal with such differences. (Frank, 1933; Thomas, 1928). One group singled out for special educational efforts were "malnourished and underweight children" (White House Conference on Children, quoted by Frank, 1933, p. 781). Overweight children, however, were not specified as a target group.

Today a different emphasis often prevails. New attention is being paid to the treatment in schools of obese children. This treatment is increasingly based on the assumption that eating behavior of such children can be changed if people accept the fact that "most divergent types are . . . but learned coping responses that occur within a complex social and cognitive environment" (Brownell & Stunkard, 1980). This orientation grows out of the past but accents different assumptions and procedures. Frank, for instance, stressed the importance of respect for the individual as a unique person in the development of well-baby clinics, parent education, and school nutrition programs (1933). Brownell, too, has pointed to the need for such programs but has noted that behavior modification directs attention "to the social learning principles which focus on the acquisition and maintenance of behavior, such as proper eating behavior, by teaching adaptive patterns of living" (1984). Although not mutually exclusive, these ways of modifying child nutrition led to different programs for children.

In the 1930s nutrition was introduced in the schools in order to combat malnutrition and underweight bodies; in the 1980s, behavior modification programs in schools emphasize combating obesity and overweight bodies. Yet, some overweight children must have been found in our society even during the Great Depression, and undernourished children are surely going to schools in the 1980s. As Foucault has helped us observe, the "political anatomy" that shapes the selection of the domains of relevance used to give meaning to bodies is reflected in our programs and policies. As Armstrong has put it, "the social space around the body delimits and constrains it, . . . It establishes, for the purposes of the investigation, the reality of the individual as a social being" (1980, p. 117).

Developmental psychologists also conceived of changing bodies with a frame of reference that linked age to physical, mental, and social development. The life course was broken into stages such as infancy, childhood, adolescence, and more recently young adulthood, middle age, late middle age, the young old, the middle old, and the oldest of the old. Each of these stages is given meaning by use of theories and research that concentrate upon the unique features of each stage.

Yet, anthropologists were simultaneously suggesting that frames of reference that compartmentalize development by chronological age lead us to overlook the continuities and discontinuities of growing up that reflect the cultures in which we are born. (Benedict, 1934). Psychoanalysts, following Freud, emphasized the unconscious connecting links between stages, persuasively arguing that eating behavior cannot be understood without paying attention to the first years of life and the unconscious determinants of subsequent behavior in childhood, adolescence, and adulthood. As our introductory quote illustrates, children have continued to grow knowing that the early shapes of their bodies have influenced their interaction with their care-givers and so have shaped their development as well.

Why is this so? As sociologists have noted, individuals grow up in social situations. From birth the meanings they give to themselves reflect the meanings they are given by others with whom they interact. Indeed, the responsibility and power of those significant others in individual destiny is another of the taken-for-granted beliefs currently being challenged. Some, for instance, accept without question that children reflect their parents' actions. (Hertzler, 1981). Kagan, however, has challenged past thinking about children by arguing that too much responsibility has been laid upon parents, particularly mothers, and not enough emphasis has been placed upon the variability of the child itself.

And so, the great debates of the twentieth century continue. Which is more significant, the individual's genetic givens or the social environment that shapes behavior? Who should have the power to decide whether we emphasize shape or feelings, individual differences or similarities, social interaction or environmental modifications? The social context of our time reflects the struggles of different theoretical positions and specialists to assert themselves as the definers of the primary domains of relevance that can and should be used to guide the meanings we give to body size and eating behavior. As these debates rage, the symbolic meanings of social interaction become even more evident; people's very sense of self are shaped from birth by the culture, as transmitted by the important people with whom they interact.

The process by which the findings of researchers are applied in clinical management and linked to the lives of ordinary people is in great need of study. Problems can be created by the premature use of findings, glossing over the lack of firm knowledge about the causes and consequences of overweight on human development. Some of these problems become evident as we look back upon past practices. In order to illustrate the importance of the social distribution of knowledge about obesity, we now turn to the beginning of the life course, when developmental obesity has been thought to occur.

The Beginning: Pregnancy

Although behavioral scientists and psychiatrists customarily begin a discussion of the life course with infancy, nutritionists turn to the pregnancy of the mother as the first event that in fact shapes us all. Although pregnancy is an option that not all adult women experience, none of us would be fat—let alone alive—were it not for the women who gave birth to us. Of course, the father's genetic makeup also has great import. However, from inception, attention is directed upon the eating behavior of the mother and its impact on the child, and there is evidence to support this taken-for-granted practice. A child's biological destiny can indeed tragically reflect a mother's malnourishment, for example. Therefore, women are taught during pregnancy to take responsibility not only for their own size and health, but also for the size and shape of their child; they are instructed to gain or lose weight according to current thoughts about the relationship between the weight of the mother, the threat of toxemia, and the health of the fetus.

The Committee on Maternal Nutrition of the American College of Obstetricians and Gynecologists (1974) and the National Research Council of the American Academy of Science have taken a strong stand, based on considerable evidence, that a weight gain of 22-27 pounds is desirable throughout the pregnancy (Committee on Dietary Allowances, 1980; Committee on Maternal Nutrition, 1970). This amount of weight gain benefits both the mother and the fetus. In particular, the birth weight of the baby is more apt to be in the desirable range. An adequate caloric intake promotes optimal utilization of the protein for growth of the fetus; a desirable weight gain of about 1.5-3 pounds during the first trimester of pregnancy and 0.8 pounds per week during the remainder is advised. This pattern is recommended even if the woman is obese at the beginning of the pregnancy. Moreover, current thinking suggests that if more than the recommended weight is gained over any time span during the pregnancy, there should be no attempt to make up for this by restricting weight gain in the remaining weeks. Controlled gain of weight is still the goal. The Recommended Dietary Allowances specify an increase of 300 calories daily above normal caloric requirements to meet the energy demands of pregnancy. This increased intake should result in the recommended weight gain (1980).

A woman who was pregnant only 15 years ago would likely be amazed at these instructions. At that time, a relationship was assumed to exist between toxemia and weight gain. Physicians advised their patients to limit weight gain to a pound a month and to eliminate salt from their diets to avoid water retention. Dire warnings of toxemia were heard as women weighed in, and those who gained more were frequently lectured about the ramifications of their "lack of self-control" upon themselves and their babies. These dietary norms created great hardship not only for the woman, but in many cases for her husband or children (Gordon and Pye, 1976). We observed cases of severe depression on the part of mothers-to-be who could not maintain such a low weight; some went on semistarvation diets prior to scheduled visits in order not to exceed the limit set by the clinic staff. One woman stopped attending the pre-natal clinic after she was strongly chastized for her weight gain and lost her baby, who might have been saved had she only continued to attend the clinic regularly. Moreover, some marriages already stressed by the pregnancy were put under additional strain as women and their husbands fought over pregnancy diets, either because the husbands tried to control all food intake of their wives, who husbands feared would "gorge" themselves and harm the baby; or because other members of the families objected furiously to dietary restrictions while the women struggled heroically to avoid the foods on the "no list" and eliminate them from the home. The family dynamics exacerbated by these past dietary injunctions were of enough concern to one obstetrical clinic that a special research and educational program was created, utilizing a team composed of a psychiatrist, sociologist, social worker, nutritionist, nurse, pediatrician, and obsterician, in order to deal with the complex troubles that arose from a now-antiquated pregnancy diet (Gordon et al., 1972).

In 1970 the Committee on Maternal Nutrition of the National Research Council reported that new evidence failed to support the relationship between caloric restriction as reflected in weight gain, the accumulation of fat, and the development of toxemia. It is now believed that toxemia may be due, particularly in lower income groups, to a lack of protein, calories, calcium, and/or salt. So, the pregnancies of an earlier cohort led to a vast array of personal difficulties because sets of dietary instructions were issued prior to more precise data. These instructions have now been reversed, because new data about the causes of toxemia have resulted in a change in management (Kaminetzky et al., 1973).

This change illustrates the processes by which scientific research becomes linked to everyday life and provides cautionary tales about the social consequences of premature applications of biomedical research findings. However, at what point should research findings be taken for granted and applied to clinical management? There is clearly a need to develop a multidisciplinary approach that can aid us in understanding the timing of health care professionals' use of scientific information and the incorporation of such findings into dietary instructions. The past alerts us to the need to connect the management of weight gain during pregnancy to the social context in which the mother lives.

For example, there is now evidence that some women encounter problems with the current instructions because of the American obsession with weight (McBride, 1982). Many women are not convinced that a weight gain of 24 pounds is desirable. In the course of nutrition education groups conducted for pregnant women, primarily from economically disadvantaged groups, we find that some women are perplexed by the fact that during pregnancy substantial weight gain is advised. As one woman put it, "How come when I look in the mirror now, I am supposed to think of myself as okay, when 3 months ago, if I looked like this people would really call me fat. In fact, before I became pregnant, my doctor told me to lose weight, and now he's telling me that I am not eating enough. How do the doctor and you people at the Family Planning Clinic know I'm not going to be fat again after I deliver? If so, won't he hassle me again, and would it be better not to gain 24 pounds now? After all, the baby won't be that big!" (Tobias, 1982).

Will this mother-to-be become depressed if after delivery she finds herself fat and encounters difficulty in losing weight? Will a woman obsessed by her own weight be able to nurture her infant easily after birth? In a culture that reacts so punitively to overweight, there is a need to take systematic account of the ramifications of these new weight norms on the mother during the postpartum period.

Suffering continues to occur when connections between societal norms and the mother's reaction to her weight and that of the newborn are ignored (McBride, 1982). As previously mentioned, research currently leads to the conclusion that, biologically, human beings take shape within their mothers' wombs and are indeed affected by the nutritional status of the women who carry them, but their shape also reflects their own biological makeup. Given such findings, should a mother-to-be still be taught that the infant's size is dependent upon her weight, though in fact the child's size also reflects his own genetic programming? Can the new knowledge at hand be distributed in such a way that a woman is not put in the position not only of weighing her body, but of weighing consequences of putting her ideas about ideal shape before of the needs of the infant? How can weight gain be handled in a way that is advantageous to both the mother and the developing fetus? In order to apply our new knowledge in a timely fashion, there is a great need to look at the ways in which it is communicated to the mother during pregnancy. The experiences of the mother may have as much bearing upon the future development of the child as his birth weight, because, sociologically, infancy reflects the interpersonal interactions between mother, child, and family that occur in the settings in which human infants are fed.

It is time to put to use what we have learned about the management of weight during pregnancy in previous years and to base prenatal dietary instructions upon the recognition that the mother's reaction to her infant, a key component of that child's growth and development, is also shaped by her reaction to herself. We need more information about the precise relationship between a woman's weight, its meaning to her, and her baby's size, in order to develop and distribute dietary instructions that take account of the sociological consequences of gestation.

Pregnancy sets the stage and lays out a script that all too often burdens the mother with the responsibility for her child's size, which does not end, but only begins, at birth. What if the baby is fat? Let us turn to the next life event: infancy.

Infancy

The knowledge at hand used to explain why babies are fat still assigns much responsibility to the mother (Jesse, 1982; Forbes, 1983, 1984 Ref.). Past developmental models have been based on the assumption that eating and the recognition of hunger signals are learned behavior and depend upon appropriate mothering. Many have believed that if an infant is fat, the mother's handling of feeding was "continuously inappropriate, be it neglectful, oversolicitous, inhibiting, or indiscriminately permissive," resulting in a child who is "confused and unable to differentiate between being hungry or other discomfort" (Bruch, 1982, p. 215).

Although, sociologically, infant feeding is shaped by the interpersonal interactions that occur in the settings in which human beings are fed—and these settings include fathers, grandparents, and siblings—much of the literature in the past was mother-centered (Hertzler, 1981). Many current obesity prevention programs continue to accept the view that an obese infant is one who is overfed, is given solids too quickly, not breastfed, and whose mother is not responsive to satiety signals. Thus breastfeeding, delayed introduction of solid foods, and allowing the infant to set the amount of food consumed are frequently recommended as ways of preventing overfeeding and subsequent obesity (Dubois, Hill, & Beaton, 1979). Even though there is little documentation supporting these propositions, so well-established are these recommendations that mothers of infants who do develop excess adipose tissue are often assumed to be guilty of not following them. Thus, a fat baby, in the eyes of some, is an indication of poor mothering, and both the mother and child interact in environments marked by social disapproval. The disapproval communicated to the mother as the infant is weighed can create strain; the resulting stress is reflected in the relationship between some mothers and their overweight infants, which intensifies as the baby reaches childhood (Tobias, 1982).

However, current research forces us to reconsider these past assumptions. Chess, Thomas, and Birch have pointed out that infants come into the world with their own energy metabolism and levels, which may or may not be related to their mothers' activities. Their observation is reinforced by the work of Dubois, Hill, and Beaton (1979), a team of Canadian researchers, who studied feeding practices commonly linked with infant obesity and found that the mothers of fat babies in their sample were not overfeeding them. They compared 42 normal and 47 obese infants aged 4-7 months with respect to energy, macronutrient intake, breast feeding history, age of introduction to solids, and maternal reliance on such external cues as time of day. The study failed to reveal any characteristic differences. In fact, on a body weight basis, the infants in the obese groups tended to eat less than their normal counterparts, particularly among those for whom maternal restriction of food intake was reported. These researchers emphasized that in the absence of a full understanding of the etiology of obesity in infants, it is most necessary to consider the possibility that a child's weight may reflect a lower than average energy need, due to genetic differences or low activity patterns.

They also found that some mothers participating in their study had restricted the food of their infants in attempts to insure that the baby conformed to the ideal weight. Such restrictions may have undesirable effects in meeting the infants' nutrient needs and may interfere with normal growth (Dubois, Hill, & Beaton, (1979). Such research cautions professionals to assess more carefully the consequences of making mothers excessively conscious of their infants' weight. What happens to babies who are denied the food they demand as infants—with all the physiological and psychological ramifications that denial imposes—in order to insure that they do not grow up obese? In order to understand the relationship of the mothers' feeding behavior to the infants' size, more attention has to be paid to the biological and sociological variables that have impact upon infancy.

Until recently the role of the father or the rest of the family during children's infancy was not discussed in relationship to feeding (Cath, Furwitt, & Ross, 1982). Currently, though, attention is being turned to fathering and family systems theory (Hertzler, 1981). However, the treatment of obese children still focuses primarily upon the involvement of the mother (Brownell, 1984). The interpretation is still being distributed that obese children are often obese because their mothers "tend to be domineering and overprotective women who treat their child as if he or she were an inanimate object to be used as compensation for the mother's true or imaginary ills, with no respect for the child's own needs" (Wolman, 1982, p. 96).

Versions of these theories have filtered down to some of the women with whom Tobias works. She has listened to the torments of those who feel blamed by pediatricians or mental health professionals for overfeeding a child during infancy, even though they swear they did not do so, and whose working relationships with such professionals reflect the strain of this felt accusation. Yet, no one can be sure that any child would have been thin if his or her mother had behaved differently. If Americans grow up obsessed with weight, such an obsession is reinforced by the unquestioning acceptance of the assumption that an infant's weight is a measure of mother's competence.

One sociological consequence of these past theories is seen in the lives of adult women who are enraged with their mothers, whom they blame for their problem of weight. Paradoxically, some who are obese or were anorexic rage at their mothers for withholding food during infancy (Orbach, 1978) or attack them for following the very instructions health care professionals have assumed they disregarded (Chernin, 1981). Others are equally infuriated because they hold their mothers responsible for overfeeding during infancy and creating too much fat (Klingman, 1981). Whether or not adult women ultimately decide to accept the interpretation that their mothers failed to feed them properly as infants, acceptance of such theories, particularly during adolescence, can contaminate the mother-daughter relationship, as published case histories demonstrate. The same finding may hold for mothers and sons as well but with the exception of Cahnman's seminal work, most of the literature at hand discusses women. Clearly, there is a need to study the total impact of restricting food intake during infancy on the development of both men and women. Attention to weight is necessary but not sufficient.

In the past, much suffering for both mothers and their fat children has grown out of the separation between biomedical and psychosocial models of development. Given current research findings, overweight infants should undergo a good multidisciplinary evaluation before it is concluded that they are becoming obese children because they are overfed or poorly mothered. Surely, their mothers, fathers, and families, regardless of etiology, should be advised by compassionate specialists who are trained to take into account the complex social interactions that infant feeding creates and expresses. Premature application of one-sided interpretations of the causes of an infant's weight can lay the foundation for a stressful childhood, as we next discuss.

Childhood

By chance alone, there should be the same proportion of fat little boys as there are fat little girls, yet, this is not the case. Although estimates of prevalence vary and reflect the lack of standard definitions, methods of measurement, and recognition of social and environmental factors, obesity is believed to be more prevalent among girls than boys (Stunkard, 1980, pp. 415-416). The reasons for this finding are not understood. They may be biological, they may be cultural. Regardless of the explanation, the trends that have emerged from studies of prevalence are also reflected in the literature on childhood obesity and weight control. For example, more girls than boys are found in the samples of investigators who have evaluated behavioral treatment of childhood obesity, whose findings Stunkard has reported (1980, Table 23). If "fat is a feminist issue," it has become so not only because women are charged with being slim in this culture or still assume major responsibilities for nurturing and feeding (Orbach, 1979, 1983). If estimates of prevalence are correct, the management of obesity in childhood may affect the life course of nearly one-third of the female population (Brownell & Stunkard, 1980). Feminist attention to weight and weight control, therefore, reflects a growing recognition of the ways in which the experience of growing up female have been linked with the experiences of growing fat (Allon, 1981; Chernin, 1981).

Current thinking emphasizes the need for weight reduction before adolescence (Brownell, 1984). The identification and treatment of childhood obesity is often based on standards used in the Ten State Nutrition Survey. According to the findings of such surveys, 10-30% of girls are obese; the values for boys are lower (Brownell & Stunkard, 1980). The claim is also being advanced that the earlier that weight control is introduced, the better the outcome (Collipp, 1980; Jesse, 1982). Accordingly, children and their families are increasingly being involved in weight management programs, often behaviorally oriented, at very young ages (Hertzler, 1981; Stunkard, 1980). Their childhoods are being shaped by the application of current thinking about obesity, for such theories become incorporated into the advice given their parents and are used to guide their eating and development.

Professionals discuss prevention in the context of the new knowledge at hand, which stresses the role of genetics. Obesity, it has been found, tends to run in families (Foman, 1982). With one obese parent, a child has a risk of about 40% of becoming an obese adult; with two such parents, the risk is increased to 70% (Collipp, 1980; Owens and Paige, 1982). Foman (1982), a noted pediatrician, points out that knowledge of parent obesity is almost certainly more useful in predicting childhood obesity than is knowledge of weight gain during infancy or weight for height of the mother during pregnancy. He directs attention to the need to determine how much of this is due to genetic, as well as environmental and social, factors.

The findings themselves are not news. These ideas were distributed to professionals and taken for granted by 1975 (Collipp). However, the emphasis on genetics requires us to look again at the ways in which this knowledge is linked to the lives of children and their families. How much of a child's weight is in fact environmentally controlled? The answer to this question may radically change the past meanings given to childhood obesity. These findings have been distributed in a fascinating way in attempts to reconcile the old nature/nurture controversy, which lies beneath the surface of debates over biomedical and psychosocial models.

The Role of Parental Intervention

In 1980 Stunkard edited a collection of papers which were contributed by "authorities in the field" in order to help "clinicians approach obese patients with new hope. The sources of this hope: basic science and treatment" (1980, p. vii). Collipp (1980), who directs one of the child obesity clinics that Allon observed, wrote the chapter on obesity. He, too, has alerted clinicians to the finding that "obesity is usually inherited as a polygenic disorder in a manner analogous to schizophrenia or juvenile diabetes mellitus" (p. 406) and has pointed to the same data Foman cited. A biological explanation that suggests that obesity is equivalent to schizophrenia does not necessarily inspire hope, but Collipp does not continue this analogy. Instead, he argues that the development of obesity is also fostered by "faulty feeding practices" (p. 407) and can be prevented and controlled by proper management in the home and in school.

The theme of parental responsibility for body size was stressed in a book written by Wilkinson (1980) that popularizes the work of Collipp among others. This paperback, entitled *Don't Raise Your Child to be a Fat Adult*, was bought at a local drugstore after a parent of an overweight child brought it to Dr. Gordon's attention. (Such serendipitous occurrences are of great value, as W.I. Thomas taught us while analyzing discarded letters from a Polish peasant.) Much of the book is based on the same information about obesity distributed to professionals.

However, nuances change when it is presented to parents. For example, Wilkinson presents the same information from the Ten State Nutrition Survey that professionals discuss and cites the same statistics about the correlation between the parent's weight and the child's. However, the emphasis is different. Wilkinson concludes, "The family with two overweight children will have to work harder. . . . The sooner parents decide to prevent their children from becoming obese, the easier the job is. The younger the children, the easier prevention is" (1980, p. 35).

Collipp, in the foreword to Wilkinson's book, applauds its optimism, but he also tells the reader immediately that his program is not 100% successful. This fact is reemphasized in the chapter entitled "Dr. Collipp's Methods," in which he is quoted noting that his rate of success is 40% (p. 88). Wilkinson, however, glosses over the fact. Over and over again, the book assures parents that children remain fat only if their parents want them to be fat. "Preventing obesity or treating obesity is simply a matter of changing habits" (p. 138).

Wilkinson is not alone in urging parents to become involved overseers of their children's eating. The instructions currently being distributed to health care professionals also advocate behavioral techniques in which mothers and families organize eating around the needs of the heaviest member (Brownell, 1984). However, the popularization of these injunctions ignores the possibility that the child may be genetically pre-programmed to be fat, regardless of the family's behavior. For instance, Wilkinson gives a seven-day sample 900-calorie diet based on Dr. Collipp's. This diet is followed by a summary of behavior modification techniques. These include asking children to keep food diaries, which parents are to read; eliminating all fattening foods from the house, even if thinner siblings want them, having children walk to school, rather than take the school bus; restricting television; instructing children not to eat birthday cake and ice cream at parties for six months; and making sure children exercise. "No boy or girl who runs five miles a day is going to be a fat child" (p. 137). These, the book concludes, are some of the "ways to attain and keep normal weight" (p. 138).

Perhaps—but is this the way to attain a normal childhood? Parents of children who are massively obese may have no other choice but to conform to such a regimen. Some intervention may be justified if an overweight child is painfully teased at school and it is thought that weight loss will relieve this stress (Brownell, 1984). However, a child's ability to make friends does not necessarily increase if the child jogs five miles alone, refuses birthday cake, doesn't take the school bus with friends, avoids going out with peers who snack on fattening foods, or no longer watches popular after-school programs because he or she is exercising. One child presented with these suggestions responded, "If I do that, I may be skinny, but I won't have anything to talk about with other kids." Although Wilkinson takes dietary instructions to their logical extreme, we can see that injunctions that focus upon weight loss without taking account of the consequences of these instructions upon the social worlds of both child and family can create dilemmas for the mothers who are asked to enforce them.

Psychosocial Repercussions

What meanings do these children give to the actions of adults? How do they react to the sudden restrictions parents place upon them in the name of weight control? Food, after all, has been equated with love. Food restriction must have emotional meaning to children who are asked to radically alter their eating behavior (Lehman, 1949). Allon's observations of overweight youth in obesity clinics led her to believe that many of these children grow up with a negative self-image and low self-esteem even if they were successful in losing weight. Others continue to gain and experience great psychological pain, even though parents try to follow dietary instructions to the letter (Bruch, 1973; Sobal, 1984). The literature is strangely silent about children's own subjective view of their dieting and development.

Adult women, looking back on such childhoods, are not silent, though. The evidence culled from the retrospective accounts of adult women leads one to reconsider the impact of dieting itself upon the child's sense of self. For instance, of the 70 women in a workshop Tobias led, 30 had dieted during childhood. Of these, 25 had been in weight control programs. All spoke with the same bitterness and anger, Bruch observed (1973), when they recounted tales of the stress generated by dieting and the cost to themselves of losing weight under their mothers' rigid surveillance. These women reported that it seemed easier for boys. Of course, there were not many boys in the programs; but those who were there appeared to manage to keep the weight off or to accept themselves if they remained 20-30 pounds overweight. They were not as distressed and retained feelings of self-worth and personal power, which the women knew they themselves lacked (Tobias, 1983). This, too, replicated Bruch's findings (1973).

Oddly enough, the sex of the child is barely mentioned in many accounts of childhood obesity. The treatment is assumed to be the same whether the child is male or female. Yet, the literature on gender roles and sex-role socialization makes it clear that gender matters and needs to be understood. For example, infants who grow up to be obese children are often assumed to be less active than infants who do not do so. Recent work on the father-infant relationship has found that men rough-house more with infants than mothers do, and there is evidence to suggest they engage male children in more physically active play at an earlier age than they do females. By age two, toddlers have already become aware of the different normative expectations for girls and boys. Girls have been taught different games than boys and have been actively discouraged from being tomboys or athletes (Goode, 1983). Moreover, the importance of physical appearance is also learned at an early age, and some investigators believe that stereotype of the ideal female are inculcated long before a child reaches adolescence. Until challenged by recent scholarship, femininity remained linked to passivity. How much of what is observed, then, reflects sex roles rather than fat?

There is a great need to incorporate additional knowledge into the treatment of childhood obesity. The pain and anger reported by the many adults whose childhoods were tragically marred because their lives were shaped by their dieting alert us to look more carefully at the long-range consequences of the early treatment of childhood obesity by behavior modification techniques. The tragedy of the lives of some children is accentuated by the fact that nutritionists have found some low-calorie diets much too severe. A 900-calorie diet, for example, can so limit food intake that it is extremely difficult for the child to get the needed proteins, vitamins, and minerals. Furthermore, nutritionists have found that encouraging a child to adopt a pattern of eating that allows growing into his or her weight has more success than attempting to bring about actual weight loss. If Felix Heald (1972), a respected pediatrician, is correct, during growth there is a period of positive nitrogen balance that corresponds with increasing lean body mass. Achieving the ideal reduction of body fat without loss of body mass may be difficult or impossible during growth, particularly pubescence.

Some children, therefore, have been asked to do the impossible. Others, will succeed at great cost, only to gain weight later. As they grow up, their lives remain organized around food and weight. If Americans are obsessed with weight, this obsession is learned at increasingly younger ages.

In the past, the inner world of the child was not viewed within the psychosocial context created by the diet regimen itself. The child who overeats continues to be described as one who expresses an unconscious wish of the mother, acted out through the child, despite a superficial struggle between mother and child over excess eating. Such mothers have very hostile feelings about their children undertaking steps in autonomy and growing up. Perhaps, but perhaps mothers who must control their children's eating behavior also end up limiting their children's autonomy by restricting activities outside the home and insisting that they eat and exercise with the family as instructed. Perhaps the instructions create additional problems for girls, because they and their mothers may be struggling with changing sex roles in a society that talks about equality but has not yet achieved it. Children, after all, desire to understand the world of adults. From the rules or patterns children extract about how adults behave, children construct models of the world and find their places in it (Cohen, 1980).

At present one body of knowledge turns attention to controlling fat, another addresses itself to the particular experiences of being fat, while yet a third turns to a child's experience of becoming an adult. In the past, these connections have been overlooked. The result, Allon has observed, was that fat teenagers often entered adolescence hating their mothers, their bodies, and themselves (Sobal, 1984).

Adolescence

As their obese children go from childhood to adolescence, mothers are given different instructions. Ironically, the very mother who became absorbed in her child's weight loss and organized the family's behavior to facilitate such loss may now find that she is held accountable not for overfeeding her child, but for overemphasing the importance of weight.

The fluctuating distribution of knowledge about the meaning of childhood weight and the treatment of obesity can be illustrated by looking at a recent collection of papers on current pediatric therapy. It was in this volume that Jesse published the paper on obesity in early childhood that we previously cited. Daniels' paper on obesity (1982) published in the same volume permits us to contrast the set of instructions given by some pediatricians in regard to child obesity with those given in regard to adolescent obesity, as the following quotation illustrates:

> There is no uniformly acceptable treatment of obesity in adolescents or adults. Most obese adolescents have been obese as children, have tried many times to lose weight and maintain lesser weight, and lack the motivation to change their lifestyles over a period of time. Almost always a method for therapeutic management of obesity in adolescents must involve other family members, who often are, and have been, critical of the adolescent's condition. Emotional support from them is needed. (p. 715)

What is this emotional support? No longer is the parent pictured as a mother who needs to control the child by overfeeding. Instead, the parent is described as a person who might have generated feelings of helplessness on the part of the child who failed to lose weight. Although exercise and dieting may be desirable, the main objective in the management of adolescent obesity is to make sure that the adolescent knows that "weight loss is not critical at this state of life," that the obese adolescent's self-esteem is of prime importance, and that these adolescents should "learn to accept themselves, whether fat or lean, as worthwhile individuals" (Daniels, 1982, p. 6).

It is no wonder that mothers of fat daughters report they are damned if they do and damned if they don't. It is also no wonder that adults who were fat children report that they grew up enraged at, and alienated from, their mothers, whom they held responsible not only for their weight, but for their pain (Chernin, 1981; Klingman, 1981).

Conclusion

The cultural contradictions about the meanings of shape, lifestyle, parental responsibility, and individual control that become manifest in adolescence play themselves out in the life course of people who struggle with body size until they die. If, as current knowledge postulates, adulthood reflects the ways in which we were mothered, parented, and socialized, the consequences of the current social distribution about weight and obesity are reflected in all of our lives.

As this paper has discussed, lives as well as bodies are being shaped by the application of current theories about obesity. It is therefore surprising to find, as we search for ways of understanding and helping, that the literature is not replete with studies of the children, parents, and families who have struggled with weight and obesity.

The family therapy literature at our disposal is far richer in regard to the families of teenagers who suffer from anorexia. Anorexia is, of course, a dramatic life-threatening condition (see other papers in this volume). Investigators have told us much about the mother-child relationships of many girls and a few boys who starve to be thin in families in which fathers, siblings, and relatives also play roles; but what about fat children and their families? We know so little about the different meanings and feelings boys and girls attach to dieting and fat as they grow. Yet, is not the loss of the ability to love oneself as is, as important as the loss of pounds? Should we not also turn to the experiences of the families, pressured as they were to change their children's shapes, who still succeeded in teaching their children to value themselves? To understand the consequences of dieting upon the life course of children, we must look at the development of the families and children who struggle with weight with the same kind of empathy, compassion, and concern that is evidenced in family therapy literature at its best.

We have much to learn about the subjective realities of fat children as they grow. Thus, we return to the separation between objective and subjective frames of reference, with which we began this paper. As Cooley long ago observed, science is "knowledge that is verifiable and cumulative" It is knowledge that "can be established to the satisfaction of an expert group and endure as the basis of new acquisitions" (1927, p. 148). The study of the subjective meanings given by children to their world is not always deemed as scientific as the objective biomedical research that concentrates upon their bodies. Yet, are not both necessary? After all, we health care professionals, biomedical researchers, and behavioral scientists grow up in the same culture and develop the same socially derived perceptions about the meaning of fat as many of the children and parents with whom we interact (Allon, 1980). We, too, live in families containing fat and thin members who struggle with illness, hardship, death, and history (Elder and Liker, 1983; Havaran, 1978). We, too, know the joys of celebrating the wonder of life and the miracles of survival. Yet, the very complexity of eating in the everyday world which we all know sometimes vanishes through the processes by which scientific knowledge is created and communicated.

The nurturance of our young, after all, depends upon more than feeding alone. Human destiny is shaped by both biology and society. Yet, often the social processes by which scientific research is shaped and funded separate the biomedical researcher from the psychosocial one. Such processes that separate one group of experts from the other are reflected in the separation between the biomedical and psychosocial approaches to obesity; this separation, in turn, is reflected in treatment and lives.

The integration of psychosocial and biological frames of reference is not an easy thing to do or to teach (Leigh & Reizer, 1980), nor is it easy to deal with the divisions between, and within, groups of experts in a time in which there is competition for funds and faculty positions. Yet, to eliminate the American obsession with weight, it is necessary to link what is known about our culture, social and economic realities, gender roles, mothering, fathering, child and adolescent development, and family integration and conflicts to what is known about the biomedical factors that influence energy intake, energy expenditure, and weight gain and loss.

The changing conceptions of childhood and adolescent obesity discussed in this paper carry with them great opportunities of multidisciplinary thinking, research, and practice, if we choose to use and distribute them. Continuing attention to the social distribution of knowledge about obesity and its management can help create the kind of humane social world in which all children, male and female, fat and thin, can live lives that are not tragically impaired by the meanings given to weight during childhood and adolescence.

Acknowledgment

The authors would like to gratefully acknowledge the generous assistance of Dr. Ellis Perlswig, Yale Child Study Center, Yale University.

References

Allon, N. (1973). The stigma of overweight in everyday life. In G.A. Bray (Ed.), *Obesity in perspective* (pp. 83-102). Washington, DC: U.S. Government Printing Office.

Allon, N. (1980). Sociological aspects of overweight youth. In R.A. Collipp (Ed.), *Childhood obesity* (2nd ed., pp. 139-156). Littletown, MA: PSG Publishing.

Allon, N. (1981). The stigma of weight in everyday life. In *Psychological aspects of obesity: A handbook* (pp. 130-174). New York: Van Nostrand Reinhold.

Anderson, L., Dibble, M., Turkk, P., Mitchell, H., & Rynbergen, H. (1982). Weight control. In *Nutrition in health and disease* (17th ed., pp. 467-486). Philadelphia: J.B. Lippincott.

Andres, R. (1983, June). *Desirable weight and longevity-status of the controversy.* Paper presented at The Brain's Control of Weight, New York, NY, sponsored by Pacific Medical Center, California.

Armstrong, D. (1980). *Political anatomy of the body: Medical knowledge in Britain in the twentieth century.* Cambridge: Cambridge University Press.

Atwood, M. (1976). *Lady oracle.* New York: Avon Books.

Barber, B., & Hirsch, W. (Eds.). (1962). *The sociology of science.* Glencoe: Free Press.

Benedict, R. (1934). *Patterns of culture.* New York: Houghton Mifflin.

Bennett, W., & Gurin, J. (1982). *The dieter's dilemma.* New York: Basic Books.

Brownell, K., & Stunkard, A. (1980a). Behavioral treatment for obese children and adolescents. In A. Stunkard (Ed.), *Obesity* (pp. 415-437). Philadelphia: W.B. Saunders.

Brownell, K., & Stunkard, A. (1980b). Behavioral treatment of obesity in children. In *Childhood obesity.* Littleton, MA: PSG Publishing.

Brownell, K. (1984). New developments in treatment of obese children and adolescents. In A. Stunkard (Ed.), *Eating and its disorders* (pp. 175-1783). New York: Ravencrest.

Bruch, H. (1973). *Eating disorders.* New York: Basic Books.

Cahnman, W. (1968). The stigma of obesity. *The Sociological Quarterly,* 283-299.

Cath, S.H., Furwitt, A.R., & Ross, J.M. (Eds.). (1982). *Father and child: Developmental and clinical perspectives.* Boston: Little, Brown.

Chaderow, N. (1978). *The reproduction of mothering.* Berkeley: University of California Press.

Chernin, K. (1981). *The obsession.* New York: Harper and Row.

Cohen, D. (1980). Constructive and reconstructive activities in the analysis of a depressed child. *Psychoanalytic Study of the Child,* 35, 237-266.

Collipp, P. (1975). *Childhood obesity.* Acton: Publishing Science Group.

Collipp, P. (1980a). Obesity in childhood. In A. Stunkard (Ed.), *Obesity* (pp. 405-414). Philadelphia: Saunders Press.

Collipp, P. (1980b). Introduction. In J.F. Wilkinson (Author), *Don't raise your child to be a fat adult.* New York: Signet.

Committee on Dietary Allowances, National Research Council, Food and Nutrition Board. (1980). *Recommended dietary allowances.* Washington, DC: National Academy of Science.

Committee on Maternal Nutrition of the American College of Obstetricians and Gynecologists, 1974.

Committee on Maternal Nutrition, National Research Council, Food and Nutrition Board. (1970). *Maternal nutrition and the course of pregnancy.* Washington, DC: National Academy of Science.

Committee on Nutrition, American College of Obstetricians and Gynecologists. (1974). *Nutrition in maternal health care.* Chicago: American College of Obstetricians and Gynecologists.

A common sense diet plan: How to lose a pound a week. (1982, April). *Ebony Magazine,* pp. 90, 92, 94.

Cooley, C. (1918). *Social process.* New York: Scribner's.

Cooley, C. (1927). Art, science and sociology. In *Life and the student.* New York: Alfred A. Knopf.

Daniels, W.A., Jr. (1982). Obesity. In S. Gelles et al. (Eds.), *Current pediatric therapy* (pp. 715-716). Philadelphia: W.B. Saunders.

Deluise, M., Blackburn, G.L., & Flier, J.S. (1980). Reduced activity of the red blood cell sodium and potassium pump in human obesity. *New England Journal of Medicine,* **303,** 1017-1022.

Denezin, N. (1970). *The research act.* Chicago: Aldine Publishing.

Dubois, S., Hill, D., & Beaton, G. (1979). An examination of factors believed to be associated with infant obesity. *American Journal of Clinical Nutrition,* **32,** 1997-2003.

Elder, G., & Liker, J. (1983). Hard times in women's lives: Historical influences across forty years. *American Journal of Sociology,* **88,** 24t-26a.

Foman, S. (1982). *Nutritional disorders of children—prevention, screening and follow-up* (DHEW Publication No. HSA 78-5104)). Washington, DC: U.S. Government Printing Office.

Forbes, G. (1977). Obesity. In H. Green & R. Haggerty (Eds.), *Ambulatory pediatrics II* (pp. 348-353). Philadelphia: W.B. Saunders.

Foucault, M. (1973). *The birth of the clinic: An archeology of medical perception.* London: Tavisock.

Frank, L. (1933). *Childhood and youth in recent social trends in the United States: Report of the President's Research Committee on Social Trends.* New York: McGraw-Hill.

Freud, S. (1974). Some psychical consequences of the anatomical distinction between the sexes. In J. Strachey (Ed. and Trans.), *The standard edition of the complete psychological works of Sigmund Freud* (Vol. 19, pp. 248-258). London: Hogarth Press. (Original work published 1925)

Goode, E. (1983). Women and men. In *Sociology*. New York: Prentice-Hall.

Gordon, J., et al. (1972). *A psycho-social approach to nutrition education in an obstetrical clinic in a metropolitan hospital.* Paper presented at the International Congress of Nutrition, Mexico City.

Gordon, J. (1977). *Obesity and the sociology of suffering.* Paper presented at the annual meeting of the Society for the Study of Social Problems, Montreal.

Gordon, J., & Pye, O. (1976). The pregnant patient and her diet. In *The Female Patient.*

Gordon, J., & Tobias A. (1984). Fat, female, and the life-course: The developmental years. *Marriage and Family Review, 7*(1), 65-92.

Havaran, T. (1978). Family time and historical time. In A. Rossi et al. (Eds.), *The family.*

Heald, F. (1972, May). Treatment of obesity in adolescence. *Postgraduate Medicine*, pp. 109-112.

Henry, J. (1965). *Culture against man.* New York: Vintage Books.

Herman, C.P., & Mack, D. (1975). Restrained and unrestrained eating. *Journal of Personality, 43*, 647-660.

Hertzler, A. (1981). Obesity-impact of the family. *Journal of the American Dietetics Association, 79*, 525-530.

Hertzler, A., & Owen, C. (1984). Culture, families and the change process—A systems approach. *Journal of American Dietetics Association, 84*, 535-540.

Himms-Hagen, J. (1982). Determinants of human obesity. *Clinical Nutrition, 1*, 4-8.

Jesse, M.J. (1982). Obesity in early childhood. In S. Gelles et al. (Eds.), *Current pediatric therapy* (pp. 2-4). Philadelphia: W.B. Saunders.

Kaminetzky, H.A., Langer, A., Baker, H., Frank, O., Thompson, A., Munves, E., Opper, A., Behrle, F., & Glista, B. (1973). The effect of nutrition in teenage gravidas on pregnancy and the status of the neonate. *American Journal of Obstetrics and Gynecology, 115*, 639-646.

Kagan, J. (1983). *Birth to maturity.* New Haven: Yale Press.

Klingman, M. (1981). *The secret lives of fat people.* Boston: Houghton-Mifflin.

Kuhn, T. (1962). *The structure of scientific revolutions.* Chicago: University of Chicago Press.

Laslett, B., & Warren, C. (1975). Losing weight: The organizational production of behavior change. *Social Problems, 23*, 69-80.

Lehman, E. (1949). Feeding problems of psychogenic origin. *The Psychoanalytic Study of the Child, 3*, 461-481.

Leigh, H., & Reiser, M. (1980). *The patient: Biological, psychological and social dimension of medical practice.* New York: Plenum Books.

Maddox, G., Back, K.W., & Liederman, V.R. (1968). Overweight as social deviance and disability. *Journal of Health and Social Behavior, 9*, 287-298.

McBride, A. (1982). Obesity of women during childbearing years. *Nursing Clinics of North America*, 17, 217-225.

Metropolitan Life Insurance Company. (1960). *Desirable weights for men and women*. (Available from Metropolitan Life Insurance Company, 1 Madison Avenue, New York, NY)

Metropolitan Life Insurance Company. (1983). *Height/weight table*. (Available from Metropolitan Life Insurance Company, 1 Madison Avenue, New York, NY)

Millman, M. (1980). *Such a pretty face*. New York: W.W. Norton.

Newsholme, E.A. (1982). The interrelationship between metabolic regulation, weight control, and obesity. *Proceedings of the Nutrition Society*, 41, 183-191.

Nisbett, R.E. (1973). Hunger, obesity and the ventromedial hypothalamus. *Psychology Review*, 79, 433-458.

Orbach, S. (1978). *Fat is a feminist issue*. New York: Berkley Books.

Orbach, S. (1982). *Fat is a feminist issue II*. New York: Berkley Books.

Owens, G., & Paige, D. (1982). Obesity in infants and children. *Clinical Nutrition*, 1, 9-13.

Paige, D. (1982). Managing the obese patient. *Clinical Nutrition*, 1, 9-13.

Reich, W. (1983, January 30). The world of Soviet psychiatry. *New York Times Magazine*, pp. 20-27.

Rodin, J. (1980). The externality theory today. In A.J. Stunkard (Ed.), *Obesity* (pp. 226-229). Philadelphia: W.B. Saunders.

Rose, M.S. (1940). *Feeding the family*. New York: Macmillan.

Schutz, A. (1964). *Collected papers II: Studies of social theory*. Edited by A. Broderson. The Hague: Martinus Nijhoff.

Sims, E.A.H. (1976). Experimental obesity, dietary-induced thermogenesis and their clinical implications. In M.J. Albrink (Ed.), *Clinics in endocrinology and metabolism* (pp. 377-395). Philadelphia: W.B. Saunders.

Sobal, J. (1984). Group dieting, the stigma of obesity, and overweight adolescents: The contributions of Natalie Allon to the sociology of obesity. *Marriage and Family Review*, 7(1), 9-20.

Stunkard, A. (1980). *Obesity*. Philadelphia: W.B. Saunders.

Sussman, M. (1956). Psycho-social correlates of obesity: Failure of calorie collectors. *Journal of the American Dietetic Association*, 32, 423-428.

Tobias, A. (1982). *Maternity infant care-family planning projects*. Unpublished manuscript, Medical and Health Research Association of New York.

Tobias, A. (1983, March). *Feminism, woman's studies, and home economics*. Paper presented at the workshop entitled "The Nutrition Connection—Fat and Food—A Conference" at Herbert H. Lehman College, City University of New York.

Tobias, A., & Gordon, J.B. (1980). Social consequences of obesity. *Journal of the American Dietetic Association*, 76, 338-342.

Thomas, W., & Thomas, D. (1928). *The child in America*. New York: Alfred A. Knopf.

Weigley, E.S. (1984). Average? Ideal? Desirable? A brief overview of height/weight tables. *Journal of American Dietetics Association,* **84,** 417-423.

Wilkinson, J.F. (1980). *Don't raise your child to be a fat adult.* New York: Signet Books.

Winikoff, B. (1983). *Handbook of health care and the health professions.* New York: The Free Press.

Wolman, B. (1982). *Psychological aspects of obesity: A handbook.* New York: Van Nostrand Reinhold.

Chapter 4

Should the Obese Child Diet?

Ellyn Satter

We are in the midst of a major attitudinal shift in our perceptions of obesity and the treatment of obesity. Our traditional way of explaining what we see is being weakened by negatives and discrepancies. We are feeling increasing pressure to come up with a new way of thinking.

The Traditional Model

In the past we have defined obesity as a major problem and have set out to cure it. We have created ingenious eating management systems. We have imposed diets (Wing & Jeffery, 1979), some of them so severe that they were potentially more harmful than the condition itself. Behaviorists got into the act, primarily because they saw weight reduction, with its objective outcome indicator, to be the ideal problem on which to ply their craft. Little did they know.

The national attitude about weight has almost taken on the character of a phobia. To achieve weight loss, people dealing with even moderate or nonexistent excesses in body weight are apparently willing to put up with (or impose) cures that are physically more harmful than the condition itself. Many commonly used weight reduction regimens are so severe they can be justified only when the obesity presents a major health risk.

Helpers, as well as sufferers,, have experienced the frustration and futility of trying to win the battle with weight. In my 15 years of weight loss counseling in a medical setting, I have seen about 100 "weight losers" a year. I have used methods ranging from nutrition education to behavioral modification. In that time, I have seen significant and sustained weight loss in perhaps five. None of them had ever dieted before: they were virgin dieters.

I read the literature and wondered why my patients were being so much less successful than those I read about. However, now long-term follow-up studies indicate that the only programs successful with sustained weight loss have been multifaceted programs that incorporate long and structured follow-up (Wing & Jeffery, 1979). Successes were moderate and the amount of investment, in some cases, enormous—far beyond what I or most of my patients could afford.

In working with patients and observing their repeated engagements and failures with the weight loss process, I began to see more and more resemblance between us and Sisyphus. He was the Greek who was condemned to an eternal afterlife of rolling a boulder up a mountain, only to have it roll back down again. Similarly, we can neither accomplish our task nor set it aside.

Childhood Intervention

In our frustration at the low success rate with adults, we have turned to preventive interventions with children. However, in working with childhood obesity, we are equally handicapped. We don't know how to define obesity in childhood, how to cure it, or even how to prevent it. We don't know what causes obesity. Obese people seemingly do little out of the ordinary to cause them to become fat, and once they are fat, only the most extraordinary behavior will allow them to become thin (Wooley & Wooley, 1979).

We have very little way of knowing what to predict or expect from a child. Some people are genetically predisposed to obesity, and we don't know who they are or how to overcome that genetic tendency (Foch & McClearn, 1980). Most children lose their baby fat as they get older (Shapiro et al., 1984). We don't know if weight loss programs help or hinder this loss. A program that sets up struggles and anxiety about eating could very well hinder weight loss.

One wonders how much good we are really doing with our interventions in childhood. Many obese adults come in to treatment having been "dieted" since childhood. They recall wistfully their moderate degree of overweight in childhood and young adulthood. They wonder if they would have been thinner if they hadn't done all that dieting.

Bruch (1973) has talked about children exposed to intense parental pressure to lose weight. She noted that for them, weight was their most centrally important feature. Their perception was that until they got thin, they could not achieve, be, and do what they wanted in life.

She contrasted these patients to others, equally fat, who had been raised with a positive and accepting attitude on the part of parents. In these instances, although patients had regretted their fatness, and perhaps even, with the help of their parents, tried to get rid of it, they felt their lives were really very full and that they could function very well (Bruch, 1973). She further made the embarrassed observation that the greater the number of helpers, the more negative the outcome in terms of the child's self-concept.

That's a pretty powerful indictment. It makes one wonder if what we have seen as "helping" has really been helping at all. Indeed, it is likely that our interventions at times have been harmful.

The Pressure to Help

We feel enormous pressure, some of it from ourselves, some from parents and the patients themselves. We want to try to help, particularly in obesity prevention. Although accurate statistics on obesity are hard to find, it appears that babies outgrow fatness (Shapiro et al., 1984). Less than 10% of infants who are obese become obese adults. However, the risk of developing adult obesity is increased to about 25% in the obese preschooler, and 70% for the obese adolescent (Weil, 1977). The person who is obese as an adult has a considerable chance of remaining obese throughout life. (Stunkard & McLaren-Hume, 1959).

It is not going to get us out of our bind to argue that the problem doesn't exist. Some have maintained that obesity is really not as much of a risk factor as it is represented to be (Mallick, 1983; Polivy & Herman, 1983). This may be true for moderate degrees of obesity and for certain people who have no other health problems. However, obesity is certainly a psychosocial risk factor. It is a handicapping condition that carries penalties in self-esteem, physical capability, and social and vocational opportunities. People learn at an early age to discriminate, at least attitudinally, against the obese.

The arguments and motivations to persist in trying for weight loss are enormously persuasive. It's nicer to be thinner. However, the unavoidable fact is that despite considerable personal disadvantage, most people are simply unable to achieve and maintain a lowered body weight (Stunkard & McLaren-Hume, 1959).

The Negative Outcome

In spite of all the energy expended, people don't seem to be getting any thinner. We all participate in instituting treatments that have been proven to be ineffective—and our patients' frustration and despair increase. Our cure, rather than resolving the problem, appears to be making it worse.

If one slants the way of looking at obesity intervention data and the case histories, one can begin to notice a trend. Many people who diet, rather than stabilizing their weight as adults or gaining slowly during aging, gain prodigiously. Many children, rather than establishing themselves in a predictable growth pattern, show periods of pronounced weight gain. Some children and adults maintain their weight at reduced levels, but at enormous sacrifice (Bruch; 1973; Wooley & Wooley, 1984). Eventually they get to the point where they can't sustain the effort anymore, and they, also, gain (Keesey, 1978).

Dieting produces behavioral and physiological reactions that increase pressure to gain weight. People who diet become preoccupied with food and prone to reactive overeating. They lose lean body tissue and regain fat. They reduce their metabolic rates and their activity levels (Keys, Brozek, Henschel, Michelson, & Taylor, 1950). Their physiological patterns of energy storage may even change as a result of heightened food awareness (Powley, 1977).

Rather than maintaining a consistent weight, the pattern in many, if not most, dieters is chronic loss and regaining. There is evidence that this unstable weight pattern is more unhealthy than maintaining a consistent, though higher, weight.

Redefining the Problem

To get out of this bind we are in, we can change how we define the problem and what we treat; we can define the problem in a way it can be solved. Instead of seeing the problem as obesity and the solution as weight loss, we can begin to see the problem as the consequences that obesity and the treatments for obesity have for peoples' lives.

Having redefined the problem, we can redefine the resolution. The resolution is not in getting rid of the obesity (although we can always hope that our interventions will accomplish that, at least for a few). It is in treating the whole cluster of attitudes and behaviors that attend obesity.

Obese patients who are chronic dieters (and most of them are) show considerable distortion in their eating attitudes and behaviors. They are anxious and confused about eating and body weight. Obese people deprive themselves of healthful exercise. Many do not observe positive health behaviors except when they are dieting. Many suffer from social isolation and low self-esteem. All these symptoms we can treat; the obesity we cannot treat.

We—and our patients—can begin to be successful when we start to define our task not as putting people on diets and getting them to be thin.

Instead, we can talk in terms of preventing (or correcting) distorted attitudes and behaviors concerning eating and weight, of teaching people to eat in a positive and deliberate fashion, of establishing positive and healthful exercise, and of instituting coping skills to help persons deal with what is really a handicapping condition. Childhood prevention in the broader definition can mean avoiding establishing negative attitudes and behaviors.

Instead of pushing for weight loss, we can collude with our patients in a realistic exploration of what holds true for them. We can't promise to make or keep people thin. We can't even be sure that we can keep a child thin. All we can do is to be moderate and consistent in our efforts and avoid doing harm. Instead of colluding with people's perceptions that weight is their most centrally important feature, we can help them get it back into perspective as only one, though perhaps regrettable, feature.

Along with exercise and personal growth, as well as eating interventions, pushing for a particular weight puts pressure on eating, on the helper, and on the helpee. Instead, we must be honest with ourselves and our patients and admit that we really don't know what to predict. We don't know whether a particular person can establish and tolerate a negative calorie balance. We don't know whether they will lose weight, even if they markedly change their eating and exercise. Some people just don't lose.

My work indicates that letting weight find its own level doesn't make people any fatter than they are now. Some even get thinner. All stop gaining too much weight—and all display markedly improved attitudes about eating, weight, and themselves in general.

An Alternate Intervention

I am going to confine my remarks primarily to eating interventions. However, I will make a few brief comments later about exercise and self-esteem.

To help patients find out what holds true for them, we can

- be realistic with them about what they are up against,
- maintain a positive feeding relationship within the family,
- avoid instituting restrained eating.

Be Realistic With the Patient

Instituting dieting implies that energy imbalance causes obesity and that correcting the energy imbalance will cure it. Obesity may indeed be caused by an energy imbalance: a person may be eating too much and exercising too little, and when this imbalance is corrected, he or she may be able to lose weight. However, we don't know this for certain. The fact that weight reduction dieting, if rigorously pursued, can help an individual lose weight does not prove a cause.

However, obesity may also be caused by a constitutional predisposition to excess adiposity (Foch & McClearn, 1980). It may be a genetic condition that is determined and defended by constitutionally based exercise and food regulation inclinations (Keesey, 1978). As such, it is likely to be overruled or overcome only with extreme difficulty, at the expense of trust and dependency on internal cues, and with a significant and unrelenting investment of time and emotional, cognitive, and physical energy. It depends on the individuals and their values whether or not it is "worth" it.

At the opposite extreme, obesity may occur because of a pattern in family dynamics making a child an "identified patient" and distorting his food intake because he is neglected, overindulged, or scapegoated (Satter, 1984). Expecting a child to adhere to a weight reduction diet and lose weight though the whole family system is set up to promote the opposite is imposing a tremendous burden on a child and increasing the negatives in an already extremely negative situation.

People can understand and accept the reality of their situations, however grim. They can understand simple explanations about the effects of negative calorie balance on metabolism, body composition, and mood. Most do not realize how much their dieting costs them in terms of physical and emotional well-being. They *can't* realize it until they start to eat normally again and discover how good that feels.

Our Limitations

Patients deserve to be told how little we know. Health workers, unlike the diet companies that say that anybody can be thin, know better and have a responsibility to say so. We know that the statistics are pretty discouraging (Stunkard & McLaren-Hume, 1959). We are in a position to say firmly, if regretfully, to patients that there is only so much we can do and are willing to do to achieve weight loss. We know that for most people, particularly for children, use of methods drastic enough to achieve weight loss will impose a cure that is worse than the disease (Mallick, 1983; Pugliese, Lifshitz, Grad, Fort, & Marks-Katz, 1983). Even maintenance of modest weight loss may be so demanding on time and energy that the cost is disproportionate.

The most difficult part of the weight loss program is maintenance. We must be realistic about what we are able to offer in this area. Programs that are energetic in the weight loss phase have a responsibility to continue to contribute energy during the maintenance phase. We, like our patients, tend to run out of steam. We owe it to ourselves to provide something we can feel confident of maintaining.

Energy for Helping

Dieting is serious business and is associated with some real risks and negative consequences. If someone is regulating body weight to begin with, even if it is at a higher level than they like, perhaps there is more to lose than to be gained by disrupting the process of food and body weight regulation. A person initiating a diet has to raise the largely unconscious process of regulation of food intake up to a conscious level. He or she has to begin ignoring and overruling, rather than gratifying, food regulation cues. Devoting the energy to live with the negative consequences of dieting can have a major impact on a person's life.

Starvation for any motive is accompanied by pronounced negative symptoms. People in negative calorie balance become tired and irritable and lose interest in other things. Their physiological and metabolic processes slow down, and they often feel dizzy and unsteady. They become preoccupied with food and eating, and they begin to eat in an urgent and intense fashion. If starvation persists, a person's entire life focus narrows to the resulting physical discomfort and the cravings for food created (Keys et al., 1950).

The stimulation of the weight loss setting, whether a group or an individual setting, enhances the patient's tolerance of the negative symptoms of starvation. To make the process work, in most cases the counselor must be willing to contribute a considerable amount of enthusiasm, approval, and ideas to keep the patient going. Eventually, though, the energy wanes, and the patient and counselor cannot sustain the effort.

Stress decreases tolerance for the negative symptoms of starvation. Furthermore, tolerance appears to decrease with repeated exposure to dieting. Some patients become so sensitized that they only have to think about deprivation to send themselves off into reactive overeating.

Stating the Hard Truth

You might react against these statements from the point of view that in being so negative, we are failing to discharge our responsibility to "motivate" the patient. I have come to see motivating patients to lose weight as being paternalistic. People deserve to know what they are up against and to have enough information to weigh the costs, risks, and benefits for themselves.

While the approach is tough and the news bad, at least patients will be relieved of the burden of thinking that excess weight is all their fault and that their failure to lose excess weight is the result of some moral weakness.

Maintain a Positive Feeding Relationship

Maintaining a positive feeding relationship between parent and child demands mutual cooperation and a division of responsibility. The parent is responsible for choosing and providing food. The child is responsible for choosing how much, and even whether, he or she eats (Satter, 1983).

When a diet is imposed, the feeding relationship is distorted. Instead of being able to support infant-controlled feeding by appropriate cue sensitivity, the parent must take charge of the child's prerogatives of quantity and, perhaps, frequency and selection. Instead of respecting a child's normal internal processes of food regulation and innate growth potential, the parent is put in the role of assuming responsibility in those areas. When parents take inappropriate responsibility, the magnitude of the distortions and losses on both sides can be very great. Consider the story of Mary.

The Story of Mary

Mary was dieted by her parents virtually from birth. When she was two days old, a nurse on the obstetrical ward brought her into her mother's hospital room and said, "Your little girl certainly eats a lot—she's had two whole bottles."

Her mother was horrified. She thought Mary's eating a lot meant that Mary was going to be fat, and she certainly wasn't going to have that. Mother was a very disciplined-looking, slender woman—more than likely what Hilda Bruch (1973) has called a "thin-fat" person. She had reportedly dieted unrelentingly to maintain her thin physique. It's possible Mary was even born hungry—at that time obstetricians were being very vehement about restraining weight gain during pregnancy.

So Mother set out to keep Mary thin. Mary didn't get "two whole bottles" from her—she got as much as Mother thought she should have. When she fussed (and she fussed a lot), Mother just put her off or put up with it. Except on the days when Mother couldn't take much, she gave in to her more. It couldn't have been much fun for either of them.

Father didn't get directly involved in the feeding, but he supported Mother in her extremes. (He was the one who told the story and made repeated references to the poor unwitting nurse who had become a family legend.)

However, Mother's interventions didn't really seem to help. Mary stayed on the chubby side through infancy and became a chubby toddler who "stole food out of the cupboards." (What toddler hasn't gotten into the food? In this family, though, this was stealing.) Her earliest memory of feeding was of her mother dishing up a carefully metered portion of carefully selected food. Mary cried, because, for her, not getting enough to eat felt very much like not getting enough love. As an adolescent, she saw herself as obese; as a late adolescent, she was anorexic.

Finally, at age 19, a beautiful and well-proportioned Mary presented herself for treatment of bulimic syndrome. She said she was fat and ugly. She was starving virtually all of the time and only eating when she gave in to food chaotically. She consumed enormous amounts at those times and then vomited repeatedly to get rid of it. On bad days she repeated the cycle as often as five or six times.

Mary's story is chilling because of the quality of insensitivity and rigidity in her parents. Year after year they kept it up, despite enormous sacrifice and little apparent benefit. Clearly, they displayed qualities that were well outside the normal range. A more flexible family would have realized how destructive they were being and would have given up.

Divide Responsibility Between Child and Parents

It is the parents' responsibility to socialize children regarding food. They can do this and avoid making a big issue about weight if they treat the fat child the same as a thin child. Parents can forbid ad-lib snacking, so that a child saves his appetite for meals and planned snacks. They can expect a child to make an effort to adjust his schedule so he can be home most times at mealtime (and they can be flexible in accomodating him).

Parents can be helpful in indirect ways. They can plan meals that are likely to be satisfying without being overwhelming in caloric density. They can put food away and keep other stimuli to eating as low as possible. They can make all of their interventions matter-of-factly, without making a big deal about what they are sacrificing for the child.

In fact, they must not sacrifice for the child. Parents have to be realistic about what they can do, without a lot of hardship on their part. There is an axiom in feeding children that the more effort one expends in providing them with special food, the more likely they are to turn it down cold. If parents are going to a lot of trouble to prepare diet food, a child's eating a bag of french fries with the gang is going to come across as a personal affront.

Parents cannot impose direct limits on the amounts and types of food a child chooses. Once parents have discharged their responsibilities of food provision and providing a positive feeding environment, they simply have to turn food selection and regulation over to their child. If they stand over him to try to get him to eat less, or different, food than he seems to want, they will only be promoting conflict and reactive overeating.

Parents also have to let go of trying to get their child's body to turn out in a way that pleases them. Some parents have an enormous amount of difficulty with that, primarily because of their bad feelings about themselves and their own bodies. If that is the case, the parent may have to be helped with personal problems before the child can be helped.

The Identified Patient

It can be dangerous to agree with parents that a child has a weight problem and to work with them in trying to get rid of it. In some distorted situations, this would be colluding with the family in creating an identified patient. These are the situations to which Bruch referred in talking about the consequences to the child of vehement family concern with treating obesity.

One can generally pick up on such situations intuitively. Mary's situation was an example. When feelings about eating and weight are enormously heightened it is likely that a distortion exists. If a parent says to you, as more than one have to me, "Get my child thin," you *know* that the problem calls for family therapy, not an eating intervention.

Avoid Instituting Restrained Eating

We owe it to Janet Polivy and Peter Herman (Herman & Polivy, 1980) for putting a name on a syndrome we have all observed in practice, and quite possibly in ourselves. It is the phenomenon of the restrained eater. The restrained eater tries not to give in to food. All restrained eaters—obese, normal, or underweight—display preoccupation with regulating food intake and distrust of their internal cues of hunger, appetite, and satiety as guides to food regulation. They attempt to overcome these internal cues and adhere only to such external standards of food regulation as the diet, and prejudices about what is good or bad.

Restrained eaters try not to eat to satiety or to include high calorie preferred foods. They respond only to overwhelming hunger or appetite and often give in to those cues chaotically or impulsively.

Restrained eaters are highly dependent on external control of eating. Dependency on externals makes them more subject to overeating in response to presence of highly salient food (Rodin, 1978), in response to emotional upset, and in response to the perception that they have overeaten (Herman & Polivy, 1980). Thus, restrained eaters are highly subject to episodes of overeating and are prone to reactive weight gain.

Restrained eaters invest considerable cognitive and emotional energy in sustaining deprivation. Chronically restrained eaters think about food and food avoidance a great deal and suffer considerable anxiety and remorse about episodes of uncontrolled eating. Some restrained eaters have been engaged in their struggle with food for so long that they are unaware of, or embarrassed by, their own preferences and desires.

Teach Internally Regulated Eating

The core issue in the attitudinal shift we have been discussing is moving away from external control of eating and back to internal control. The trick is to stop depriving. This is not the same thing, as some patients fear, as giving up on all control.

If one is to avoid instituting restrained eating, the patient can be taught to eat based on internal cues of hunger, appetite, and satiety. Interventions can be catered to set up the environment (and the child's eating habits) so internal regulatory mechanisms are distorted as little as possible by outside interference.

We can teach children and parents food composition and food selection, not to encourage undereating, but so they know how to put together a meal or snack that is likely to be satisfying and that will provide sustained energy and keep away hunger and food-seeking. To be satisfying, a meal should have protein, fat, and carbohydrates; should offer something chewy and something that is bulky and low in caloric density; and should certainly contain something that is delicious.

An essential corollary to internally regulated eating is adjustment in the weight goal. Rather than seeking a particular level, the subject must allow weight to respond as it will to internally determined food intake regulation and to moderate and consistent exercise. In short, the goal is to allow weight to find its own level, rather than encouraging deprivation and loss.

The body *will* regulate, based on internal cues of hunger, appetite, and satiety. Using the same behavioral techniques as have been used to institute weight reduction, people can be taught to eat in a positive and deliberate fashion. We can teach attentive eating, stimulus control, and environmental control. Yet, the intent is not to help people trick themselves out of eating, but rather to help them make deliberate and positive decisions *to* eat.

Maintain Positive Eating Attitudes

We must at all times be positive, rather than negative, about food and eating. Sharing our own love of food and good eating is a powerful way of doing that. We probably wouldn't be in this business if we didn't have a heightened interest in food. We might as well start owning up to this.

Beyond that, we must be careful to avoid imposing anything that even *feels* like deprivation, because that sets up food-seeking reactions. Food deprivation can be disguised in many forms: as portion control, as "eating for good health," as a very liberal pattern that includes a treat every day or every week. However, external control is still just that, and sooner or later external constraints are going to be perceived as deprivation, which can form the basis for reactive overeating.

Many times parents are restrained eaters and have passed their attitudes and anxieties about eating along to their children. In such cases it may be necessary to cure the parents' restrained eating in order to help the children.

Discovering Internally Regulated Eating

People who begin to give themselves permission to eat and discover the ability of their bodies to regulate react with delight and relief. Their panic about being able to control their eating and weight drops away. They achieve their dreams of eating all they want without gaining weight. However, they do not eat the enormous quantities they had imagined; they eat in a positive and deliberate fashion.

Paradoxically, their overeating episodes become less frequent or stop. Patients discover that they don't have to go out of control to eat what they want or to get enough to eat.

Exercise and Self-Esteem

I have not yet said anything about exercise and building self-esteem. I consider each to be an important part of the adolescent treatment package.

Instituting realistic, comfortable, and challenging exercise can help a child be healthier and feel more physically capable. One doesn't have to be skinny to have a good body, and kids can be helped to know this. It's a trap, however, to promote exercise on the basis of producing weight loss. A child might lose some weight if he consistently increases his exercise; he might not. Whether he perceives weight loss as his major reward depends a great deal upon his initial assumptions.

A certain minimum of physical activity appears to enhance accurate food intake regulation. People who are at very low levels of physical activity tend to eat disproportionately great amounts (Mayer, 1959).

Children can be helped with coping and self-enhancement for the way they are right now, not just for the way they hope to become. Helping them come to terms with who they are helps them get on with their lives, rather than waiting until they get thin to do it. Obesity has the distinction of being the only handicapping condition that is blamed on the sufferer, often by the sufferer himself. Kids shouldn't have to do that to themselves.

Treatment Outcomes

The approach I have described is intended to prevent overeating, not to promote undereating. As outlined in Table 1, there are four possible outcomes, which are diagnostic of the problem.

If one establishes normal eating and exercise based on internal controls, and a child loses weight, it is highly likely that he was overeating or underexercising previously. If one does the same thing and he doesn't lose, it appears that his calorie balance previously was appropriate and that the extra fat is part of his constitutional inheritance.

Table 1   Outcomes of Normalizing Eating

Outcome	Problem
Family responds appropriately, child loses weight	Energy imbalance
Family responds appropriately, child doesn't lose weight	Genetics
Family overreacts, child doesn't lose: Is angry at the child Is rigid and domineering Intrudes on child's prerogatives	Family dynamics
Family underreacts, child doesn't lose: Doesn't provide meals Makes no attempt at supportive food planning Expects child to deprive Fails to set appropriate limits on eating behaviors	Family dynamics

If, however, the family fails to cooperate, it won't be possible to establish normal eating and exercise. One still won't know whether the subject's excess weight comes from energy imbalance or genetics, but one does know that he is up against a tough family situation.

It might be possible to interest a family in psychotherapy to help them be less chaotic or less rigid (Satter, 1984). This is valid, because if they are unable to be of any help to one child with weight management, it is unlikely they are able to be of much help to any of their children's needs. The child's weight may or may not go down once the family problem is resolved. However, if the family lets go of weight as an issue, the child will have a chance of increased emotional health.

If a family refuses to try to change itself, it is probably just as well to wait to intervene until the child leaves home. One might be able to be helpful once he gets more control over his environment. In the long run, this can be more productive for him. Unsatisfactory intervention attempts tend to close people's minds for further help. Weight loss attempts tend to be less successful with each repetition.

Summary

We professionals are stymied in our efforts to help patients lose weight. Dieting doesn't work, and we don't know what does.

As an alternative to the weight loss process, this paper suggests that we define the problem in a way it can be solved. We have seen the issue as excess weight and the solution as getting rid of the weight. Instead, we can begin to see the problem as the whole cluster of distorted attitudes and behaviors that surround obesity. This presents a clear direction, helping our patients institute positive eating, exercise, and self-enhancement attitudes and behaviors.

References

Bruch, H. (1973). *Eating disorders: Obesity, anorexia nervosa and the person within.* New York: Basic Books.

Foch, T.T., & McClearn, G.E. (1980). Genetics, body weight and obesity. In A.J. Stunkard (Ed.), *Obesity.* Philadelphia: W.B. Saunders.

Herman, C.P., & Polivy, J. (1980). Restrained eating. In A.J. Stunkard, *Obesity* (pp. 208-225). Philadelphia: W.B. Saunders.

Keesey, R.E. (1978). Set-points and body weight regulation. *Psychiatric Clinics of North America, 1*, 523-544.

Keys, A.J., Brozek, A., Henschel, O., Michelsen, O., & Taylor, H.S. (1950). *The biology of human starvation* (Vols. 1, 2). Minneapolis: University of Minnesota Press.

Mallick, M.J. (1983). Health hazards of obesity and weight control in children: A review of the literature. *American Journal of Public Health, 73*, 78-82.

Mayer, J. (1959). Exercise and weight control. *Postgraduate Medicine, 3*, 25-37.

Polivy, J., & Herman, C.P. (1983). *Breaking the diet habit: The natural weight alternative.* New York: Basic Books.

Powley, T. (1977). The ventromedial hypothalamic syndrome, satiety, and a cephalic phase hypothesis. *Psychological Reviews, 85*, 89-126.

Pugliese, M.T., Lifshitz, F., Grad, G., Fort, P., & Marks-Katz, M. (1983). Fear of obesity; a cause of short stature and delayed puberty. *The New England Journal of Medicine, 309*, 513-518.

Rodin, J. (1978). Has the distinction between internal versus external control of feeding outlived its usefulness? In G.A. Bray (Ed.), *Recent advances in obesity research.* London: Newman.

Satter, E.M. (1983). *Child of mine: Feeding with love and good sense.* Palo Alto: Bull Publishing.

Satter, E.M. (1988). Feeding in the family context. In K. Clark, R. Parr, & W. Castelli (Eds.), *Evaluation and management of eating disorders: Anorexia, bulimia, and obesity.* Champaign, IL: Human Kinetics.

Shapiro, L.R., Crawford, P.B., Clark, M.J., Pearson, D.J., Raz, J., & Huenemann, R.L. (1984). Obesity prognosis: A longitudinal study of children from the age of 6 months to 9 years. *American Journal of Public Health, 74*, 968-972.

Stunkard, A., & McLaren-Hume, M. (1959). The results of treatment for obesity: A review of the literature and report of a series. *Archives of Internal Medicine, 103,* 79-85.

Weil, W.B. (1977). Current controversies in childhood obesity. *Journal of Pediatrics, 91,* 175-187.

Wing, R.R., & Jeffery, R.W. (1979). Outpatient treatments of obesity: A comparison of methodology and clinical results. *International Journal of Obesity, 3,* 261-279.

Wooley, S.C., & Wooley, O.W. (1979). Obesity and women: I. A closer look at the facts. *Women's Studies International Quarterly, 2,* 69-79.

Wooley, S.C., & Wooley, O.W. (1984). Should obesity be treated at all? In A.J. Stunkard & E. Stellar (Eds.), *Eating and its disorders.* New York: Raven.

Chapter 5

Obesity Intervention in Youth: Who? What? When?

M. Joan Mallick

The title of this chapter may be interpreted in two ways. First, it may be understood to mean "Prescribing Obesity Regimes in Youth: For Whom? What Type of Regime? When?" Second, it may be read as "Obesity Intervention in Youth: Who Undertakes Weight Control? What Do They Do? When Do They Do It?" In order to understand one's role as a health professional in relation to childhood weight control, both interpretations must be addressed. It is the purpose of this chapter to examine both versions of the basic question and to demonstrate that the answer to the second version provides the basis for professional intervention in weight control matters.

Prescribing Obesity Regimes in Youth: For Whom? What Type of Regime? When?

Medicine being a compendium of the successive and contradictory mistakes of medical practitioners, when we summon the wisest of them to our aid, the chances are that we may be relying on a scientific truth the error of which will be recognized in a few years' time. [Marcel Proust, Remembrance of Things Past. The Guermantes Way (1913-1927)]

Today's scientific truth about obesity and youth includes the following logical deduction: Premise 1: Overweight and obesity are dangerous conditions in youth not only because of the health risks during the childhood and adolescent years, but also because of the health risks carried into adulthood. Premise 2: Except for a few acute and mild side effects, weight control measures for young people are relatively safe. Conclusion: Therefore, children and adolescents judged to be overweight should be placed on weight reduction regimes.

Those who have studied logic know that in order for a deduction to be valid, the premises themselves must be correct. The purpose of this portion of the discussion is to illustrate the fallacy of the premises related to childhood obesity, thereby illustrating the invalid nature of the conclusions drawn from them. This having been done, the answers to the questions "Obesity intervention: Who? What? When?" should become evident.

Shortcomings of Research

Overweight and obesity in childhood have rarely been associated with mortality, as they have been in adult populations (Powers, 1980). However, there is a general consensus that childhood overweight poses serious physical and psychological problems to afflicted youth. This "fact" is so well-accepted that researchers often do not even state it explicitly in justifying research endeavors (Hooper, 1971). The consensus that overweight in childhood is a serious health problem seems to be based on a handful of oft-quoted research studies that profess to scientifically prove the existence of weight-related health risks. However, a careful examination of these studies reveals methodological or logical errors that invalidate the conclusion that weight-related risks exist.

One frequently quoted study purporting to illustrate the physical risks of overweight among children was done by Hooper and Alexander (1971). These researchers purported to examine the incidence of weight-related illness among 151 children followed in their pediatric practice from birth on. They concluded that overweight children experienced more illnesses than their lean counterparts. However, these authors made several serious mistakes in their research. First, they included in their calculations episodes of illnesses which have never been associated with weight. For instance, they included excema and respiratory illnesses in the total number of illness episodes used to calculate illness rates. Second, in their calculations they did not truly compare overweight and lean children. Rather they compared subjects in three categories: breast-fed, bottle-fed, and obese. When they found that obese infants had an illness rate of 2.3 episodes per infant, whereas breast- and bottle-fed infants had illness rates of only 1.9, they concluded that obesity among infants was associated with greater morbidity.

These authors provided enough data to permit calculations of the true incidence rates of illnesses among obese and lean children. The recalculated statistics show the illness rate of 2.85 among nonobese children is greater than the rate of 2.3 for obese infants. Even if one accepts that the illnesses studied are related to weight status, calculations indicate that the Hooper and Alexander conclusions directly contradict their research data.

Another frequently quoted study was conducted by Tracey and Harper (1971). These authors studied the incidence of respiratory infections among normal- and above-average-weight children aged 3 months to 2 years and reported statistically greater incidence rates among overweight children. Methodological problems, however, abound in this study. For instance, many respiratory illnesses included in the calculations were not directly diagnosed by the researchers. An illness was counted in the study if the parents reported by phone respiratory symptoms lasting 3 or more days. Another methodological flaw was that children in two weight categories were excluded from analysis. The incidence rates of illnesses among lean children—that is, those at or below the 25th percentile—and moderately overweight children—that is, those between the 76th and 89th percentile—were not included in the calculations. Therefore, the researchers have not demonstrated a linear relationship between weight and frequency of illness.

Obesity is perceived to be a particular risk factor for coronary disease. Several studies have examined the relationship between childhood weight status and hypertension. Although the conclusions of most of these studies is that overweight and hypertension are related, close examination of these studies indicates that evidence may not support these conclusions. For instance, Lauer, Connor, Leaverton, Reiter, and Clark (1975) concluded that because weight is related to elevated systolic and diastolic blood pressure among school children independent of height, it was a significant risk factor in coronary disease. However, they ignored their own statistical calculation that showed that age was more highly correlated to increased blood pressure than weight was.

Levine, Lewy, and New (1976) studied the relationship between adolescent weight status and hypertension. Participants in their study were drawn from a population of 1,863 high school students who were screened for hypertension. Of the 110 students found to be hypertensive, 28 consented to be admitted to a hospital for extensive examination. The researchers found that family history of hypertension and obesity were the factors most frequently associated with hypertension. They concluded, therefore, that obesity was a significant risk factor in development of hypertension. They failed, however, to address the possibility that these factors may not have been as prominent among the 82 hypertensive students who did not participate in the extensive hospital exams. Furthermore, they failed to compare their subjects to others of the same weight who may not have been hypertensive. The results of this study, therefore, provide no assurance that obesity is always associated with hypertension.

Court, Hill, Dunlop, and Boulton (1974) studied the relationship between obesity and blood pressure by measuring the blood pressures of 209 obese children who were referred to their clinic for treatment. Because they found that 77% of the subjects studied were not hypertensive, they concluded that elevated blood pressure is not consistently associated with obesity in childhood.

There are few *longitudinal* studies which examine the delayed risks of disease among persons who were overweight as children. However, those which have been conducted indicate that no such relationship exists (Higgins, Keller, Metzner, Moore, & Ostrander, 1980; Kuller et al., 1980).

An interesting study by Abraham, Collins, and Nordsieck (1971) has called into question the perception that childhood obesity is a serious adult risk factor. These researchers located and examined 902 males whose childhood weight and health status had been monitored as part of the U.S. Public Health Service study in Hagerstown, Maryland. The authors found no association between childhood weight status and adult blood sugar and blood cholesterol levels, cardiovascular disease, atherosclerosis, or diabetes. Furthermore, they found an inverse relationship between childhood weight status and hypertensive vascular disease. That is, those persons who were below average weight as children had the greatest incidence of hypertensive vascular disease as adults. This finding is more in agreement with the revised statistics of the Hooper and Alexander study, which showed that leanness is a greater risk factor than obesity.

Thus, there is little evidence in the literature that indicates that above-average weight in children presents either short- or long-term risks for physical health problems. The literature which is used to support the assumption that such risks exist is either methodologically or logically flawed and presents no basis for this commonly accepted premise.

Psychological Problems as Effect, Not Cause, of Childhood Obesity

Studies examining the relationship of overweight and obesity with psychological problems are more methodologically sound than those examining the relationship of weight to physical problems. The former do indicate that childhood obesity is associated with psychosocial problems. For instance, Stunkard and Mendleson (1969) found that many obese individuals have body image disturbances, as evidenced by preoccupation with their weight status, often to the exclusion of any other positive personal characteristics. Subjects viewed themselves with contempt and felt that others viewed them likewise. Body image disturbances were found to be related to age of onset of weight problems. Monello and Mayer (1963) found that obese girls showed heightened concern and sensitivity to words related to weight control and by giving negative responses to a battery of projective tests, indicated their sense of alienation from their peer group.

Jourard and Secord (1955) found that college-aged women held body ideals lower than actual body measurements and that these restrictive ideals were a source of anxiety and insecurity in some instances. Likewise, Bruch (1957, 1958, 1973, 1977) has indicated that women who desire to be thinner than their genetic make-up permits sacrifice serenity, relaxation, and efficiency and live instead tension-filled existences that may ultimately require psychotherapy.

Results of several studies indicate that overweight individuals may be correct in their perceptions that society devalues them. For instance, Canning and Mayer (1966) found that although overweight teenage girls performed as well academically as their normal or lean counterparts, they had lower admission rates to college. The authors concluded that high school counselors writing letters of recommendation to admission committees may unconsciously write less enthusiastic endorsements for heavy, than for normal-weighted, students. Goodman et al. (1963) found that when asked to indicate those with whom they were likely to be friends, most children reacted negatively to pictures of obese and physically handicapped children. Furthermore, reactions to overweight children were more negative than reactions to children with other types of physical aberrations.

The general belief exists that overweight children become overweight because of underlying psychological problems. However, Dwyer (1973) has indicated that the converse is most likely true. That is, it is likely that overweight children develop psychosocial problems because society stigmatizes them and prevents them from participating with peer groups on a normal basis. Cahnman (1968) and Louderback (1970) agree that many overweight individuals develop psychological problems because they are forced to accept society's judgment that they are lazy, slovenly, and generally lack self-control.

Weight Control Among Children Not Justified by Health Risks

The literature review discussed above indicates that the short- and long-term risks of overweight to the physical health of children have not clearly been established. Therefore, weight control regimes cannot be justified by the supposed risks of developing physical problems during childhood or adult life. Some, however, may argue that the psychological problems associated with overweight in childhood may warrant weight control measures for this group. However, it is illogical to conclude that the appropriate remedy for these ills is to treat the overweight person, for, in Ryan's (1973) term, this is an instance of blaming the victim.

In a victim-blaming situation, an individual or social group is relegated to a powerless status by society. However, society disregards the powerless status of the group and expects the group members to perform "powerful" acts such as improving their status in society (i.e., pulling themselves up by their bootstraps). Of course, because the victim is powerless, such feats are nearly impossible, whereupon society blames the victim for being in the powerless position.

Overweight persons may be considered social victims. Society has made them feel worthless, and as a result they often display signs of psychological stress, including depression. They are blamed by society for their inability to lose weight, an accomplishment well known to be hindered by depression. This additional blame adds to their depression, which adds to their weight problems, and so on. Several authors have more logically concluded that the remedy to so-called weight problems lies in altering society's perception of the meaning of overweight, rather than in the manipulation of what appears to be a biologically predetermined and unchangeable condition (Fisher, 1973; Louderback, 1970; Ryan, 1973).

Health Risks Associated With Weight Control Measures in Children

The discussion above has indicated that the physical and psychological health risks associated with childhood obesity do not warrant weight control measures in this group. Some professionals, however, may argue that as long as these measures do no harm, prescribing them may be considered a matter of personal, aesthetic preference and that such practices are to be neither advocated nor condemned. Before accepting this argument, it is important to review the literature, which provides evidence about the safety of weight control programs among children and adolescents.

Few studies have examined the risks, as well as the benefits, of weight control regimes among children and adolescents. However, those that have examined risks have concluded that the risks do not outweigh the purported benefits.

Several researchers have examined the effects of nutrient restriction as early as the stage of fetal development. Simpson, Lawless, and Mitchell (1975) conducted a 20-year study during which they examined weight gain during pregnancy and infant birthweight. They found that many white pregnant women were weight-conscious and voluntarily restricted their intake during pregnancy, resulting in lower birthweight infants. The mortality rate was six times higher for low-birthweight infants than for normal-weight infants.

Singer, Westphal, and Niswander (1968) studied 10,000 infants, analyzing the relationships between maternal weight gain, birthweight, length of gestation, and subsequent growth and performance of infants up to 1 year of age. They found that the lower the maternal weight gain during pregnancy, the poorer the infant weight and height gain, and the poorer the performance on motor, mental, and neurological measurements.

Churchill and Berendes (1969) studied the effects of low maternal weight gain on birth characteristics and mental functioning at 4 years of age. They found no immediate differences between infants born to high- and low-maternal-weight-gain mothers. However, they found that at 4 years of age, infants of low-weight-gain mothers had lower IQs than those whose mothers gained a normal or above-normal amount of weight during their pregnancies. Furthermore, they found a difference in IQs dependent upon the time when weight gain was restricted. That is, the infants who experienced calorie deficiencies during their last trimester of gestation had lower IQs than those who experienced calorie deprivation during the first or second trimester.

Several researchers have studied the direct effects of calorie restriction among children and adolescents. Stoch and Smythe (1976) conducted a longitudinal study of youths who experienced severe undernutrition during infancy, in order to determine permanency of effects. They found that despite improved subsequent nutrition, those who were deprived of nutrition during infancy were at age 15 still significantly below age norms for height, weight, and skull size. Dreizen, Spirakis, and Stone (1967) studied 60 adolescent girls, 30 of whom exhibited sustained nutritional deprivation, and 30 of whom were adequately nourished. A significant finding of the study was that menarche was later in the undernourished group by an average of 24 months.

Brook, Lloyd and Wolff (1974) studied the effects of dietary restriction (to 350 Kcal) in a group of 20 obese youngsters aged 1.5-16.5 years and found a reduction in height velocity. Rayner and Court (1974) found a similar decrease in linear growth velocity in overweight children who were being treated for overweight by both dietary restrictions and anorectic drugs. These decreases did not seem to be significantly different from similar decreases among intake-restricted, normal-weighted youths. Thus, the effects of nutrient restriction did not seem to be mitigated by the fact that the subjects were overweight.

Some have suggested that the adverse effects of dieting in youth may be reduced by altering the quality of nutrients included in the reducing diet. Heald and Hunt (1965) explored this possibility by altering the diets of four obese youngsters. Subjects between the ages of 12 and 15 were given diets of varying caloric amounts and varying protein portions for periods of 24 days to 10 months. Researchers analyzed nitrogen retention during periods of adequate and reduced caloric intake. They found that three subjects who were in their growth spurt period experienced negative nitrogen balance (that is, dietary proteins were converted for use as sugar, rather than being used for muscle building) when caloric intake was restricted. This negative nitrogen balance occurred regardless of the percentage of protein included in the diet. These investigators concluded that adolescents, even obese ones and those given nutritionally sound reducing diets, could not safely be subjected to calorie restriction.

Two studies (Mallick, 1982; Nylander, 1971) have indicated that a variety of acute health problems may be associated with dieting in teens. These problems include constipation, headaches, nervousness, dizziness, depression, nausea, weakness, and hunger. Although these problems do not seem as serious as the others mentioned above, the fact that they are caused by dieting, which has not been proven to be medically warranted, makes their occurrence troublesome. Of further concern is the prevalance of anorexia nervosa and bulimia, two eating disorders often beginning with childhood attempts to control weight.

The conclusion from review of literature discussing the hazards of weight control among children must be that calorie deprivation in childhood poses serious risks relative to growth, development, and general health. Thus, in light of the lack of evidence that overweight poses serious health risks to children, the conclusion that weight control measures may be prescribed for young people without concern for adverse consequences is invalid. Thus, the answer to the question, "For whom?" is "No young person, whether overweight or not." The answer to the question, "What Type?" is "Since no diet has been shown to be free of harmful side effects, none should be prescribed for young people." The answer to the question "When?" is "Reducing regimes can be considered safe only after the growth spurt has been completed."

Obesity Intervention: Who Undertakes It? What Do They Do? When Do They Do It?

If not to prescribe reducing regimens, what is the role of health professionals in relation to weight control in children and adolescents? Based on an understanding of who is most likely to try weight reduction, what types of weight control programs they try, and the age at which they begin to control weight, the answer is that the role of the health professional is to intervene to discourage weight control among young people.

Subjects of Weight Control

Teenage girls are believed to be the largest group of dieters in the population. Hueneman, Shapiro, Hampton, and Mitchell (1966) found that two-thirds of 9th grade girls and one-half of 9th grade boys were trying to do something about their weight. Guggenheim, Poznanski, and Kaufman (1973) found similar proportions among the 13- and 14-year-old Israeli children they studied. Dwyer, Feldman, and Mayer (1970) found that of the 446 suburban, middle-class girls they studied, 61.4% had at some time dieted to lose weight. These figures are somewhat higher than those for adult males and females (Ashwell & Etchell, 1974; McKenzie, 1967).

Of more significance than the proportion of teenagers who diet is the fact that for the most part, dieters are not overweight by customary standards (Dwyer et al., 1970; Guggenheim et al., 1973; Hueneman et al., 1966; Mallick, 1982). This is important because the health problems described above will occur sooner among leaner individuals than among normal or overweight individuals (VanItallie & Yang, 1977). Thus, those who are not overweight but are following reducing regimens represent a special risk group for developing health problems related to dieting.

Types of Reducing Regimes and Their Time Span

Another reason why self-directed adolescent dieters represent a special risk group is that they are likely to try a variety of fad diets or to try diets that are suited to adult metabolic needs. Mallick (1982) found that teenagers tried a variety of diets ranging from zero-calorie diets (i.e., starvation) to balanced, low-calorie regimes. Consistent with laboratory findings (Berland, 1979), those teens who undertook the most rigorous diets experienced more serious health problems.

There is little research data to indicate how early children and adolescents undertake weight control efforts. Mallick (1980) asked subjects when they first perceived they had weight control problems and several answered "all my life," whereas others indicated they had begun controlling their eating as early as age five. Pugliese, Lifshitz, Grad, Fort, and Marks-Katz, (1983) found that of 201 children referred to their practice for treatment of short stature and delayed puberty, fourteen experienced these problems due to self-imposed malnutrition. The youngest of these patients, all of whom cited fear of obesity as their motivation, was 9 years old.

Childhood and adolescent years are the years when the greatest nutritional demands are made upon the body (Heald, 1979). Calories are used in great quantities to achieve the growth and development genetically programmed into each person. There is little wasted intake in relation to the body build, height, and weight that heredity has predestined. Nutrient restriction during childhood and adolescence always results in a deficit in growth and development, rather than merely a reduction in body mass (as might occur with adults). Thus, any degree of calorie restriction during childhood becomes significant, making weight control regimes among this group particularly risky.

Concluding Remarks

A final reason why young people represent a high risk group for health problems related to dieting is their tendency to believe that they are invulnerable to serious health problems related to dieting. Many who have overcome anorexia nervosa have reported that during the time when weight loss was most severe, they persisted in believing they were not at risk of death. They believed, rather, that they were in control of their situations and could not only recognize "serious" symptoms when they occurred, but reverse them with little effort. Mallick (1980) found a comparable sense of invulnerability among a group of dieting teens, a majority of whom indicated that they were willing to tolerate the health problems associated with dieting in order to achieve the goal of weight loss.

Thus, young people are the most likely to be dieting, the most vulnerable to the health problems associated with dieting, and the most likely to deny or fail to respond to the health problems they experience while dieting. Because of these circumstances, health professionals should undertake health promotion activities that will reduce the number of teenagers engaging in weight control activities. Several strategies may be employed to achieve this goal. First, health professionals should alert youngsters to the potential hazards of dieting and lack of risk associated with above-average weight. Second, health professionals in schools should monitor weight control activities of students to identify those who may be on weight control programs. These students should then be counseled about good nutrition. Third, all students should be included in discussion sessions that address the relationship of self-worth and weight status.

The above-mentioned strategies are difficult for most health professionals to perform, because of the current medical belief that overweight is a hazard and weight control efforts are more effective the sooner they are begun. Perhaps, as Proust states, it may be our fate to commit successive and contradictory mistakes before stumbling onto an appropriate medical regime. However, with regards to weight control for children, there are some road signs indicating the correct path. Failure to read the signs not only prolongs the journey but leads others down a path that is likely to be fraught with detours and dead ends.

References

Abraham, S., Collins, G., & Nordsieck, M. (1971). Relationship of childhood weight status to morbidity in adults. *Public Health Report*, **86**, 273-284.

Ashwell, M., & Etchell, L. (1974). Attitude of the individual to his own body weight. *British Journal of Preventive Social Medicine, 28,* 127-132.

Berland, T. (1979). Diets '79: Consumer guide magazine health quarterly. New York: Rand McNally.

Brook, C.G.D., Lloyd, J.K., & Wolff, O.H. (1974). Rapid weight loss in children. *British Medical Journal, 3,* 44.

Bruch, H. (1957). The emotional significance of the preferred weight. *American Journal of Clinical Nutrition, 5,* 192-196.

Bruch, H. (1958). Psychological aspects of obesity in adolescence. *American Journal of Public Health, 48,* 1349-1353.

Bruch, H. (1973). *Eating disorders.* New York: Basic Books.

Bruch, H. (1977). Psychological antecedents of anorexia nervosa. In R.A. Vigersky (Ed.), *Anorexia nervosa.* New York: Raven Press.

Cahnman, W.J. (1968). The stigma of obesity. *Sociology Quarterly, 9,* 283-299.

Canning, H., & Mayer, J. (1966). Obesity: Its possible effect on college acceptance. *New England Journal of Medicine, 257,* 1172-1184.

Churchill, J.A., & Berendes, H.W. (1969). Intelligence of children whose mothers had acetonuria during pregnancy. In *Pan American Health Organization: Perinatal factors affecting human development* (pp. 30-35). Washington, DC: Science Publications.

Court, J.M., Hill, G.J., & Boulton, T.J.C. (1974). Hypertension in childhood obesity. *Australian Pediatrics Journal, 10,* 296-300.

Dreizen, D., Spirakis, C.N., & Stone, R.E. (1967). A comparison of skeletal growth and maturation in undernourished and well-nourished girls before and after menarche. *Journal of Pediatrics, 70,* 256-263.

Dwyer, J.T. (1973). Psychosocial aspects of weight control and dieting behavior in adolescents. *Medical Aspects Human Sexuality, 82,* 82-107.

Dwyer, J.T., Feldman, J.J., & Mayer, J. (1970). The social psychology of dieting. *Journal of Health and Social Behavior, 11,* 269-287.

Epstein, L.H. et al. (1983). Effects of weight loss on fitness in obese children. *American Journal of Diseases in Children, 137,* 654-657.

Fisher, S. (1973). *Body consciousness: You are what you feel.* New Jersey: Prentice-Hall.

Goodman, N., et al. (1963). Variant reactions to physical disabilities. *American Sociological Review, 28,* 429-434.

Guggenheim, K., Poznanski, R., & Kaufman, N.A. (1973). Body build and self perception in thirteen and fourteen year old Israeli children and their relationship to obesity. *Israel Journal of Medical Science, 9,* 120-128.

Heald, F.P., & Hunt, S.M. (1965). Calorie dependency in obese adolescents as affected by degree of maturation. *Journal of Pediatrics, 66,* 1035-1041.

Higgins, M.W., Keller, J.B., Metzner, H.L., Moore, J.T., & Ostrander, L.D. (1980). Studies of blood pressure in Tecumseh, Michigan. II: Antecedents in childhood of high blood pressure in young adults. *Hypertension*, **2**, 117-123.

Hooper, B.D., & Alexander, E.L. (1971). Infant morbidity and obesity. *Practitioner*, **207**, 221-235.

Hueneman, R.L., Shapiro, L.R., Hampton, M.C., & Mitchell, B.F. (1966). A longitudinal study of gross body composition and body conformation and their association with food and activity in a teenage population. *American Journal of Clinical Nutrition*, **18**, 328-338.

Jourard, S.M., & Secord, P.R. (1955). Body cathexis and the ideal female figure. *Journal of Abnormal Social Psychology*, **50**, 243-246.

Kuller, L.H., et al. (1980). Dormont High School (Pittsburgh, Pennsylvania) blood pressure study. *Hypertension*, **2**, I-109–I-116.

Lauer, R.M., Connor, W.E., Leaverton, P.E., Reiter, M.A., & Clark, W.R. (1975). Coronary heart disease risk factors in school children: The Muscatine Study. *Journal of Pediatrics*, **86**, 697.

Levine, L.S., Lewy, J.E., & New, M.I. (1976). Hypertension in high school students. *New York State Journal of Medicine*, **76**, 40-44.

Louderback, L. (1970). Fat power: Whatever you weigh is right. New York: Hawthorn Books.

Mallick, M.J. (1980). *The adverse effects of weight control in teenage girls.* Unpublished doctoral dissertation, Case Western Reserve University, Cleveland, OH.

Mallick, M.J. (1982). Health problems associated with dieting activities of a group of adolescent girls. *Western Journal of Nurses Research*, **4**(2), 167-177.

Mann, G.V. (1971). Obesity: The nutritional spook. *American Journal of Public Health*, **61**, 1491-1498.

McKenzie, J.C. (1967). Profile and slimmers. *Commentary*, **9**, 77-83.

Monello, L.F., & Mayer, J. (1963). Obese adolescent girls, an unrecognized minority group? *American Journal of Clinical Nutrition*, **13**, 35-39.

Nylander, I. (1971). The feeling of being fat and dieting in a school population. *Acta Sociologica Scandinavica*, **1**, 17-26.

Powers, P.S. (1980). *Obesity: The regulation of weight.* Baltimore: Williams and Wilkins.

Pugliese, M.T., Lifshitz, F., Grad, G., Fort, P., & Marks-Katz, M. (1983). Fear of obesity: A cause of short stature and delayed puberty. *New England Journal of Medicine*, **309**, 513-518.

Rayner, P.H.W., & Court, J.M. (1974). The effect of dietary restriction and anorectic drugs on linear growth velocity in childhood obesity. *Archives of Disease in Childhood*, **49**, 822-823.

Ryan, W. (1973). *Blaming the victim.* New York: Random House.

Shapiro, L.R., Crawford, P.B., Clark, M.J., Pearson, D.L., Raz, J., & Hueneman, R.L. (1984). Obesity prognosis: A longitudinal study of children from the age of 6 months to 9 years. *American Journal of Public Health*, **74**, 968-972.

Simpson, J.W., Lawless, R., & Mitchell, A.C. (1975). Responsibility of the obstetrician to the fetus: II. Influence of pregnancy weight and pregnancy weight gain on birthweight. *Obstetrics and Gynecology*, **45**, 481-487.

Singer, J.E., Westphal, M., & Niswander, K. (1968). Relationship of weight gain in pregnancy to birthweight and infant growth and development in the first year of life. *Obstetrics and Gynecology*, **31**, 417-423.

Stoch, M.B., & Smythe, P.M. (1976). Fifteen-year developmental study on the effects of severe undernutrition during infancy on subsequent physical growth and intellectual functioning. *Archives of Disease in Childhood*, **51**, 327-336.

Stunkard, A., & Mendelson, M. (1967). Obesity and the body image: Characteristics of disturbances in the body image of some obese persons. *American Journal of Psychiatry*, **123**, 1296-1300.

Tracey, V.V., & Harper, J.R. (1971). Obesity and respiratory infection in infants and young children. *British Medical Journal*, 16-18.

VanItallie, T.B., & Yang, M. (1977). Current concepts in nutrition. *New England Journal of Medicine*, **297**, 1158.

Chapter 6

Weight Loss: Its Effect on Normal Growth Patterns

Richard B. Parr

Adolescence is a period of growth that has many social, psychological, and maturational implications. The adolescent period represents a transition from childhood to adulthood; the adolescent is playing the role of a child and young adult at the same time. There is great variability in stature as well as behavior patterns, making life confusing, frustrating, and unpredictable. The most significant observable change during adolescence is that of growth and maturation, so much so that the definition of adolescence is based on growth factors.

Pubescence begins with the first increase in hormone secretions and the appearance of secondary sex characteristics. Pubescence ends when sexual reproduction become possible and is followed by the adolescent period, which terminates with the completion of physical growth and maturation (Roche, 1976). There is a rapid growth spurt during puberty that lasts eight to fourteen months and usually occurs between the ages of 9 to 13 for females and 12 to 16 for males. The adolescent growth period continues to approximately age 17 for females and age 21 for males.

Figures 1 and 2 show variations between males and females in the maximal growth spurt. The time of onset, duration, and magnitude of growth are important considerations for nutritional status (McKigney & Munro, 1976). Boys have a longer growth period than girls, and their maximal rate of growth exceeds the girls'. Within each sex there are early and late onset maturers, with maturation affected by heredity, nutrition, socioeconomic factors, illnesses, and exercise habits (Alford & Bogle, 1982). The range of variation is greatest between the ages of 10 and 16, during which boys of the same chronological age can vary as much as five years in skeletal age, accounting for variations of 12-15 inches in height and 75-90 pounds in weight. Hereditary factors, including the onset and

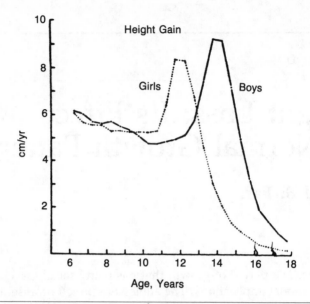

Figure 1. Mean height for males and females between 6 and 17 years of age. From *Nutrition During the Life Cycle* (p. 76) by B.B. Alford and M.L. Bogle, 1982, Englewood Cliffs, NJ: Prentice-Hall. Reprinted by permission.

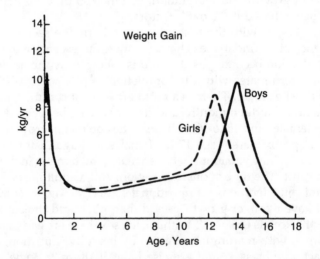

Figure 2. Mean weight gain for age of males and females between infancy and 18 years. From *Nutrition During the Life Cycle* (p. 77) by B.B. Alford and M.L. Bogle, 1982, Englewood Cliffs, NJ: Prentice-Hall. Reprinted by permission.

velocity of growth, account for variations in growth more than the influence of nutrition. However, it is during this unpredictable period of growth that the individual is most vulnerable to poor nutrition resulting from weight loss.

During adolescence, nutritional requirements are based on physiological growth, rather than on chronological age. Chronological age is used only as a practical estimate of the growth pattern. Early and late maturers are most vulnerable to unanswered nutritional recommendations. Furthermore, the recommendations for nutritional requirements are based on very limited data and are estimates determined from adult nutritional requirements, based on ages not specific to the growth spurt. The precise onset and magnitude of the growth spurt can be most accurately determined with serial clinical measures over a three-month period. Especially important is skeletal maturity, determined by epiphyseal fusion in the hand. Because such measures are impractical, various landmarks are used as an indication of the growth curve. These landmarks, however, assess the end of the growth spurt, not the velocity or length of the growth spurt. As a result, optimal nutrition becomes an afterthought rather than a practice to assure optimal growth. Menarche is a landmark for females, yet most of the female height and lean body mass has already been acquired, and nutritional requirements decrease from their peak levels to those required for adults. Unfortunately, the male adolescent has no identifiable landmarks to estimate optimal growth.

During the period of the adolescent growth spurt, the peak growth velocity often requires double the nutritional intake rate of the remainder of the adolescent period. (Mahan & Rees, 1984). Males increase their lean body mass and skeletal mass while decreasing body fat. Females gain proportionately more fat, so that by the end of adolescence, they have approximately twice the fat content of their male counterparts (Nutritional Concerns During Adolescence, 1981). A segment of our population has a mild degree of growth retardation; however, it is not clear whether the cause is nutritionally dependent or only a reflection of genetic potential (McGaity, 1976). It is often difficult to assess whether a child is weight-retarded based on growth charts or that low weight is a secondary effect of height deficit.

Teenagers' appetites tend to parallel their growth spurt, as well as their overall growth during adolescence; therefore, adequate nutrition generally meets growth requirements when a variety of foods are selected from recommended food groups. Growth-related nutritional problems may occur when adolescents choose, either on their own or through peer pressure, foods of low nutritional density. Following hypocaloric diets also represents a threat to growth, even when foods of high nutritional density are chosen.

Groups most vulnerable include teenagers voluntarily reducing weight by fad diets and dietary practices, complete vegetarians, anorexics and bulimics, and athletes determined to reduce body weight for competition. Major food qualities of concern include protein, calcium, and iron, as well as total energy (calorie) intake. Low calorie diets (less than 1,000 calories for females and 1,200 calories for males) over a long period of time create a high risk of calcium and iron deficiency, especially in women.

Body Composition

Males and females enter puberty with similar body compositions. Males enter with 15% body fat, and girls enter at 19% body fat (Mahan & Rees, 1984). Boys gain twice as much lean tissue as girls, whereas girls increase fat tissue. When boys exit adolescence, they carry approximately 12% body fat, whereas girls measure 23% fat. Because boys gain more lean tissue, they incur a greater metabolic expenditure and a greater demand for caloric and protein intake.

Nutritional Needs

Standards for nutritional requirements for adolescents are based on little scientific research. Current Recommended Dietary Allowances (RDAs) (Food and Nutrition Board, 1980) for adolescents are derived from adult maintenance figures, with additional values added for growth. From a practical point of view, RDAs are given for chronological ages; however, requirements would be more appropriate if based on physiological or developmental age. It is evident that more research from serial clinical studies is necessary to establish more precise nutrient requirements based on growth patterns. Until such data is available, much can be gained by educating adolescents about proper nutrition during their primary growth years. The Ten-State Survey (United States Department of Health, Education, and Welfare, 1972) showed no evidence of extensive deprivation of nutrients for adolescents relative to growth; however, the effects of weight loss and related nutrient intake has not been studied. This is not to be interpreted that adolescents regularly meet their RDAs for all nutrients. On the contrary, more than one-half of the female adolescents surveyed consumed less than two-thirds the 1979 RDAs for iron, calcium, and vitamin A.

Energy Requirements for Growth

Adequate energy intake is important during the growth spurt but is no less important throughout adolescence. It should be emphasized to

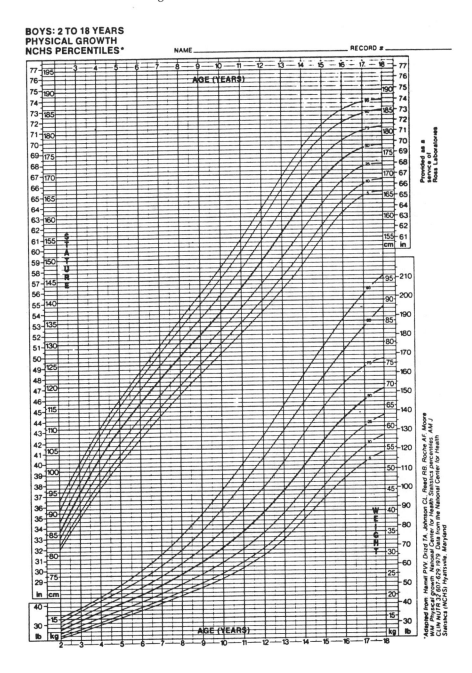

Figure 3. Physical growth chart: males. From *Nutrition in Adolescence* (p. 279) by L.K. Mahan and J.M. Rees, 1984, St. Louis: Times Mirror/Mosby. Reprinted by permission.

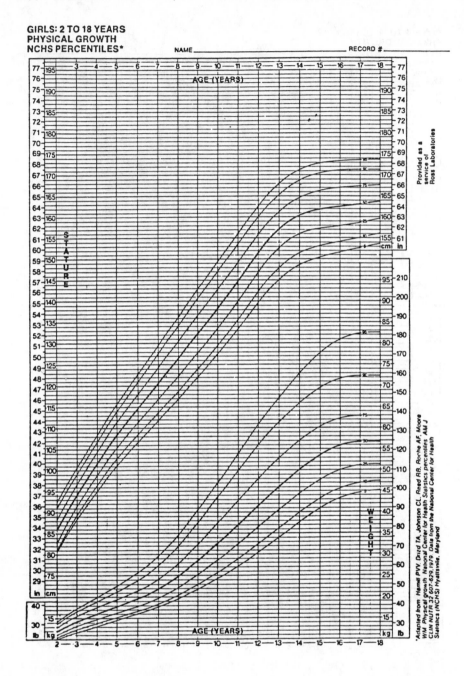96   Parr

Figure 4. Physical growth chart: females. From *Nutrition in Adolescence* (p. 280) by L.K. Mahan and J.M. Rees, 1984, St. Louis: Times Mirror/Mosby. Reprinted by permission.

Table 1   Recommended Energy Allowances for Adolescence, Based on 1980 RDAs

Subject and Age (Years)	Energy Recommendations (kcal)
Children	
7–10	2,400 (1,650–3,300)
Males	
11–14	2,700 (2,000–3,700)
15–18	2,800 (2,100–3,900)
19–22	2,900 (2,500–3,300)
Females	
11–14	2,200 (1,500–3,000)
15–18	2,100 (2,100–3,000)
19–22	2,100 (1,700–2,500)

teenagers that appropriate selection of energy foods also includes nutrients necessary for proper growth. As a point of reference, caloric intake can be derived from RDAs. A more practical approach is to follow a sequential plotting of height and weight to assess the rate of growth (Mahan & Rees, 1984). Growth charts (Figures 3 and 4) are useful in channeling growth patterns and can be used as a crude measure of energy intake. Too often, however, these growth charts are inappropriately used to determine an ideal weight by comparing all individuals' growth to the norm.

Table 1 shows the recommended energy intake for males and females (Food and Nutrition Board, 1980) and can be used as a guide for adolescents engaged in weight loss. Energy intake of less than 1,800 calories makes it difficult to meet the RDAs for calcium and iron; it is highly unlikely that requirements for these nutrients are met with energy intake of less that 1,000 calories for females or 1,200 calories for males.

Protein

The protein RDAs (Food and Nutrition Board, 1980) for adolescents vary from 44 to 56 grams, depending on sex and age (Table 2). The highest protein requirement for males begins at age fifteen (56 g) and continues through adulthood. For the female the peak protein requirement is at age eleven (46 g) and decreases to 44 g in adulthood. Other methods of recommending protein requirements are based on either body weight or protein percentage of total caloric intake. Adolescents should include in their diet one gram of protein for each kilogram of body weight. As a guideline to this goal, approximately 12 percent of caloric intake should

Table 2   Recommended Nutrient Allowances for Adolescence, Based on 1980 RDAs

Subject and Age (Years)	Calcium (mg)	Iron (mg)	Protein (g)
Children			
7–10	800	10	34
Males			
11–14	1,200	18	45
15–18	1,200	18	56
19–22	800	10	56
Females			
11–14	1,200	18	46
15–18	1,200	18	46
19–22	800	18	44

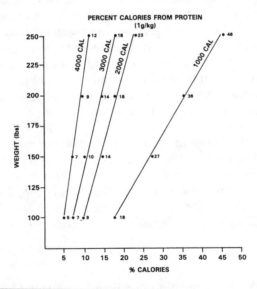

Figure 5.   Percentage of calories from protein.

be from protein sources. Figure 5 shows the relationship between absolute protein intake, protein relative to body weight, and protein as a percentage of total caloric intake. Adolescents with low caloric intake cannot rely on adequate protein intake by selecting 12 percent of their calories as protein. Following the recommendation of 1 gram protein per kilogram of body weight may require 25 percent of caloric intake as protein for the average weight adolescent on a weight loss diet of 1,000 calories. Teenagers should be counseled toward high quality protein during their growing years. Females are more likely to be deficient in milk intake and therefore risk quality, as well as quantity, of protein intake.

Calcium

Calcium requirements increase with growth of bone and muscle mass. Forty-five percent of skeletal growth occurs during adolescence (Beal, 1980), and the adolescent growth spurt contributes 15% to final adult height. It is likely that low calcium intake during this critical time can limit length of bone growth and, therefore, final adult height. Growth in bone density and thickness, however, continues after adolescence. The significance of bone density and the quality of growth during the adolescent years has recently been associated with osteoporosis in later life (Allen, 1984). RDAs for calcium increase from 800 milligrams (mg) for ages 7-10 to 1,200 mg for ages 11-18 in both males and females (Table 2). After age 18 the RDA for calcium is 800 mg per day.

There is a still lower threshold of calcium intake, below which adaptive mechanisms such as increased parathyroid secretions to promote vitamin D synthesis cannot occur. In adults the lower limit appears to be 600 mg/day, which is three-fourths of the RDA. Although similar data is not available for adolescents, extrapolation of data would indicate the lower level of calcium intake would be 900 mg/day. Because the precise skeletal growth spurt is ill-defined, such extrapolation is, at best, a liberal interpretation of minimal calcium needs.

Calcium/phosphorus (Ca/P) ratios have gained greater recognition in recent years because of the increased incidence and attention given to osteoporosis (Allen, 1984; Beal, 1980; Mahan & Rees, 1984). Ca/P ratio appears to affect the homeostasis of calcium and phosporus and, thus, the integrity of skeletal structure. The RDAs for calcium and phosphorus are 1,200 mg each; therefore, the Ca/P ratio is 1:1. The Ca/P ratio may be reduced to 1:.71 in female adolescents when their milk consumption is decreased (Beal, 1980). Furthermore, Ca/P ratio is even more disturbed because of increased consumption of phosphorus-containing soft drinks, combined with reduced milk intake (Nutritional Concerns, 1981).

Calcium is one of the nutrients found to be deficient in the teenage diet (Mahan & Rees, 1984). About three-fourths of calcium intake is supplied by milk and milk products (Allen, 1984), with the rest coming from green leafy vegetables (broccoli and collards), salmon, almonds, shellfish, and tofu (soybean curd). Trends in consumption—a 22% decrease for milk and an 11% increase for soft drinks—are partially responsible both for a deficiency in total calcium intake (Figures 6 and 7) and for reduced Ca/P ratio.

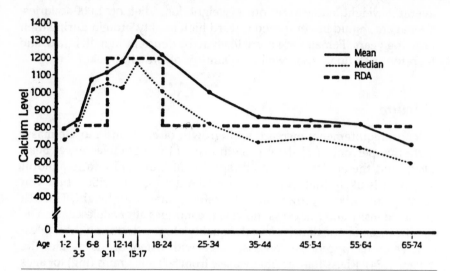

Figure 6. Daily calcium intake (mg) for males in U.S. population, 1976 to 1980. From "The Role of Calcium in Health" by the National Dairy Council, January-February 1984, *Dairy Council Digest,* 55(1), p. 2. Reprinted by permission.

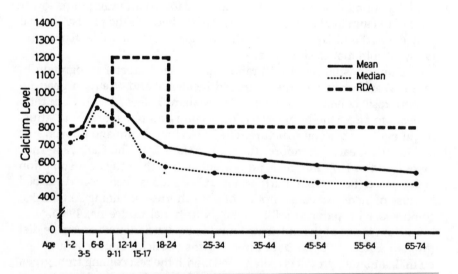

Figure 7. Daily calcium intake (mg) for females in U.S. population, 1976 to 1980. From "The Role of Calcium in Health" by the National Dairy Council, January-February 1984, *Dairy Council Digest,* 55(1), p. 2. Reprinted by permission.

Inadequate calcium intake during adolescence appears to be an important criteria related to bone loss (demineralization) in later life, because of calcium's role in skeletal growth and development (Matkovic, Kostial, & Semovoic, 1979; Recker, 1984). Peak skeletal mass is attained early in life; however, little is known about either minimal or optimal calcium requirements during adolescence (Recker, 1984). Other factors related to reduced bone growth during adolescence include unusually high protein intake, inactivity, and amenorrhea in young women. High protein intake has been shown to cause a negative calcium balance (Recker, 1984). Although protein intake in amounts taken by most Americans is not high enough to interfere with calcium absorption, the effects of dietary protein and supplements common to some athletes have not been studied adequately. Exercise also plays a role in optimal bone growth, for it increases bone mass during the growing years. Amenorrhea associated with heavy exercise, reduced body weight, or reduced body fat has recently been associated with slightly lower skeletal mass. The implications of reduced skeletal mass on later life, however, have not been determined. At any rate, it is becoming more apparent that osteoporosis is more related to the density of bone during the growth period than it is to calcium intake in old age (Mahan & Rees, 1984).

Rising Iron Needs

Iron requirements increase with rapid growth, muscle mass, blood volume, and metabolic enzymes. In females, additional requirements are necessary at menarche because of loss of iron during menstruation. Male adolescents, however, require more dietary iron than the menstruating female, because of increased blood volume and muscle mass. The demands are so great that iron requirements may vary fourfold between early- and late-maturing males. During the growth spurt, males may require 25.8 mg iron/day; whereas at the same age, early or late maturers may require 6.6 mg iron/day (McKigney & Munro, 1976). Iron requirements for female adolescents may vary twofold.

The RDA (Food and Nutrition Board, 1980) for iron is shown in Table 2. There is an average concentration of 6 mg iron/1,000 calories in the American diet (Finch, 1977). Based on the range of recommended caloric intake (Table 1), the equivalent intake of iron would be 12-22 mg iron for males and 7-18 mg for females. Girls between the ages of 12 and 16 have been reported to consume 9-13 mg iron/day; boys of the same ages consumed 10-16 mg iron/day (Food and Nutrition Board, 1976). Even when caloric intake is within recommended levels, there is difficulty in meeting the RDA for iron. When adolescents are on restricted caloric diets, it is doubtful that iron intake is adequate for growth (Nutritional Concerns, 1981).

Weight Loss in Adolescents

It is well-established that optimal nutrition, especially during the growth spurt, is necessary for optimal growth and attainment of genetic potential. The National Academy of Science (Food and Nutrition Board, 1980) has set nutrient recommendations high enough to include variations in timing and magnitude of the growth spurt. These recommendations are designed to meet the needs of the fastest growth patterns over the entire span of adolescence. Previous discussion in this chapter has indicated that undernutrition (based on RDAs) is not uncommon with nondieting teenagers (Food and Nutrition Board, 1976; Mahan & Rees, 1984). It is more apparent that dieting adolescents, especially those on quick weight-loss fad diets, are at higher risk for undernutrition. Dieting adolescents (especially girls), anorexics, and bulimics are at the highest risk to interference with growth patterns; however, little substantial data has been reported relative to the effects of these behaviors on growth. It is generally agreed, though not yet substantiated, that undernutrition resulting from acute weight loss at worst delays, rather than prevents, growth. Still, there is not enough data to attribute delays in growth to nutritional deficiencies, as opposed to hereditary predisposition.

The effects of weight loss have been studied in greatest detail in wrestlers who purposely reduce below optimal weight in order to make certain weight classes (American College of Sports Medicine, 1976; Freischlag, 1984; Hansen, 1978). However, focus has been directed toward rapid weight loss and performance (American College of Sports Medicine, 1976; Freischlag, 1984; Hansen, 1978; Houston, Murrin, Green & Thomson, 1981; Tipton, 1982), rather than the effects of persistent weight loss on growth.

The purpose of weight loss in wrestlers is to qualify for lower weight classes for competition, in order to gain advantage over opponents who may be inferior in size, strength, and mechanical advantage. Weight loss of 3-20% during preseason and prior to certification is not uncommon (Houston et al., 1981). Short-term weight loss of less than 4% has not been shown to be detrimental to performance; however, studies have not included repetitive weight loss on growth. Four percent weight loss becomes pronounced when considering that nondieting athletes are simultaneously gaining 4-5% body weight through natural growth (Freischlag, 1984). Although weight loss of this degree has not been associated with interference with growth, it is significant that the most prominent change is in the lower weight classes, which represents the youngest athletes, who are more vulnerable to the practice of weight loss. The American Medical Association and the American College of Sports Medicine (ACSM, 1976) have issued position statements on quick weight loss for athletes and are opposed to rapid and significant weight loss when rapid growth is taking place.

Summary

There is a lack of significant information regarding the effects of weight loss on growth patterns in adolescents. The onset, duration, and velocity of the growth spurt is not well-defined. Adequate nutrition is agreed to be important but often is blamed for delaying growth, though heredity is perhaps the limiting factor. Recommended dietary values for most nutrients have been established to meet the needs of growth; however, minimal or maximal requirements have not been defined. The acute or chronic effects of undernutrition on growth are not known.

On the other hand, health professionals must understand that interrelationships of hereditary potential and diet are difficult to delineate. Heredity sets the limits of growth; yet, adequate nutrition allows hereditary characteristics to develop to their full potential. More important, we know more than we put into practice. The potential problems related to weight loss and growth are primarily attributed to poor dietary and nutritional practices.

References

Alford, B.B., & Bogle, M.L. (1982). *Nutrition during the life cycle.* Englewood Cliffs, NJ: Prentice Hall.

Allen, L.H. (1984). Calcium absorption and requirements during the life span. *Nutrition News, 47,* 1-3.

AMA Committee on the Medical Aspects of Sports. (1967). Wrestling and weight control. *Journal of the American Medical Association, 201,* 541-543.

American College of Sports Medicine. (1976). Position stand on weight loss in wrestlers. *Sports Medicine Bulletin, 11,* 1-2.

Beal, V.A. (1980). *Nutrition in the lifespan.* New York: John Wiley and Sons.

Finch, C.A. (1977). Iron nutrition. *Annals of the New York Academy of Science, 300,* 221-227.

Food and Nutrition Board, National Research Council. (1980). *Recommended dietary allowances* (9th ed.). Washington, DC: Author.

Food and Nutrition Board, National Research Council. (1976). *Iron nutriture in adolescence* (HEW Publication No. HSA 77-5100). Washington, DC: U.S. Government Printing Office.

Freischlag, J. (1984). Weight loss, body composition, and health of high school wrestlers. *The Physician and Sportsmedicine*, **12**, 121-126.

Hansen, N.C. (1978). Wrestling with "making weight." *The Physician and Sportsmedicine*, **6**, 107-111.

Houston, M.E., Murrin, D.A., Green, H.J., & Thomson, J.A. (1981). The effects of rapid weight loss on physiological functions in wrestling. *The Physician and Sportsmedicine*, **9**, 73-78.

Mahan, L.K., & Rees, J.M. (1984). *Nutrition in adolescence*. St. Louis: Times Mirror/Mosby.

Matkovic, V., Kostial, K., & Semovoic, I. (1979). Bone status and fracture rates in two regions of Yugoslavia. *American Journal of Clinical Nutrition*, **32**, 540-549.

McGaity, W.J. (1976). Problems of nutritional evaluation of the adolescent. In J.I. McKigney & H.N. Munro (Eds.), *Nutrient requirements in adolescence*. Cambridge, MA: The MIT Press.

McKigney, J.I., & Munro, H.N. (Eds.). (1976). *Nutrient requirements in adolescence*. Cambridge, MA: The MIT Press.

Nutritional concerns during adolescence. (1981). *Dairy Council Digest*, **52**, 1-8.

Recker, R.R. (1984). The role of calcium in bone health. *Nutrition News*, **47**, 5-6.

Roche, A.F. (1976). Some aspects of adolescent growth and maturation. In J.I. McKigney & H. N. Munro (Eds.), *Nutrition requirements in adolescence*. Cambridge, MA: The MIT Press.

Tipton, C.M. (1982) Consequences of rapid weight loss. In W.L. Haskell, J.H. Whittam, & J. Scala (Eds.), *Nutrition and athletic performance* (pp. 176-197). Palo Alto, CA: Bull Publishing.

Part III

Activity

The role of exercise is fully accepted as an important adjunct in the treatment and management of obesity. This section discusses the relationship between eating and inactivity, and their interaction on obesity. The need for nutritional supplementations for physically active youth is included in the discussion. Finally, the importance of creating a positive exercise environment is emphasized.

Chapter 7

Eating Versus Inactivity

Ann C. Grandjean

Obesity is a major health problem in the United States. It has been estimated that approximately 15-20% of school-age children in the United States are overweight (Greenwood, 1983). Eating and activity level are instrumental in both the etiology and treatment of obesity.

A study of nursery school children in New York City revealed that 13% of the children were obese ($\geq$ 95th percentile). Fourteen percent of children under 6 years of age surveyed in the California component of the Ten-State Nutrition Survey had weights above the 84th percentile values of the Iowa Standards. The Ten-State Nutrition Survey also revealed that 5-7% of children in the 3- to 6-year-old group had skinfold measurements above the 95th percentile (Neumann, 1977).

Johnson and colleagues estimated the incidence of obesity in Boston high school students to be 12.9% in girls and 9.5% in boys. The Ten-State Nutrition Survey similarly found that approximately 12% of girls and 11% of boys had triceps skinfolds exceeding the 95th percentile (Meyer & Neumann, 1977).

Etiology

The research on the etiology of obesity reveals numerous theories and the realization that obesity is not a single disorder but, rather, a collection of disorders:

- Inability to monitor internal satiety signals
- Brown fat
- Fat cell number/size
- Genetic makeup
- Environment
- Metabolism
- Set point

Irrespective of the theory or theories one may ascribe to, they can all be reduced to energy imbalance. On the other hand, if energy intake is equal to energy expenditure, constant weight results.

The average energy requirement for children of both sexes declines gradually from 105 kcals/kilogram of body weight at age one to about 80 kcals/kg through 10 years of age. After age 10, average energy requirements decline further to 45 kcals/kg for adolescent males and 38 kcals/kg for adolescent females (Food and Nutrition Board, 1980).

It is common knowledge that obese parents tend to have obese children. It is highly likely that the mechanism is multifactorial and that heredity and cultural and familial eating patterns are factors (Taitz, 1977).

There are several environmental factors known to have impact on obesity (Guthrie, 1979). *Availability of food* is one such factor. Obesity is a significant problem for large portions of the population only in countries in which the food supply exceeds the demand. Additionally, a *comfortable environment* and the products of high technology contribute to the problem. Due to heating in homes, cars, and work sites, one can dress lightly and still stay warm in the winter without having to expend a great deal of energy in doing so. Labor-saving devices contribute to a reduced energy expenditure.

Another contributing factor is the use of foods and beverages as *expressions of hospitality*. Almost all social functions (weddings, funerals, and other gatherings) include food as part of the occasion. Additionally, to refuse these expressions of hospitality is not acceptable, in some cases. Compounding the problem, the types of food served at social occasions are often very caloric dense.

Learned food habits are another factor which can have impact on obesity. Food habits, usually learned from the family, are transferred from generation to generation. Many may still cook as though feeding farmhands, instead of low-energy-expending office workers. Additionally, the perceptions of what constitutes a meal—for example, that a meal isn't complete without dessert—are learned. *Responses to external stimuli,* such as food cues and other stimuli, and *infant feeding practices* are additional environmental factors that have impact on obesity.

Research has indicated the following as some of the predisposing factors of obesity (Tullis & Tullis, 1977):

- Being the youngest or only child
- Being the product of an unwanted pregnancy
- Experiencing psychological trauma
- Having obese parents or siblings
- Having physical handicaps that limit mobility
- Having a family structure in which the father is subordinate to the mother

Many researchers agree that one type of juvenile onset obesity is a functional disorder resulting from a *low level of physical activity* (Tullis & Tullis, 1977). There are wide individual variations in the physical activity of infants and children. Inactive children may become obese even when their energy intake is well below the average allowance, whereas extremely active children require more calories. Adolescents also exhibit marked variations in energy output (Food and Nutrition Board, 1980).

Adolescents who exercise infrequently run a high risk of becoming obese. Additionally, lack of exercise coupled with boredom can result in increased food intake and puts the adolescent in double jeopardy (Paige, 1983). A study of obese adolescent girls in a summer camp, using time-lapse photography during periods of mandatory physical activity, revealed that the obese girls were less active than normal-weight girls (Bullen, Reed, & Mayer, 1964). For example, during swimming periods, obese girls spent less time swimming and more time floating. During tennis, the obese girls were active 23% of the time, compared to 44% for normal-weight girls.

Treatment

The best treatment for the overweight child is to maintain weight and allow the child to "grow into the weight." In the case of the grossly overweight child or the adolescent who has reached his or her mature height with epiphysial closure, weight reduction is indicated.

Several successful programs with children and adolescents have been reported. Most of these involve the social support of parents and/or school, behavior modification, and/or physical activity.

A study by Colvin and Olson (1983) on adult men and women who had been successful at weight loss and maintaining that loss reported that improved nutrition, increased exercise, and self-monitoring were characteristics seen in both the men and the women. Additionally, the majority of female subjects assumed responsibility for their need to lose weight; developed their own diet, exercise, and maintenance plan; and became more involved in business and other activities outside the home.

A study by Brownell and colleagues has suggested that in a program of behavior modification, parent involvement appears to be important (Brownell, Kelman, & Stunkard, 1983). Young children may need more supervision from their parents, whereas adolescents may require more independence. Brownell reported that when mother and child met in separate groups, there was a greater weight loss than when the mother and child met together or when the mother did not take part in the treatment program.

The benefits of exercise in a weight loss program are several. There is the calorie expenditure required for the exercise, in addition to an increase in the basal metabolic rate. Along with creating these physiological benefits, exercise is also associated with creating a feeling of well-being, and improved mood and self-concept (Collingwood & Willett, 1971; Folkins & Sime, 1981). Children who show a tendency toward obesity should be encouraged to participate in the more active types of recreation.

The important role of exercise in treatment of overfatness was demonstrated in a study by Zuti and Golding (1976). Women participating in this 16-week study were randomly assigned to one of three groups: a diet group, an exercise group, or a combination group. The caloric deficit for all three groups was 500: the women in the diet group achieved this deficit entirely by reduction in caloric intake, the women in the exercise group increased energy expenditure by 500 calories per day, and the women in the combination group reduced caloric intake by 250 calories and increased energy expenditure the same amount. The average weight loss for each group was not significantly different from the others, with the group averages being 11.7, 12.0, and 10.6 pounds for the diet group, combination group, and exercise group, respectively. The women in both the exercise and combination groups had increases in lean tissue, with the dieters the only group losing lean tissue.

Because the primary concern in the treatment of overfatness is the loss of fat mass, exercise obviously plays an important role. "It makes me hungry" is one of the arguments frequently heard for not exercising. Research does not support this argument. Studies by Woo, Garrow, and Pi-Sunyer evaluating the effect of prolonged exercise on food intake in obese women revealed that the increase in energy requirements of long-term moderate exercise was not compensated by an increase in caloric intake (1982a,b).

Prevention

Of utmost importance in discussing prevention is the question, "Do obese infants become obese adults?" Although the research in this area is very difficult to evaluate, there is reason to believe that obesity in school-aged children and adolescents predisposes them to obesity in adult life. Whether obesity in infancy predisposes them to obesity as school-aged children or as adults is even more difficult to evaluate than is the relationship between adolescent and adult obesity. In short, the question cannot be answered at this time. Until the answer is known, however, it seems desirable to avoid obesity during infancy and childhood.

Prevention of obesity is clearly preferable to treatment and should be approached by educating parents with respect to feeding practices during infancy (Fomon, 1974). The probability is high that an obese child or adolescent will continue to be troubled by obesity in later life. Habits that promote a sound balance of energy output and intake should therefore be developed in early childhood.

In view of the association between obesity and hypertension, atherosclerosis, diabetes, cancer, and many other conditions, it appears obvious that an ounce of prevention is indeed worth a pound of cure. In 1958, in a paper on obesity, Sebrell stated, "It is clear that the time is here for us to start a preventive program aimed primarily at mothers and children." Considering the current statistics on the incidence of obesity, it is clear that the need for a preventive program still exists.

References

Brownell, K.D., Kelman, J.H., & Stunkard, A.J. (1983). Treatment of obese children with and without their mothers: Changes in weight and blood pressure. *Pediatrics*, **71**(4), 515-523.

Bullen, B.A., Reed, R.B., & Mayer, J. (1964). Physical activity of obese and non-obese adolescent girls appraised by motion picture sampling. *American Journal of Clinical Nutrition*, **14**, 211-223.

Collingwood, T.R., & Willett, L. (1971). The effects of physical training upon self-concept and body attitude. *Journal of Clinical Psychology*, **27**, 411-412.

Colvin, R.H., & Olson, S.B. (1983). A descriptive analysis of men and women who have lost significant weight and are highly successful at maintaining the loss. *Addictive Behaviors*, **8**(3), 287-295.

Folkins, C.H., & Sime, W.E. (1981). Physical fitness, training and mental health. *American Psychology*, **36**, 373.

Fomon, S.J. (1974). *Infant nutrition* (2nd ed.). Philadelphia: W.B. Saunders.

Food and Nutrition Board, National Research Council. (1980). *Recommended dietary allowances*. Washington, DC: Author.

Greenwood, M.R.C. (1983). Preface. In M.R.C. Greenwood (Ed.), *Obesity* (pp. xi-xiii). New York: Churchill and Livingstone.

Guthrie, H.A. (1979). *Introductory nutrition* (4th ed.). St. Louis: Mosby.

Meyer, E.E., & Neumann, C.G. (1977). Management of the obese adolescent. In C.G. Neumann & D.B. Jelliffe (Eds.), *The pediatric clinic of North America, symposium on nutrition in pediatrics* (pp. 123-132). Philadelphia: W.B. Saunders.

Neumann, C.G. (1977). Obesity in pediatric practice: Obesity in the preschool and school-age child. In C.G. Neumann & D.B. Jelliffe (Eds.) *The pediatric clinic of North America, symposium on nutrition in pediatrics* (pp. 117-122). Philadelphia: W.B. Saunders.

Paige, D.M. (1983). *Manual of clinical nutrition*. Pleasantville, NJ: Nutrition Publications.

112   Grandjean

Sebrell, W.H. (1958). Weight control through prevention of obesity. *Journal of the American Dietetic Association*, **34**, 920-923.

Taitz, L.S. (1977). Obesity in pediatric practice: Infantile obesity. In C.G. Neumann & D.B. Jelliffe (Eds.), *The pediatric clinic of North America, symposium on nutrition in pediatrics* (pp. 107-115). Philadelphia: W.B. Saunders.

Tullis, I.F., & Tullis, K.F. (1977). Obesity. In H.A. Schneider, C.E. Anderson, & D.B. Coursin (Eds.), *Nutritional support of medical practice* (pp. 392-406). Hagerstown, MD: Harper & Rowe.

Woo, R., Garrow, J.S., & Pi-Sunyer, F.X. (1982a). Effect of exercise on spontaneous calorie intake in obesity. *American Journal of Clinical Nutrition*, **36**, 470-477.

Woo, R., Garrow, J.S., & Pi-Sunyer, F.X. (1982b). Voluntary food intake during prolonged exercise in obese women. *American Journal of Clinical Nutrition*, **36**, 474-478.

Zuti, W.B., & Golding, L.A. (1976, January). Comparing diet and exercise as weight reduction tools. *The Physician and Sportsmedicine*, 49-53.

Chapter 8

Nutrition Supplementation: Needs of the Physically Active Youth

Ann C. Grandjean

"Nutritional supplement" is often used interchangeably with "vitamin/ mineral pill." A more accurate definition—and the one adopted for the purpose of this paper—is anything consumed in addition to the normal diet.

Nutritional Status and Eating Habits of Today's Youth

There are several national surveys that assess food and nutrient intake of Americans. One such survey is the USDA Food Consumption Survey. Data from the USDA 1977-78 Nationwide Food Consumption Survey indicated that three vitamins and three minerals may be problem nutrients for a number of sex-age groups in the United States (Pao & Mickle, 1981), the vitamins being vitamin B_6, A, and C, and the minerals being calcium, iron, and magnesium.

Mean intakes of nutrients indicate that calcium, iron, magnesium, and vitamin B_6 are problem nutrients for some sex-age groups. Using frequency distribution, the percentage of individuals with intakes below 70% of their RDA for those nutrients are shown in Table 1.

Pragmatically, it is more meaningful to look at specific groups. The sex-age groups in which low intakes (less than 70% RDA) are most prevalent (greater than 33% of the group) are as follows (Pao & Mickle, 1981):

- Calcium—females over 11 years of age, males 35 and over
- Iron—infants aged 1-2, children 3-5, females 12-50, males 12-14

Table 1   Percentage Distribution of 37,785 Individuals
With Nutrient Intakes at Specified Levels of 1980 RDAs

Nutrient	% of Individuals Receiving:		
	100% and Over of RDA	70-99% of RDA	Less Than 70% of RDA
Energy	24	44	32
Protein	88	9	3
Calcium	32	26	42
Iron	43	25	32
Magnesium	25	36	39
Phosphorus	73	19	8
Vitamin A	50	19	31
Thiamine	55	28	17
Riboflavin	66	22	12
Preformed niacin[a]	67	24	9
Vitamin B_6	20	29	51
Vitamin B_{12}	66	19	15
Vitamin C	59	15	26

Note.   From "Problem Nutrients in the United States" by E.M. Pao and S.J. Mickle, 1981, Food Technology, 35(9), p. 58. Reprinted by permission.
[a]Based on RDA values as milligrams of preformed niacin.

- Magnesium—females over age 11, males 12-22, males 65 and over
- Vitamin A—females aged 12-51, males 19-50, females and males 75 and over
- Vitamin B_6—females aged 9 and over, males 19 and over
- Vitamin C—females aged 19-50

Although group data are useful when used in the right contexts and can be indicative of problem areas, they must be used with caution when applied to individuals.

Specific Considerations

There are several nonpathologic conditions or situations which can affect the nutritional quality of the diet.

Weight Loss and Gain

One condition affecting the nutritional quality of the diet is consuming a low-calorie diet, the most frequent reason for which being weight control. Persons consuming low-calorie diets frequently have difficulty obtaining the recommended levels for some vitamins and minerals. In our study of athletes, data show that once caloric intake drops below 2,000 calories, it is increasingly difficult, although possible, to meet nutrient recommendations (Grandjean & Lolkus, 1981-1984). When, for whatever reason, food intake is being restricted, supplementation with a multivitamin/mineral pill may be indicated.

Surveys have shown that whereas female adolescents feel they should be smaller, male adolescents feel they should be larger. Bulking-up, or gaining weight in the form of muscle mass, is not uncommon among athletes. Muscle mass increases only after a sufficient period of progressive weight training and cannot be increased simply by altering the diet. Although increased calorie and protein needs must be met, adequate protein can be obtained by diet, and protein supplements are not necessary or recommended. The protein needs of the adolescent should be calculated on per kilogram of body weight, considering the age-specific recommended dietary allowances.

Athletics

More than 7 million boys and girls take part in competitive sports in high school, and nearly 20 million are engaged in out-of-school recreation and competitive sports (Committee on Sports Medicine, 1983). These athletes are in an age group documented to be at the highest risk of nutrition problems and inadequate diets (Committee on Sports Medicine, 1983). In their desire to excel, they are vulnerable to adopting unorthodox eating habits and are prey for quackery. For example, crash dieting in order to drop 10-20 pounds is not uncommon. Water restriction by coaches is still practiced, and promotion of supplements to athletes is common.

For the athlete making weight, the responsibility of the health professional is to advise and guide the athlete in a reasonable program. Because any program most likely involves food restriction, vitamin/mineral supplementation may be indicated, but indiscriminate use of supplements is not recommended.

Many athletes feel that because of the grueling demands of their training program, they require more vitamins than non-athletes (Grandjean, Hursh, Majure, & Hanley, 1981). This is one of several reasons they are susceptible to taking high doses of vitamins and minerals. It is the health professional's responsibility not only to evaluate the athlete's diet for deficiencies, but also to consider intake levels that can be toxic.

Because of their role in energy metabolism, thiamine and riboflavin requirements should be calculated on a per-thousand-calorie basis. Although it is true that the requirements for these vitamins increase as caloric intake increases, meeting caloric needs most often results in meeting thiamine and riboflavin requirements. However, the caloric requirement of an athlete is more dependent on body size than on the energy demands of the sport and/or training program. Therefore, a small athlete, such as a female figure skater, gymnast, or low-weight class judo player, may routinely consume less than 2,000 calories per day.

For the young athlete who is a serious competitor, it is not uncommon to spend several hours a day in training, in addition to school and other responsibilities. In order to train, the youth may be required to attend early morning, late afternoon, or evening practices that may necessitate missing a meal. In such a situation, snacking can provide the needed nutrients and energy, provided a wise selection of snack foods is used. Another alternative is a nutritionally complete liquid meal replacement. Such products are nutritionally complete, convenient, and can be consumed while the athlete is at home or on the go.

Body Size/Surface

The primary factor in determining caloric requirement is body size, specifically surface; the larger the person, the higher the caloric requirement. Older children and teenagers who are small, especially if they are inactive, may have caloric requirements below 2,000 calories a day, making it difficult to consume the RDA for some nutrients. Of particular concern are the iron and calcium needs of teenage females. As previously stated, surveys indicate that these are problem nutrients for this age group and therefore deserve particular attention, due to their critical roles in anemia and osteoporosis.

Vegetarian Diets

Vegetarianism is not new. Ancient Greek athletes trained on vegetarian diets. In Sparta the basic diet was barley, wheat bread, porridge, fruits, vegetables, olive oil, honey, eggs, and goat cheese, which by today's nomenclature would be classified as a lacto-ovo-vegetarian diet (Grandjean, 1984).

Vegetarian diets can be put on a spectrum ranging from fruitarian to lacto-ovo-vegetarian. The total vegetarian, or vegan, avoids all foods of animal origin, whereas the lacto-ovo-vegetarian eats eggs, milk, and milk products, and lacto-vegetarians exclude eggs and meat. Some people who simply avoid red meats still consider themselves vegetarians. A less common vegetarian diet, the fruitarian diet, usually includes only fruits, nuts, seeds, honey, and vegetable oil.

If care is taken to include sufficient variety of allowed foods and to combine nutritionally complementary foods, vegetarian diets, with the exception of the fruitarian diet, can be nutritionally adequate (The American Dietetic Association, 1980). Because of the high nutrient density of eggs, milk, and cheese, with a possible lack of iron, the lacto-ovo- and lacto-vegetarian diets are very similar in nutrient content to diets containing meat.

The total vegetarian diet must be carefully planned to meet the requirements for some nutrients. Vitamin B_{12} is not found in plants; animal products are the only practical dietary sources of this vitamin. Therefore, the pure vegetarian, not consuming any animal products, should use soybean meal fortified with vitamin B_{12} or a vitamin B_{12} supplement. Meatless dishes are likely to be of marginal content in calcium, iron, zinc, and riboflavin. Additionally, the iron from vegetable sources is absorbed less efficiently than the heme-iron in meat.

Careful planning of the diet to include sources of needed nutrients is especially important during periods of rapid growth, specifically, childhood and adolescence. Calcium and riboflavin can be obtained from milk and milk products, almonds, vegetables such as broccoli and asparagus, and enriched bread products. Soy milk fortified with riboflavin can be a good source of riboflavin and a fair source of calcium. Although red meats are the richest source of iron, iron is also found in fish and poultry, as well as in enriched breads and cereals, legumes, and nuts. Vitamin D can be supplied by products fortified with vitamin D, such as milk. However, vitamin D deficiency is not a problem for most children if they have adequate exposure to sunshine.

In planning nutritionally adequate vegetarian diets, consideration must be given to protein quality. Awareness of foods which complement each other in amino acid content can assure adequate protein intake. Although some of the nutrients commonly missing in ill-planned vegetarian diets—particularly calcium, iron, vitamin B_{12}, zinc and riboflavin—can be replaced with nutritional supplements, this is not necessarily the case with protein.

The Role of Supplements

In view of survey data showing less-than-adequate diets for many children and teenagers, and in view of the fact that meal skipping, snacking, and fast foods are a part of the lifestyle of youths today, a daily multivitamin/mineral tablet may be indicated when there is doubt regarding the nutritional adequacy of the diet. However it should be stressed that not more than 100% of the RDA should be provided via supplements daily. Therapeutic doses are not indicated for healthy individuals.

Although nutritional supplements (liquid meal replacements and pills) can be useful in replacing missed meals or helping to ensure nutritional adequacy, it must be stressed that it is impossible for supplements to be a replacement for a normal diet or to correct poor eating habits. Although there is a role for supplements, they should not be used in place of nutrition education.

References

The American Dietetic Association. (1980). Position paper on the vegetarian approach to eating. *Journal of the American Dietetic Association,* **77**, 61-69.

Committee on Sports Medicine, American Academy of Pediatrics (1983). *Sports medicine: Health care for young athletes.* Evanston, IL: Author.

Grandjean, A.C. (Ed.). (1984). *Nutrition for sport success.* Reston, VA: American Alliance for Health, Physical Education, Recreation, and Dance.

Grandjean, A.C., Hursh, L.M., Majure, W.C., & Hanley, D.F. (1981). Nutrition knowledge and practices of college athletes. *Medicine and Science in Sports and Exercise,* **13**(2), 82.

Grandjean, A.C., & Lolkus, L.J. (1981-1984). *Dietary habits of athletes.* (Available from Swanson Center for Nutrition, Inc., Omaha, Nebraska)

Pao, E.M., & Mickle, S.J. (1981). Problem nutrients in the United States. *Food Technology,* **35**, 58-69.

Chapter 9

Creating a Positive Exercise Environment for Obese Individuals

Kristine Larson Clark

Despite conclusive evidence that obese persons can, and should, exercise as part of comprehensive fitness and weight control strategies, exercise programs designed specifically for these people are rare. Moreover, though extensive research has focused on how much and what types of exercise are appropriate for obese persons, the literature regarding obesity, exercise, and weight control offers few strategies for keeping them exercising. It is the purpose of this paper to introduce the notion of therapeutic touch as a method for increasing compliance in programs for obese persons. The use of therapeutic touch has been implemented in the "Nutri-Fit" program at the University of Wisconsin-La Crosse. "Nutri-Fit," one of the offerings of the La Crosse Exercise Program, is a fitness and weight control program specifically designed for obese people.

Exercising the Consumer

Exercise programs designed to meet the needs of recreational athletes and exercise enthusiasts are growing in number. In many towns, high school gymnasiums are being utilized for community fitness programs at night. In larger cities, the growth of the fitness and weight control industry is more visible. The emergence of health spas, weight lifting centers, on-site employee fitness programs, and chain-operated fitness and weight control centers reflects the diverse needs of consumers. Operators of exercise facilities have reassessed their programs and have designed marketing strategies geared to attract all types of exercisers. Competition for participants has forced facilities to add new equipment and programs.

This increased diversification of programs should attract a more diverse clientele, which, in turn provides a greater likelihood of financial and program stability.

Target audiences for an exercise program can include infants, pre-schoolers, adolescents, high-school-aged children, young adults (aged 18-25), adults (age 26-60), and seniors (over 60). Some exercise facilities are now including programs for the physically impaired and for pregnant women. Yet, very few of these facilities are designing and marketing programs aimed specifically at the obese person. This segment of the population requires programs that are sensitive to the physical restrictions accompanying obesity, such as lack of muscular strength and poor mobility and flexibility. Perhaps more important is the recognition of the psychological liabilities of obesity, such as a general sense of low self-esteem and the fear of failure or injury.

Understanding the Reasons Behind Low Participation

Obese persons rarely seek out formal exercise programs designed for the general public. Fear of being unable to "keep up" in a generic class, of being "the fattest person in the class," of being injured, of being embarrassed by their awkwardness and by the type of clothes they must wear to cover up their bodies are a few reasons listed by obese women either for not enrolling in exercise programs or for dropping out soon after joining (Foss, 1984). Yet, these fears are, in part, legitimate responses to the situations that prevail in most exercise programs. Operators of exercise facilities, seeking to reap the greatest economic benefits from their programs, have largely ignored the special needs of obese individuals precisely because these individuals have not been a source of enrollment and revenues to offset facility costs and program expenses. To resolve this dilemma, health and fitness administrators need to develop programs that will be profitable because they appeal to a segment of the population that has largely been untouched by the fitness revolution.

Obese persons can exercise and should learn how to exercise as part of a proper weight reduction program (Foss, 1981). The benefits of exercise include raising the metabolic rate and increasing flexibility, muscle strength, and cardiovascular endurance. Exercise has been shown to be a factor in reducing blood sugar and blood pressure in obese subjects (Farebrother, 1979; Foss, 1984; Hage, 1982). Obese individuals have been able to either reduce or stop using medications as a result of consistent exercise (Bray, Whipp, Koyal, & Wasserman, 1977). When asked, clients frequently cite an improvement in sleep habits, along with decreased stress and negative coping behaviors.

Despite the benefits of exercise, most obese individuals avoid physical activity and thus pose a problem for the health educator, physician, and/or dietitian concerned with their well-being. General reasons cited for exercise noncompliance are well-documented in the literature (Dishman, 1982; Hayes, 1984; Oldridge, 1984; Oldridge & Jones, 1983; Wankle, 1984). The most commonly cited reasons are

1. not enough time,
2. too busy,
3. boring,
4. don't want additional work,
5. money (can't afford program),
6. inconvenient location,
7. lack of support from family and friends,
8. not motivated,
9. work conflicts,
10. embarrassed,
11. too tired,
12. too difficult,
13. wasn't working.

Although none of these reasons explicitly refers to a negative exercise environment as a cause for noncompliance, several can be interpreted in this manner. The obese individual in a generic exercise program could list reasons #10—"embarrassed," #11—"too tired," #12—"too difficult," and #13—"wasn't working." These reasons could be associated with the possibility that the exercise class did not provide a supportive exercise environment. Again, the operators of exercise facilities can hardly be blamed for targeting their programs toward the physical abilities of their present clientele. Since few obese people seek out formal exercise classes, their special needs are easily overlooked. The few obese persons who do join probably don't continue, because the workouts are too strenuous (reasons "too tired" and "too difficult"), thin women and even the presence of men can be intimidating (reason "embarrassed"), they tried very hard and became sore or injured (reasons "too difficult," "wasn't working"), and lastly, they felt too alone and misunderstood (reasons "embarrassed," "wasn't working").

Rather than simply accepting the notion that exercise programs cannot appeal to obese persons, health professionals need to consider the possibility that programs structured to meet the unique needs of the obese could increase both participation rates and length of commitment by these people.

Structuring a Supportive Environment

As mentioned in the first part of this chapter, obese persons are uniquely sensitive to exercise programs in which they feel out of place. Although many people enter exercise programs from sedentary lifestyles, the obese person is conspicuous not only for lack of exercise experience, but also for being overweight and perhaps the largest person in the gym. Embarrassment and a sense of alienation could be avoided if each obese person were welcomed into his or her program in a personalized manner. Because large classes seldom offer the opportunity for instructors to meet or acknowledge individual participants, little direct encouragement is given. With this in mind, the following concepts should be considered in creating an exercise environment for the obese participant:

- Small group exercise sessions, allowing no more than 10-15 in the class, reduce anxiety over exercising in public. The small size also facilitates group interaction and personal exchange between the exercise leader and the participants.
- The program should be carefully marketed as a program for persons who are 30 or more pounds overweight. This should screen out those individuals who perceive themselves to be overweight but who are either at or below their ideal weight. A physician's referral to the program could also aid in attracting only those considered clinically obese.
- Classes could be taught by a leader who is overweight. A participant who is enthusiastic and exhibiting success would be an ideal candidate to recruit for developing exercise leadership skills. The participant could either accompany the ''official'' exercise leader or lead a class solo. The nonverbal statement being made by the program is one that fosters support, stimulates self-respect, and negates the notion that approval, accomplishment, and success can result only when thinness is achieved. An overweight exercise leader, recognized as being in the process of losing weight and gaining strength, presents a more realistic role model for an obese participant.
- The exercise leader should allow participants the freedom to wear ''nonregulation'' exercise apparel, provided it is comfortable and does not restrict movement. Body size can be embarrassing for the obese woman in an exercise program, and covering up with slacks and long-sleeved shirts or sweat suits is not uncommon. If participants choose to exercise in a water program, they are frequently faced with the dilemma of not having a swimming suit. In cases such as these, the exercise leader should be encouraging and suggest that the new participant wear whatever is comfortable. Comfort in this case can mean psychological comfort, as well as physical comfort. A large T-shirt

and shorts (perhaps made from a discarded pair of slacks) can be worn for water exercises. Clients may find that their willingness to give up their cover-up clothes for more cool, lighter weight clothing is directly related to the degree of their psychological comfort in the exercise class.

Leadership Techniques for Personalizing the Program

By maintaining a class size of no more than 15 persons, the group leader will be able to meet each participant. This individual attention contributes to a sense of self-worth for clients. Introducing participants to each other is an additional way of initiating a "bonding process." This concept of a bonding process is the foundation for creating the type of setting or atmosphere to which participants would like to return. A program offering this positive setting emphasizes the development of relationships within the group, the fostering of group interaction, the personal attention provided by the exercise leader, and the safety and support provided by an environment uniquely structured for obese persons.

One technique that has facilitated the bonding process in an exercise program for obese clients is *therapeutic touch*. Delores Krieger, professor of nursing at New York University, was instrumental in developing the technique of therapeutic touch in this country and is noted for her research on the healing aspects of touch. According to Krieger, therapeutic touch involves the "laying on of hands," which invites an exchange of human energy between two persons. One has an abundance of energy to share with the other, who is in need of "healing" energy. Therapeutic touch has been used in the treatment of terminal illnesses and with infants failing to thrive.

The stimulation derived from human touch triggers a physiological response which is not completely understood. However, Krieger's research reveals two interesting ideas. The first is that therapeutic use of the hands affects the patient's blood components and brain waves and that it elicits a generalized relaxation response. The second idea is that this highly personalized interaction invokes in the patient or client a sense of self-responsibility for his or health (Krieger, 1979). Both of these ideas have merit when considering using therapeutic touch in an exercise program for the obese.

Implementation of Therapeutic Touch

To define therapeutic touch for purposes of using it as a behavior modification technique, it is a hug, an arm around a shoulder, a pat on the back, or any other nonsexual touching that demonstrates caring, support, encouragement, approval, and acceptance. Exercise leaders can implement therapeutic touch in their classes through self-initiation and invitation. Exercise sessions might conclude with ten minutes of therapeutic touch as part of the cool-down period. Leaders should remind participants that the cool-down phase of an exercise bout allows the body to relax and gently recover from the aerobic phase just accomplished. Focusing attention on the need to relax and on the new energies from the exercise is an appropriate lead-in to the three following therapeutic touch techniques:

- Participants are invited to form a circle and stretch their arms out in front until all fingertips are touching in the center of the circle (see Figure 1). The exercise leader invites all participants to "share their energies"—in other words, to consciously support each other. For example, participants can be invited to express a problem or a concern, in response to which the group can provide input and encouragement. This personalized interaction may provide the client with a sense of belonging and assist in bonding with the group. A renewed sense of confidence and self-worth may ward off a binge eating episode and increase the likelihood that this particular client will return for another session.
- Participants are invited to put their arms around each other's shoulders and massage the shoulder muscles (Figure 2). This touching results in comments such as "Oh, that feels so good," "I haven't

Figure 1.

Figure 2.

Figure 3.

Figure 4.

had that done for me in a long time," and "No one ever rubs my shoulders!" Obese individuals enjoy the pleasures of a caring touch as much as anyone, but their low self-esteem may usually leave them feeling unworthy of touch. The structured environment of an exercise program can be invaluable in providing a setting in which touching is permissible and welcome.

• Participants are invited to find someone in the class and give that person a hug (Figures 3 and 4). This technique emphasizes the need and desire for human support in all efforts and especially in those efforts that can be difficult, embarrassing, or lonely. Obese individuals are chronically faced with society's verdict that their bodies are unattractive and unacceptable. The touch of a hug reinforces the acceptability of the person inside the body. Feeling good about themselves and about the others in the class is the memory with which they leave and return.

Conclusion

In summary, exercise programs would benefit from classes designed specifically for the obese individual. Restricting enrollment to clinically obese individuals; structuring the exercise environment to promote a positive body image, health, and fitness; and implementing the component of therapeutic touch are critical to a successful program for obese individuals. The exercise leader has a major responsibility for implementing these techniques.

References

Bray, G.A., Whipp, B.J., Koyal, S.N., & Wasserman, K. (1977). Some respiratory and metabolic effects of exercise in moderately obese men. *Metabolism*, **26**, 403-412.

Dishman, R.K. (1982). Compliance/adherence in health-related exercise. *Health Psychology*, **1**, 237-267.

Farebrother, M.J.B. (1979). Respiratory function and cardiorespiratory response to exercise in obesity. *British Journal of Diseases of the Chest*, **73**, 211-229.

Foss, M.L. (1981). Exercise prescription and training programs for obese subjects. In P. Bjorntop, M. Cairella, & A.N. Howard (Eds.), *Recent advances in obesity research* (pp. 81-100). London: Libbey.

Foss, M.L. (1984). Exercise concerns and precautions for the obese. In J. Starlie & H.A. Jordan (Eds.), *Nutrition and exercise in obesity management* (pp. 123-147). New York: Spectrum Publications.

Hage, P. (1982). Diet and exercise programs for coronary heart disease: Better late than never. *The Physician and Sportsmedicine*, **10**, 121-126.

Hayes, R.B. (1984). Compliance with health advice: An overview with special reference to exercise programs. *Journal of Cardiac Rehabilitation*, **4**, 120-127.

Krieger, D. (1979). *The therapeutic touch.* Englewood Cliffs, NJ: Prentice-Hall.

Oldridge, N.B. (1984). Efficacy and effectiveness: Critical issues in exercise and compliance. *Journal of Cardiac Rehabilitation*, **4**, 119-121.

Oldridge, N.B., & Jones, N.L. (1983). Improving patient compliance in cardiac exercise rehabilitation: Effect of written agreement and self-monitoring. *Journal of Cardiac Rehabilitation*, **3**, 257-262.

Wankle, L.M. (1984). Decision-making and social-support strategies for increasing exercise involvement. *Journal of Cardiac Rehabilitation*, **4**, 124-134.

Chapter 10

Exercise Programming for the Moderately Obese Adult: Rationale and Procedures

Barry A. Franklin

Reduction of body weight and fat stores is often recommended as part of the medical treatment of several chronic health problems (Buskirk, 1974). Endurance exercise training, when maintained on a regular basis, has a favorable influence on body composition, resulting in moderate reductions in body weight, moderate to large losses in body fat, and small to moderate increases in lean body weight (Wilmore, 1983). Unfortunately, conventional exercise programs are often ineffective in achieving these outcomes, with poor patient compliance a big part of the problem (Franklin & Rubenfire, 1980; MacKeen, Franklin, Nicholas, & Buskirk, 1983).

The purposes of this paper are (a) to review the physiological basis and rationale for exercise training in weight reduction programs for the moderately obese adult, and (b) to provide the exercise leader with examples of innovative and enjoyable recreational activities to employ in the implementation of such programs.

Keys to the Successful Exercise Program

Exercise programs for the moderately obese adult should meet four specific criteria: (a) safety, (b) effectiveness, (c) education and motivation components, and (d) fun or pleasure principle. Obese adults embarking on physical conditioning programs often have unrealistic impressions of safe and effective exercise practices. The exercise leader should select activities that minimize the potential for musculoskeletal and orthopedic complications, yet meet a threshold exercise dosage (frequency, intensity, duration) that will increase cardiorespiratory fitness and, perhaps more importantly, promote a negative caloric balance. Undue fatigue, extreme muscle soreness, and injury must be avoided to achieve long-term compliance.

Education of adults on *why* and *how* they should exercise should serve as an integral part of the exercise program. Participants should receive substantive information on body mechanics, energy expenditure, exercise prescription (Hellerstein & Franklin, 1984), importance of warm-up and cool-down, ineffective gadgets and gimmicks, exercise myths and misconceptions (Franklin, 1984a), guidelines on appropriate exercise clothing and shoes, nutrition, and the effect of ambient temperature and humidity on performance (Franklin, 1978). The participant should be cautioned against certain proscribed behaviors that counteract the benefits of exercise or that may be potentially hazardous, i.e., sporadic high intensity exercise, performance of the Valsalva, exercise during illness, ingestion of large meals or alcohol before or after exercise, etc. (Hellerstein & Franklin, 1984). In addition to educating participants, it is necessary to motivate them to continue exercise training (Franklin, 1978; Franklin, 1984b). Since poor exercise compliance is associated with low enjoyability ratings (Martin & Smith, 1981), participants should engage in physical activities that are fun or pleasurable. The "games-as-aerobics" approach provides a format that facilitates this objective (Franklin, Oldridge, Stoedefalke, & Loechel, in press).

The Games-as-Aerobics Approach

The games-as-aerobics approach provides an ideal complement to an endurance training program. The approach emphasizes fun, pleasure, and repeated success, in contrast to the pain and discomfort associated with many traditional preventive and rehabilitative exercise programs. Activities may vary with each workout, being limited only by the creativity of the exercise leader. Stretching and flexibility calisthenics and dynamic aerobic exercises are frequently camouflaged as games, relays, or stunts, incorporating ball passing and other movement skills for variety (see Figure 1). The participant exercises at his or her own pace, rather than being directed in a format in which all persons are expected to perform the same activity at the same cadence, as in Marine Corps calisthenics. Complementary equipment may include hula hoops, medicine balls, cage balls, playground balls, jump ropes, parachutes, heavy-hands (Schwartz, 1984), and playbuoy arm exercisers (Frost, 1977).

This approach differs from conventional exercise programs in that total body movement is generally greater, maximizing the potential for a negative caloric balance. Participants are required to keep moving for a prescribed period of time. Repeated flexion and extension of the upper

Figure 1. The "games-as-aerobics" approach to exercise. Calisthenics are modified to incorporate ball passing and other movement skills for variety.

and lower limbs and slow walking (i.e., 1.5-2.0 mph) are encouraged even during rest breaks (Franklin et al., in press).

There are four phases to the program format: warm-up; endurance, sustained activity; modified recreational games; and cool-down.

Phase I: Warm-Up

Warming up about 5-15 minutes prepares the body for vigorous exercise. It serves as a period of adaptation by increasing cardiac output and skeletal muscle blood flow; it stretches postural muscles, it minimizes oxygen deficit and the formation of lactic acid, and it increases skeletal muscle and body core temperatures, which enhance muscular efficiency and oxyhemoglobin dissociation (Astrand & Rodahl, 1970). Warm-up decreases muscle viscosity, the susceptibility to injury, and the occurrence of electrocardiographic abnormalities indicative of the myocardial ischemia and/or ventricular irritability that may occur following sudden strenuous exertion (Barnard, Gardner, Diaco, MacAlpin, & Kattus, 1973). Thus, warmup exercises have preventive value and enhance performance capacity (Hellerstein & Franklin, 1984).

Warm-up exercises should include both musculoskeletal (i.e., static stretching, flexibility, muscle-strengthening exercises) and cardiorespiratory activities. An initial period of calisthenics, involving stretching and flexibility movements, may include flexion, extension, circling, rotation, abduction, and adduction (Franklin et al., in press). The cardio-respiratory warm-up should follow, involving total body movement to include an intensity of activity (i.e., alternate walking-jogging, swimming-recovering, moderate cycling) sufficient to evoke a heart rate within 20 beats per minute of the "target heart rate" recommended for endurance training (Hellerstein & Franklin, 1984).

Our experience suggests that the ideal warm-up for an endurance activity is that very activity, only at a lower intensity. Hence, participants who require brisk walking during the endurance phase should conclude the warm-up with slow walking. On the other hand, fast walking (i.e., 3.5-4.5 mph) serves as an optimal warm-up for participants who jog. Cardiorespiratory warm-up activities can be modified to incorporate playground balls and to include individual, partner, or group activities or relays. However, with partner or small group activities, participants should be grouped homogeneously to include individuals with similar aerobic capacities ($\dot{V}O_2$max).

Phase II: Endurance and Sustained Activity

The endurance phase (at least 30 minutes) serves to directly stimulate the oxygen transport system and maximize caloric expenditure. This phase should be prescribed in specific terms of intensity, frequency, and duration (Hellerstein & Franklin, 1984). However, interrelationships among these variables may permit a subthreshold level in one factor to be partially or totally compensated for by appropriate increases in one or both of the others. Exercise training at 60-70% of maximal heart rate, equivalent to 45-57% $\dot{V}O_2$max, should facilitate this objective (Sharkey, 1975). During this relative exercise intensity, blood lactate levels generally remain low, allowing the individual to exercise for sustained periods, whereas free fatty acids are used preferentially as a fuel source (Girandola, 1976; Katch & McArdle, 1977). In contrast, exercise training above 60% $\dot{V}O_2$max is associated with decreased fat and increased carbohydrate utilization (Figure 2) (Astrand & Rodahl, 1970). These data highlight the importance of mild- to moderate-intensity exercise, the "long, slow distance concept," when targeting adipose tissue stores as the energy substrate during exercise.

During the endurance phase, exercise intensity may be regulated by several popular methods (Hellerstein & Franklin, 1984): a prescribed training heart rate range; assigned pace for walking or jogging; recommended work load for the stationary cycle ergometer; and the Borg scale (Borg, 1970) for rating of perceived exertion (RPE). This latter method, particularly when used in conjunction with other clinical, psychological, and physiological information (i.e., pulse rate), provides a reliable method for regulating exercise intensity within safe and effective limits. The Borg scale consists of 15 grades from 6 to 20: 7 = very, very light; 9 = very

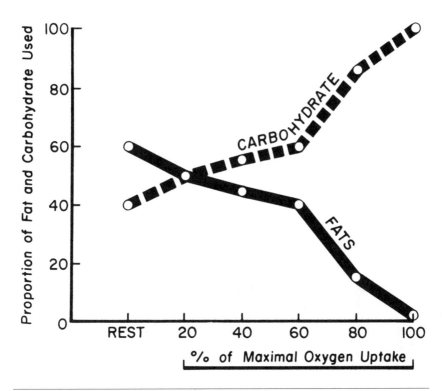

Figure 2.   Relative contributions from fat and carbohydrate as a function of exercise intensity, expressed as a percentage of the maximal oxygen uptake (V̇O₂max). During mild- to moderate-intensity exercise (e.g., below 60% V̇O₂max), fat serves as an important energy substrate. From *Textbook of Work Physiology* (p. 460) by P.O. Astrand and K. Rodahl, 1970, New York: McGraw-Hill. Copyright 1970 by McGraw-Hill, Inc. Adapted by permission.

light; 11 = fairly light; 13 = somewhat hard; 15 = hard; 17 = very hard; 19 = very, very hard. The ratings are based on one's overall feeling of exertion and physical fatigue. Participants are cautioned not to overemphasize any one factor, such as leg pain or dyspnea, but to try to assess their total, inner feeling of exertion. Among healthy young persons, the RPE number during exercise generally approximates one-tenth of the number of heart beats per minute.

Exercise rated as 11 to 13, between "fairly light" and "somewhat hard," is generally appropriate for weight reduction programs, corresponding to 60-70% of the maximal heart rate and equivalent to 45-57% V̇O₂max (Figure 3). In contrast, exercise rated 13 to 16, between "somewhat hard" and "hard," is generally considered more appropriate for cardiorespiratory conditioning, corresponding to 70-85% of maximal heart rate and equivalent to 57-78% V̇O₂max (Hellerstein & Franklin, 1984).

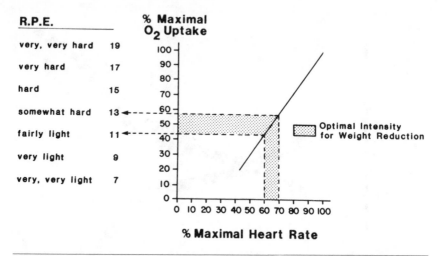

Figure 3. Relationships among percentage of maximal oxygen uptake, percentage of maximal heart rate, and Borg's rating of perceived exertion (RPE) scale, at the optimal exercise intensity for reduction of body weight and fat stores. From "Exercise Testing and Prescription" by H.K. Hellerstein and B.A. Franklin, 1984, in N.K. Wenger and H.K. Hellerstein (Eds.), *Rehabilitation of the Coronary Patient* (2nd ed., p. 241). New York: John Wiley, Copyright 1984 by John Wiley & Sons. Adapted by permission.

An American College of Sports Medicine position paper (American College of Sports Medicine, 1979) suggests that exercise training programs for reduction of body weight and fat stores include sustained exercise of an endurance nature for at least 20-30 minutes duration, an exercise intensity sufficient to expend 300 or more kcal per session, with a minimum of three exercise sessions per week. Exercise programs lasting less than 3 months, or those performed twice a week—regardless of the intensity, duration, or both—are generally ineffective in reducing adipose tissue stores (Bjorntorp, 1978; Pollock, Wilmore & Fox, 1978).

The most effective exercises for the endurance phase employ large muscle groups, are maintained continuously, and are rhythmical and aerobic in nature, e.g., jogging (in place or moving), running, stationary or outdoor cycling, swimming, skipping rope, rowing, climbing stairs, and stepping on and off a bench. Other exercise modalities commonly used in activity programs for the overweight include calisthenics, particularly those involving sustained total body movement (e.g., jumping jacks, hops, sailor's hornpipe), recreational games, and weight training (Foss & Strehle, 1984).

Walking, in particular, has several advantages over other forms of exercise for moderately obese adults. It offers an easily tolerable exercise intensity and causes fewer musculoskeletal and orthopedic problems of the legs, knees, and feet (Pollock et al., 1971). Furthermore, walking is a "companionable" activity that requires no special equipment other than a pair of well-fitted athletic shoes. Ad libitum and fastest-pace walking programs have been successfully used with moderately overweight (Franklin et al., 1979; Gwinup, 1975; Leon, Conrad, Hunninghake, & Serfass, 1979; Lewis et al., 1976) and extremely obese subjects (Foss, Lampman, & Schteingart, 1976; Foss, Lampman, & Schteingart, 1980; Goodman & Kenrick, 1975; Kenrick, Ball, & Canary, 1972), particularly when the walking duration exceeds 30 minutes (Gwinup, 1975).

The gross caloric cost of walking approximates 1.15 kcal/kg/mile (Franklin & Rubenfire, 1980). Moreover, unless the individual walks at extremely slow or fast paces (i.e., < 1.9 mph or > 3.7 mph), the caloric cost per mile is relatively independent of speed (American College of Sports Medicine, 1986), increasing linearly as a function of body weight (Figure 4) (Franklin & Rubenfire, 1980). Although many obese persons may be unable to jog or run, a substantial energy expenditure can result by moving excessive body weight over an extensive distance.

GROSS CALORIC REQUIREMENTS
PER MILE FOR WALKING

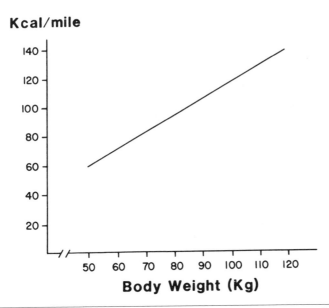

Figure 4.   Gross caloric requirements per mile of walking, expressed as a function of body weight. From "Losing Weight Through Exercise" by B.A. Franklin and M. Rubenfire, 1980, *Journal of the American Medical Association,* **244,** p. 378. Copyright 1980 by The American Medical Association. Adapted by permission.

Recently, several innovations in conventional walking programs have been suggested for moderately obese adults. Swimming pool walking has been used successfully in weight reduction programs (Kindl & Brown, 1977). Walking in water requires considerably more energy than walking on land (Evans, Cureton, & Purvis, 1978), and the buoyancy of the water acts to reduce strain on muscles and joints—particularly important among the extremely obese. Walking with ankle weights or a backpack also offers another practical option for those who wish to lose weight and improve fitness (Schoenfeld, Keren, Shimoni, Birnfeld, & Sohar, 1980).

As a variation to the standard walking format, several other activities can also be used during the endurance phase. For example, instead of 30-40 minutes of walking alone, a 15-minute walk may be supplemented by 15-25 minutes of noncompetitive relays and individual, group, or partner activities. Many forms of human locomotion can be employed during this phase, including walking, striding, jogging, skipping (forward, rearward, sideward), and hopping (for brief periods) (Franklin et al., in press). Participants may carry playground balls, foot- or hand-dribble balls, pass them to one another, or bounce them off gymnasium walls. The scope of these activities is limited only by the creativity of the exercise leader.

Phase III: Modified Recreational Games

Conventional exercise programs, including a warm-up, walk jog, and cooldown sequence, offer little in terms of fun or enjoyment. A recreational game, appropriately modified, should be incorporated as an added option to this format. Game modifications that serve to minimize required skill and competition and maximize participant success and energy expenditure are particularly important in exercise programs for the obese. To this end, the imaginative exercise leader may recommend a larger court size, frequent player rotation, continuous movement, adjusted scorekeeping, or other subtle rule changes. If volleyball nets are employed, they may be at heights lower than recommended for official tournament play. Through such modifications, the exercise leader is better able to emphasize play, as opposed to points won or a team victory (Franklin, 1978).

Recreational games that are particularly popular in exercise programs for the obese include cageball soccer, one-bounce volleyball, and kickball golf. A brief description of each follows, with specific reference to the playing area, number of players, playing time, equipment, rules, and scoring and penalties.

Cageball Soccer.

- Playing area: Gymnasium floor or basketball court, with a rectangular goal at each end, goal size: 9-12 feet. Goals may be constructed from tape (on walls), pylons, cages, or floor mats placed against walls.

- Number of players: Equal number on each team.
- Playing time: First team to score a designated number of goals, or time arbitrarily determined by the exercise leader.
- Equipment: Cageball (3-5 foot diameter)
- Rules/scoring: All players begin in the seated position, hands on the floor for support (Figure 5). The game is started by a face-off in the center of the court. The ball may be kicked with the feet only, hand-ball contact is not permitted. The objective is to advance the cageball toward the opponents' goal. Contact of the ball with the goal scores a point, followed by a new face-off. Player movement up and down the court is by crab-walk only. Goalies are frequently alternated. There are no out-of-bounds, because the gymnasium walls may be used to pass the ball from one player to another. The winner is the team with the most goals.
- Penalties: This is no-hands game. A penalty is charged against the team using their hands: the opposing team receives the ball side out.

Figure 5. Cageball soccer is a popular game in exercise programs for over-weight adults.

One-Bounce Volleyball.

- Playing area: Volleyball court with a net height of 6-8 feet.
- Number of players: Any number may play, generally, 5-9 players per side works best. When a team has a player talent advantage, the exercise leader should move selected players to the opposing side to facilitate comparable playing ability between the teams.
- Playing time: The first team to reach 11, 15, or 21 points; the winner must be ahead by 2 points.
- Equipment: Volleyball
- Rules/scoring: The game is started by a volley for serve, during which the ball must cross the net a minimum of three times. The winner of the volley serves first. Standard volleyball rules are followed, *except* one floor bounce and as many as 3 hits per side are permitted (allowing one bounce of the ball per side facilitates longer play and provides additional fun, while minimizing the skill level required to play the game). The serving team wins a point when their opponents are unable to return the ball over the net. Failure of the serving team to successfully return the ball over the net results in the loss of service. Player rotation can occur after each point or service.
- Penalties: Side out is declared when the ball is struck more than one time in succession by a single player or more than three times in succession by one team.

Kickball Golf.

- Playing area: Any grassy outdoor area (80-300 yards). The ideal playing area might include water hazards, small rolling hills, and trees, telephone poles, or implanted utility poles.
- Number of players: Any number of players can be involved. There may be individual, partner, or team play.
- Playing time: Determined by the exercise leader.
- Equipment: A wide variety of sport balls (e.g., volleyball, soccer ball) may be used. An inflated rubber playground ball (10-12 inches in diameter) is ideal.
- Rules/scoring: Rules are similar to conventional golf, except that sport balls and wooden stakes (as "holes") are employed (Franklin et al., in press; see Figure 6). Cardboard or cloth flags designating the hole number may be mounted at the top of each wooden stake. The number of holes is determined by the exercise leader, as is the arbitrarily established tee for each hole. The success of the game depends on the exercise leader's ability to create a golf course that is interesting and challenging. Many variations are possible: doglegs, water hazards, placing the stakes on hilly terrain. Before the players tee off, the leader determines the par for the hole by evaluating the distance

Figure 6. A participant plays a round of kickball golf. Rules are similar to conventional golf, except that playground balls and wooden stakes (as "holes") are employed.

and hazards that may be encountered. For example, a 200-yard hole might be considered a par 5, whereas a 60-yard hole may be a par 3. The ball is kicked from the ground; *players must walk briskly or jog between kicks.* The object of the game is to strike the wooden stake (hole) in the fewest number of strokes. Scores may be recorded on real golf cards. The tee for the next hole is adjacent to the hole that was recently completed. The lowest score on a predetermined number of holes is the winner.

Phase IV: Cool-Down

The cool-down (5-8 minutes) provides a gradual recovery from the sustained, mild- to moderate-intensity activities of the two previous phases (endurance and recreational games). During exercise, vasodilatation in the active muscles accommodates the blood flow necessary for increased metabolic demands. The potential for accumulation of blood in the lower extremities is countered by a "milking action" of the muscles on the veins, augmenting venous return and stroke volume. To assist in this process, the veins have one-way valves that permit blood flow in an upward direction only (Figure 7). Following abrupt cessation of exercise, there is no muscle pump action to return blood to the heart. Consequently, blood may pool in the legs. The subsequent decrease in venous return to the brain, heart, or intestines may result in dizziness or fainting, dysrhythmias, or nausea.

The best way to prevent venous pooling after vigorous exercise is to maintain the massaging action of the muscles through continued movement involving slow walking or low intensity exercise (Hellerstein & Franklin, 1984). Activities of a muscle-stretching or -lengthening nature are encouraged during this period, particularly involving extensor muscles of the back, lower legs, and upper extremities (Franklin et al., in press). The cool-down permits appropriate circulatory readjustments and return of the heart rate and blood pressure to near-resting values, facilitates dissipation of body heat, promotes more rapid removal of lactic acid than stationary recovery (Belcastro & Bonen, 1975), and combats the potentially deleterious effects of the postexercise rise in plasma catecholamines (Dimsdale, Hartley, Guiney, & Ruskin, 1984).

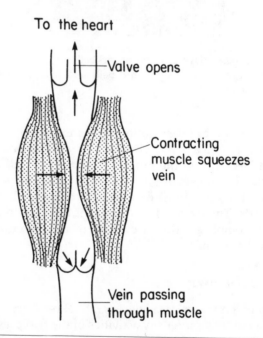

To the heart

Valve opens

Contracting muscle squeezes vein

Vein passing through muscle

Figure 7.   Contraction of skeletal muscle squeezes veins, forcing blood toward the heart. One-way valves prevent the blood from flowing backward.

Conclusion

It is not easy to maintain fitness motivation among previously sedentary overweight adults. The obese individual must develop an attitude toward exercise that reinforces adherence. This is particularly important over the initial 90 days of participation during which time dropouts are most likely to occur (Stoedefalke & Hodgson, 1975). Perhaps the most significant factor shaping this attitude is the type of physical activity that is employed in the exercise program. Exercise leaders should be imaginative in their selection of activities that are safe, effective, and enjoyable.

Acknowledgment

The author gratefully acknowledges Brenda White for her assistance in the preparation of this manuscript.

References

American College of Sports Medicine. (1986). *Guidelines for graded exercise testing and exercise prescription* (3rd ed.). Philadelphia: Lea and Febiger.

American College of Sports Medicine. (1979). The recommended quantity and quality of exercise for developing and maintaining fitness in healthy adults. *Medicine and Science in Sports, 10,* 7-9.

Astrand, P.O., & Rodahl, K. (1970). *Textbook of work physiology.* New York: McGraw-Hill.

Barnard, R.J., Gardner, G.W., Diaco, N.V., MacAlpin, R.N., & Kattus, A.A. (1973). Cardiovascular response to sudden strenuous exercise—heart rate, blood pressure and ECG. *Journal of Applied Physiology, 34,* 833-387.

Belcastro, A.N., & Bonen, A. (1975). Lactic acid removal rates during controlled and uncontrolled recovery exercise. *Journal of Applied Physiology, 39,* 932-936.

Bjorntorp, P. (1978). Physical training in the treatment of obesity. *International Journal of Obesity, 2,* 149-156.

Borg, G. (1970). Perceived exertion as an indicator of somatic stress. *Scandinavian Journal of Rehabililation Medicine, 2,* 92-98.

Buskirk, E.R. (1974). Obesity: A brief overview with emphasis on exercise. *Federation Proceedings, 33,* 1948-1951.

Dimsdale, J.E., Hartley, L.H., Guiney, T., & Ruskin, J.N. (1984). Postexercise peril: Plasma catecholamines and exercise. *Journal of the American Medical Association, 251,* 630-632.

142   Franklin

Evans, B.W., Cureton, K.J., & Purvis, J.W. (1978). Metabolic and circulatory responses to walking and jogging in water. *Research Quarterly,* **49,** 442-449.

Foss, M.L., Lampman, R.M., & Schteingart, D.E. (1976). Physical training program for rehabilitating extremely obese patients. *Archives of Physical Medicine and Rehabilitation,* **57,** 425-429.

Foss, M.L., Lampman, R.M., & Schteingart, D.E. (1980). Extremely obese patients: Improvements in exercise tolerance with physical training and weight loss. *Archives of Physical Medicine and Rehabilitation,* **61,** 119-124.

Foss, M.L., & Strehle, D.A. (1984). Exercise testing and training for the obese. In J. Storlie & H.A. Jordan (Eds.), *Nutrition and exercise in obesity management.* New York: Spectrum Publications.

Franklin, B.A. (1978). Motivating and educating adults to exercise: Practical suggestions to increase interest and enthusiasm. *Journal of Health, Physical Education and Recreation,* **49,** 13-17.

Franklin, B.A. (1984a). Myths and misconceptions in exercise for weight control. In J. Storlie & H.A. Jordan (Eds.), *Nutrition and exercise in obesity management* (pp. 53-92). New York: Spectrum Publications.

Franklin, B.A. (1984b). Exercise program compliance: Improvement strategies. In J. Storlie & H.A. Jordan (Eds.), *Behavioral management of obesity* (pp. 105-135). New York: Spectrum Publications.

Franklin, B., Buskirk, E., Hodgson, J., Gahagan, H., Kollias, J., & Mendez, J. (1979). Effects of physical conditioning on cardiorespiratory function, body composition and serum lipids in relatively normal weight and obese middle-aged women. *International Journal of Obesity,* **3,** 97-109.

Franklin, B.A., Oldridge, N., Stoedefalke, K., & Loechel, W. (in press). *On the ball: Innovative activities for adult fitness and cardiac rehabilitation programs.* Indianapolis: Benchmark Press.

Franklin, B.A., & Rubenfire, M. (1980). Losing weight through exercise. *Journal of the American Medical Association,* **244,** 377-379.

Frost, G. (1977). The playbuoy exerciser. *American Corrective Therapy Journal,* **31,** 156.

Girandola, R.N. (1976). Body composition changes in women: Effects of high and low exercise intensity. *Archives of Physical Medicine and Rehabilitation,* **57,** 297-300.

Goodman, C., & Kenrick, M. (1975). Physical fitness in relation to obesity. *Obesity and Bariatric Medicine,* **4,** 12-15.

Gwinup, G. (1975). Effect of exercise alone on the weight of obese women. *Archives of Internal Medicine,* **135,** 676-680.

Hellerstein, H.K., & Franklin, B.A. (1984). Exercise testing and prescription. In N.K. Wenger & H.K. Hellerstein (Eds.), *Rehabilitation of the coronary patient* (2nd ed., pp. 197-284). New York: John Wiley.

Katch, F.I., & McArdle, W.D. (1977). *Nutrition, weight control, and exercise.* Boston: Houghton Mifflin.

Kenrick, M.M., Ball, M.F., & Canary, J.J. (1972). Exercise and weight reduction in obesity. *Archives of Physical Medicine and Rehabilitation,* **53,** 323-327.

Kindl, M.M., & Brown, P. (1977). Successful treatment of obesity. *Modern Medicine,* **45,** 49-51.

Leon, A.S., Conrad, J., Hunninghake, D.B., & Serfass, R. (1979). Effects of a vigorous walking program on body composition and carbohydrate and lipid metabolism of obese young men. *American Journal of Clinical Nutrition,* **32,** 1776-1787.

Lewis, S., Haskell, W.L., Wood, P.D., Manoogian, N., Bailey, J.E., & Pereira, M. (1976). Effects of physical activity on weight reduction in obese middle-aged women. *American Journal of Clinical Nutrition,* **25,** 151-156.

MacKeen, P.C., Franklin, B.A., Nicholas, W.C., & Buskirk, E.R. (1983). Body composition, physical work capacity and physical activity habits at 18-month follow-up of middle-aged women participating in an exercise intervention program. *International Journal of Obesity,* **7,** 61-71.

Martin, J.E., & Smith, P.O. (1981, November). *Factors predicting exercise adherence: A two-year evaluation.* Paper presented at the 15th annual convention of the Association for Advancement of Behavior Therapy, Toronto.

Pollock, M.L., Miller, H.S., Janeway, R., Linnerud, A.C., Robertson, B., & Valentino, R. (1971). Effects of walking on body composition and cardiovascular function of middle-aged men. *Journal of Applied Physiology,* **30,** 126-130.

Pollock, M.L., Wilmore, J., & Fox, S.M. (1978). *Health and fitness through physical activity.* New York: John Wiley.

Schwartz, L. (1984). *Heavyhands.* New York: Warner Books.

Sharkey, B.J. (1975). *Physiological fitness and weight control.* Missoula, MT: Mountain Press.

Shoenfeld, Y., Keren, G., Shimoni, T., Birnfeld, C., & Sohar, E. (1980). Walking: A method for rapid improvement of physical fitness. *Journal of the American Medical Association,* **243,** 2062-2063.

Stoedefalke, K.G., & Hodgson, J.L. (1975). Exercise Rx—designing a program. *Medical Opinion,* **4,** 48-55.

Wilmore, J.H. (1983). Body composition in sport and exercise: Directions for future research. *Medicine and Science in Sports,* **15,** 21-31.

Part IV

Eating Disorders

Anorexia and bulimia are phenomena of a society that rewards thinness and visualizes even mild obesity as undesirable. These eating disorders present complex etiologies. This section discusses complications of eating disorders and nonmedical treatments.

Chapter 11

To Eat or Not to Eat: Toward a Sociology of Anorexia

Judith Bograd Gordon

Anorexia nervosa, as Stevenson has pointed out, is a terrifying phenomenon. In societies blessed with food for all, increasing numbers of people, particularly teenage girls, starve themselves by choice. Some starve to the point of death, though they carefully feed family members. Daily these human beings view themselves in the mirror with feelings of fear and trepidation, dreading any sign of fat. Eating, yet not eating—their lives and behavior are organized around food intake. Families in desperation turn to health care professionals. In turn, physicians, dietitians, mental health professionals, nurses, and researchers search scientific disciplines for concepts and tools to help them intervene successfully and save the lives of the people they treat.

As part of this effort, renewed attention is being paid to the societies and cultural groups in which anorexics are found in attempts to prevent anorexia and check the burgeoning numbers of people engaged in self-starvation. The purpose of this paper is to add some sociological frames of reference and concepts to the repertoires of people engaged in the search for understanding of this most perplexing activity. Sociology, too, can contribute to the search for the means to resurrect the will to eat in those people, who must themselves choose to eat if they are to thrive.

For the most part, sociological theory and research has not been integrated into current thinking about anorexia. The reasons for this are intriguing. Since the 1950s, sociologists have paid some attention to the study of eating behavior in general, and obesity in particular (Allon, 1980). However, can sociological understandings of the painful suffering of

people who weigh too much contribute to our search for an understanding of people who starve to avoid such pain?

The following poem by Susan McCabe (1983) reassured me that, indeed, a sociological approach to anorexia is not only relevant, but needed.

Though we were both fat
you wore a bikini at the beach
while I rarely went
you went to parties to get drunk
while I talked softly with my own
you rarely smiled
while I prided myself in making you laugh
now you are thin
while I am not
each morning you take a kaleidoscope of pills
a yellow appetite suppressant
a white thyroid pill
a blue water pill
two, three, four brown ex-lax
and now when you look great on a tennis court
you are too weak to play

As this poem reflects, the process of self-starvation in large measure
is initiated by social interaction and the search for social approval. Attention paid to the medical and psychological aspects of anorexia is surely
necessary, but not sufficient. The emaciated condition of anorexic
teenagers brought to medical attention is a phenomenon that also calls
for sociological attention and explanation.

Since the publication of Werner Cahnman's seminal article on the stigma
of obesity in 1968, sociologists have looked at the personal and social
troubles of those who are fat in societies that prize thinness (Schwartz,
1984; Allon, 1980). However, there has been no similarly influential article on the stigma of anorexia. Skeleton-like anorexics, not only the obese,
can cause negative reactions from others who judge psychological stability on the basis of physical appearance. Yet, the autobiographies of
anorexics, even those who nearly starved themselves to death, do not
report encountering the kind of discrimination and prejudice directed
toward those labeled fat (MacLeod, 1981; O'Neill, 1982). Why not?

Feminists, such as Chernin (1981), have looked at anorexia as the extreme product of this society's obsession with weight. Yet, the literature
on the social worlds of anorexics is as shrunken as their bodies. Surely
they, as do the fat, live in the everyday world and interact with people
besides their families, doctors, dieticians, nurses, and therapists.

In some ways anorexics are natural sociologists, for they are keen observers of the social scene. They know that regardless of efforts to eliminate the stigma of obesity, it is still better to be thin than fat in contemporary societies. They know that many health care professionals advocate thin bodies, and they can recite the risks to health of overweight. They understand all too well how their families function. They may even accurately perceive, as some claim, the advantage of avoiding adult roles and responsibilities by perpetuating their own needs for care through self-starvation and patienthood. How then does sociological theory and research contribute to our understanding of anorexics in society?

I was asked at this conference to clarify what a sociologist does that is different from members of other professions more frequently included in multidisciplinary health care teams. As I thought about this question, I began to review what sociologists do. Sociologists, it is claimed, often talk and write in their own jargon. Some are seen as people who attack physicians and the medical model (Peterdorf & Feinstein, 1981). Yet, some of our best friends are physicians. One of the most useful studies of mental hospitals, for example, was done by Stanton, a psychiatrist, and Schwartz, a sociologist (1954). Sociologists frequently are asked to analyze large data sets, often gathered by epidemiologists and others. Sometimes sociologists serve as "super-clerks" to help health care professionals secure grants by formulating ideas in other professional groups' vocabularies. Sociologists also frequently collaborate on quantitative studies and often specialize in survey and community research.

However, sociologists do other things. Historically, sociologists have raised provocative questions (Berger, 1963). We are eclectic and linked into many bodies of knowledge. Most importantly, we use a distinct orientation to human action. We never assume that individuals can operate independently of their society or that any behavior, including eating behavior, can be understood without taking account of the complex interaction between individuals, groups, and social structure. As Cooley put it, "Self and Society are intertwined. We know one as we know the other" (1907).

Currently, some sociologists are paying renewed attention to what is called "the existential self in society" (Kortoba & Fontona, 1984). Moreover, following the work of Wirth (1931), a new association of sociologists interested in the clinical applications of their discipline has emerged (Clinical Sociology Review, 1982; Glassner & Freedman, 1979). Clinical sociology, too, provides what W.I. Thomas called a "beneficent frame" (quoted by Wirth), which adds dimensions to the study of anorexia. In the remainder of this paper, I will illustrate the use of a few sociological concepts in making sense of the phenomenon of anorexia. Then I will suggest some payoff features of these notions by indicating their relevancy to the treatment and prevention of anorexia.

The Looking Glass Self

Social psychology has not been widely applied in the study and treatment of eating disorders. Behavioral psychology has had far more impact. An informal survey revealed that nearly three-fourths of participants here have used behavior modification techniques and theories in their own work. However, only three people have heard of Charles Cooley, and not one has used the concept of the "looking glass self" in treatment or prevention programs. Yet, Cooley's work has had great bearing upon our understanding of anorexics. By 1902 Cooley had already suggested that people's opinions of themselves reflect their view of other's opinions of them. He elaborated upon this concept by specifically focusing upon people's views of the appearance of their bodies.

> We see . . . our face, figure, and dress in the glass and are interested in them because they are ours, and are pleased or otherwise with them according to whether they do or do not answer to what we should like them to be. . . .

> A self-idea of this sort seems to have three principal elements: the imagination of our appearance to the other person; the imagination of his judgement of that appearance; and some sort of self-feeling, such as pride or mortification. (1902, p. 184)

The looking glass self, therefore, develops in interaction with those around us. By toddlerhood, children know the ways in which adults in this society judge whether they are good or bad girls and boys.

The child who becomes anorexic, the literature points out, is not initially viewed as a bad or deviant child. The opposite is true; these children are very in tune with adult expectations for them. They are often described as children who do everything right. They behave correctly and, most importantly, they look right—and, they often begin to diet when someone whose opinion they value makes a comment about their appearance and weight (Sour, 1980).

Unlike their obese peers, they diet by choice. Indeed, their choices reflect the fact that, as adolescents often do, they take onto themselves exaggerated versions of ordinary cultural values. While growing up, the child who becomes anorexic has seen fat children ridiculed and parents dieting. They don't wait for others to put them on a diet. They do it themselves.

Parr (1988) has reported that many ordinary adolescents also self-diet. All children are taught at increasingly younger ages that to have others reflect back one as worthwhile, it is best to be slim. Anorexics, in search of this reflection, distort their appearance. Propelled by forces not yet fully understood, some human beings can initiate a process in which they starve themselves to the point of death. Yet, the time lag before some of these people enter treatment is disturbing, given their low weight. Granted, adolescents have a great sense of their own privacy and may be able to mask their low weight by clothing. Granted, families become just plain accustomed to their children's looks.

Still, the increasingly lower weights reported for anorexics at the point of their entry into treatment suggests that others in their lives do not look at them with disapproval at the start of the process (Brockopp, 1984). As their own autobiographies point out, are they not at first praised for dieting? Salesladies don't tell them their hips are too big for slim fashions anymore. Parents pressed by rising cost of living initially may be grateful for a child who does not "eat like a pig." Ballet teachers reward them with praise, toe shoes, and parts in productions. Gym teachers applaud their attention to exercise. Siblings envy their slimness. Friends comment approvingly about how much weight they have lost. Modeling agencies recruit them, in an era that has not changed very much since Twiggy reigned supreme. Even the Playmate of the Year has grown slimmer during the past couple of decades. Thus, many begin their diets unimpeded and are rewarded for initial weight control by the important people in their lives.

It is true that by the time anorexic adolescents enter treatment, they often have distorted body images (Sour, 1980). They imagine that others see them as slim, whereas, in fact, they appear emaciated. They think others see fat on their bodies where they themselves see fat, but others do not. It is surely a shocking experience that must shake their sense of the self for dieting adolescents to be forced to realize that thinness has become illness and that a biological process is underway that can destroy their lives. Indeed, this realization shakes up everyone involved in the life of the anorexic. How can some teenagers diet to such low weights? Why were they not stopped earlier, before their very lives were put in jeopardy?

Given the individualistic bias of this culture, psychological answers to these questions are the first given (Ching, 1983). It is hypothesized that anorexics may be unconsciously suicidal or troubled by their developing sexuality. For some, dieting to the point of death may indicate a psychotic process. Surely, ordinary people lack the capacity to engage in such drastic self-starvation (Ching).

In addition, attention is paid to their families. An anorexic child calls family functioning into question. Some families are clearly too ashamed to seek help early; others, too busy. Yet, the perplexing questions about anorexia remain unanswered, for some anorexics are not psychotic and some families try desperately to intervene. The literature suggests that these adolescents, psychotic or not, want what all adolescents want: peer approval, parental love, and social recognition of themselves as worthwhile human beings. Are they so wrong in thinking they can win all three by a frantic pursuit of slimness in a culture that takes so long to reflect back a different reaction to their actions and shrinking body size?

Where were the anorexics' teachers? Why didn't their pediatricians intervene earlier? As Allon has observed, many physicians, too, initially praise children who strives to control weight gain during puberty (1980). When children's life-threatening dieting is finally recognized for what it is, their behavior, and sometimes their selves, is reflected back in a new way. They find themselves categorized as "anorexic," "sick," or even "crazy." Their families find themselves viewed by others as pathological because they have produced a starving child. However, underlying the psychological traits and family malfunctioning are the social processes that affect the emergence and early identification of anorexia nervosa, for anorexics, like us all, reflect the ways in which human beings give meanings to themselves and others within a social context.

The concept of the looking glass self, therefore, directs our attention to the judgments of others, as well as to anorexics' views of such judgments and themselves. Cooley's work can guide us to search for intervention and prevention strategies that are based upon the recognition of the ongoing interaction between human beings and the social order.

Significant Others

Following Cooley and William James, George Herbert Mead elaborated upon the interactional processes by which selves are shaped, and noted that some people's reactions have more symbolic meaning than others' (Lester, 1984). For instance, an adolescent may care far more about what his friends think about his appearance than what his math teacher thinks; the opinion about weight of a dancing teacher may mean far more to an aspiring teenage ballerina than that of her mother. Yet, the opinions of parents and other family members remain of paramount importance as children grow up.

The concept of the significant other was developed to delineate individuals and groups whose definitions or interpretations enter into one's own self-definitions (Lester, 1984). Societal values and norms, such as the importance of a thin body, are reinforced or challenged by groups and members of groups who matter to each other.

As Stephenson (1988) has noted, the earlier that intervention is made in cases of anorexia, the more likely the person can go on to a better, less tormented, existence. Other papers in this collection also call attention to the issue of cultural values that overstress the desirability of a slim body as a means to a good life. It is these values that may in fact blind significant others to the beginning development of anorexia, which manifests itself in the early teenage years. By the time an adolescent is near death, such blinders are removed.

We professionals can hope to modify the culture with time. The presentations in these proceedings on obesity suggest that a struggle is taking place in regard to our cultural orientation to body size, dieting, and lifestyle. For some, the quality of the lived life, even with extra pounds, supplants the search for an extended life with fewer pounds. Surely a sensible adult way of coming to terms with genetics, weight, longevity, and dieting would be of benefit to our children, for children model themselves after adults and reflect back the values they are taught. More rational adult approaches to weight and dieting can help modify the cultural set that contributes to the early development of anorexia. Cultures, after all, are transmitted by people; therefore, more attention needs to be paid to the adults whose judgments have impact upon the lives of children and adolescents.

Attention is already being turned to the need to develop educational programs about anorexia nervosa for parents, physicians, school personnel, and teenagers. Guidance counselors, school social workers, and nurses, as well as teachers and peers, are being trained to become cognizant of the signs of anorexia and to cooperate in the early identification of cases. Self-help groups are coming into existence for teenagers who are anorexic (Ching, 1983). However, teenagers are known to be resistant to formal health education in the schools, and anorexic teenagers may be even more resistant. Indeed, once the process is underway, some lose their ability to control it, no matter how much rational information is given to them (Sour, 1980). Education about the disease, its consequences, and its early recognition is necessary, of course, but we need to explore additional ways of influencing eating behavior of our young before anorexia develops.

Mead and Cooley's work points to additional strategies. As attention is turned to reflecting others, it can be seen that some are more significant than others. For instance, children may worship their parents far more than adolescents, who listen to their peers. As with drug education and sex education, nutrition education must be geared to children's and families' readiness to receive and work with the information. Just as we professionals assess readiness to read, so we should begin to assess the readiness of children to understand the relationship between eating and their growth and development.

Education is still a powerful tool in shaping behavior. Preventative efforts can be initiated in elementary schools by holding workshops on eating and adolescense for parents of elementary-age children. Parents can be helped to anticipate reactions to eating during puberty and to identify early signs of trouble. In both elementary and junior high schools, school dieticians can do more than just plan menus. Nutrition educators can serve as resources to classroom and science teachers, giving guest lectures on the nutitional requirements of childhood growth and puberty, the dangers of fad dieting, and the consequences of underweight and self-starvation.

As Mead has observed, as children age, their peer groups become increasingly significant. Health care professionals can also speak informally to social groups of both children and adolescents. Given the prevalence of anorexia in early adolescents, junior-high-age students (aged 12-14) are one group to target (Ching, 1983). It has been suggested that teasing about being fat is most pronounced in this age group (Allon, 1980). Since the peer group during adolescense often has a powerful impact on the social behavior of its members and in some cases has more impact than the family itself, attention must be turned to teaching teenagers about genetics, bodies, and shapes. Feedback from valued significant others can mitigate against the fantasy of approval of extraordinary thinness, particularly if the teenager is already cognizant of the long-range negative consequences of self-starvation.

Efforts are already underway to combat what is being called the "epidemic of anorexia" (Brockopp, 1984). Of course, it is not easy to challenge the deeply ingrained cultural fear of fat that is reflected in anorexic teenagers. Equally importantly, experts have yet to reach agreement on the ways to manage children and adolescents whose bodies weigh more than the amount some health care professionals postulate is best (Gordon & Tobias, 1988). In addition, different socioeconomic and ethnic groups have different genetic make-ups and cultural values that impinge upon body shape. Preventive programs, like dietary instructions, must be adapted to the needs of particular communities and schools, as well as families. Sociologists can contribute a needed perspective in the development and evaluation of such programs because of their use of concepts that link self and society.

Cooley and Mead's work reminds us that social behavior is shaped by fantasy, feelings, and symbolic meanings, as well as by facts, rewards, and punishments. Most adolescents and young adults, for instance, do not dream of positive recognition for being heroin addicts. They are aware that the majority of people in their lives do not praise hard-core drug addiction and that society as a whole condemns such behavior. The majority of teenagers are sensible enough to avoid heroin after they learn about its dangers. It thus seems reasonable to assume that many 13-year-olds would also avoid extreme dieting if they understood its dangers. Some adolescents may be encouraged to eat differently if valued others change their stances toward dieting, body size, and weight loss during puberty. However, society does not generally condemn underweight, so reshaping the responses of significant others to body size is not simple. Applying sociology in this social context is not easy, but it's worth a try.

Some teenagers, of course, defiantly starve no matter how much information they receive. Given the life-threatening reality of anorexia, there is often a need for medical intervention to save their lives. However, we still do not know the best way to insure that the fortunate ones who survive will choose to eat to thrive. A variety of treatment strategies is being tried. Sociologists can contribute a perspective on the development and evaluation of such strategies, as a discussion of role theory and the study of deviance illustrates.

Social Role and Social Deviance

The concept of social role directs our attention to the requirements that apply to the behavior of a specific category of people in particular situational contexts. (Vander Zanden, 1984). Briefly put, a role is the behavior expected in a particular position. In this society, it is easier to define the concept of role than to know what the requirements are for our behaviors.

For example, take the roles of men and women. Each of us performs many tasks, some of which have been required by the fact of our genders, especially in the past. Anorexics do so, too. They also encounter the debates over today's changing social requirements of their gender role. As Tobias (1988) has noted, investigators are examining the connections between feminism, changing sex roles, and the prevalence of anorexia and bulimia in contemporary society. Unlike bulimics, anorexics for the most part, are not yet adults, but are adolescents. Thus, anorexia must often be viewed as deviant adolescent, and not adult, behavior.

How then do anorexics perform the role of adolescents, male or female? I have found few discussions of the ways in which anorexics are like other teenagers; more attention is given to the ways in which they differ. Yet, from a sociological point of view, one must "situate" deviant behavior by searching for an understanding of the normal social conventions governing the role behavior of particular types of persons, families, and groups. (Glassner and Freedman, 1979).

How then do anorexics deviate? Anorexics are often described as difficult people. Not only are they impossible to predict, swinging from mood to mood, but they are prone to angry outbursts and devastating attacks on those who care for them. They are given to rages, they lie, they manipulate, and they insist on doing things their own way. Capable of deep despair, they might commit suicide. They defy authority and simply do not abide by the sensible teachings of people who know what's best for them.

Sometimes, such behavior is explicitly described as pathological. Levenkron, for instance, described anorexic girls as "obsessive-compulsives'' who ''experience parents as depleted, exhausted, dependent (upon her), and insubstantial'' and who are ''afraid of their own anger and ashamed of feeling contempt for their parents, whom they view as insubstantial'' (1982). He assumed that much of their eating behavior reflects such feelings, as do their open or muted conflicts with their parents.

However, do other adolescents lack such feelings? As Douglas has pointed out, it is the very role of the adolescent to partially reject or rebel against parents' attempts to determine his or her patterns of actions and self-image. ''Instead of meekly seeing himself in the mirror of his parents' ideas and values for himself, the adolescent shatters (or at least cracks) the mirror and belligerently insists on seeing himself as a new person, as a self of his own choosing'' (Douglas, 1984, p. 71). One can focus on anorexics by concentrating upon eating behavior and family interaction, but, sociological theory and research also enjoins one to look more carefully at anorexics as teenagers who deviate not in their defiance, but only in their starvation.

As other papers in these proceedings have pointed out, many non-anorexic teenagers also have a fear of fatness, and some, such as anorexic teen-agers, follow diets which their families reject (Parr & Sutter, 1988). Though we professionals are aware of the destructive intensity that accompanies meals in families with anorexic children, at the same time, other adolescents are driving their parents to exhaustion by their use of drugs and alcohol. Still others refuse to do homework, or they may insist upon wearing strange clothing and even coloring their hair bright pink right before their grandmother's visit from out of town. Still others won't obey curfews.

Most manage to get through adolescence by performing well enough to go on to the stage of early adult development, though. Indeed, Kleeber has suggested that the task of parenting adolescents is complicated by the need to find ways of dealing with their rebellion in such a way that they can constructively express their deviance from family norms without harming themselves (1977). Anorexics, however, mar their future by their present handling of their biological selves, and it is this deviance that shapes their adult lives.

From a sociological perspective, therefore, anorexics are not being deviant when they disagree with their parents, physicians, or therapists. Nor are they being deviant when they struggle for autonomy and manipulate others in acting upon their own desires. As all who have parented teenagers know, angry scenes are not unique to the families of anorexics. Hell, I have been told, has no fury like a teenager who has been informed that he cannot have the car to drive 100 miles through a blizzard to a rock concert.

Most importantly, anorexics are not being deviant when they find it difficult to come to terms with their feelings and families. Indeed, when frightened of their anger, they are quite conventional, as Williams reminds us:

> Adolescents are frightened by their rage and destructive potential, particularly in reaction to their parents. The rage often relates to inner struggles over autonomy and is projected onto the parents. . . . At other times, the teenager's rage represents a defense against positive erotic feelings toward parents and siblings. . . . Fighting it out can help the adolescent test the limitations of his murderous rage in terms of potential action, as well as the extent and limitation of his parents' and siblings' murderous rage in terms of potential danger. Some adolescent peer groups maintain an ideology of love. The proclamation "We love everyone, including the parents who hassle us" may serve as a defense against the eruption of repressed or supressed feelings of rage toward family members. (1983, pp. 286-287)

Unlike other teenagers, however, anorexics cannot easily avail themselves of peer-group solace. In their desperate struggles to be thin, they commit the unpardonable adolescent sin: they starve to a point at which they not only look different from adults, but they behave differently from others their own age. Compelled by forces they cannot control, they can no longer engage in mundane adolescent encounters.

As Bruch (1983) has pointed out, the social isolation of the dieting anorexic intensifies the loneliness and despair teenagers experience when they feel rejected and set apart from their peers. The routine established by their dieting and exercise may preoccupy them and provide an explanation that controls the pain of their separatedness. However, from a sociological point of view, constricted peer group membership in adolescence is also deviant behavior. This behavior must be of concern, for the lives of adolescents are difficult indeed without the refuge, even with its stresses, provided by the peer culture. Anorexics, like other adolescents, do not have an easy time, due to the situation in which their role is performed.

The Situational Context of Adolescence and Deviant Behavior

The concept of the situation, as sociologists employ it, requires professionals to look at the total configuration of social factors that influence a person's behavior or experience (Vander Zanden, 1984). To understand the behavior of adolescents, attention to the family is necessary, but not sufficient, for other organizations and social factors also make up the world in which adolescent development takes place.

In this society, we do not have a clear definition of adolescence that can be used to consistently guide behavior. For example, at 16 persons can drive; at 18, marry or die in war; but they cannot drink in some states until they are 21. It was not very long ago that adolescents could die in battle, but not vote, at 18. The structure of adolescence reflects not only the family, but other adult organizations in the community, nation, and the world.

One of the most powerful organizations affecting adolescent behavior is the school. As Henry (1965) and Sarason (1982) have recorded, adolescents need solace from peers, and not only because of their inner rage against parents; friends help to channel the impotent fury that is generated by the cruelty our society inflicts upon teenagers as it sorts them into occupations, colleges, and marriages.

As Jules Henry put it in *Culture Against Man* (1965), human beings wring from this culture whatever satisfaction they can. Anorexic teenagers are not deviant, because they, at times, are unhappy, despairing, and overwhelmed with the task of finding their way to an adult future. All adolescents cope with their emerging biopsychosexual selves in an often hostile environment.

The particular stresses teenagers and young adults encounter vary with social class and personal aspirations. However, all are faced with the pressure to make something of themselves. Each school day, many teenagers experience frustration, humiliation, and rejection from teachers whose power over their lives is nearly unlimited, dispensing grades and judgments. As Herbert Birch (1973) put it, the repressive and controlling atmosphere of far too many schools resembles that of a penal institution, and neither prisons nor schools create carefree persons.

Only on television does high school consist only of happy days. Surveys of adolescents report that they more frequently note difficulties with school than with families or peers. Even when adolescents are fortunate enough to find caring and compassionate teachers who enrich their ability to discover and enhance themselves, their situations still remain difficult, because of the tasks of adolescence itself.

> The terminal stage of adolescence, reached at different chronological ages by children in different socioeconomic classes or families, requires all to renounce a host of expectations and wishes. Up to this stage, many lives seemed possible. Approaching adulthood requires the pursuit of limited goals and the commitment to selective values. The magnitude of the task is usually understated. (Blos, 1983)

The task is great. What, then, is the normal role of the adolescent? How does this bear upon the skills needed to treat anorexia?

Considerations for Treatment Providers

Role theory alerts professionals to the need to have the knowledge and training to help sort out what is different about treating anorexic adolescent patients from other teenagers. What do treatment providers expect teenagers to be and do, both within treatment and without? Who defines their social roles?

Customary child development and behavior has often been delineated by pediatricians, child psychiatrists, and psychologists. There is also a rich, but not as well-known, sociological literature on children, schools, and juvenile deviant behavior, primarily delinquency. However, adolescence is only currently coming into attention as a specialized area of medicine (Kallen, 1984; Barnes, 1980).

In the past some mental health professionals would not treat adolescents, because the normal developmental tasks and the stressful social situations of the period cause so much turbulence that many believed it was impossible to separate normal adolescents from abnormal ones. Only teenagers whose behavior was an overt threat to themselves or others were treated (Lauffer, 1983).

Many health care professionals, as illustrated by this audience, have not had a course in adolescent development. Nor have they been asked to read the studies of American schools and teenagers. Some of us learn more about normal adolescence while working with anorexic teenagers than we knew before.

Yet, shouldn't it be the other way around? To work with anorexics requires knowledge of adolescence. Otherwise, just like parents, dieticians and other health care professionals have trouble dealing with anorexics' intense reactions to them. The treatment of anorexic teenagers is a complicated therapeutic endeavor not only because they can die, but because of the very complexity of the social roles of adolescents.

Not everyone is suited to work with teenagers. It takes a lot of patience and tolerance, and an acceptance of one's own orientation to the world, to work successfully with this age group. If some health care professionals do not like doing so, they are not alone. Others find themselves in situations in which they are urged to fall back upon strategies that concentrate on weight gain and eating behavior, disregarding the other components of their patients' lives. Surely it is necessary to do all one can to ensure that a starving patient does not die, but adolescents, like other people, do not live by bread alone; anorexics need to do more than regain weight in hospital or outpatient clinics to survive.

There is a great need for workshops, continuing education courses, conferences, and support groups for dieticians and other health care professionals who are being asked to work with these troubled teenagers

/revious training in the newly emerging specialites that focus
)lescents. In these days of volunteerism, the treatment of anorexia
is not one of the problems for which professional knowledge and
se can be discounted, for it takes a great deal of knowledge—
:d from many disciplines—to re-engage anorexics in the ordinary
life of the world.

From one perspective, anorexia is not only a disease that needs treatment, but a lifestyle. Teenagers suffering in this condition have found a solution to the social tasks of adolescence, which, if we are not careful, can be accentuated by treatment itself. These young people have became anorexics, and as having diagnostic nomenclature implies, anorexics have become a category of people whose behavior is socially shaped and defined. In order to illustrate the utility of a clinical application of sociogical frames of reference, I turn now to the last concept I will discuss: social identity.

Social Identity

Like other stages in the life cycle, adolescence and young adulthood are shaped by the culture and societies in which human beings mature. After all, it is not enough for teenagers to know who they are and what they want. Such wants and desires are channeled into avenues of expression human communities permit. In some, lives are determined by tradition. Born into communities, one's meaning to oneself is clearly defined and shared by others. In our society, this is not the case. One's sense of oneself is not always recognized by others. One's social identity may be at variance with one's hopes and aspirations. As Fontana has noted, existential sociology directs attention toward the struggle for identity. "Put simply, identity is the perception of the self by others, the ways it is defined, controlled, supported, and challenged by the social world" (Fontana, 1984, p. 11). Like all of us, the human beings who become known as anorexics must find ways of giving meaning to themselves in the world of everyday life.

Erikson (1982) has noted that the very basic process of forming one's identity must emerge from the selective affirmation and reputation of an individual's childhood identifications, and the way in which the social process of the time identifies young individuals—at best, recognizing them as persons who had to have become the way they are and who, being the way they are, can be trusted. The community feels recognized by the individual who cares to ask for such recognition. By the same token, however, the community can feel deeply and vengefully rejected by the individual who does not care to be accepted, in which case it thoughtlessly dooms many whose ill-fated search for community it cannot fathom and absorb.

The young people whom we identify as anorexics are not immune from the complexity of the processes of identity formation, even if some choices are abruptly foreclosed to them by the consequences of anorexia itself. Society, as transmitted largely by their families, clearly shapes the process by which this identity emerges (MacLeod, 1981), yet sociologically, we cannot overlook the importance of the social processes that identify them. The young anorexic calls out for social recognition by the very act of self-starvation, and we do recognize them. We do respond. We label them "anorexics" and treat them. The entry into the treatment process, forced upon both us and them by the need to save their lives, may disrupt their need to find an alternative and better identity, if we do not look at the interactive processes set off by treatment itself.

MacLeod (1981) has suggested that these young girls themselves recognize that anorexia is a solution to the "problem" of being in the world. Faced with the complexities of becoming an adult woman in an often sexist society, MacLeod herself developed anorexia. Although her dieting was not always within her control, her search for autonomy and selfhood became linked to her identity as an anorexic. When this identity was challenged by others who could not reflect back her self with the approval she envisioned, she became massively depressed. As she put it, "to save a life is easier than to make that saved life acceptable to the person who has to live it." Anorexia, therefore, is not only a medical problem. It is also, as MacLeod has noted, a psychological, social, and even a philosophical, one. As she has summed it up, "An anorexic is not simply a girl or young woman who doesn't eat and can be considered cured when she resumes eating. She is someone who doesn't know how to live, except by non-eating" (1981, p. 172). If this is so, the behavior of anorexics can be comprehended as a deviant means to find a social identity—an identity from a sociological point of view, defined, maintained, and transformed through social interaction. This concept of identity has profound implications for treatment, because it provides another way to evaluate, and choose among, the options before us.

Implications for Treatment and Research

As Wirth has argued, the function of the sociologist on the clinical team is not to displace anyone from other disciplines, but to lend an additional point of view and method that can enrich the treatment of particular cases. Sociologists can also contribute to an evaluation of the social, as well as the psychological and biological, consequences of different research and treatment protocols.

Hospitalization

One debate found in the literature concerns hospitalization. Sometimes the physical conditions of patients offer no alternative but inpatient treatment. However, anorexics, historically have been hospitalized to isolate them from their families (Sour, 1980). Currently, some enter via protocols or research studies that begin by stabilizing weight and modifying eating in hospital settings.

Given the low weights of such patients at the time they appear for treatment, the decision of where to locate such treatment can have life-and-death consequences. The responsibility upon the therapist who manages anorexics in outpatient settings is awesome indeed. Each case must be evaluated (Anyan & Schowalter, 1983). Part of the evaluation should include assessment of the impact of hospitalization upon the adolescent patient's social world and the ability of each to use hospitalization constructively in the ongoing search for a social identity.

Sour (1980) has pointed out that physical separation from the family in itself may not be an adequate enough reason to hospitalize a teenager. The psychological and social bonds of a family, after all, are not be rent asunder during hospitalization. If family therapy is initiated, it needs to be continued on an outpatient basis. Respite care may be indicated, but outpatient management has fewer long-term negative consequences upon the patient's social world.

Why is this so? Anorexics are often good students; any long illness that removes an adolescent from the normal school routine creates additional stresses when the student returns, even if classwork is carried on at the hospital. Most importantly, from the point of view of the adolescent peer culture, any hospitalization, especially a lengthy one, is disruptive. For some anorexics, friends are few and precious. Teenagers like to drop in and visit; the anorexic teenager is further separated from ordinary peer group interaction in hospital units in which visits from friends and family are rewards to be earned by increased weight. Anorexics may gain pounds under such circumstances, but do they retain friends? What is the consequence of this kind of hospital treatment upon the peer group to which they return? The ability to talk to friends without interference means a great deal to teenagers. In evaluating the costs and benefits of hospitalization, one must consider how teenagers and their networks interpret the visibility of their treatment and its impact not only upon their roles as children or patients, but as adolescents.

Hospitalization clearly has different social meanings and impact on medical, adolescent, or psychiatric units. Entry into psychiatric treatment settings, no matter how humane and benign, adds an additional problem to the future life of the anorexic. Psychiatric hospitalization leads to a new stigma, not from anorexia, but from being a former mental patient. This stigma, no matter how much we deplore its existence and strive to overcome it, can be as powerful in shaping the future course of life as the experience of anorexia itself (Bruch, 1903). More research is needed upon the sociological consequences of the treatment settings and their impact upon the teenager's self-development and subsequent social identity.

Medication

A second debate concerns the efficiency of drug treatment. Much of current research does not focus upon anorexics in their social context, but turns instead to studies of drugs and modifications of eating behavior. The search for pharmacological treatments of any disease is always engaging and promising. Yet, drug research for helping adolescents is extremely complicated, as Stephenson (1988) has noted, because of the complex biological changes that take place during these years. In addition, as he has stressed, the complex developmental processes of normal adolescence are even more complicated by the ramifications of starvation. Until such ramifications are under control, the impact of new mood-altering drugs may be even harder to evaluate.

The decision to use drugs, particularly new ones, also calls for multidisciplinary evaluations. From a sociological point of view, the complex social roles of adolescents can be complicated by medication. For example, some people experience side effects that are very intrusive. Drugs that slow down thinking processes hardly help teenagers perform well on the tests needed to gain entry into college or jobs. Drug-produced stiffness or tardive dyskinesia distinquish adolescents from their peers, no matter what their weight. Drugs that have impact upon sexual feelings and performance cannot help but be additional disruptions in the lives of anorexics, whose very illness some believe is caused by their unconscious troubled responses to their developing sexuality.

Medications may have other unintended sociological consequences as well. Some anorexics may like taking drugs. Teenagers often do. Among competing peer cultures are those based on using drugs as a way out of pain, struggles, and loneliness. Some anorexics have already become accustomed to use drugs to control weight, as McCabe's poem (1983) quoted earlier illustrates. How do they relate to the drug scene, both before and after treatment? When discharged, do many of these teenagers move from legal to illegal drugs or the other way around? Do they share mood-altering drugs with friends? Little research has been done on the impact of legal drug use in the life of these teenagers who, like others, live in a culture that too easily turns to the "magic" of pills as a solution to social troubles. Both biologically and sociologically, anorexic teenagers may not be the most ideal population upon which to initiate drug research, unless all other modalities are failing.

Participation in Research

What about participation in research itself? Concern has been expressed that anorexics are too compliant and enjoy being research subjects far too much. Observers have noted that they cooperate willingly in experiments that require them to drink all kinds of substances in order to be compared with normal or obese subjects. They agree to try new medications whose long-term side effects are unknown. Some volunteer for inpatient units experimenting with drugs and behavior modification approaches. Some return over and over, participating in new studies as they age.

Of course, rehospitalization in a research unit precipitated by the return of self-starvation to dangerously low weights may signal the failure of the initial treatment or may be due to the course of the disease itself. However, the concept of social identity alerts us to another possibility. To be a patient in a prestigious medical school research unit is a social identity. Hall has argued that being a chronic anorexic patient can become a way of life. For some, becoming a chronic anorexic research patient may be a way to resolve the search for a social identity. We must guard against such iatrogenic outcomes.

However, participation in research studies that pose no risk to biological development could have functional consequences, if such participation broadens an anorexic teenager's choice of adult roles. For example, it is true that many anorexics exhibit what psychiatrists describe as obsessive-compulsive traits—but so do many researchers. The very traits and intelligence that permit some anorexics to perform complex calculations of calories and study the chemical composition of food can be rechanneled. The ability to stick to a routine or schedule is also advantageous in laboratory research. Depending upon their social class or experiences, some anorexic teenagers know very little about the world of science or careers in fields that are food-related. Hospitals and research units, after all, are places where other young people learn occupations; could not anorexics be helped to being thinking about their own vocations there as well?

Current programs often assess the social interactions of anorexic patients on the hospital wards or within their families. Since anorexic teenagers are considering various adult roles, during the course of treatment, they could also be helped to identify vocational possibilities manifested in the treatment setting. Children and teenagers, even sick ones, are inquiring people who learn a great deal from any situation in which they are placed. Sociologists can be of use, therefore, in developing evaluation studies that look at the negative and positive impact of the research process upon anorexics' subsequent selections of adult roles.

Behavior Modification

The sociological frames of reference presented in this paper also have a bearing upon current debates over the utility of behaviorist techniques. For instance, sociological conceptualizations of the self in society turn attention to anorexics not only as deviants, but as conformists. Anorexics are not a monolithic group, even though they share a common eating disorder. Their sociological heterogeneity has a bearing upon the use of particular behavior modification techniques.

In may ways, behavior modification programs that focus attention upon weight control fit into the dominant cultural value system. For example, the rewards used in some programs reflect current fashions, because new clothing is an incentive for weight gain. However, not everyone accepts the same values. As Bruch (1983) and others have cautioned, the search for autonomy must be respected, no matter what treatment is advocated. This includes a respect for the right to chose cultural values as well.

The dangers of behavior modification are as relevant as its advantages, in the treatment of teenagers whose very starvation may represent a defiant desire to do things in their own way. In an era when women's roles are shifting, the choice to conform to current ideological values is, of course, as valid as the choice to deviate. Occupational anorexia is found in professions such as modeling or ballet, in which the ideal weight specified for the job may be so low that menarche ceases. Some women choose to be thin for a livelihood. Perhaps we can convince them to become healthier, but some girls reject weight goals that jeopardize their professional aspirations.

Not all anorexics are rebels. Some may want very traditional women's roles. Some male anorexics aspire to conventional male roles. In many ways, behavioral modification programs are best suited to anorexics who need help to conform. We can ask whether some teenagers, via entry into behavior modification protocols, are finding more sociologically acceptable ways of being obsessed with food, body, and appearance in a culture that continues to reward such obsessions? Former anorexics are found, for instance, in such occupations as dietetics that permit them to utilize their own interests in diet to help others deal with weight and food. Others find their way into the many commercial enterprises that have sprung up to help normal people lose weight and maintain health.

Behavior modification programs may work best when the values of the program designer are shared by the participant. However, anorexics, especially young women struggling with feminist aspirations, may not feel rewarded by new clothing or family visits. The values implicit in such rewards may well meet the needs of some, but not all. Sociologists could be of use in identifying some of the underlying cultural values and assumptions that affect the design of treatment programs, and aid in more appropriately matching options to people.

Considerations in Choosing Treatment

As Bruch has noted, some young women are struggling with ways of successfully breaking free from past cultural restraints. The task of adolescent women, after all, is not only to find ways of being daughters or high school students, but to find ways for self-expression and -realization in an environment that provides more choices than women ever had in the past. Some anorexic teenagers are also feminists, and they come of age in a world in which the ideology of the women's movement has not become reality. How, then, does this affect the treatment we offer them?

If one is studying satiety, hunger, or appetite, the social meanings given to the role of women may be as irrelevant as the meanings experimental rats give the maze. If one is studying the treatment of developing adolescent women or men who are choosing to starve themselves to the point of death social meanings may be of paramount importance. Granted that biology is destiny, as Lacan and Freud observed (Mitchell, 1984), however, human destiny is also shaped by the ways in which women and men understand the implications of the physical being upon their lives. Ellen West, for example, played out the conflicts in our culture over inequality and women's work in her own starvation (Binswanger, 1958). Should not such interactions between self and society also guide our evaluation of treatment modalities?

Some debates currently pit one form of treatment against another (aided by third party payers who shape insurance benefits). Such debates also should involve more sociological assessments of outcome. For instance, family therapy does address one major component of an adolescent's life and can aid some adolescents in resolving the family issues that anorexia may manifest (Williams, 1983). However, other adolescents need to be helped to free themselves from family values and norms they cannot use in guiding their lives. Both professionally led and self-help groups may be beneficial for some anorexics, providing the needed peer support to feel less alone. For others, groups based on diagnostic categories intensify their feelings of apartness. Some thrive in psychoanalytic therapy, because they can use such a relationship to feel understood and accepted and to learn to live with themselves. Others find little benefit in such an approach and prefer behavior modification programs.

The task of matching modalities to people becomes even more complicated in a moment of historical time when women and men are reexamining the relationship between their bodies, their selves, and their societies. In a culture that provides alternative pathways for identity development, some adolescent anorexics may require individual, as well as group or family, therapy in order to address such choices while they struggle to no longer concentrate their quest for meaning upon body shape.

In theory, we need not think in either/or terms; for example, Freud was not a disbeliever in the efficacy of biological interventions. Nor need we ignore the efficacy of some behavioral approaches for weight restoration. Weight gain and maintenance is, of course, necessary for physical survival. However, as Bruch has pointed out, the adult suicides of treatment failures suggest that for some women and men, survival depends upon more than pounds. Sociological theory and research can contribute to a reassessment of current social policy decisions as they affect the choice and delivery of appropriate treatments.

The Importance of Social Policy

As a sociologist, I cannot conclude this paper without directing attention toward society, as well as self. In an era in which the family is being lauded and urged to take responsibility for the care and treatment of its ill, public policy has lagged behind in helping families do so. Take the families of anorexics: they are offered many kinds of treatments, such as family therapy, individual psychoanalysis, long hospitalizations, and outpatient behavioral interventions, as well as needed medical care. The economic resources directed toward the care of an anorexic child surely can be a way of expressing love or assuaging guilt. Providing treatment is, in fact, the obligation of such families. If they do not do so, they are further blamed for their child's condition.

Yet, do the poor and middle-class, in fact, have the resources to provide optimal treatment to their children? When the poor starve or are malnourished, they do not always turn to pediatricians or psychiatrists. Indeed, as the alarming incidence of poverty increases in female-headed families whose food and health benefits are being slashed, a child who eats little is a blessing. When such children become anorexic, as is happening in increasing numbers, poverty itself may shape their initial desire not to be fat. Far more attention has been paid to self-starvation in the rich and middle class than in the poor. This in part reflects prevalence, but self-starvation in America grows out of the total situation, and we need to look more carefully at the eating problems of the poor as well.

The rich can afford treatments, of course. The very poor also can avail themselves of a variety of treatment modalities, including family therapy and individual treatments available at public clinics for which they qualify. Middle-class people struggle. Yet, anorexia frequently is found among upper-middle-class children, whose parents cannot easily afford out-patient treatments. For example, having two children attend Ivy League colleges costs over $30,000 per year. Even with financial aid, the middle class does not have an easy time educating its young. It has an even harder time treating them.

Family therapy usually is not covered by medical insurance. The number of outpatient therapy sessions is often restricted to a very few, if any. HMOs require patients to work with the staff they hire; if an anorexic teenager cannot get along with the staff at that HMO, families may not have the needed resources to help them select their own physicians or therapists. Anorexia is also found in the children of upwardly mobile, lower-middle-class ethnic families. For such aspiring families, anorexia is a great burden.

The economics of health care has a great impact on family and individual functioning. Surely some of the anger, despair, depression, and desperate need to control the situations observed in the families of anorexics do not arise only out of the psychological needs of the parents. Sometimes the lives of the other children are constantly disrupted as hard choices must be made between psychoanalysis for their anorexic sibling, family treatment for all, or a child's college selection. Thus, the lives of anorexics are shaped by yet another social variable not of their own making.

Social policy impinges upon treatment providers, too. As these proceedings illustrate, the treatment of all eating disorders reflects the knowledge base gathered by research. The functioning of multidisciplinary teams reflects the education, training, and areas of expertise of the members. Both knowledge and practice, therefore, are shaped by available economic resources.

Currently, political leaders of both parties, as well as the general public, are searching for ways to cut large-scale government spending. There is more readiness to curtail government spending on domestic programs than on national defense (Brofenbrenner & Weiss, 1983). Proposals are being made to drastically reduce the public monies available for research, education, and training. The cost of care is tied to the cost of the health care team; efforts are being made to reduce the expenses of both health and social services. Budgetary allocations to all programs for children and their families are being scrutinized and questioned (Zigler, Kagan, Klugman, 1983). These ongoing social policy debates over the distribution of public resources impinge upon everyone's social situations and actions.

Conclusion

The sociological imagination directs attention to the connections between personal troubles and social issues (Mills, 1959). Sociologists, therefore, can be of great use in formulating studies and collecting data to help understand and shape social factors that bear upon the delivery of services to anorexics and their families.

The answer to the questions "What is the unique contribution of sociologists to the team?" is simply that sociologists contribute a knowledge of sociological theory and research. That knowledge, as this paper argues, is of great relevancy for the study and treatment of anorexia. As Wirth (1931) observed, clinical sociologists do not argue that they can understand phenomenon such as anorexia without cooperating with other professions; why then, do other professions so often assume they can understand the self in society without sociologists? By working together with others, he argued, we each do not merely promote our own field. We aid in building cooperative groups of scholars, each conscious of their own limitations and dependence upon others for finding solutions to a common problem. Surely we can find the means to join forces and look for a common understanding of the human beings who become anorexics. As we all search for solutions to the problem of anorexia nervosa, together we can develop ways to aid them in choosing to continue to live and enhance themselves in their social worlds.

Acknowledgments

The author would like to acknowledge gratefully the generous assistance of Dr. Ellis Perlswig, Yale Child Study Center, Yale University, and Dr. Alice Tobias, Department of Health Services, Herbert H. Lehman College, CUNY.

References

Agras, W.S., et al. (1984). The treatment of anorexia nervosa. Do different treatments have different outcomes? *Res public assoc. res nero mental disorders*, **62**, 193-207.

Allon, N. (1973). The stigma of overweight in everyday life. In G.A. Brayleal (Ed.), *Obesity in perspective* (pp. 83-102). Washington, DC: U.S. Government Printing Office.

Allon, N. (1980). Sociological aspects of overweight youth. In P. L. Collib (Ed.), *Childhood obesity* (pp. 134-156). Littletown: PSG Publishing.

Allon, N. (1981). The stigma of overweight in everyday life. In B. J. Wallman (Ed.), *Psychological aspects of obesity: A handbook* (pp. 130-174). New York: Van Nostrand Reinhold.

Anyan, W., & Schowalter, J. (1983). A comprehensive approach to anorexia nervosa. *Journal of the American Academy of Child Psychiatry,* **22**, 122-127.

Barnes, H. (1980). Growth: A new journal—challenge and responsibility. *Journal of Adolescent Health Care,* **1**, 64.

Berger, P. (1963). *Invitation to sociology.* New York: Doubleday Anchor.

Binswanger, L. The case of Ellen West. In R. Mayo (Ed.), *Existence* (pp. 237-364). New York: Simon and Schuster.

Binswanger, L. The case of Ellen West. In R. Mayo, R. Mag, E. Angel, & H. Ellenberger (Eds.), *Existence* (pp. 237-364). New York: Simon and Schuster.

Blos, P. (1983). Intensive psychotherapy in relation to the various phases of the adolescent. In A. Esman (Ed.), *The psychiatric treatment of adolescence* (pp. 281-302). New York: International Universities Press.

Brady, J., & Brodie, M. (Eds.). (1978). *Controversies in psychiatry.* Philadelphia: W.B. Saunders.

Brockopp, D.Y., et al. (1984). Eating disorders: A teenage epidemic. *Nursing Practice,* **9**, 32, 34-35.

Brofenbrenner, U., & Weiss, H. (1983). Beyond policies without people: An ecological perspective on child and family policy. In E. Zigler, S. Kagan, & E. Klugman (Eds.), *Children, families and government: Perspectives on American social policy.* Cambridge: Cambridge University Press.

Bruch, H. (1983). Psychotherapy in primary anorexia nervosa. In A. Esman (Ed.), *The psychiatric treatment of adolescence* (pp. 445-482). New York: International Universities Press.

Cahnman, W. (1968). The stigma of obesity. *The Sociological Quarterly,* **9**, 283-299.

Chernin. (1981). *The obsession.* New York: Harper and Row.

Ching, C.L. (1983). Anorexia nervosa: Why do some people starve themselves? *The Journal of School Health,* **53**, 22-25.

Clinical Sociology Review. (1982). Symposium V. 1, pp. 3-6.

Cooley, C. (1902). *Human nature and the social order.* New York: Scribner's.

Cooley, C. (1907). Social consciousness. *American Journal of Science,* **12**, 675-687.

Douglas, J. (1984). The emergence, security and growth of the sense of self. In J. Kortoba & A. Fontona (Eds.), *The existential self in society* (pp. 69-99). Chicago: The University of Chicago Press.

Erikson, E. (1982). *The life cycle completed: A review.* New York: Norton.

Fontona, A. (1984). Introduction: Existential sociology and the self. In J. Kortoba & A. Fontona (Eds.), *The existential self in society* (pp. 2-17). Chicago: The University of Chicago Press.

Freud, S. (1961). Some psychological consequences of the anatomical distinction between the sexes. In J. Strachey (Ed. and Trans.), *The standard edition of the complete psychological works of Sigmund Freud* (Vol. 19). London: Hogarth Press. (Original work published 1923).

Glassner, B., & Freedman, J. (1979). *Clinical sociology.* New York: Longman.

Gordon, J., & Tobias, A. (1984). Fat, female and the life course. *Marriage and Family Review, 7,* 67-92.

Hall, A. (1982). Deciding to stay an anorectic. *Postgraduate Medical Journal, 58,* 641-647.

Halmi, K., et al. (1983). Treatment of anorexia nervosa with behavior modification: Effectiveness of formula feeding and isolation. In A. Esman (Ed.), *The psychiatric treatment of adolescence* (pp. 281-302). New York: International Universities Press.

Henry, J. (1965). *Culture against man.* New York: Vintage Books.

Johnson, C. (1984). A bio-psycho-social theory of bulimia.

Johnson, C., et al. (1982). A descriptive study of dieting and bulimic behavior in a female high school population. *Understanding anorexia nervosa and bulimia.* Columbus: Ross Laboratories.

Kallen, D. (1984). Clinical sociology and adolescent medicine: The design of a program. *Clinical Sociology Review, 2,* 78-93.

Kleeber, H. (1978). Unpublished manuscript, Yale University, Department of Psychiatry, New Haven.

Kortoba, & Fontona, A. (Eds.). (1984). *The existential self in society.* Chicago: The University of Chicago Press.

Lauffer, M. (1983). Preventive intervention with adolescents. In A. Esman (Ed.), *The psychiatric treatment of adolescence* (pp. 281-302). New York: International Universities Press.

Levenkron, S. (1982). *Treating and overcoming anorexia nervosa.* New York: Warner Books.

Lester, M. (1984). Self: Sociological portraits. In J. Kortoba & A. Fontona (Eds.), *The existential self in society* (p. 193). Chicago: University of Chicago Press.

MacLeod, S. (1981). *The art of starvation: A story of anorexia and survival.* New York: Schocken Books.

Maloney, M.J. (1983). Anorexia and bulimia in dancers. *Clinical Sports Medicine, 2,* 549-555.

McCabe, S. (1983). A poem about my sister Caroline. In L. Schoenfielder & B. Wieser (Eds.), *Shadow on a tightrope.* Iowa City: Aunt Lute.

Mills, C. (1959). *The sociological imagination.* New York: Oxford Press.

Mitchell, J. (1984). Freud and Lacan: Psychoanalytic theories of sexual difference. *Women: The longest revolution* (pp. 248-277). New York: Pantheon Books.

O'Neill, C. (1982). *Starving for attention.* New York: Dell.

Parr, R.B. (1988). Weight loss: Its effect on normal growth patterns. In K. Clark, R. Parr, & W. Castelli (Eds.), *Evaluation and management of eating disorders: Anorexia, bulimia, and obesity.* Champaign, IL: Human Kinetics Publishers.

Petersdorf, R., & Feinstein, A. (1981). An informal appraisal of the current status of "medical sociology." *Journal of the American Medical Association,* **245,** 943-950.

Proceedings: International Conference on Anorexia Nervosa and Bulimia. (1983). *The International Journal of Eating Disorders,* **2.**

Rubel, J. (1984). The function of self-help groups in recovery from anorexia nervosa and bulimia. *The Psychiatric Clinics of North America.* Philadelphia: W.B. Saunders.

Sarason, S. (1982). *The culture of the school and the problem of change.* Boston: Allyn and Bacon Press.

Satter, E. (1988). Should the obese child diet? In K. Clark, R. Parr, & W. Castelli (Eds.), *Evaluation and management of eating disorders: Anorexia, bulimia, and obesity.* Champaign, IL: Human Kinetics.

Silber, J.J. (1984). Anorexia nervosa in black adolescents. *Journal of the National Medical Association,* **76,** 29-32.

Sour, J. (1980). *Starving to death in a sea of objects.* New York: Jason Aranson.

Stanton, A., & Schwartz, M. (1954). *The mental hospital.* New York: Basic Books.

Stephenson, J. (1988). Pathophysiology of eating disorders—What can it tell us? In K Clark, R. Parr, & W. Castelli (Eds.), *Evaluation and management of eating disorders: Anorexia, bulimia, and obesity.* Champaign, IL: Human Kinetics.

Tobias, A. (1988). Bulimia: An Overview. In K. Clark, R. Parr, & W. Castelli (Eds.), *Evaluation and management of eating disorders: Anorexia, bulimia, and obesity.* Champaign, IL: Human Kinetics.

Tobias, A., & Gordon, J. (1980). Social consequences of obesity. *Journal of the American Dietetic Association,* **76,** 338-342.

Vander Zandem, J. (1984). *Social psychology.* New York: Random House.

Vigersky, R. (Ed.). (1977). *Anorexia nervosa.* New York: Raven Press.

Williams, F. (1983). Family therapy: Its role in adolescent psychiatry. In A. Esman (Ed.), *The psychiatric treatment of adolescence* (pp. 281-302). New York: International Universities Press.

Wirth, L. (1931). Clinical sociology. *American Journal of Sociology,* **37,** 49-66.

Zigler, E., Kagan, S., & Klugman E. (Eds.). (1983). *Children, families and government: Perspectives on American social policy.* Cambridge: Cambridge University Press.

Chapter 12

Bulimia: An Overview

Alice L. Tobias

How does she do it?
Easy: She throws up.
Easy?
Well, she never learned to accept her body. She still stares at the
 Coppertone suntan ads.
That's disgusting. I thought she's a feminist. . . .
She's thin.
Yes, but she throws up her food.
But why?
I told you. She never learned to accept her body.
I thought you said she's a feminist.
I did, but it's her outlet. Whenever she gets nervous or anxious,
 angry, or depressed—she eats more than you or I could ever
 imagine, and throws it up! No consequences.
No consequences . . . (Goldner, 1983, pp. 183-184)

The pathetic woman Robin Goldner describes in her poem "Fat, Not
Fat" suffers from an eating disorder variously known as bulimia, bulimia
nervosa, and bulimarexia. This disorder would be a serious problem in
itself if it merely represented an obsession with dieting and weight, but
it also results in insults to the body and psyche.

The vicious cycle of binging and purging, and/or starving, is part of
a syndrome characterized by a lowered self-esteem, social isolation, and
a deviant lifestyle that is often devoid of fun and pleasure. The known
medical consequences include depression, dental erosion, esophageal
irritation, and fluid and electrolyte imbalance.

While some mental health professionals and nutritionists show disbelief,
eating disorders seem to have increased markedly in Western culture during the last 10-15 years. Indeed, there is speculation that the number of
individuals suffering disoriented eating patterns (for example, obsessive

dieters, bingers, and the binge-purgers) has now reached epidemic proportions.

To date, the study of eating disorders has focused on three recognizable syndromes: anorexia nervosa, bulimia nervosa, and certain forms of obesity. The food consumption patterns, food-related activities, and resulting weights associated with these eating disorders give rise to a sort of overlapping continuum. At one end of the spectrum are the people with anorexia nervosa. They have lost 20-25% of their original body weight and have no known physical illness that would account for the weight loss. There are two types of anorexics: restrictors and bulimics. Restrictors maintain relentless control over their eating, limiting their intake to 500 to 600 calories per day (on average). Bulimic anorexics also severely restrict their intake but alternate their bouts of starvation with an occasional binge and purge.

At the midpoint are those who suffer from bulimia but maintain nearly normal weight. They regularly binge, sometimes consuming as much as 20,000 calories in a day but later vomiting up much of this food to avoid weight gain. Although the typical bulimic is attached or addicted to dieting or vomiting, some may use laxatives and diuretics to limit weight gain.

At the other end of the spectrum is noncompensatory bulimia, an eating disorder that contributes to certain forms of obesity. Noncompensatory bulimics are those who eat compulsively but do not regularly vomit, nor do they regularly use laxatives or diuretics following the binge to avert weight gain. Noncompensatory bulimia is more often a feature of early onset obesity than of adult onset obesity.

All along the spectrum, sufferers abuse food and hold in common certain basic and underlying developmental problems. It is, however, important to distinguish between the various eating disorders, because these differences may determine correct management and referral strategies.

First, I will focus on basic information about bulimia nervosa and will differentiate between anorexia nervosa, binge eating, and true bulimia. Then I will pinpoint and describe bio-psycho-social factors believed to play an important role in the etiology of bulimia. Finally, I will indicate how clinicians and educators can play a role in its management.

Comparison of Eating Disorders

Bulimia is a complex problem requiring intervention. It is characterized by powerful and intractable urges to binge—to ingest large amounts of food in an uncontrollable fashion—and then, for all bulimics have a morbid fear of becoming fat, to avoid the fattening effects of ingestion by vomiting, purging, or dieting.

According to the *Diagnostic and Statistical Manual of Mental Disorders* (DSM-III) (American Psychiatric Association, 1980) anorexia nervosa and bulimia are separate syndromes. However, those who suffer from these disorders exhibit symptoms, signs, and patterns of behavior in common. A high percentage of people fulfilling the criteria for anorexia nervosa exhibit bulimic behavior, and those with bulimia often pass through a phase of anorexia and/or exhibit anorexic behaviors.

Studies and clinical observations show that both anorexics and bulimics are likely to have been brought up in middle-class, upwardly-mobile families and to have had histories of being "good girls." Both anorexics and bulimics tend to use compliance and achievement to elicit the love and approval of others (Boskind-White & White, 1983).

In view of the close relationship between these disorders, it is necessary to consider their similarities and differences, because such differentiation has important implications for referral, diagnosis, and treatment of individuals who suffer from these disorders.

In both anorexia nervosa and bulimia, there exist a concern with body weight and an obsession with food. The pursuit of thinness is the driving force in each, whereas other aspects of life become secondary and are often manipulated to fit the obsessional pattern.

In anorexia nervosa, the obsession is to severely restrict caloric intake not only in spite of hunger sensations but also despite the unsatisfied demands of a severely undernourished body. The average anorexic has an extremely low caloric intake. Episodes of binge-purge occur rarely. In contrast, the binge-purge cycle of the bulimic is associated both with ritualistic behavior and with response to stress. Between binge-purge episodes, the bulimic usually consumes a low-calorie, highly nutritious diet in an effort to compensate for the harm done to her body.

A significant difference between the two eating disorders relates to the typical body weight of sufferers. As the anorexic woman becomes more and more cachectic, the physical, mental, and emotional complications that are associated with starvation take command; starvation naturally tends to compound and perpetuate the illness. Therefore, aggressive nutritional support and weight gain are required before the seriously malnourished anorexic can respond to others' insight or behaviorally oriented psychotherapy.

The apathy and irritability contributing to the anorexic's unyielding stance in therapeutic situations is not prominent among bulimics. This appears to be due to the fact that their weight is usually only 15% above or below normal body weight. Fluctuating weight is common among bulimic women. A weight history with cyclic gains and losses ranging from 20-30 pounds in a 2-3 month period is not uncommon.

In both anorexics and bulimics, secrecy about weight control, including dieting, binging, exercising, and vomiting, is common. The bulimic, though, unlike the anorexic, recognizes that her eating pattern is not normal and is anxious to receive help. However, she is often afraid to reveal enough of the details of her eating pattern. It is therefore difficult for her to receive help in altering this behavior.

On average, anorexia nervosa involves young adolescent women (11-19 years of age) who are far less socially competent than bulimics and much more dependent on their families. Although bulimia may begin in adolescence, the majority of bulimics are young adult women who have left their parental homes and established a degree of autonomy. Therefore, family therapy, so often favored in the treatment of anorexia nervosa, is rarely appropriate here.

The criteria for diagnosing anorexia nervosa and bulimia as described in DMS-III (American Psychiatric Association, 1980) given in Tables 1 and 2) have some limitations. It is often difficult to assign a particular patient

Table 1 Clinical Diagnosis of Anorexia Nervosa

The criteria for the clinical diagnosis of anorexia nervosa include:
1. weight loss of at least 25% of original body weight;[a]
2. intense fear of becoming obese, which does not diminish as weight loss progresses;
3. distortion of body image; for example, thin or cachectic patients considering themselves normal or overweight;
4. loss of menstrual period;
5. excessive physical activity;
6. food binges followed by fasting, vomiting, or using laxatives.

[a]Some experts diagnose anorexia nervosa onset at only 15% weight loss minimum.

Table 2 Clinical Diagnosis of Bulimia

The criteria for the clinical diagnosis of bulimia include:
1. inconspicuous, recurrent episodes of binge eating;
2. consumption of high-calorie, easily ingested food in the course of binging;
3. termination of such eating episodes by abdominal pain, by sleep, through social interruption, or by self-induced vomiting;
4. repeated attempts to lose weight by severely restrictive diets, self-induced vomiting, or use of cathartics or diuretics;
5. frequent significant weight fluctuations due to alternating binges and fasts;
6. awareness that the eating pattern is abnormal and fear of not being able to stop voluntarily;
7. depressed mood and self-deprecating thoughts following eating binges.

to one unique category. For example, some bulimics would have been classified anorexics earlier in their lives, whereas others would be called obese during their fat phase. The criteria for bulimia, in addition, does not specify how frequently binges must occur to qualify for diagnosis. Finally, the guidelines do not provide a means for differentiating between bulimia nervosa and other, related eating problems, such as binging and vomiting.

Binge Eating Versus True Bulimia

At present there is no widely accepted, uniform definition for binge eating or, in fact, for bulimia itself. According to DMS-III, a binge is the rapid consumption of large amounts of food in a discrete time period, usually less than 2 hours. A binge is also accompanied by fear of not being able to stop eating voluntarily and is followed by a period of self-deprecating thoughts (American Psychiatric Association, 1980).

Current research suggests that a substantial number of teenage girls and young women are binge eaters, purgers, and/or engage in fasting at various times. Their chaotic eating habits often are associated with an ideal body image that is unrealistically thin, and dieting for weight loss that distorts their concepts of food, good nutrition, and appropriate body weight.

Do all these people now suffer from true bulimia? Probably not! Furthermore, psychiatrists and psychotherapists report that not all people who binge and purge have the associated personality disturbances either of anorexia nervosa or of true bulimia; they believe that some merely get into the self-denial and overeating as compensatory habits. Others—such as professional dancers, athletes, and fashion models—develop bulimia hyperemesis, an eating disorder in which vomiting is used as an "easy" method to keep slim (Levenkron, 1982); these people are particularly vulnerable because they often are forced as a condition of employment to keep their weights much lower than ideal body weights.

It is evident from the data cited previously that binge eating is not synonymous with true bulimia nervosa. Though far less serious, binge eating and vomiting, even in the absence of deep personality problems associated with anorexia nervosa or bulimia nervosa, can result in physical, emotional, and social trauma. Far more serious than any eating disorder that develops when dieting gets out of control is bulimia nervosa. It often requires long-term psychological intervention. The diverse nature and extent of the psychological and physical problems associated with true bulimia, as well as the various types of potential interventions that are required to overcome true bulimia, mandate expert screening and assessment throughout a range of known binge eaters. This is best done by a team of health care professionals that includes a mental health practitioner as well as a nutritionist. With the binge type eating disorders other than true bulimia, various modes of intervention can help sufferers effect behavioral changes. Among these are psychotherapy, behavioral therapy, and self-help groups.

Etiology and Pathogenesis of Bulimia

Unanswered questions remain concerning the etiology and pathogenesis of bulimia. A biopsychosocial model is currently being proposed to explain what we know, and to focus and organize new data, about bulimia. Initially this model was used by Lucas (1981) to explain anorexia nervosa, but it also helps explain and link a number of major factors that seem to play a role in the development of bulimia.

This model represents the interaction of three major etiological factors:

- Biological vulnerability or predisposition, resulting from undefined genetic, physiologic, endocrine, and biochemical mechanisms
- Psychological predisposition, by virtue of early negative experiences and family interactions that foster developmental problems within the sufferer
- Sociocultural influences, such as negative female stereotyping and role playing; related is an obsession with thinness that can propel one beyond dieting toward an eating disorder.

The relative importance of each of the above etiological factors—biological predisposition, psychological factors, and sociocultural influences—varies with each case.

Biological Vulnerability

A certain kind of susceptibility to binging may be the result of dieting to lose weight or to maintain weight below the biological norm or "preferred weight." Boskind-Lodahl and Sirlin (1977) noted that when 100 women displaying symptoms of bulimarexia were asked to describe the circumstances that led each to her first binge episode, each cited rigid dieting.

Hawkins and Clement (1980) have found that food consumed during binge episodes relates to dieting concern. The more severe the binge eating problem, the more stringent the prior attempt at restraint eating.

The biologically preferred weight is often referred to as the "set point" because it is felt that fat stores appear to be regulated by a sensitive feedback mechanism involving the hypothalmus. The set point theory may have significance in explaining the seeming paradoxical relationship of dieting to binge eating. According to Herman and Mack (1975), extreme dieting concern may present a chronic deprivational state in which persons try to maintain their weights below their set points. According to Herman's hypothesis, these individuals are in a state of deprivation because they habitually restrain their eating, but they also may run the risk of counterregulatory eating responses aimed at restoring the fat mass to its preferred level. If this hypothesis is correct, then when restraints are removed, persons who maintain weight at levels below their set points would be expected to demonstrate latent externality responses to food cues. For example, according to Herman, restraint eaters would be highly responsive to such environmental cues as the sight or smell of food.

Latent externality was assessed by Herman and Mack (1975) in normal-weight subjects who differed only in the degree to which they demonstrated evidence of dieting or weight suppression. As expected, Herman found that when the normal restraints to eating were overcome—by forcing the subjects to drink milk shakes—the subjects who scored highest on the restraint eating scale subsequently consumed more ice cream than those who scored lowest on the restraint scale.[1]

Moreover, the clinical observations of Mahoney and Mahoney (1976) have indicated that overly strict and unrealistic dieting produces hunger, and triggers obsessions about eating, as well as feelings of self-denial and deprivation that correlate with an assumed right to indulge in binge eating. Many psychologists and nutritionists therefore believe that dieting per se plays a role in initiating and perpetuating the vicious, repetitive pattern of chaotic eating characteristic of bulimia.

Psychological Factors

Various theories have been offered to explain the psychological antecedents to bulimia that promote and support it. Bruch (1973) was one of the first investigators to describe the principal psychological feature of anorexia nervosa and bulimia as a misuse of the eating function in an effort to solve or camouflage problems that appear otherwise insoluble to the subject. Bruch has emphasized that the disease ensues from ego deficits that result from arrested development, and not merely from dieting that has gotten gradually out of control.

Since the pursuit of thinness is currently a sociocultural epidemic, it is important to note the difference between the anorexic or bulimic and the average dieter who sets out to lose a few pounds. The key is the degree of compulsion with which the disoriented individual pursues her plans

---

[1]The restraint scale was determined by a brief questionnaire designed to determine the extent of dieting behavior and concern with restraint in food consumption. It presumed that those with a high score exercised greater restraint in maintaining their weight below their biological set point.

for achieving a more "perfect" weight. The bulimic is obsessed with dieting, food intake, and body weight. She is often unable to experience such bodily sensations as hunger and satiety as normal and valid. Therefore, she gives herself over to ritualistic food behaviors to limit her intake. It appears that the mistrust of her own internal visceral impulses leads to a sense of helplessness and ineffectiveness. The negation of the body allows her to develop a pattern of displacing all fears and concerns onto the area of weight control.

Bruch (1973) has noted that eating disorders may originate in families that are highly controlling and in which boundaries between family members are vague. Through the descriptions of disturbed mother-child relationships, she has shown how the inability to develop a distinct identity apart from the mother may predispose a child to such an eating disorder.

Minuchin's theory of psychosomatic disease also describes problem relationships with the mother, but also goes on to stress other negative family patterns that serve as antecedents to eating disorders. The four characteristics of the overall functioning family that encourage somatization include enmeshment, overprotectiveness, rigidity, and lack of conflict resolution (Minuchin, Rosman, & Baker, 1978). *Enmeshment* refers to the extreme proximity and intensity of family interactions. The individual gets lost in the family system because boundaries of personal autonomy are so weak that his or her ability to function independently is severely handicapped. The *overprotectiveness* of the family can be seen in the inappropriately high degree of concern of family members for each others' welfare. In such families, the parents' overprotectiveness discourages development of the child's autonomy and competence. It also interferes in activities outside the family unit. *Rigidity* within families commits members to maintain the status quo. Thus, they experience great difficulty during periods in which growth and change are necessary. *Lack of conflict resolution* becomes a concern when a family's threshold for resolving conflict appears very low. Religious or ethical codes are sometimes used to rationalize avoidance; as a result, conflicts go unresolved and family members repeatedly impinge upon one another.

In addition, Minuchin has noted that these families, wherein anorexics are frequently reared, focus on diets, food fads, and physical appearance in their verbal interactions (Minuchin et al., 1978). I propose that these same characteristics also describe the families in which bulimics are reared.

Bulimia can begin at any age, from teens well into middle age. White, middle-class adolescent girls, and women in their twenties with a strong orientation toward academic achievement and traditional values, are most vulnerable. Boskind-White and White (1983) have bulimarexics as "stronger carbon copies of their younger anorexic sisters." They see adolescence as the critical stage in which such food obsession takes hold of girls with low self-esteem. They furthermore said:

Many women teeter on the brink of anorexia or bulimia during adolescence. This is a time when girls become acutely aware of other girls who seem more successful and attractive than themselves. As a result, they feel inadequate or self-conscious by comparison. In searching for "magical cures" for their existential crises, both groups—preanorexics and prebulimarexics—focus on the diet as their ticket to success and happiness. What happens after this first diet is crucial and critical. Their ability to resolve the frequently unfulfilled expectations about weight loss is often dependent on support from family, as well as on the life experience the young women already possess. The more isolated and locked into family they are, the greater the chance they will "choose" anorexia. Anorexia represents a pathetic attempt to assert control over their lives and also over the lives of others. Women who veer toward bulimarexia are more tenacious. They do not have to "show" their pain to the extreme evidenced in anorexia. However, this passivity and desperation and their attempts to maintain control are a matter of degree. (p. 35)

Many women who survive adolescence without these food obsessions become vulnerable during their early years at college as new opportunities and new pressures threaten them. This explains the high incidence of bulimia currently seen in college students and young career women.

Sociocultural Factors

Bulimia and anorexia nervosa have been called "diseases of the 1980s" because they are increasingly common in our culture. Though the etiology of the disorder in young women who seem most vulnerable is not yet well defined, many experts believe that it is related to the condition of women in current society. In fact, there is virtual agreement in numerous articles in professional journals and popular magazines in women being far more susceptible to eating disorders than men because they are the principal victims of our cultural obsession with thinness.

Boskind-White is among the leading exponents of this sociocultural theory that hypothesizes that disoriented eating is a symptom of contemporary women's desperate striving to conform to the traditional role of women. She has described her bulimarexic patients as relentless in their pursuit of thinness but passive, accommodating, and helpless in their approaches to life (Boskind-White & White, 1983). Orbach (1978), on the other hand, has noted that her patients do not always accept, nor do they always conform to, the traditional role of women. She describes her patients' compulsive eating in symbolic terms and suggests that binge eating is often a manifestation of the patient's unconscious rejection of the stereotype that femininity is equal to being slim, weak, and incompetent.

Rost, Neuheus, and Florin (1982) have argued that these seemingly contradictory conclusions of Boskind-White and Orbach are not necessarily incompatible. Their data on sex role attitudes (SRA) and sex role behavior (SRB) indicates a marked discrepancy between bulimic women's general attitudes toward the role of women, and their actual behavior as women. In spite of rather liberated attitudes, bulimic women may in their behavior tend to adapt to the demands of their male partners and to follow a pattern of passivity, dependency, and unassertiveness. Furthermore, a comparison of the SRA and SRB of bulimic subjects and of matched controls indicates that bulimics' sex role behaviors are more conservative than those of nonbulimic women. The researchers have concluded that bulimics' inability to live by their general sex role attitudes contributes to their sense of loss of control and their feelings of helplessness (Rost et al., 1982). These feelings often serve as a precipitant to binging.

Treatment

Patients with bulimia need help and support in their struggles to overcome their problem. Specific strategies for intervention are beginning to be discussed in the literature. Most of the programs can be described either as psychodynamic psychotherapy, behavioral modification, or an eclectic, balanced therapy. Nutritional counseling and/or drug therapy have also been used as adjuncts to some of these programs. To date, no one style of treatment or specific protocol seems to be effective with every patient.

In this paper, I will describe some general guidelines for the eclectic, balanced approach combining individual therapy, group therapy, and nutritional counseling. This treatment approach involves the application of psychoanalytic, behavioral, and nutritional counseling techniques.

Individual sessions allow the patient to gain insights into conflicts that may have caused the symptoms (e.g., low self-esteem, sense of incompetence, mistrust of internal impulses and feelings, as well as chaotic eating). It is believed that once the underlying conflicts are understood and discussed, they can eventually be resolved. The symptoms will then disappear.

Group therapy allows the use of behavioral techniques to expose and analyze the physiological, emotional, and psychological cuing of binge eating while it develops and to reinforce desirable eating behavior.

Individual and group therapy sessions work together and should not be considered in isolation from one another. Both focus on the following themes:

- *Getting in touch with physiological hunger and the appetite for specific foods.* Because they use food to ward off unpleasant feelings and to relieve stress caused by unresolved conflicts, compulsive eaters often are unable to recognize and respond to physiological hunger.

Also, the pressure to conform to the thinness "ideal" produces tension and guilt, especially when the bulimic goes off her Spartan diet. Food seems to be an enemy or an evil and is feared. Thus, Orbach (1982) has stressed, the bulimic can break the diet-binge cycle only by beginning to see herself as a normal person who need not fear food. According to Orbach, diets, with their rules and regulations, reinforce a deviant self-image. They serve as a constant reminder that the dieter cannot be trusted around food. Assignments, exercises, and group discussions help the bulimic learn to recognize and respond to the appropriate physiological cues for food and hunger. She learns to identify her appetite for certain foods and her hunger.

- *Developing a more realistic view of femininity.* The compulsive pursuit of thinness is often an expression of the bulimic's stereotyped image of femininity, which includes a passive, dependent woman who functions as a sexual object. Boskind-White has explained that the bulimic's attempts to control her physical appearance reflect a disproportionate concern with pleasing others, particularly men (Boskind-White & White, 1983). A common fantasy is that by pleasing others, she will be able to get what she wants (i.e., a more desirable marital partner and a higher paying job), if only she gets thinner. Psychotherapeutic sessions can be used to dispel such fantasies and to show women how they turn themselves into sexual objects through a narcissistic preoccupation with their weight and appearance (Boskind-White & White, 1983). Other myths and misconceptions about the thinness ideal can also be addressed during group sessions by focusing on the realities of the human body.

A counselor may present the following facts to help the bulimic woman establish a more realistic assessment of her body. First, a relationship between weight, body fat, and the menstrual cycle exists. A minimum weight relative to height is necessary for the onset and maintenance of menstrual cycles. Frisch and McArthur (1974) have said that a 17% body fat ratio is necessary for the maintenance of the menstrual cycle in women age 16 years and over. Because fashion models, actresses, and others revered for their thinness are often dangerously close to the minimum level of body fat necessary to maintain the normal reproductive cycle, some fall below and develop amenorrhea. The female body was not meant to be so thin that bones protrude. The normal body range for total fat in females is 18-32% whereas it is only 7-22% for males.

Moreover, a bulimic must learn to assess the possibilities for self-realization as a woman by learning to identify and act on authentic needs and values. Emotional factors can play a pivotal role in triggering binges.

Such feelings as frustration, disappointment, anger, rebellion, and perceived rejection can trigger binge eating. A bulimic often stuffs herself in an effort to suppress these feelings and because she is eager to please others and avoid conflict at any cost. This is a masochistic pattern that can be broken only when the woman learns to identify, accept, and act on her own perceived needs.

A bulimic woman usually assumes a traditional role in her relationship with a male partner; she is highly adaptive to the needs and demands of others, particularly men. Studies indicate that such women demonstrate a high level of acceptance of external control (i.e., they depend too much upon others), act as though their male partners are superior to themselves, and lack the ability to assert their sexual wishes to their partners. Many bulimic women are in conflict because of their liberated attitudes towards their social and sexual roles as women. Their behavior and beliefs oppose one another. Binge eating is often a furtive and distorted means of rebelling against the sense of helplessness and frustration imposed by that conflict. Assertiveness training in group therapy may reduce this discrepancy while building the woman's sense of internal control, competence, and self-respect.

Another treatment technique, nutrition counseling, focuses on correcting misconceptions about food, nutrition, and body weight while reinforcing the psychological insights made during individual and group sessions. The counselor presents information on the basic principles of nutrition, so that the bulimic can adapt a more physiologically normal eating pattern when she is ready to give up the chaotic diet-binge-purge cycle.

Nutritional counseling may be on an individual basis, or it may be part of the group sessions. The nutrition counselors must understand the psychological issues connected with bulimia. Also, they should be professionally trained in nutrition. Ongoing collaboration between the psychotherapist, group leader, and nutritionist is essential for effective treatment.

Lacey (1983) has reported that patients who do well in his treatment program, using similar techniques to the model described above, tend to be ambitious and hard-working women whose prominent clinical non-diet symptoms were sadness and anger. In general, these women appear to be resourceful, but neurotic. On the other hand, a poor prognosis was associated with such negative factors as abuse of alcohol, presence of frequent binge episodes, and to a lesser extent, a previous history of anorexia nervosa. Lacey has stressed that when these negative factors are taken into account, the prognosis of bulimic patients is better than formerly supposed.

Outcome data from a number of other sources also indicates that bulimics can make significant gains as a result of treatment. Virtually all aspects of the disorder are potentially improved when certain principles are followed during the course of treatment. Andersen (1983) has given the following guidelines for an effective and comprehensive program:

1. Correct identification of the syndrome by history and mental examination
2. A balanced approach, which includes changing the eating pattern and understanding and correcting the predisposing and underlying psychodynamics
3. An empirical and practical approach to treatment that avoids speculative concepts relative to origin
4. An understanding of the natural history and underlying psychopathology of the disorder
5. A nonblaming and supportive approach, which includes flexibility as to the specific kind of psychotherapy that is chosen, according to the needs and abilities of the patient
6. Global treatment goals, which include psychologic, biologic and social improvement aims
7. Avoidance of procedures with high morbidity, such as high-dosage medications
8. An attitude of realistic optimism toward improving the bulimic's disorder for a successful outcome

Summary

Recent data indicates that we are beginning to identify the biopsychosocial factors involved in the development of bulimia. This complex eating disorder seems to occur in young females brought up in middle-class, upwardly mobile families who lack self-esteem and a sense of effectiveness. Their sense of helplessness seems to be associated with a marked discrepancy between their sex-role attitudes and sex-role behavior. The apparently increasing incidence of this syndrome seems to be related to the cultural obsession with an unrealistically thin body image.

Disclosure appears to be essential before any treatment approach has an opportunity for success. An effective treatment program must address all of the factors involved in the development of the disorder. As we learn more about these etiological factors, treatment will become increasingly effective. However, many questions about the etiology and management of bulimia remain unanswered. Until long-term, multidisciplinary research studies are designed, implemented, and evaluated, the efficacy of existing treatment protocols will remain unclear.

Acknowledgment

The author would like to gratefully acknowledge the feedback of Judith Bogard Gordon, Ph.D., Department of Sociology, University of New

Haven and Lecturer, Department of Psychiatry, Yale University, on this paper.

References

American Psychiatric Association. (1980). *Diagnostic and statistical manual of mental disorders* (3rd ed., pp. 67-71). Washington, DC: Author.

Andersen, A.E. (1983). Anorexia and bulimia. Diagnosis and comprehensive treatment. *Psychiatry and Behavioral Sciences*, **9**, 9-16.

Boskind-Lodahl, M., & Sirlin, J. (1977, March). The gorging purging syndrome. *Psychology Today*, pp. 50-51, 82-83.

Boskind-White, M., & White, W. (1983). *Bulimarexia. The binge purge cycle.* New York: W.W. Norton.

Bruch, H. (1973). *Eating disorders.* New York: Basic Books.

Frisch, R.E., & McArthur, J.W. (1974). Menstrual cycles. Fatness as a determinant of minimum weight for height necessary for their maintenance or onset. *Science*, **85**, 949-951.

Goldner, R. (1983). Fat, not fat. In L. Schoenfield & B. Wieser (Eds.), *Shadow on a tightrope* (pp. 183-184). Iowa City: Aunt Lute.

Hawkins, R., & Clement, P. (1980). Development and construct validation of a self-report measure of binge eating tendencies. *Addictive Behaviors*, **5**, 219-226.

Herman, C.P., & Mack, D. (1975). Restrained and unrestrained eating. *Journal of Personality*, **43**, 647-660.

Lacey, J.H. (1983). Bulimia nervosa, binge eating, and psychogenic vomiting. A controlled treatment study and long-term outcome. *British Medical Journal*, **286**, 1609-1613.

Levenkron, S. (1982). *Treating and overcoming anorexia nervosa.* New York: Warner Books.

Lucas, A. (1981). Toward the understanding of anorexia nervosa as a disease entity. *Mayo Clinic Proceedings*, **56**, 254-264.

Mahoney, M.J., & Mahoney, K. (1976). *Permanent weight control. A total solution to the dieter's dilemma.* New York: Norton.

Minuchin, S., Rosman, B., & Baker, L. (1978). *Psychosomatic families. Anorexia nervosa in context.* Cambridge: Harvard University Press.

Orbach, S. (1978). Social dimensions in compulsive eating in women. *Psychotherapy, Theory, Research, and Practice*, **15**, 180-189.

Orbach, S. (1982). *Fat is a feminist issue II. A program to conquer compulsive eating.* New York: Berkeley Books.

Rost, W., Neuheus, M., & Florin, I. (1982). Bulimia nervosa. Sex role attitude, sex role behavior, sex role related locus of control in bulimarexic women. *Journal of Psychosomatic Research*, **26**, 403-408.

Chapter 13

Bulimia

Craig Johnson
Stacey Steinberg
Christin Lewis

The recent increase in the incidence of bulimic behavior, predominantly in young adult women, has generated a substantial treatment demand and curiosity regarding the disorder. In an historical review of the symptoms of bulimia, Casper (1983) found that though clinical descriptions of bulimia date back to the late 1800s, it was not until the 1940s that more detailed accounts of bulimic behavior began to emerge in the literature. In these early reports, however, the symptomatic behavior was always referred to as a symptom of anorexia nervosa. Bulimia among individuals who did not have histories of weight disorders such as anorexia nervosa and obesity was first observed in 1976 by Boskind-Lodahl, who coined the term *bulimarexia* to describe this disorder. Shortly thereafter emerged such descriptive labels as bulimia nervosa (Russell, 1979), dietary chaos syndrome (Palmer, 1979), and abnormal weight control syndrome (Crisp, 1981). Bulimia emerged as a distinct diagnostic entity with publication of the third edition of the *Diagnostic and Statistical Manual* (DSM-III) (American Psychiatric Association, 1980). The suggestion in DSM-III was that episodic binge eating was not only an isolated symptom, but an essential component of a specific syndrome of disordered eating.

Bulimia, as defined by the DSM-III, is characterized by repeated episodes of the rapid ingestion of large amounts of food in a discrete amount of time, typically less than 2 hours. The individual is aware that these eating binges are abnormal, fears the inability to terminate eating voluntarily, and experiences depressed mood and self-depreciating thoughts following the episodes. According to the DSM-III criteria, inconspicuous eating; weight fluctuations of greater than 10 pounds; consumption of high caloric, easily digested food during the binge; repeated attempts to lose weight by means of severely restricted diets or purging behaviors;

and the termination of binges by pain, sleep, social interruption, or self-induced vomiting are also characteristic of bulimia. The DSM-III stipulation that the bulimic episodes not be due to anorexia nervosa or any physical disorder limits the syndrome to persons who are at, or above, normal weight.

The elevation of bulimia to a syndrome in the DSM-III has spawned both a rapidly growing body of literature and a fair amount of controversy and confusion. The controversy and confusion revolves around two major issues that reflect the newness of the area of conceptualization. The first area of controversy arises from the fact that the symptoms of bulimia occur along a continuum of weight disorders including anorexia nervosa (Garfinkel, Moldofsky, & Garner, 1980; Casper, Eckert, Halmi, Goldberg, & Davis, 1980; Hsu, 1979) and obesity (Stunkard, 1959; Wardle, Beinhart, 1981). According to DSM-III a history of anorexia nervosa precludes a primary diagnosis of bulimia.

Recent research, however, has suggested that the symptoms of bulimia occur frequently, and have significant prognostic implications, among anorexia nervosa patients. Furthermore, anorexia nervosa patients who manifest bulimic symptoms appear to be more similar to bulimic patients who do not have histories of weight disorders than they are to anorexia nervosa patients who do not manifest bulimic symptoms during the courses of their disorders. Garner, Garfinkel, and O'Shaughnessy (1983) have compared normal-weight bulimics, anorexics with bulimic symptoms, and anorexics without bulimic symptoms (restrictors) on demographic, clinical, and psychometric variables. Results have indicated that the normal-weight bulimics closely resembled anorexics with bulimic symptoms and that these two groups could be distinguished from anorexic restrictors on many dimensions, including age of onset, highest and lowest premorbid weight, duration of illness, histories of substance abuse, mood fluctuations, sexual activity, body-image distortion, and family characteristics. The implication of this early research is that presence or absence of weight disorders may have less diagnostic and prognostic value than presence or absence of bulimic symptoms.

The second area of confusion relates to the ability of the current DSM-III criteria to distinguish clinically pathological levels of bulimic behavior. Prevalence studies surveying binge eating behavior, body dissatisfaction, dieting behavior, etc., have indicated that these are very prevalent, highly endorsed behaviors among adolescent and young adult women (Halmi, Falk, & Schwartz, 1981; Pyle, Mitchell, Eckert, & Halvorson, 1983; Johnson, Lewis, Love, Lewis, & Stuckey, 1984; Johnson, Lewis, Love, Stuckey, & Lewis, 1983). It remains to be demonstrated which of the current DSM-III criteria are sufficient or necessary to identify individuals whose bulimic behavior is interfering in some significant way with their life adjustment.

Despite the confusion regarding the syndrome of bulimia, the inclusion of the symptom picture in the DSM-III has resulted in a newly developing area of research. The purpose of the current chapter is to review and synthesize the current body of literature related to bulimia among patients at normal weight and those with histories of anorexia nervosa. In addition to reviewing demographic features, clinical characteristics, personality variables, medical consequences, and treatment strategies, the chapter attempts to synthesize these findings into a biopsychosocial model that explains the etiology and perpetuation of the disorder.

Bulimia in Normal Weight Population

Although there has been substantial speculation that bulimia is a highly prevalent disorder, very few studies exist that have attempted to document its incidence. Strangler and Prinz (1980) reviewed the psychiatric diagnosis in a sample of 500 students seen at a university psychiatric clinic. Results indicated that among all the student patients, 3.8% met the newly established DSM-III criteria for bulimia, including 5.9% of the women seen. Several recent investigations have further attempted to estimate the incidence of this eating behavior among college students. Halmi et al. (1981) surveyed 539 college students during the summer session at a suburban liberal arts university. Three hundred thirty-five students (66% of the total population) completed a questionnaire regarding the behavioral symptoms of bulimia. Overall, 13% of the population endorsed statements that indicated they met the essential DSM-III criteria for a probable diagnosis of bulimia. Within the bulimic group, 87% were female, which was 19% of the female population that responded to the questionnaire. Unfortunately, in this study no data was available regarding the frequency of bulimic episodes. Although 9.9% of the sample reported the use of self-induced vomiting, only 1.7% reported they engaged in the behavior on a weekly or greater basis.

Pyle et al. (1983) also surveyed a college population. Thirteen hundred fifty-five college freshmen completed a self-report questionnaire regarding their eating behaviors. This represented 98.3% of the total freshman population (n = 1,379) at a midwestern university. Using somewhat modified DSM-III criteria for bulimia, the results indicated that 4.1% of the overall population met the DSM-III criteria for probable diagnosis of bulimia (7.8% of the female population and 1.4% of the male population). With the addition of a frequency variable of at-least-weekly episodes of binge eating, the percentage dropped to 2.1% of the population (4.5% of the females and 0.4% of the males). The use of self-induced vomiting was reported by 6.2% of the sample, but only 1.9% reported vomiting on a weekly or greater basis.

Johnson et al. (1983) found results strikingly similar to the Pyle et al. (1983) study among a high school population of 1,268 females (97% response rate). Using conservative criteria to identify bulimia among the female students, their findings indicated that 4.9% of the students reported clinically significant levels of bulimic behavior. Inclusion in the bulimic group required that the students endorse statements taken from the DSM-III criteria for diagnosing bulimia and that they be engaged in weekly or greater episodes of binge eating. Results also indicated that 1% of the sample were both binge eating and purging on a weekly or greater basis. Johnson and his colleagues noted, however, that 21% of the sample reported weekly or greater episodes of binge eating and that the criteria used to identify bulimia probably resulted in a significant number of false negatives, thus producing a conservatively low estimate of the prevalence.

Although further studies are needed to identify the prevalence of bulimia, the two studies with the most rigorous sampling validity suggest that the incidence of bulimia is approximately 5% among high school and college females. Further prevalence studies, it is hoped, will be able to overcome the limitations of self-report data, sampling biases, and the confusion regarding how to differentiate clinically significant levels of bulimia from episodic binge eating.

Demographic Profile

Studies that have reported demographic information about bulimic individuals have been fairly consistent in their findings. The typical bulimic reported is a white, single, college-educated female in her early to mid-twenties who comes from a family of more than one child and who has been struggling with the bulimic symptoms from 4-6 years (Johnson, Stuckey, Lewis, & Schwartz, 1982; Herzog, 1982; Pyle, Mitchell, & Eckert, 1981; Lacey, 1982, Fairburn & Cooper, 1982).

Pyle et al. (1981) and Herzog (1982) have reported demographic information from groups of bulimic women presenting at outpatient clinics. The sample of 34 patients described by Pyle et al. averaged 24 years of age and reported a mean duration of symptoms of 4 years before seeking treatment, with a mean age at onset at 18 years. Seventy-three percent of this sample had at least some college education, and the majority (64%) had never been married. Of this group, 41% were living independently, 32% lived with parents, and the remainder lived either in a conjugal setting or with other relatives. The bulimic patients studied by Herzog were similarly found to be predominantly single, middle- or upper-class college graduates. They averaged 25 years of age, with an average duration of over 6 years.

Demographic and symptom-related information from large samples of bulimic women in the community were gathered by Johnson et al. (1982) and Fairburn and Cooper (1982) by means of questionnaires sent and returned via the mail. Johnson et al. (1982) have reported on data obtained from respondents to a mail survey sent in response to requests from women seeking help and information on eating disorders. Of the 509 individuals completing the survey, 316 endorsed items suggesting that they met the DSM-III criteria for bulimia. Fairburn and Cooper (1982), in England, identified 499 women who fulfilled their diagnostic criteria for bulimia nervosa from 669 respondents to a notice placed in a popular women's magazine requesting people who were using self-induced vomiting as a means of weight control and who were willing to complete a confidential questionnaire. Due to the method of data collection and the inferred diagnosis from self-report, results need to be interpreted cautiously. However, despite this consideration, as well as despite the fact that 62% of Johnson et al.'s sample and 70% of the Fairburn and Cooper sample had never sought medical attention for their problem, these groups did not differ in terms of major demographic characteristics from the clinical samples of Pyle et al. (1981) and Herzog (1982) of persons who had sought treatment for their bulimia.

The Johnson et al. (1982) sample of 316 was predominantly comprised of Caucasian females, averaging 24 years of age and reporting an average duration of symptoms of 5 years 6 months, with an average age of onset at 18. Eight-four percent of the women reported a minimum of some college education, consistent with the fact that nearly one-half were students at the time of completing the survey. Most of the women had never been married (70%) and lived either with parents, boyfriends, or alone. Less than 5% lived with other women. Examination of the socioeconomic status of the respondent's family of origin, as determined by the father's occupation and education (Hollingshead, 1957), indicated clustering in categories I (graduate level education and holding high administrative or professional positions), III (administrative personnel, small independent business owners, and semi-professionals), and IV (clerical and sales workers, technicians, owners of smaller businesses.) In terms of socioeconomic status, Lacey (1982) reported that of a series of 20 successive bulimic patients who did not have a history of anorexia nervosa, 14 of their fathers came from social classes IV and V (semiskilled-unskilled), whereas 13 of the patients themselves would be classified in social classes I and II (professional and managerial). These findings are significant in that they reflect a greater heterogeneity of socioeconomic status than is typically cited for the person with anorexia nervosa.

Similarly, the group identified by Fairburn and Cooper (1982) averaged 23.8 years of age, with a mean age of onset of binge-eating of 18.4 years. The average duration of binge eating was reported as 5.2 years. Vomiting was reported to begin approximately 1 year after the onset of binge eating, with the mean age of onset being 19.3 years, with a duration of 4.5 years. Of the women identified as bulimic, 20.7% were married, 5.1% reported being housewives, 24.8% were students, and 12.9% were in medical or paramedical professions. It also was reported that 3.4% of the women were in food-related professions.

Clinical Profile

Symptomatic Food-Related Behavior. The bulimic eating pattern is characterized by "binges," the rapid consumption of a large quantity of food that the persons experience as being outside of their control. The binge state is often experienced as an altered state of consciousness or dissociative experience, with the events of the binge being somewhat blurred. The subsequent reliance on evacuation techniques to undo the eating and prevent weight gain is one of the most pernicious aspects of bulimia. Based on data collected by Johnson et al. (1982) and Fairburn and Cooper (1982), it has been suggested that these behaviors appear approximately 1 year after the individual has begun the binging behavior.

Although the DSM-III states that the bulimic episodes not be due to anorexia nervosa or any other known physical disorder and includes reference to frequent weight fluctuations, there are no specific criteria with regard to the weight of bulimic individuals. An examination of current and past weights of bulimic subjects reveals somewhat inconsistent information, although trends do emerge. Based on actuarial tables of the Metropolitan Life Insurance Company (1979), the majority of bulimic women are of normal weight for their height at the time weight data was collected. Pyle et al. (1981) reported that only 2 of 34 patients weighed more than 5 kilograms above the medial weight for their height, but 17.5% of the Johnson et al. (1982) sample were judged to be currently overweight (defined as more than 110% of the norm for their height). Fairburn and Cooper (1982) reported that 83.2% of their sample was between 85% and 115% of the matched population weight at the time of assessment. An additional 20% of the Johnson et al. respondents and 35% of Pyle et al. sample were determined to be underweight at the time of assessment.

In terms of past weight, Pyle et al. (1981) reported that 17% of their patient group had a history of weighing more than the maximum acceptable weight for their height, whereas fully half of the 316 women surveyed by Johnson et al. (1982) reported a history of being overweight. Almost one-half the women surveyed by Fairburn and Cooper (1982) also reported a history of overweight, with 45.2% reporting a highest weight since menarche of over 115%, with 65.7% of this group having once weighed over 120% of the matched population mean weight. Forty-three percent of this sample reported a lowest weight of less than 85% since menarche, indicating that they may have at one time had a sufficiently low weight to fulfill accepted diagnostic criteria for anorexia nervosa. Of Pyle et al.'s sample, 50% were seen as possibly having a history compatible with a diagnosis of anorexia nervosa, but only 6.1% of the Johnson sample endorsed criteria that would lead to the speculation that they could be considered to be suffering from a current (0.9%) or past (5.2%) episode of anorexia nervosa.

The severity of the eating pathology reported by bulimic women varies in relation to the nature in which the population was identified. Not surprisingly, frequency of binge eating was highest among women assessed while initiating treatment for their eating disorders and lower among persons identified as meeting bulimic criteria merely by the utilization of population survey methods. However, data from the three samples are consistent in that both groups reported that on the average, the disordered eating had begun around the age of 18 and the data was gathered after they had been struggling with the disordered eating for 4-5 years.

Of the 34 bulimic patients assessed by Pyle et al. (1981), all reported at least weekly binge eating and 89% reported binge eating at least daily. Vomiting was self-induced at least daily by 78.4% and at least weekly by 86.5% of this same group. The use of laxatives and diuretics was less frequent, with the use of each on a weekly basis being reported by 27% of the women. Thirty-two percent of the bulimic patients engaged in at least weekly 24-hour fasting.

Although only 38% of the population surveyed by Johnson, Stuckey, Lewis, and Schwartz (1982) had sought professional help for their disordered eating, the fact that they had contacted the Eating Disorders Project indicates that they all had identified themselves as having a problem in this area. Of this group, 51% were binge eating at least daily, and an additional 42% at least weekly. Comparable to Pyle's figures, 86% induced vomiting at least weekly with 59% reporting daily vomiting. Laxative use was somewhat more common among this group, with 54% reporting at least weekly use of this purging method.

Of the women identified by Fairburn and Cooper (1982) as suffering from bulimia nervosa, 27.2% reported binge eating at least once daily, with an additional 32.6% reporting at least weekly binges. Paralleling the figures reported by Pyle, Mitchell, and Eckert (1981) and Johnson, Stuckey, Lewis, and Schwartz (1982), 56.1% of this sample reported vomiting at least once daily, and an additional 17.5% reported more than once weekly vomiting. The abuse of purgatives was reported by 18.8% of the sample.

Other population surveys that have attempted to identify bulimic individuals using a variety of assessment strategies reveal a somewhat lower frequency of bulimic behaviors among persons labeled bulimic. Typically, although reported frequency of binge eating remains quite high, purging behaviors are reported less frequently. Of the 7.8% of a female college freshman class which Pyle et al. (1983) identified as meeting the criteria for bulimia following DSM-III guidelines (minimum frequency of binge eating not included), 73.2% reported at least weekly binge eating. However, only 20% reported inducing vomiting at least weekly. Laxative and diuretics were used on at least a weekly basis by 13.2% and 18.5%, respectively. Of the 4.9% of female high school students identified by Johnson et al. (1984), 11% reported the weekly use of laxatives, 17% were inducing vomiting at least weekly, and only .04% reported weekly use of diuretics.

It is possible that these young women reporting lower frequencies of purging behavior are in an earlier stage of the disorder. The bulimic high school students averaged 15.5 years of age (Johnson et al., 1984), and the bulimic students surveyed by Pyle et al. (1983) were all freshmen in college. Although duration of binge eating behavior was not reported for these groups, it is likely that given their younger age, their binge eating behavior was of more recent onset than those presenting at Pyle's clinic or responding to the Eating Disorders Project survey (average age—24). The speculation that the lower frequency of purging behaviors may be due to a more recent onset of binge eating symptoms is consistent with the speculation advanced by Johnson et al. that evacuation techniques emerge as a consistent feature of the disorder after the binging behavior has been exhibited for approximately 1 year.

Pyle et al. (1983) also noted that among college students, the use of fasting is more prevalent for weight control than purging is, and suggested that being overweight and fasting might be common in the earlier stages of the bulimic syndrome or in mild cases of this problem. Possibility of the greatest significance in understanding the varying frequencies of bulimic behaviors, however, is the fact that it has yet to be determined whether there is a need for a measure of severity in the DSM-III criteria to aid in the classification of persons who exhibit varying degrees of bulimic behavior.

In an attempt to gather more precise information about the symptomatic behavior, Mitchell, Eckert, and Pyle (1981) collected data on the duration and frequency of binge eating and vomiting episodes for 40 patients who met the DSM-III criteria for bulimia. This group, who kept careful records for a week prior to beginning a group therapy program, reported an average of 11.7 binge-eating episodes per week, with a range of 1-46 episodes. The mean duration of each binge-eating episode was reported to be 1.18 hours, with a range from 15 minutes to 8 hours. Among this group, the most common pattern was for the individual to binge eat at least once each day, spending on the average 13.7 hours each week binge eating, with a range from 30 minutes to 43 hours. Of the 40 patients, 37 vomited as part of the syndrome, with a mean frequency of vomiting episodes among these individuals being 11.7 per week.

Both Pyle et al. (1981) and Johnson et al. (1982) have reported that binge eating episodes are most likely to occur when persons are alone, primarily in the evening hours. Most binges consist of sweet or salty carbohydrates, foods which are otherwise "forbidden." A subgroup of 25 patients in the study conducted by Mitchell et al. (1981) reported the foods they ate during their binges. These data revealed that during an average binge episode 3,415 calories were consumed (range of 1,200-11,500). The sample surveyed by Johnson et al. reported consuming an average of 4,800 calories per binge. This figure, however, reflected their estimations and was not based on actual reports of food eaten. Also, because the altered state of consciousness associated with a binge is believed to interfere with accurate reporting of amount of food consumed, the estimated average amount of money spent per binge was also elicited. The average of $8.30 spent per binge (range $1.00-$55.00) may represent a more reliable estimate of the severity of a binge for a particular individual. In addition, the majority of Pyle et al.'s clinical sample indicated that they had strong appetites with poor control, and most had difficulty eating regular meals when they were not binge eating. Fasting between binges was also common, and the women reported difficulty in knowing when they were full at the end of a "normal" meal.

The DMS-III defines a binge as the "rapid consumption of a large amount of food in a discrete period of time." In addition, both anecdotal and data-based reports often emphasize the large quantities eaten by bulimic women during a binge. As more is learned about bulimia, however, it is becoming unclear as to whether the large quantity of food is critical to defining a binge and making a diagnosis of bulimia. Of 25 subjects reporting food eaten during binges, 5 reported consuming less than 2,000 calories during an average binge (Mitchell et al., 1981). Professionals working clinically with bulimic women are noting that it is often the phenomenological experience of being out of control, rather than the amount of food eaten, that defines a binge. This aspect of the disordered eating pattern of the bulimic clearly requires further investigation.

Personality and Psychological Characteristics

Several recent investigators have attempted to identify personality characteristics of normal-weight bulimics. Two studies using the MMPI have indicated that bulimic patients have difficulties with impulse control, chronic depression, exaggerated sense of guilt, intolerance for frustration, and recurrent anxiety. Interpersonally, the studies suggest, bulimic patients feel alienated and self-conscious, and have difficulty with direct expression of feelings, particularly anger (Norman & Herzog, 1983; Pyle et al., 1981).

Much attention has been focused recently on the extent and nature of depression among bulimic patients. Several studies have demonstrated that bulimics report significant levels of depression that seems to center around themes of learned helplessness, hopelessness, pessimism, self-criticism, and guilt (Stuckey & Johnson, 1984; Pyle et al., 1981; Russell, 1979). In addition to the psychological experience of depression, researchers have been finding that bulimic patients have affect instability, which may be characteristic of primary affective disorder. Johnson and

Larson (1982) have demonstrated that bulimics have significantly lower and more volatile moods than a normal control group. In their discussion, they observed that the nature of the affective instability among the bulimic group was suggestive of an agitated depressive state that might be responsive to antidepressant medication.

Several investigators have pursued more fully the possible role of primary affective disorder among bulimic patients. In a series of studies, Hudson, Pope, Jonas, and Yurgelund (1983) have indicated that bulimic patients have a morbid risk factor for primary affective disorder of 28%. Citing the high prevalence of concomitant DSM-III diagnosis of major affective disorder, results on the dexamethazone suppression test that are most similar to comparison group of patients with affective disorder, and a high incidence of primary affective disorder among first-degree relatives (44 of 251 relatives), they have argued that bulimia may simply be a "forme fruste" of affective disorder. The suggestion that bulimia patients may be suffering from major affective disorder has resulted in several investigations on the use of antidepressant medication, which will be reviewed in the treatment section.

Life Adjustment

Early observers suggested that bulimics at normal weight had good life adjustment, despite the severity of their food related behavior. Unfortunately, only one study has investigated the life adjustment of normal-weight bulimics. Johnson and Berndt (1983), using the Weisman Social Adjustment Scale (Weisman, Drusoff, Thompson, Harding, & Meyers, 1978) found that normal-weight bulimics' functioning at work, social and leisure activities, family activities, and overall adjustment to be significantly more disturbed than a normal control sample, but comparable to a sample of female alcoholics.

Although only further research can continue to elucidate the complexities of the personality and psychological characteristics of bulimic individuals, taken together the studies to date reveal the normal-weight bulimic woman as someone troubled by feelings of helplessness and inadequacy, someone who is more anxious, depressed, self-critical, impulsive, and concerned with issues related to food and body dissatisfaction than women with normal eating patterns. Research in this area, however, will continue to be compromised by the heterogeneity of the patient population. The increased incidence of the disorder has predictably also increased the variability within the group. Clearly, future research on psychological characteristics needs to focus on attempting to articulate subgroups within the overall patient population, and needs to identify the ways these patients are similar to, and different from, other psychiatric populations.

Medical Complications

Unfortunately, long-term outcome studies on bulimia are not currently available. Consequently, the medical complications that might arise from recurrent binge eating and purging are largely unknown at this time. However, several reports have begun to emerge that indicate that several side effects may arise as a result of the disorder.

Pyle et al. (1981) reported that 51.8% of the 85 bulimic patients they studied had abnormal balances of electrolytes. Common abnormalities were metabolic alkalosis, hypochloriemia (low blood levels of chlorine), and hypokalemia (low blood levels of potassium). The depletion of chlorine and potassium is associated with fatigue, muscle weakness, constipation, and dysphoria, all of which mimic depression. Also reported are edema and possible kidney dysfunction, and a predisposition to cardiac arrythmias. Furthermore, laxative abuse has been associated with damage to submucosal nerve fibers in the intestines (Freeman & Schmidt, 1980). Gastric dilitation has been reported in two case studies (Saul, Dekker, & Watson, 1981; Mitchell, Pyle, & Miner, 1982), with one case resulting in death due to rupturing of the intestines. Other associated medical problems are parotid enlargement from vomiting and poor diet (Ahola, 1982; Hasler, 1982), and dental caries and enamel erosion from frequent exposure to hydrochloric acid from vomiting (Gallo & Randel, 1981).

Theories of Etiology

Understanding the processes by which the symptoms of bulimia emerge in patients remains a critical aspect of the disorder that has yet to be adequately delineated. There is, however, concensus among investigators that bulimia is a multidetermined disorder that can serve a variety of biological, psychological, and sociocultural adaptations. As Figure 1 depicts, some preliminary data is available on the biological, familial, and sociocultural milieu of the bulimic patient. The following section on etiology attempts to review and synthesize how these different factors may contribute to personality difficulties that have been observed among bulimic patients. Also, an explanation is offered regarding why the specific symptoms of bulimia would emerge as an adaptation to these difficulties.

Biological Factors

The contribution of organic factors to the onset of bulimia is unclear. Although there are often medical side effects associated with bulimia, which include electrolyte abnormalities, dehydration, edema, parotid

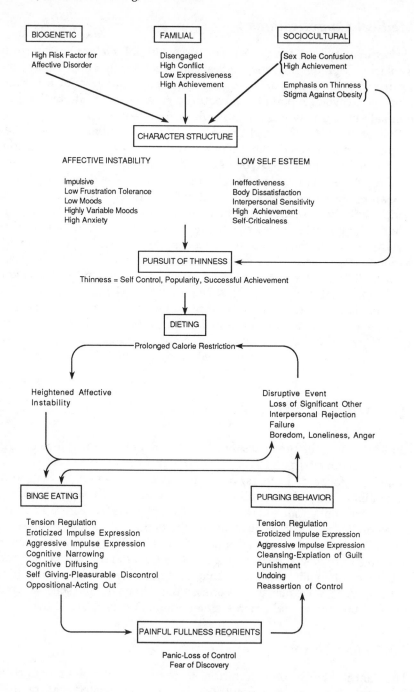

Figure 1.   An etiological model of bulimia.

gland enlargements, dental decay, anemia, gastrointestinal problems, and menstrual difficulties (Ahola, 1982; Gallo & Randel, 1981; Hasler, 1982; Mitchell & Bantle, 1983), to date there has not emerged any consistent endocrine finding of etiological significance.

Over the last several years, however, there has been an increasing body of literature that suggests that bulimia may be a symptom expression of a biologically mediated affective disorder. Several converging pieces of evidence have been offered in support of this hypothesis. The first line of evidence is related to preliminary findings that have indicated that a large number of bulimic patients report symptoms characteristic of unipolar and bipolar illnesses. These symptoms include a persistence of low, and highly variable, mood states; low frustration tolerance; anxiety; and suicidal ideation (Glassman & Walsh, 1983; Hudson et al., 1983; Johnson & Larson, 1982; Pyle et al., 1981; Russell, 1979).

Although these early reports have suggested that bulimic patients present with vegetative symptoms similar to patients with major depression, the etiology of the depressive experience remains unclear. It is possible that the depressive symptoms either may be physiological side effects from weight loss or fluctuations in nutritional status, or may be psychological side effects from repeated exposure to a pattern of thoughts and behavior that result in feelings of helplessness, shame, guilt, and ineffectiveness.

The most compelling evidence for the depression hypothesis comes from family studies, which indicate a high incidence of major affective disorder among first- and second-degree relatives of bulimic patients. Using the family history method among a sample of 75 patients with bulimia, Hudson and his colleagues (Hudson, Laffer, & Pope, 1982; Hudson et al., 1983) found that 53% had first-degree relatives with major affective disorder. Likewise, substance abuse disorder was found to be highly prevalent (45 of 350 relatives). Results further indicated that the morbid risk factor for affective disorder in relatives was 28%, which was similar to that found in families of patients with bipolar disorder. Strober and his colleagues (Strober, 1981; Strober, Salkin, Burroughs, & Marrell, 1982) found strikingly similar results among anorexic patients who manifested bulimic symptoms. Their findings indicated a 20% morbid risk factor for affective disorder in the bulimic families. They also noted that 18% of the first- and second-degree relatives reported histories of alcoholism.

There has also been a preliminary attempt to identify biological markers that are associated with depression and bulimia. Although consistent markers that are predictive of affective disorder have not been isolated, two that are under consideration are suggestive of major depression among bulimic patients.

The dexamethasone suppression test and the thyroid releasing hormone stimulating test have been found positive in bulimic patients with the same frequency as in patients with major depression and much more frequently than would be expected in normal control populations (Gwirtsman, Roy-Byrne, & Yager, 1983; Hudson et al., 1982). Also, sleep lab research has recently indicated that a subgroup of bulimics at normal weight (with previous histories of anorexia nervosa) displayed sleep disturbance (shortened REM latency) characteristic of patients with affective disorders (Katz et al., 1984).

Finally, support is marshaled for this hypothesis by early findings regarding the effectiveness of antidepressant pharmacotherapy. Both open trials and double-blind placebo studies of tricyclic and MAO inhibitor treatment have resulted in significant improvement in frequency of bulimic symptoms (Brotman, Herzog, & Woods, 1984; Jonas, Pope, & Hudson, 1983; Mendels, 1983; Pope & Hudson, 1982; Pope, Hudson, Jonas & Yurgelund, 1983; Sabine, Yonace, Farrington, Barratt, & Wakeling, 1983; Walsh et al., 1982).

Although further research is necessary to substantiate the prevalence of affective disorders among bulimic patients, it is clear that overall the group experiences significant affective instability that may have predated the onset of bulimic symptoms. Furthermore, given the high incidence of affective disorder and substance abuse among the parents of these patients, we can speculate that the family environment is likely to reflect some of the instability the parents experience.

Family Characteristics

Few studies have investigated the nature of the family environment among bulimic patients. Results from preliminary studies are promising, however, in that there appears to be some agreement about what things characterize these families. Most investigators have used self-report measures of family interaction style. Johnson and Flach (1985) and Ordman and Kirschenbaum (1984) have reported that compared to normal control families, the families of normal-weight bulimics express greater anger, aggression, and conflict, a more indirect pattern of communication, give less support and commitment to each other, less emphasis on assertiveness and autonomy, and are less interested in political, social, cultural and recreational events despite expressing higher achievement expectations. Strober (1981) has found similar results from comparing the families of anorexic bulimics to those of anorexic restrictors. In addition, he has reported higher levels of discord between the parents, higher overall level of life stresses within the family, and more alienation between the anorexic bulimic patient and her family, especially her father. He has described mothers of anorexic bulimics as more hostile and depressed, whereas the fathers are more impulsive and irritable, have poorer frustration tolerance, and are more often alcoholic (Strober et al., 1982). Humphrey (1984a) has compared anorexic bulimic families to normal control families; she has found virtually the same results.

Garner, Garfinkel, and Olmsted (1983) have compared normal-weight bulimic families to families of anorexics who binged and to families of restricting anorexics. These investigators have found that normal-weight bulimics' families were strikingly similar to the anorexic bulimics' families on 6 of 8 measures of family interaction style, including communication, affective expression, affective involvement, control, values and norms, and social desirability. In addition, they have reported that the degree of problems in these areas suggested significant overall pathology, well above the families of the restricting anorexics.

Two recent investigations have utilized direct observational measures of bulimics' family interaction styles. Humphrey (1984b) and Humphrey, Apple, & Kirschenbaum (1984) have reported that compared to normal control families, the families of bulimic anorexics are more belittling and appeasing, and less helping, trusting, nurturing, and approaching. In addition, these parents give more negative, less positive, more contradictory (double bind) messages to their daughters, especially concerning issues of being controlled versus having autonomy. These direct observations are consistent with, and provide validation of, the self-report data.

Taken together, these early studies suggest that bulimics' families generally can be characterized as disengaged, chaotic, highly conflictful, and having a high degree of life stress. Furthermore, they use indirect and contradictory patterns of communication, are deficient in problem-solving skills, are less supportive, and are less intellectually and recreationally oriented, despite their higher achievement expectations.

At this point in the etiological model, we have a child who is at risk for affective instability and who has a high probability of being in a family that is volatile and disorganized, with parents who themselves may have difficulty with affective disorder. Unfortunately, as we move to the broader sociocultural context, we find that, particularly for young women, it is a milieu that simultaneously exacerbates feelings of instability and suggests an adaptation to the instability they are experiencing.

Sociocultural Factors

Obviously, biological and familial factors alone could not explain why one would be observing an increase in a specific symptom picture among a rather homogeneous cohort (15–25-year-old, middle- to upper-class, Caucasian, college-educated women in westernized countries). Consequently, one has to turn to the broader sociocultural context to see whether any events occured during the period of increased incidence that would selectively bias the group at risk, as well as bias the specific symptom expression.

Retrospectively, it appears that two cultural events that have occurred simultaneously could account for this. The mean age of the patient population indicates they are the first generation of young women raised at the onset of the feminist movement. Several authors have observed that during these years, the sociocultural milieu for young women was in substantial transition, which appears to have contributed to role and identity confusion among at least a subpopulation of this age group (Bardwick, 1971; Garner, Garfinkel, & O'Shaughnessy, 1983; Lewis & Johnson, in press; Palazzoli, 1974; Schwartz, Thompson, & Johnson, 1982). Garner, Garfinkel, and O'Shaughnessy (1983) have reviewed evidence that these shifting cultural norms force contemporary women to face multiple and ambiguous, and often contradictory, role expectations. These role expectations included accommodating more traditional feminine expectations such as physical attractiveness and domesticity, incorporating more modern standards for vocational and personal achievement, and taking advantage of increased opportunity for self-definition and autonomy. Garner and his colleagues have suggested that though "the wider range of choices made available to contemporary women may have provided personal freedom for those who were psychologically robust, it may have been overwhelming for the field-dependent adolescent who lacked internal structure" (Garner, Garfinkel, & O'Shaughnessy, 1983, p. 77). Consequently, this cohort appears to represent a transitional group, within which at least a subgroup may be at increased risk for experiencing anxiety (affective instability) in reaction to the shifting role expectations and increased demand for achievement.

A second cultural shift, having emerged concomitantly with the feminist movement, appears to have biased the specific symptom expression of food- and body-related behavior. More specifically, during the mid-1960s, an emphasis on thinness for women emerged. Amid a milieu of increasing emphasis on achievement and confusion about how to express the drive to achieve, it appears that the pursuit of thinness emerged as one vehicle through which young women could compete among themselves and demonstrate self-control. In fact, the accomplishment of thinness has increasingly become a very highly valued achievement that secures envy and respect among women in the current culture.

Conversely, the absence of weight control, leading to even moderate obesity, leads culturally to social discrimination, isolation, and low self-esteem, which begin early in life. Wooley and Wooley (1979) reviewed numerous studies that document the stigma of obesity in childhood and adolescence. They have asserted that the overweight child is regarded by others as responsible for his or her condition, and that failure to remediate the situation is viewed as personal weakness. Both normal-weight and overweight children themselves describe obese silhouettes with pejorative labels, such as *stupid, lazy, dirty, sloppy, mean,* and *ugly*. Female children add *worried, sad,* and *lonely* to the list of adjectives, which suggests that for them obesity carries with it connotations of social isolation (Allon, 1975; Staffieri, 1967, 1972).

This negative attitude toward endomorphic children prevails for both sexes; however, there is increasing evidence that in adolescence and adulthood, females are more affected than males by this antifat prejudice. Empirical research has shown that obese girls have greatly reduced chances of being admitted to college, compared to nonobese applicants (Canning & Mayer, 1966); obese job applicants are less likely to be hired than their slimmer counterparts (Roe & Eickwort, 1976); once hired, their job performance is more likely to be negatively evaluated (Larkin & Pines, 1979); they are less likely to make as much money, and they are less likely to get top spots when promotions come around (Fat execs get slimmer paychecks, 1974). Finally, compared to nonobese women, overweight women are much more likely to achieve a lower socioeconomic status than their parents (Goldblatt, Moore, & Stunkard, 1965). This was not found to be true among men.

Against the backdrop of confusing cultural expectations and high achievement expectations, it appears that the pursuit of thinness (which can be scaled and measured) and avoidance of obesity has emerged as one very concrete activity through which young women can compete and obtain consistently favorable social responses, which hold the possibility of enhancing self-esteem. It is extremely important to note, however, that not all young women exposed to this cultural milieu have developed eating disorders. Therefore, one must attempt to look more closely at the personality characteristics thought to be associated with patients who develop bulimia.

Personality Factors

Although personality trait findings among this group are quite variable, as one reviews the data-based research, two consistent factors seem to emerge. First, as mentioned earlier, there is substantial evidence that bulimics experience significant affective instability, which is manifested in depressed and highly variable mood states, impulsive behavior (frequently including drug and alcohol abuse), low frustration tolerance, and high anxiety. Although data-based research has not clearly indicated that reported affective instability predates the onset of the bulimic symptoms, clinical observations suggest that the affect regulation difficulties are long-standing side effects, resulting both from biogenetic vulnerabilities and from maladaptive parenting styles. Consequently, these patients have long histories of feeling somewhat out of control, and perhaps helpless, in relation to their bodily experience, which undoubtedly contributes significantly to the second prominent personality trait among bulimics, low self-esteem (Boskind-Lodahl, 1976; Conners, Johnson, & Stuckey, 1984; Garfinkel & Garner, 1982; Love, Ollendick, Johnson & Shlesinger, in press).

Although low self-esteem is commonly associated with any genre of psychopathology, there appear to be certain features that are characteristic of bulimic patients. Several investigators have observed that many bulimic patients have difficulty identifying and articulating different internal states (Bruch, 1973). This incapacity appears to contribute to a feeling of being undifferentiated (Lewis & Johnson, in press), which leads to feelings of ineffectiveness and helplessness in controlling these internal states. It is interesting to note that in addition to the sociocultural factors that might contribute to women feeling dissatisfied with their bodies (imperfect appearance), women who experience difficulty modulating internal states may feel more dissatisfaction, perhaps even rage, at bodies they experience as being defective containers of their affective states. Further exacerbating self-esteem problems is the fact that interpersonally, bulimic patients are quite rejection-sensitive, which results in feelings of social discomfort and nonassertive behavior (Boskind-Lodahl, 1976; Conners, Johnson & Stuckey, 1984; Johnson et al., 1982; Norman & Herzog, 1983; Pyle et al., 1981; Schneider & Agras, in press). Finally, amid these various vulnerabilities, these patients have very high expectations of themselves, which results in persistent shame, guilt, and self-criticism over the continuous discrepancy they feel between their actual and ideal selves (Goodsitt, 1984; Kohut, 1971).

At this point in the etiological model, we have a situation in which the biological, familial, and sociocultural milieus have combined to shape an individual who is at high risk for feeling fundamentally out of control in her internal life. Given these circumstances, it is likely that the person would begin to seek some external adaptation in an attempt to gain control of her internal experience. Given the issues related to bodily experience, it would seem obvious that the adaptation would need to be focused in that arena. This raises the question as to why food-related or dieting behavior would be selected, rather than other potential behaviors, such as drug abuse, promiscuity, delinquency behavior, or a more primitive form of self-mutilation. The following section presents comments on how the pursuit of thinness would have emerged for these patients as a viable adaptation to the self-regulatory deficits that have been reviewed.

Other Psychological Motives for the Pursuit of Thinness

Clinical observations and data-based research has documented that an early and primary source of feelings of mastery for children comes from successful control of bodily functions and movements. As suggested earlier, biogenetic and parental factors appear to have predisposed these patients to have long-standing difficulty identifying and modulating internal affective states. It was further suggested that these repeated difficulties might result in feelings of helplessness, ineffectiveness, and being out of control. Over the last several decades, an emphasis on women taking control of their bodies has emerged. A demonstration of being in control of one's body appears to have become, more generally, a demonstration that one is in control of one's life. More specifically, for this group of patients, the accomplishment of thinness, or control of amount and distribution of fat, has become a demonstration to themselves that they can control the container that houses their affective states. Furthermore, in the absence of knowing how to determine whether they are in control or not, they simply have to weigh themselves in order to obtain some external, concrete indicator of their level of control, which could be quite reinforcing.

It was also suggested earlier that many bulimic patients lack confidence interpersonally and feel self-conscious and unattractive. The accomplishment of thinness among these women not only enhances self-confidence but also often results in significant social transformations. Many women report dramatic increases in their social desirability (popularity) as a result of weight loss.

Finally, the pursuit of thinness has also become a vehicle to express achievement. As mentioned earlier, one dimension of change that has occurred during the time frame of increased incidence has been an increased emphasis on achievement for young women. Unfortunately, at the time of increased emphasis on achievement, there were relatively few areas in which young women could compete directly that were socially valued. It appears that the pursuit of thinness has emerged as one way in which young women can compete and demonstrate intrapsychic and interpersonal achievement. This avenue for achievement and competition not only has appeared benign but has been socially sanctioned.

Therefore there are several reasons why the pursuit of thinness would become a functional adaptation to the personality vulnerabilities mentioned earlier. Although it seems clear how the pursuit of thinness and the accompanying dieting behavior would increase in incidence, it remains unclear how the symptoms of bulimia also increase in incidence. The following section presents a synthesis of how the symptoms of bulimia might emerge.

The Adaptive Context of Binge Eating

As suggested earlier, over the last two decades a cultural milieu has progressively emerged, particularly for women, conveying the attitude that if one can control weight and achieve thinness, this is a demonstration of self-control, which is intrapsychically and interpersonally reinforcing. Of course, thinness results from extended calorie restriction. Consequently, the increase in the incidence of bulimic behavior has occurred during the time period in which large numbers of adolescent and young adult women have been pursuing thinness through highly restrictive dieting.

Predictably, research has indicted that the onset of bulimic symptomatology is often caused by periods of prolonged calorie deprivation. (Pyle et al., 1981; Johnson et al., 1981). Over the last several years a growing body of research has documented both that physiological and psychological side effects result from semi-starvation and that counterregulatory behaviors such as binge eating also occur in reaction to prolonged states of calorie deprivation (Garfinkel & Garner, 1982; Garner, Rockert, Olmsted, Johnson & Coscina, 1984; Glucksman & Hirsch, 1969; Herman & Mack, 1975; Herman & Polivy, 1980; Keys, Brozek, Henschel, Mickelson, & Taylor 1950; Rowland, 1970). The physiological side effects that have been reported include gastrointestinal discomfort, decreased need for sleep, dizziness, headaches, hypersensitivity to noise and light, reduced strength, poor motor control, edema, hair loss, decreased tolerance for cold temperatures, visual disturbances, auditory disturbances, and parastesia. Additional side effects include persistent tiredness, weakness, listlessness, fatigue, and lack of energy. Psychological side effects include increased depression, irritability, rage outburst, increased anxiety, social withdrawal, and loss of sexual interest. Specific increases in food-related behavior that occur from semistarved states include an increased obsession with food, food hoarding, prolonged eating behavior during meal times, peculiar taste preferences, and hyperconsumption of substances such as coffee and gum.

The explanation offered for the appearance of these side effects is that as the body drops below a minimal biogenetically mediated range of weight (set point), the body initiates a variety of compensatory behaviors designed to conserve energy and to begin to increase the body weight to the internally prescribed weight range that is normal (Garner et al., 1984; Keesy, 1980, 1983; Mrosovsky & Powley, 1977; Nisbett, 1972). This is particularly true for women, who must maintain approximately 13% adipose tissue in order to menstruate (Frisch, 1983). Any time the body fat threatens to drop below this range, a specific biological imperative would ensue that would involve a persistent and intense drive toward caloric intake because if a female's body weight drops below a menstrual threshold, the species' perpetuation is in danger, due to the accompanying infertility of amenorrhea. A similar imperative does not appear to occur among men.

Foremost among the compensatory behaviors that emerge in reaction to caloric deprivation is an increased vulnerability to binge eat (to rapidly consume a large quantity of food in a short space of time). As with a person who gulps water after being fluid-deprived, persons who are calorie-deprived are at increased risk for rapidly consuming food.

Consequently, as Figure 1 depicts, at this point in the etiological model, we have a person who has attempted to compensate for a variety of self-regulatory and self-esteem deficits by accomplishing thinness. Unfortunately, if her success in accomplishing thinness drops her near her set point (and menstrual threshold), a variety of physiological and psychological side effects occur that not only exacerbate her original affective instability but threaten the self-esteem she had developed through the accomplishment of the low weight. Unfortunately, at this point the person is at what could be referred to as a "psychobiological impasse." Essentially, the psychological adaptation she has developed is at odds with her biology. In fact, it is likely that the person interprets the body's relentless drive to consume calories as the body once again being out of control. As Figure 2 demonstrates, a belief system that is logically consistent could emerge that would result in her interpreting the internal experience of hunger as a signal that she was out of control and failing at her appointed task. This guarantees that times she would have multiple internal experiences (hunger) every day that she would interpret as evidence that she was ineffective and a failure. Paradoxically, then, the effort at compensation results in an exacerbation of the original difficulties.

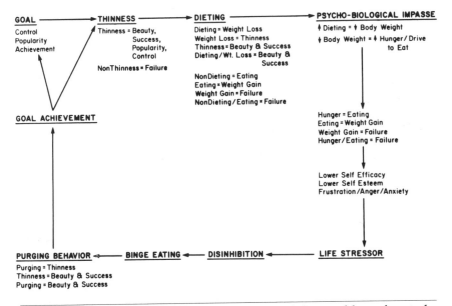

Figure 2. Belief system that interprets hunger as failure and loss of control.

Binge Eating

Against this backdrop of heightened affective instability, lowered self-esteem, and semistarvation, any stressful life event would be taxing to the failing defensive adaptation (of thinness being equated with control and achievement). If disinhibition occurred, given the semistarved state, binge eating would be the most likely expression of the breakdown in defenses.

Despite the fact that most bulimic patients feel that episodic binge eating is a shameful and humiliating experience of being out of control, the act of binge eating can offer a number of compensatory adaptations that become quite reinforcing. Mentioned below are a number of the adaptations that have been observed.

Affect Regulation.   Given the evidence for affective instability, it is easy to see how binge eating could emerge as a relatively safe mechanism for regulating different tension states. As noted earlier, research has indicated that bulimics often experience a wide range of highly variable mood states that they have difficulty identifying, articulating, and controlling. These moods include anxiety, panic, depression, boredom, irritability, anger, and euphoria. Throughout the day the variability, range, and seeming unpredictability of the different mood states may become overwhelming and disorganizing for the patient. Concrete and repeated acts of binging and purging can serve an integrating function for these patients, allowing them to reliably create a predictable affective and cognitive state by means of the behavioral sequence. Essentially, when overwhelmed by confusing and variable mood states, the binging and purging becomes both an explanation of the dysphoria ("I am feeling bad because I have binged") and a mechanism for actually helping to regulate the dysphoria ("I feel relieved after I have binged").

Impulse Expression.   As suggested earlier, bulimic patients are vulnerable to impulsive behavior. Episodic binge eating can be a relatively safe mechanism for being impulsive, for binge eating does not carry significant moral, legal, or medical consequences in the same way that promiscuity, delinquent behavior, or drug abuse do. More specifically, bulimic patients can eroticize the binge eating episodes, thus offering an alternative response to sexual feelings if they have conflicts about masturbation or heterosexual activity. Similarly, binge eating and subsequent purging behavior can become an effective mechanism for expressing aggressive feelings that, research indicates, these persons have difficulty expressing interpersonally.

More obsessive, overcontrolled patients also use binge eating to temporarily be out of control or have the phenomenological experience of letting go or spacing out. These patients create an experience of controlled discontrol. They invest food, an inanimate object that has no volition and can only have as much power as they grant it, with the power to overcome them and make them become impulsive. This allows them some relief from an overcontrolled psychological world, without having to take responsibility for the impulsive episodes.

Self-Nurturance. Some bulimic patients are tormented by a profound sense of guilt, which results in a belief that they should deny themselves pleasurable or self-enhancing activities. They are quite self-sacrificing, and their continuous efforts to care for others often leaves them feeling depleted and exhausted. The act of binge eating (with the attendant attribution that the event was externally determined) among these patients can serve as a mechanism for briefly greedily and selfishly consuming for themselves.

Along similar lines, some bulimic patients experience a basic mistrust of others, which prevents them from receiving emotional support from the outside. Consequently, they invest food and the act of binge eating with the ability to soothe, comfort, and gratify themselves. In this regard, they often project onto the food humanlike qualities that allow them the illusion of receiving emotional supplies from a source other than themselves. The fact that food (an inanimate object) can only behave as they desire allows them to simultaneously refuel and yet be protected from the potential disappointment of human relationships.

Oppositionality. Binge eating can also serve as a mechanism for expressing oppositionality. For patients who feel that external authority figures have imposed significant restraints on them, binge eating can become an expression of "acting out" or of defiance. This is particularly true of bulimics who were raised in families in which weight control and dieting were highly emphasized by the parents. The act of binge eating, for these patients, becomes a statement of protest and expression of autonomy.

Whatever specific adaptation binge eating serves, once an episode has ended, the patients generally feel some combination of guilt, shame, disgust, and fear of being discovered. These feelings become concretely manifested in a sense of panic that they will gain weight, which would be an observable indication that they are out of control, disorganized, undisciplined, greedy, etc. Consequently, the use of evacuation techniques, such as self-induced vomiting, laxative abuse, and enemas, emerges as a viable mechanism for undoing the binge eating.

Purging Behavior

Like binge eating, purging behavior can serve a variety of different adaptive functions, some of which may become more important than the actual act of binge eating in the psychic economy of the bulimic. As with binge eating, the act of purging can serve as a mechanism for tension regulation. This is particularly true of aggressive feelings. Self-induced vomiting can be a rather violent act, and the physical process of vomiting can be quite cathartic for aggressive feelings. For patients who feel especially guilty and self-critical about the binge eating episodes, the purging can serve as a self-punishment and an act of undoing or penitence that pays for the crime of impulse expression. For the oppositional patient, it allows her to get away with something without "getting caught" or having to pay the price of her overeating.

For patients more on the borderline, the act of purging (primarily through laxative abuse) appears to serve an integrating function similar to other forms of self-mutilatory behavior. The intense pain created by persistent diarrhea appears to make them feel alive and in touch with reality.

Most importantly, as Figure 2 depicts, the purging behavior becomes highly reinforcing because it allows the individual to avoid the psychobiological impasse of restrained eating. Essentially, the purging allows the individual to eat in any compensatory way she desires, without the negative consequence of weight gain. Several investigators have noted that the purging behavior can become so highly reinforcing that for some patients, a transformation occurs from purging so that they can binge eat, to binge eating so that they can purge (Johnson & Larson, 1982; Rosen & Leitenberg, 1982).

Unfortunately, similar to the adaptive effort of the pursuit of thinness, the purging adaptation simultaneously creates and solves a problem. In the absence of immediately apparent negative consequences, the binging and purging progressively increases until the sufferer is using the cycle to regulate a variety of affective and cognitive states. Eventually, she feels addicted to, and controlled by, the process, which again results in lower self-esteem and heightened affective instability.

Treatment

The recent increase in the incidence of bulimia has placed a significant clinical demand for treatment on the professional community. Prior to the last several years, virtually no studies existed that had reported on treatment strategies for this patient population. More recently, however, studies have begun to emerge, documenting the effectiveness of various treatment modalities. Included in this section is a review of the data-based reports of treatment that currently exist. The review is divided into four sections, which include behavioral, cognitive behavioral, group, and psychopharmacological interventions.

Behavioral Interventions

Although aversion therapy has been employed quite frequently in the treatment of patients who are overweight due to compulsive eating, few reports deal specifically with patients identified as bulimic. Several reports do, however, provide insight into how these techniques have been utilized in the treatment of bulimic symptoms. Wijesinghe (1973) employed massed electrical aversion to control the compulsive eating of two overweight female patients, aged 37 and 20 years. For both women the compulsive eating behavior apparently developed in response to separation from significant persons in their lives. Case descriptions would argue for at least one of these subjects being bulimic. During treatment, a mild shock and buzzer, or buzzer alone, was activated by the therapist at varying stages of the patient handling, touching, and nibbling the food that she had identified as being most problematic for her. Complete cessation of the compulsive eating was reported for both patients after six treatment sessions, all of which were held in 1 day. Following these sessions, the patients were seen every 2 weeks for several months, during which there was no return of symptomatology; at 1 year posttreatment, they remained symptom-free. However, the author did not report whether the patients maintained the ability to eat the specific foods in a noncompulsive fashion. The author does state, though, that if the initial overeating is maintained by anxiety, it is necessary to treat the anxiety before considering aversion treatment.

Aversion techniques were also utilized by Kenny and Solyom (1971) in their treatment of a 22-year-old female patient who binged and vomited an average of three times daily. The behavior apparently began at the age of 14 as a method of weight control and became progressively worse and more difficult to control, until she finally entered therapy. During treatment the patient received electroshock at pain threshold intensity to a middle finger while she visualized herself at each step of the compulsive eating and vomiting sequence. Twenty-two sessions were completed in a 5-week period, at the end of which the binging and vomiting had ceased. Several weeks of therapy followed, during which the patient was helped to regain normal eating activities. A 3-month follow-up revealed that although her eating behavior was still somewhat erratic, the compulsive vomiting had not recurred. The authors suggest that since vomiting often becomes a habit no longer related to original sources of conflict, the disruption of the mental images and the focus on the elimination of the habit itself may be a critical treatment component.

Following up on Kenny and Solyom's (1971) and Johnson and Larson's (1982) speculations that the purging, rather than the binge eating, was the primary reinforcer in the binge-purge cycle, Rosen and Leitenberg (1982) have constructed a Response Prevention Model for intervention.

Rosen and Leitenberg have hypothesized that vomiting among bulimic patients served an anxiety-reducing function similar to compulsive hand-washing and checking rituals in obsessive-compulsive neurosis. Consequently, an exposure plus response prevention model might be effective. Essentially, an exposure plus response prevention model operates on the assumption that repeated exposure to a feared stimulus (eating frightening foods) while preventing the customary response that previously mediated the anxious event (vomiting after eating anxiety-producing foods) eventually reduces anxiety through desensitization and allows for the development of normal eating.

Five patients were treated in a 6-week program in which they were exposed to the treatment regime three times per week. The protocol involved a therapist sitting with a patient consuming a meal that provoked an urge to vomit, then remaining with the patient until the anxiety related to the food consumption had abated. During the meal sessions, the therapist would elicit from the patient different feeling states that arose as a result of eating threatening foods and preventing the vomiting response. Post-treatment and 6-month follow-up results indicated that two of the five patients had completely stopped vomiting. Two others had substantially improved, and one remained unchanged. Significant improvements in eating attitudes, depression, and self-esteem were also reported.

Cognitive Behavioral Strategies

Although several authors have recommended the use of cognitive behavioral techniques (Garner & Bemis, 1982; Loro & Orleans, 1981), only one study has reported on its effectiveness as an intervention (Fairburn, 1982). Essentially, cognitive behavioral strategies focus on challenging attitudes and beliefs that are thought to mediate the disturbed eating behavior. Fairburn (1981) applied a cognitive behavioral approach to the individual treatment of 11 bulimic women. This two-part treatment program consisted of first interrupting the binge-purge episode, then teaching cognitive strategies for self-control. During the second phase of the treatment, each patient was helped to modify abnormal attitudes toward food, eating, body weight, and shape, and to maintain progress. Normally restricted foods (sweets, breads, etc.) were introduced gradually into the patient's diet to make the desire to binge on these foods less overwhelming. The patient was helped to identify situations in which loss of control occurred. In addition, the patients were prepared for future relapse events. The mean duration of treatment was 7 months. Nine of the 11 patients reduced their binge eating and vomiting of three times daily to less than once a month. At 1-year follow-ups on six of the patients, one patient had ceased to binge and vomit, four reported binging and vomiting two to three times a month, and one patient failed to benefit. Follow-up data were not available for the other five patients.

Group Interventions

Several investigators have reported on the use of group therapy for the treatment of bulimia. Lacey (1983) reported on a short-term outpatient treatment program for 30 women who met the DSM-III criteria for bulimia. After evaluation and random assignment of subjects to treatment or an assessment-only control, a 10-week treatment was conducted. Experimental subjects received treatment, consisting of a half hour of individual therapy and 1-1/2 hours of group therapy weekly. Patients contracted to attend sessions, maintain their weight, and eat a prescribed diet. Each patient carried a diet diary in which she recorded eating behavior, thoughts and feelings. The sessions gradually moved from behavioral strategies to more inside-oriented material. Results indicated that the control program had no significant effect but that 24 patients (80%) within the experimental group stopped binging and vomiting completely by the end of the 10 treatment group sessions. An additional four patients stopped within 4 weeks after the end of treatment, for an overall remission rate of 93%. Twenty-eight patients were monitored for as long as 2 years of follow-up. Twenty patients were completely free of binging, and 8 patients had occasional episodes (on average, 3 per year).

Psychoeducational group formats were used by Johnson et al. (1983) and Connors et al. (1984) to treat bulimic patients. Using a multiple baseline design, the authors treated two groups of 10 patients over a 12-week period. The group used a psychoeducational format that combined didactic presentations and process group therapy. The didactic presentations were designed to inform, and challenge beliefs, about issues such as overevaluation of thinness and distorted ideas about food, weight, and dieting. They were designed also to teach behavioral strategies to reduce binging and purging and to normalize eating through self-monitoring and self-paced goal-setting. Postgroup and 6-month follow-up results indicated that overall the weekly number of binge-purge episodes among group members had been reduced by 70%. Three patients were symptom-free, eight patients had reduced their frequency of episodes by more than 50%, and six others had reduced their frequency by 30-50%. Three patients were unchanged at follow-up. Additional measures showed significant improvement in self-esteem, depression, assertiveness, and beliefs about thinness and food-related behavior.

Psychopharmacological Interventions

Over the last 3 decades, various psychopharmacological interventions have been used in the treatment of anorexia nervosa and bulimia (Johnson et al., 1983). Two groups of medications, anticonvulsants (phenothyin) and antidepressants (tricyclics and mao inhibitors), have been investigated under controlled circumstances.

Antidepressants. As reported earlier, evidence has begun to accumulate that suggests that at least a subgroup of bulimic patients has biological and familial characteristics indicative of major affective disorders that would be responsive to antidepressant medication. To test this hypothesis, Pope et al. (1983) conducted a placebo control double-blind study, using principally the tricyclic imipramine (200 mg daily). The sample consisted of 22 women who met the DSM-III criteria for bulimia. After a random assignment and 6 weeks of treatment or placebo, the results indicated that the number of binges in the experimental group had declined by 70% overall, whereas there was virtually no change in the placebo group. Of the nine patients in the experimental group, three were symptom-free at the end of treatment, five had reduced their binge eating by more than 50% and one remained unchanged. In the placebo group, eight were unchanged, one was worse, and one reported moderate improvement. Imipramine treatment, compared to the placebo group, was also associated with a significant improvement on self-rating scales related to intensity of binges, preoccupation with food, depression, and an overall subjective sense of global improvement.

Following the double-blind phase of the investigation, the placebo group was also given a trial on the medication. Results indicated that among the nine patients who agreed to treatment, three became symptom-free, four decreased their binge-purge frequency by more than 50%, and two remained unchanged. Follow-up, conducted up to 8 months after the double-blind phase of the study, indicated that of the 20 patients who had received imipramine or another antidepressant, 18 (90%) showed moderate or marked reductions in binging. Seven patients (35%) had stopped binging entirely.

Similar results were also reported in a noncontrolled report of six bulimic patients treated with the MAO inhibitor phenelzine (60-90 mg daily) Walsh et al. (1982). Although the treatment period was unspecified, and follow-up data was not reported, posttreatment results indicated that four of the six patients treated were symptom-free; the other two had reduced their binge-purge frequency by greater than 75%.

Anticonvulsant. There has been considerable speculation in recent years that anorexia nervosa and bulimia may be related to certain neurophysiological abnormalities. One reason for this hypothesis has been the demonstrated association between abnormal eating behaviors and certain neurological conditions such as partial complex seizures (Remick, Jones, & Compos, 1980) and certain central nervous system tumors (Kirschbaum, 1951). Another line of findings suggesting this hypothesis has come from the presence of electroencephalogram abnormalities in patients with eating disorders. Crisp, Fenton, and Strotton (1968) have found an increased incidence of EEG abnormalities in patients with active anorexia nervosa, compared to controls.

Much of the recent research in this area has been reported by Rau and Green (Green & Rau, 1974, 1977; Rau & Green, 1978; Rau, Struve, & Green, 1979). A total of 47 patients were reported to have had adequate trials of phenytoin (Rau et al., 1979). Operational criteria based on patients' reports of their progress were included. Analysis revealed a higher percentage of abnormal EEGs among compulsive eaters, when compared to normal controls. The authors concluded that patients with abnormal EEGs were more likely to respond to drug treatment. With the exception of four patients described in 1977 (Green et al., 1977) and two patients described in 1979 (Rau et al., 1979), all of the subjects reported by Rau and Green were treated in open, nonblind protocols. Blood levels of anticonvulsants were not reported.

The recent work of Wermuth, Davis, Hollister, and Stunkard (1977) has addressed some of the methodological problems in the Rau and Green studies. This group originally reported EEG abnormalities in four or five patients with bulimia (Davis, Qualls, Hollister, & Stunkard, 1974). A subsequent trial (Wermuth, Davis, Hollister, & Stunkard, 1977) compared phenytoin to placebo double-blind in 19 bulimic women, one of whom had anorexia nervosa. The study involved a crossover design with random assignment to treatment groups. Treatment phases lasted 6 weeks. Three subjects had definitely abnormal EEGs, and four had questionably abnormal EEGs. There was no significant relationship between drug response and EEG abnormality. Phenytoin was found to be associated with fewer eating binges overall. Eight patients showed "marked" to "moderate" improvement, and 11 showed "slight" to "no" improvement. Interestingly, the authors reported that patients with anorexic histories were among the least improved. In the phenytoin to placebo sequence, the number of binge-eating episodes decreased during drug treatment; however, this improvement continued when the subjects were placed on placebo. This finding complicates the interpretation of the results. Five additional instances of phenytoin treatment of bulimia have appeared, all unsuccessful (Greenway, Dahms, & Brag, 1977; Weiss & Levitz, 1976).

All the studies reported suffer from two fundamental problems. Foremost, the sample sizes are small, which prevents more sophisticated data analysis that would yield important information regarding characteristics of responders and nonresponders among the patients in the different treatment conditions. Secondly, the posttreatment follow-up periods are too short to adequately assess the effectiveness of the various treatment strategies. Despite methodological limitation, it is important to note that preliminary reports suggest that a variety of treatment interventions appear to be useful in the treatment of bulimia. These findings contradict early clinical observations that bulimia was a tenaciously intractable disorder.

Bulimia Versus Anorexia Nervosa

Bulimia has long been recognized as one aspect of the disordered eating habits of anorexia nervosa patients. Meyer (1961) and Dally (1969) first attended to phenotypic differences between anorexics who maintain subnormal body weights by rigidly controlled intake (typically referred to as "starvers" or "restrictors") and anorexics who manifested eating patterns characterized by binge eating episodes followed by the use of evacuation techniques, such as self-induced vomiting and laxatives. Since these early reports, several investigators have indicated that the presence of bulimic symptoms does reflect a behavioral phenotype within anorexia nervosa that has prognostic, clinical, and etiological implications.

Incidence and Outcome

Basic descriptive studies have reported varying findings regarding the incidence of bulimia among anorexia nervosa patients. Several studies indicate that 44-55% of anorexia nervosa patients develop the symptoms of bulimia during the course of the disorder (Casper et al., 1980; Garfinkel et al., 1980; and Hsu, 1979). Other investigators have reported lower frequencies, including 16% (Theander, 1970) and 27% (Rollins & Piazza, 1978). Garfinkel and Garner (1982) have agreed with Crisp's (1980) observation that taking the different selecting biases among the different studies into consideration, it is reasonable to estimate that approximately 30% of anorexia nervosa patients manifest bulimic symptoms during the course of the disorder. The presence of bulimic symptoms among anorexics has also been demonstrated to be a poor prognostic indicator. Several investigations have indicated that bulimic anorexics experience a more chronic course to their illness than do restricting anorexics (Crisp, Kalucy, Lacey, & Harding, 1977; Garfinkel, Moldofsky, & Garner, 1977; Morgan & Russell, 1975; Hsu, 1979).

Clinical Characteristics

As a result of research that has occurred within the last decade, there appears to be an emerging consensus regarding some of the clinical characteristics that distinguish bulimic anorexics from restricting anorexics. Several investigations have shown that the bulimic symptoms generally develop with 1 or 1-1/2 years of the point when the patient began to diet (Dally, 1969; Russell, 1979; Garfinkel et al., 1980) and that, premorbidly, the bulimic anorexics had histories of obesity and were observed to have a higher incidence of stressful life events prior to the onset of the illness, in comparison to restricting anorexics (Strober, 1981). Interpersonally, bulimic anorexics have been found to be more sexually active (Beaumont,

1977; Beaumont, George & Smart, 1976; Casper et al., 1980; Garfinkel et al., 1980; Beaumont, Simpson, & Abraham, 1981) and more extroverted (Beaumont, 1977; Casper et al., 1980) than their restricting counterparts. Garfinkel and Garner (1982) have pointed out, however, that the natures of both the sexual and social relationships of the bulimic anorexics are most often experienced as being transient and nonsatisfying.

Standard indices of psychiatric symptoms have also differentiated between the two groups. In comparison to restricting anorexics, bulimic anorexics have been found to be more depressed (Casper et al., 1980; Strober, 1981), to have more labile moods (Garfinkel et al., 1980), to be more anxious (Stonehill & Crisp, 1977), and to have more somatic complaints (Casper, 1980). Palazzoli (1974) has reported finding more serious thought and communication disorder among bulimic anorexics. Casper, Eckert, Halmi, Goldberg, and Davis (1980) have further demonstrated that patients who had daily bulimic episodes showed significantly elevated MMPI scores on the schizophrenia, depression, psychopathic deviant, paranoia, and psychasthenia subscales.

Impulse-related difficulties have also been found to differentiate bulimic anorexics from restricting anorexics. Bulimic anorexics have been found to have higher incidences of drug and alcohol use (Casper et al., 1980; Garfinkel et al., 1980), histories of compulsive stealing (usually food items) (Casper et al., 1980; Garfinkel et al., 1980), and more suicide attempts and reports of self-inflicted injuries (Casper et al., 1980; Garfinkel et al., 1980).

Character Organization

Some early investigators attempted to identify personality types differing between bulimic and restricting anorexics. In a series of 31 anorexics, Beaumont, George, and Smart (1976) found bulimic anorexics to have more histrionic personalities than restrictors and that both groups scored high on the Leighton Obsessional Inventory.

More recent inquiry has focused on whether bulimic anorexics in particular have borderline personality organizations. Garfinkel and Garner (1982) have offered a well-substantiated argument for a borderline diagnosis with bulimic anorexics. The evidence they cite for offering such a diagnosis includes impulse control difficulties, labile moods, sexual activity that is usually unpleasurable and that appears to be more an attempt at closeness, interpersonal relationships that fluctuate between intense dependency and transient superficiality, and brief, but repeated, depersonalization experiences. Garfinkel and Garner have wisely urged caution making a character diagnosis with anorexia nervosa patients, given that the usual age of the onset occurs during a maturational period in which character development is in flux.

Despite what appears to be a more disorganized and impulse-ridden personality style among bulimic anorexics, Strober et al., (1982) have found bulimic anorexics to be more psychologically minded and flexible on the California Personality Inventory.

Family Environment

In a series of studies, Strober and his colleagues (1981, 1982) identified several distinctions between bulimic and restricting anorexics' families. On the Family Environment Scale (Moos, 1974), bulimic anorexics' families were characterized as having higher levels of conflictual interactions and expressions of negativity among family members. In contrast, mutual support and concern (cohesiveness) and clarity of structure of rules and responsibilities (organization) were more strongly associated with restrictors' families. In addition, parents of bulimics reported higher marital discordance than parents of restrictors, and bulimic anorexics reported feeling more distant from both parents—particularly their fathers—than restrictors.

Several personality attributes on the MMPI were also found to differentiate parents of bulimics from parents of restrictors. Fathers of bulimics scored significantly higher on scales measuring general maladjustment, impulsivity, low frustration tolerance, hostility, activity level, and excitement (hypomania). In contrast, fathers of restrictors scored higher on scales assessing emotional sensitivity and passivity, and submissiveness and withdrawal from social interactions (social introversion).

Mothers of bulimic anorexics were also distinguished from mothers of restrictors. Mothers of bulimics scored significantly higher on scales measuring psychosomatic preoccupation (hypochondriasis) and depression. Mothers of restrictors obtained higher scores on masculinity-femininity, social introversion, and phobia content scales, indicating they had more neurotic fears and anxieties. On the content scales of the MMPI, both mothers and fathers of bulimics scored significantly higher in the family problems and hostility scales, indicating greater intrafamilial disturbance and a lesser degree of inner control. When a multiple regression analysis was performed, maternal depression and paternal impulse disturbance and depression were found to be predictive of greater severity of bulimia among the patients.

Family Psychiatric Morbidity

In an effort to further articulate familial differences between bulimic and restricting anorexics, Strober (1981) explored the prevalence of psychiatric disorders among first- and second-degree relatives. His findings indicated that relatives of bulimic and anorexics have a much greater liability to affective disorder than either restricting anorexics or the general population. Furthermore, maternal affective disorder was far more prevalent for the bulimic anorexics. Overall, the familial prevalence for affective disorder, considering both first- and second-degree relatives, was 13% for bulimics and 6% for restrictors. The raw prevalences were equivalent to morbid risk for affective disorder of 20% in bulimic families, compared to 9% in restrictor families (the estimated morbid risk factor in the general population is 6%). It was also noted that when bipolar illness could be identified, it more frequently affected the relative of a bulimic patient. Histories of alcoholism also differentiated the two groups. Pooling across first- and second-degree relatives, the overall rate of alcoholism among relatives of bulimics equaled 18%, compared to 8% in relatives of restrictors. Alcoholism was three times more prevalent in fathers of bulimics than fathers of restrictors.

In reviewing the biological, familial, and psychological characteristics of anorexia nervosa patients who manifest bulimic symptoms, one is struck by the similarity to the clinical picture of bulimics at normal weight and by the differences from the restricting anorexics. These findings raise significant questions about whether information regarding cognitions and behavior related to disturbed *eating* patterns have more diagnostic utility than information related to *weight* patterns. Clearly, more research comparing biological, familial, and personality variables across weight categories is necessary to further articulate the similarities and differences between the groups.

Concluding Remarks

The task of the current chapter has been to review the extent of our data-based knowledge regarding the syndrome of bulimia among patients at normal weight and those with anorexia nervosa. The prevalence studies indicate that bulimia is a significant problem, with an incidence rate of approximately 5% among adolescent and young adult women. Furthermore, between 30-50% of patients with anorexia nervosa develop the symptoms of bulimia during the course of the disorder. An etiological model has been proposed that synthesizes available data, indicating that young women who are at risk for developing bulimia appear to have a biological vulnerability to affective instability, family environments that are conflictful and disorganized, and a variety of personality traits that result in low self-esteem and self-regulatory difficulties. It has been further proposed that a sociocultural milieu has emerged that has suggested to young women that the achievement of thinness offers a remedy for self-esteem difficulties. Binge eating has been presented as a counter-regulatory reaction to prolonged caloric restriction (dieting in the pursuit of thinness). Finally, the variety of psychological adaptations the binge-purge cycle could serve has been reviewed. A review of the treatment literature has indicated that although most of the studies were quite preliminary, encouraging results have been found using response prevention, cognitive behavioral and group interventions, and antidepressant pharmacotherapy. The multidetermined nature of bulimia and the variety of adaptations the behavior can serve is striking. Future research, it is hoped, will enhance our understanding of the relative contributions and interactive effects of each of the various factors presented.

References

American Psychiatric Association. (1980). *Task force on nomenclature and statistics. Diagnostic and statistical manual of mental disorders* (3rd ed.). Washington DC: Author.

Ahola, S. (1982). Unexplained parotid enlargement. A clue to occult bulimia. *Connecticut Medicine, 46*, 185-186.

Allon, N. (1975). Latent social services in group dieting. *Social Problems, 32*, 59-69.

Bardwick, J. (1971). *Psychology of women: A study of bio-cultural conflicts.* New York: Harper & Row.

Beaumont, P.S.V. (1977). Further categorization of patients with anorexia nervosa. *Australian and New Zealand Journal of Psychiatry, 11*, 223-226.

Beaumont, P.J.V., George, G.C.W., & Smart, D.E. (1976). Dieters and vomiters and purgers in anorexia nervosa. *Psychological Medicine, 6*, 617-622.

Beaumont, P.J.V., Simpson, K.G., & Abraham, S.F. (1981). The psychosexual histories of adolescent girls and young women with anorexia nervosa. *Psychological Medicine, 11*(1), 131-140.

Boskind-Lodahl, M. (1976). Cinderella's stepsisters: A feminist perspective on anorexia nervosa and bulimia. *Journal of Women in Culture and Society, 2*, 342-356.

Brotman, A., Herzog, P., & Woods, S. (1984). Antidepressant treatment of bulimia: The relationship between binging and depressive symptomatology. *Journal of Clinical Psychiatry, 45*(1), 7-9.

Bruch, H. (1973). *Eating disorders: Obesity, anorexia nervosa, and the person within.* New York: Basic Books.

Canning, H., & Mayer, J. (1966). Obesity—Its possible effect on college acceptance. *New England Journal of Medicine, 275*, 1172-1174.

Casper, R.C. (1983). On the emergence of bulimia nervosa as a syndrome: A historical view. *International Journal of Eating Disorders*, 2(3), 3-16.

Casper, R.C., Eckert, E.D., Halmi, K.A., Goldberg, S.C., & Davis, J.M. (1980). Bulimia: Its incidence and clinical significance in patients with anorexia nervosa. *Archives of General Psychiatry*, 37, 1030-1035.

Connors, M., Johnson, C., & Stuckey, M. (1984). Brief psychobehavioral group therapy. *American Journal of Psychiatry*, 141(2), 1512-151.

Crisp, A.H. (1980). *Anorexia nervosa: Let me be*. London: Academic Press.

Crisp, A.H. (1981). Anorexia nervosa at a normal weight! The abnormal weight control syndrome. *International Journal of Psychiatry in Medicine*, 11, 203-234.

Crisp, A.H., Fenton, G.W., & Strotton, L. (1968). A controlled study of the EEG in anorexia nervosa. *British Journal of Psychiatry*, 114, 1149-1169.

Crisp, A.H., Kalucy, R.S., Lacey, J.H., & Harding, B. (1977). Long-term prognosis in anorexia nervosa: Some factors predictive of outcome. In R.A. Vigersky (Ed.), *Anorexia nervosa* (pp. 55-66). New York: Raven Press.

Csikzentmihalyi, M., & Graef, R. (1980). The experience of freedom in daily experience. *American Journal of Community Psychology*, 8, 401-414.

Dally, P. (1969). *Anorexia nervosa*. New York: Grune & Stratton.

Davis, K.L., Qualls, B., Hollister, L., & Stunkard, A.J. (1974). EEG's of "binge eaters." *American Journal of Psychiatry*, 19, 331-335.

Fairburn, C.G. (1981). A cognitive behavioral approach to the treatment of bulimia. *Psychological Medicine*, 11, 707-711.

Fairburn, C.G. (1982). Binge eating and its management. *British Journal of Psychiatry*, 141, 631-633.

Fairburn, C.G., & Cooper, P.J. (1982). Self-induced vomiting and bulimia nervosa: An undetected problem. *British Medical Journal*, 284, 1153-1155.

Fat execs get slimmer paychecks. (1974). *Industry Week*, 180, 21, 24.

Frisch, R.E. (1983). Fatness and reproduction: Delayed menarche and amenorrhea of ballet dancers and college athletes. In P.L. Darby, P.E. Garfinkel, D.M. Garner, & D.V. Coscina (Eds.), *Anorexia nervosa: Recent developments* (pp. 343-363). New York: Alan R. Liss.

Gallo, L., & Randel, A. (1981). Chronic vomiting and its effect on the primary dentition: Report of a case. *Journal of Dentition Child*, 48, 383-384.

Garfinkel, P.E., & Garner, D.M. (1982). *Anorexia nervosa: A multidimensional perspective*. New York: Brunner, Mazel.

Garfinkel, P.E., Moldofsky, H., & Garner, D.M. (1977). The outcome of anorexia nervosa: Significance of clinical features, body image, and behavior modification. In R.A. Vigersky (Ed.), *Anorexia nervosa* (pp. 315-330). New York: Raven Press.

Garfinkel, P.E., Moldofsky, H., & Garner, D.M. (1980). The heterogeneity of anorexia nervosa: Bulimia as a distinct subgroup. *Archives of General Psychiatry*, **37**, 1036-1040.

Garner, D.M., & Bemis, K. (1982). A cognitive behavioral approach to anorexia nervosa. *Cognitive Therapy Research*, **6**, 123-150.

Garner, D.M., Garfinkel, P.E., & Olmsted, M. (1983). An overview of sociocultural factors in the development of anorexia nervosa. In P.L. Darby, P.E. Garfinkel, D.M. Garner, & D.V. Coscina (Eds.), *Anorexia nervosa: Recent developments in research* (pp. 65-82). New York: Alan R. Liss.

Garner, D.M., Garfinkel, P.E., & O'Shaughnessy, M. (1983). Clinical and psychometric comparison between bulimia in anorexia and bulimia in normal-weight women. *Report of the Fourth Ross Conference on Medical Research* (pp. 6-13). Columbus, OH: Ross Laboratories.

Garner, D.M., Rockert, W., Olmsted, M.P., Johnson, C., & Coscina, D.V. (1984). Psychoeducational principles in the treatment of bulimia and anorexia nervosa. In D.M. Garner & P.E. Garfinkel (Eds.), *A handbook of psychotherapy for anorexia and bulimia* (pp. 513-572). New York: Guilford Press.

Glassman, A.H., & Walsh, B.T. (1983). Link between bulimia and depression unclear. *Journal of Clinical Psychopharmacology*, **3**, 203.

Glucksman, M.L., & Hirsch, L. (1969). The response of obese patients to weight reduction. *Psychosomatic Medicine*, **31**, 1-7.

Goldblatt, P.B., Moore, M.E., & Stunkard, A.J. (1965). Social factors in obesity. *Journal of the American Medical Association*, **192**, 1039-1044.

Goodsitt, A. (1983). Self-regulatory disturbances in eating disorders. *International Journal of Eating Disorders*, **2**(3), 51-60.

Goodsitt, A. (1984). Self-psychology and the treatment of anorexia nervosa. In D.M. Garner & P.E. Garfinkel (Eds.), *A handbook of psychotherapy for anorexia nervosa and bulimia* (pp. 55-82). New York: Guilford Press.

Green, R.S., & Rau, J.H. (1974). Treatment of compulsive eating disturbances with anticonvulsant medication. *American Journal of Psychiatry*, **131**, 428-432.

Green, R.S., & Rau, J.H. (1977). The use of diphenylhydantoin in compulsive eating disorder: Further studies. In R.A. Vigersky (Ed.), *Anorexia nervosa* (pp. 377-382). New York: Raven Press.

Greenway, F.L., Dahms, W.T., & Brag, D.A. (1977). Phenytoin as a treatment of obesity associated with compulsive eating. *Current Therapeutic Research*, **21**, 338-342.

Gwirtsman, H.E., Roy-Byrne, H.E., & Yager, J. (1983). Neuroendocrine abnormalities in bulimia. *American Journal of Psychiatry*, **140**, 559-663.

Halmi, K.A., Falk, J.R., & Schwartz, E. (1981). Binge eating and vomiting: A survey of a college population. *Psychological Medicine*, **11**, 697-706.

Hasler, J. (1982). Parotid enlargement. A presenting sign in anorexia nervosa. *Oral Surgery, Oral Medicine, Oral Pathology*, **53**, 567-573.

Herman, C.P., & Mack, D. (1975). Restrained and unrestrained eating. *Journal of Personality*, **43**, 647-660.

Herman, C.P., & Polivy, J. (1980). Restrained eating. In A.J. Stunkard (Ed.), *Obesity* (pp. 208-225). Philadelphia: W.B. Saunders.

Herzog, D.B. (1982). Bulimia: The secretive syndrome. *Psychosomatics*, **23**(5), 481-487.

Herzog, F.S., & Kaufman, A. (1981). Vomiting and parotid enlargement. *Southern Medical Journal*, **74**(2), 251.

Hollingshead, A.B. (1957). *Two factor index of social position.* (Available from author, 1965 Yale Station, New Haven, CT.)

How you can control your weight. (1979). Pamphlet available from Metropolitan Life, One Madison Avenue, New York. Originally published 1959.

Hudson, J.I., Laffer, P.S., & Pope, H.G., Jr. (1982). Bulimia related to affective disorder by family and response to the deamethasone suppression test. *American Journal of Psychiatry*, **137**, 695-698.

Hudson, J.I., Pope, H.G., Jonas, J.M., & Yurgelund, T.D. (1983). Family history study of anorexia nervosa and bulimia. *British Journal of Psychiatry*, **142**, 133-138.

Humphrey, L.L. (1984a). *Family relations in bulimic-anorexic and nondistressed families.* Manuscript submitted for publication.

Humphrey, L.L. (1984b). *A comparison of bulimic-anorexic and nondistressed family processes using structural analysis of social behavior.* Manuscript submitted for publication.

Humphrey, L.L., Apple, R., & Kirschenbaum, D.S. (1984). Differentiating bulimic-anorexic from normal families using an interpersonal and a behavioral observation system. Manuscript submitted for publication.

Hsu, L. (1979). Outcome of anorexia nervosa. *Archives of General Psychiatry*, **37**, 1041-1046.

Johnson, C.L., & Berndt, D.J. (1983). Preliminary investigation of bulimia and life adjustment. *American Journal of Psychiatry*, **140**(6), 774-777.

Johnson, C., Connors, M., & Stuckey, M. (1983). Short-term group treatment of bulimia. A preliminary report. *International Journal of Eating Disorders*, **2**(4), 199-208.

Johnson, C., & Flach, R.A. (1985). *Family characteristics of bulimia and normal women—A comparative study.* Manuscript submitted for publication.

Johnson, C.L., & Larson, R. (1982). Bulimia: An analysis of moods and behavior. *Psychosomatic Medicine*, **44**(4), 333-345.

Johnson, C.L., Lewis, C., Love, S., Lewis, L., & Stuckey, M. (1984). Incidence and correlates of bulimic behavior in a female high school population. *Journal of Youth and Adolescence*, **13**, 15-26.

Johnson, C.L., Lewis, C., Love, S., Stuckey, M., & Lewis, L. (1983). A descriptive survey of dieting and bulimic behavior in a female high school population. *Report of the Fourth Ross Conference on Medical Research* (pp. 14-18).

Johnson, C.L., & Maddi, K. (1985). The Etiology of bulimia: A biosycho-social perspective. *The Annals of Adolescent Psychiatry*, **13**, 253-273.

Johnson, C.L., Stuckey, M.K., Lewis, L.D., & Schwartz, D.M. (1982). Bulimia. A descriptive survey of 316 cases. *International Journal of Eating Disorders*, **2**(1), 3-18.

Johnson, C.L., Stuckey, M., & Mitchell, J. (1983). Psychopharmacological treatment of anorexia nervosa and bulimia: Review and synthesis. *Journal of Nervous and Mental Disease*, **171**(9), 524-534.

Jonas, J.M., Pope, H.G., Jr., & Hudson, J.I. (1983). Treatment of bulimia with MAO inhibitors. *Journal of Clinical Psychopharmacology*, **3**, 59-60.

Katz, J.L., Kuperberg, A., Pollack, C.P., Walsh, B.T., Zumoff, B., & Werner, H. (1984). Is there a relationship between eating disorder and affective disorder? New evidence from sleep recordings. *American Journal of Psychiatry*, **141**(6), 753-759.

Keesy, R.E. (1980). A set point analysis of the regulation of body weight. In A.J. Stunkard (Ed.), *Obesity*. Philadelphia: W.B. Saunders.

Keesy, R.E. (1983). A hypothalamic syndrome of body weight regulation at reduced levels. In *Understanding anorexia nervosa and bulimia. Report of the Fourth Ross Conference on Medical Research* (pp. 60-66). Columbus, OH: Ross Laboratories.

Kenny, F.T., & Solyom, L. (1971). The treatment of compulsive vomiting through faradic disruption of mental images. *Canadian Medical Journal*, **105**, 1072-1073.

Keys, A., Brozek, J., Henschel, A., Mickelsen, O., & Taylor, H.L. (1950). *The biology of human starvation* (Vol. 1). Minneapolis: University of Minnesota Press.

Kohut, Heinz. (1971). *The analysis of the self*. New York: International Universities Press.

Kirschbaum, W.R. (1951). Excessive hunger as a symptom of cerebral origin. *Journal of Nervous and Mental Disease*, **113**, 95-114.

Lacey, J.H. (1983). Bulimia nervosa, binge eating, and psychogenic vomiting: A controlled treatment study and long term outcome. *British Medicine Journal*, **286**(6378), 1609-1613.

Lacey, J.H. (1982). The bulimic syndrome at normal body weight: Reflections on pathogenesis and clinical features. *International Journal of Eating Disorders*, **2**(1), 59-66.

Larkin, J.E., & Pines, H.A. (1979). No fat persons need apply. *Sociology of Work and Occupations*, **6**, 312-327.

Lewis, L., & Johnson, C. (in press). A comparison of sex-role orientation between women with bulimia and normal controls. *International Journal of Eating Disorders*.

Loro, A.D., & Orleans, C.S. (1981). Binge eating in obesity—Preliminary findings and guidelines for behavioral analysis and treatment. *Addictive Behaviors*, **6**(2), 155-166.

Love, S., Ollendick, T. H., Johnson, C.L., Schlesinger, S.E. (in press). A preliminary report of the prediction of bulimic behaviors: A social learning analysis. *Bulletin of Psychologist in Addictive Behaviors.*

Mayer, J. (1968). *Overweight: Causes, cost and control.* Englewood Cliffs, NJ: Prentice-Hall.

Meger, J.E. (1961). The anorexia nervosa syndrome: Catamnestic research. *Archives Psychiat. Nervenkr.*, **202**, 31-59.

Mendels, J. (1983). Eating disorders and antidepressants. *Journal of Clinical Psychopharmacology*, **3**, 59-60.

Meyer, J.E. (1961). The anorexia nervosa syndrome: Catamnestic research. *Archives Psychiat. Nervenkr.*, **202**, 31-59.

Mitchell, J., & Bantle, J. (1983). Metabolic and endocrine investigations in women of normal weight with the bulimia syndrome. *Biological Psychiatry*, **18**(3), 355-365.

Mitchell, J.E., Eckert, E.D., & Pyle, R.L. (1981). Frequency and duration of binge eating episodes in patients with bulimia. *American Journal of Psychiatry*, **138**(6), 835-836.

Mitchell, J.E., & Pyle, R. (1982). *Electrolyte abnormalities in patients with bulimia.* Unpublished manuscript.

Mitchell, J.E., Pyle, R.L., & Miner, R.A. (1982). Gastric dilation as a complication of bulimia. *Psychosomatics*, **23**, 96-99.

Moos, R. (1974). *Family environment scale manual.* Palo Alto, CA: Consulting Psychologists Press.

Morgan, H.G., & Russell, G.F. (1975). Value of family background and clinical features as predictors of long-term outcome in anorexia nervosa: Four-year follow-up study of 41 patients. *Psychological Medicine*, 355-372.

Mrosovsky, N., & Powley, T.L. (1977). Set points for body weight and fat. *Behavioral Biology*, **20**, 205-223.

Nisbett, R.E. (1972). Eating behavior and obesity in men and animals. *Advances in Psychosomatic Medicine*, **7**, 173-193.

Ordman, A.M., & Kirschenbaum, D.S. (1984). *Bulimia: Assessment of eating, psychological, and familial characteristics.* Manuscript submitted for publication.

Norman, D.K., & Herzog, D.B. (1983). Bulimia, anorexia nervosa, and anorexia nervosa with bulimia: A comparative analysis of MMPI profiles. *International Journal of Eating Disorders*, **2**(2), 43-52.

Palazzoli, M.S. (1974). *Self-starvation.* (A. Pomerans, Trans.). London: Chaucer.

Palmer, R.L. (1979). The dietary chaos syndrome: A useful new term? *British Journal of Medical Psychology*, **52**, 187-190.

Pope, H.G., Jr., & Hudson, J.I. (1982). Treatment of bulimia with anti-depressants. *Psychopharmacology*, **78**, 176-179.

Pope, H.G., Hudson, J.I., Jonas, J.M., & Yurgelund, D. (1983). Bulimia treated with imipramine: A placebo-controlled, double-blind study. *American Journal of Psychiatry*, **140**(5), 554-558.

Pyle, R.L., Mitchell, J.E., & Eckert, E.D. (1981). Bulimia: a report of 34 cases. *Journal of Clinical Psychiatry*, **42**(2), 60-64.

Pyle, R.L., Mitchell, J.E., Eckert, E.E., & Halvorson, P.A. (1983). The incidence of bulimia in freshman college students. *International Journal of Eating Disorders*, **2**(3), 75-85.

Rau, J.H., & Green, R.S. (1978). Soft neurologic correlates of compulsive eating. *Journal of Nervous and Mental Disorders*, **166**, 435-437.

Rau, J.H., Struve, F.A., & Green, R.S. (1979). Electroencephalographic correlates of compulsive eating. *Clinical Electroencephalography*, **10**, 180-188.

Remick, R.A., Jones, M.W., & Compos, P.E. (1980). Postictal bulimia [letter to the editor]. *Journal of Clinical Psychiatry*, **41**, 26.

Roe, D.A., & Eickwort, K.R. (1976). Relationships between obesity and associated health factors with unemployment among low income women. *Journal of the American Medical Women's Association*, **31**, 193-204.

Rollins, N., & Piazza, E. (1978). Diagnosis of anorexia nervosa: A critical reappraisal. *Journal of the American Academy of Child Psychiatry*, **17**, 126-137.

Rose, D.A., & Eickwort, K.R. (1976). Relationships between obesity and associated health factors with unemployment among low income women. *Journal of the American Medical Women's Association*, **31**, 193-204.

Rosen, J.C., & Leitenberg, H. (1982). Bulimia nervosa: Treatment with exposure and response prevention. *Behavior Therapy*, **13**, 117-124.

Rowland, C.V. (1970). Anorexia nervosa: A survey of the literature and review of 30 cases. *International Psychiatric Clinics*, **7**, 37-137.

Russell, G. (1979). Bulimia nervosa: An ominous variant of anorexia nervosa. *Psychological Medicine*, **9**, 429-448.

Sabine, E.J., Yonace, A., Farrington, A.J., Barratt, K.H., & Wakeling, A. (1983). Bulimia nervosa: A placebo-controlled therapeutic trial of mianersin. *British Journal of Clinical Pharmacology*, **15**, 195S-202S.

Saul, S., Dekker, A., & Watson, C. (1981). Acute gastric dilatation with infarction and perforation. Case report. *GUT*, **22**, 978-983.

Schneider, J.A., & Agras, W. (in press). A cognitive behavioral group treatment of bulimia. *British Journal of Psychiatry*.

Schwartz, D.M., Thompson, M.G., & Johnson, C. (1982). Anorexia nervosa and bulimia: The sociocultural context. *International Journal of Eating Disorders*, **1**(3) 23-25.

Staffieri, J.R. (1967). A study of social stereotype of body image in children. *Journal of Personality and Social Psychology*, **7**, 101-104.

Staffieri, J.R. (1972). Body build and behavior expectancies in young females. *Developmental Psychology,* **6**, 125-127.

Stonehill, E., & Crisp, A.H. (1977). Psychoneurotic characteristics of patients with anorexia nervosa before and after treatment and at follow-up 4-7 years later. *Journal of Psychosomatic Research,* **21**, 187-193.

Strangler, R.S., & Printz, A.M. (1980). DSM-III: Psychiatric diagnosis in a university population. *American Journal of Psychiatry,* **137**, 937-940.

Strober, M. (1981). The significance of bulimia in juvenile anorexia nervosa: An explanation of possible etiolgical factors. *International Journal of Eating Disorders,* **1**(1), 28-43.

Strober, M., Salkin, B., Burroughs, J., & Marrell, W. (1982). Validity of the bulimia-restrictor distinction in anorexia nervosa. Parental personality characteristics and family psychiatric morbidity. *Journal of Nervous and Mental Disease,* **170**(6), 345-351.

Stuckey, M.K., & Johnson, C.L. (1984). *Bulimia among normal weight women: A manifestation of learned helplessness?* Manuscript submitted for publication.

Stunkard, A. (1959). Obesity and the denial of hunger. *Psychosomatic Medicine,* **21**, 281-289.

Theander, S. (1970). Anorexia nervosa: A psychiatric investigation of 94 female patients. *Acta Psychiatrica Scandinavica Supplementum 214* (pp. 14-26). Copenhagen: Munksgaard.

Walsh, T., Stewart, J., Wright, L., Harrison, W., Roose, S.P., & Glassman, A. (1982). A treatment of bulimia with monoamine oxidase inhibitors. *American Journal of Psychiatry,* **139**(12), 1629-1630.

Wardle, J., & Beinhart, H. (1981). Binge eating: A theoretical review. *British Journal of Clinical Psychology,* **20**, 97-109.

Weisman, M.M., Drusoff, B.A., Thompson, W.D., Harding, P.S., & Meyers, J.K. (1978). Social adjustment by self-report in a community sample and in psychiatric outpatients. *Journal of Nervous and Mental Disease,* **166**, 317-326.

Weiss, T., & Levitz, L. (1976). Diphenylhydantoin treatment of bulimia [letter to the editor]. *American Journal of Psychiatry,* **133**, 1093.

Wermuth, B.M., Davis, K.L., Hollister, L.E., & Stunkard, A.J. (1977). Phenytoin treatment of the binge-eating syndrome. *American Journal of Psychiatry,* **134**, 1249-1253.

Wijesinghe, B. (1973). Massed electrical aversion treatment of compulsive eating. *Journal of Behavior Therapy and Experimental Psychiatry,* **4**, 133-135.

Wooley, S., & Wooley, O. (1979). Obesity and women: I. A closer look at the facts. *Women's Studies International Quarterly,* **2**, 69-79.

Chapter 14

The Major Complications Associated With Eating Disorders and Their Pathophysiology

John N. Stephenson
Elizabeth S. Ohlrich

Eating disorders have been of interest to the medical profession for at least the past several centuries. Today we are inclined to roughly categorize as having anorexia nervosa those patients who have an intense fear of obesity, a disturbed body image, and who pursue thinness regardless of their emaciated state. A companion syndrome known as bulimia consists of an uncontrollable food craving that leads to gorging, followed by self-induced purging.

In the course of the elucidation of any disease, its pathophysiology is ordinarily defined long after its description and natural history have been established. With respect to the eating disorders, this has been a confusing, drawn-out, and highly conflictual process. Even the term *anorexia nervosa* is a misnomer because loss of appetite is experienced by no more than half of patients ill enough to require hospitalization, according to one study (Halmi, Brodland, & Rigas, 1975). Similarly, bulimia, which means "ox hunger," is infrequently associated with hunger during the planning or binging phase of the disorder.

Historical Overview

More than a century ago, Lesegue and Gull described anorexia nervosa and emphasized its psychological origins and absence of somatic pathology (Gull, 1874; Lasegue, 1873). Gull further noted the occasional presence of voracious appetite and uncontrolled eating behavior.

The concept of a psychological etiology was seriously challenged when in 1914 Simmons, a pathologist, reported destructive lesions in the pituitary gland of an emaciated woman who had died following delivery (Simmons, 1914). Thereafter, cases of otherwise unexplainable emaciation were thought to be the result of endocrine dysfunction. The legacy of this period remains with us to this day, for contemporary research and publications continue to address complications and their pathophysiology, rather than the formulation of a more unifying etiology.

Since the 1960s, with reports based on larger patient groups, a true anorexia nervosa syndrome has emerged. The intrapsychic theories of Bruch and Palazzoli and the family systems approach by Minuchin and colleagues have added a richness to an already impressive, but still incomplete, understanding of this disorder (Bruch, 1973; Minuchin, Rosman, & Baker, 1978; Palazzoli; 1974).

Bulimia has been classified as a distinct disorder only since 1980, when it was entered into APA's *Diagnostic and Statistical Manual* of Mental Disorders (DSM-III). In the preceding decade, the binge-purge syndrome had been identified as occurring in increasingly alarming numbers among women, and less frequently among men, of normal weight and often not in association with a previous history of anorexia nervosa or obesity (Boskind-Lodahl, 1976).

Etiology

The etiology of eating disorders is an area of intense investigation and theorization at present. Although there is considerable overlap in the eating disorders, they are distinct syndromes. There is no proof of any simple somatic or psychological etiology. The possibility that the medial hypothalamus, the locus of a neurochemical system believed to stimulate appetite and weight gain, may be directly linked to symptoms of anorexia nervosa is supported only by animal studies at the present time (Leibowitz, 1983). On the other hand, considerable attention is now being focused on the possible connection between the bulimia and bipolar depression. The bulimic is commonly depressed, and Hudson et al. have pointed out that 22% of the relatives of their bulimic patients had affective disorders, compared to 10% of relatives of normal control probands (Hudson, Laffer, & Pope, 1982).

It is essential to approach eating disorders patients from a combined biopsychosocial perspective, whether or not the patients have any one or a combination of the following: a biological vulnerability resting within the hypothalamus; an unusual psychological response to malnutrition or binge-purge behavior; or a malady significantly interrelated to depression, as is thought to be the case in bulimia. This has important ramifications not only in the current clinical management of these patients but also for productive research in this field.

For example, a currently popular clinical and research question is why one-third of anorexic women develop their secondary amenorrhea before the onset of any weight loss. If the weight loss cannot always account for reduction in plasma estradiol levels, serum luteinizing hormone (LH), and follicle-stimulating hormone (FSH), then perhaps one might wish to consider the hyperactivity of some of these patients or their high levels of emotional distress (Gwirtsman, Roy-Byrne, Yager, & Gerner, 1983). Endorphins and, subsequently, prolactin levels are sometimes elevated in these persons. Prolactin may in turn suppress LH and FSH, with resulting low levels of estradiol. Research findings are contradictory in this area. Although many of the details of this phenomenon remain to be delineated, the blending of psychosocial and organic issues is useful to the health professional when generating a differential diagnosis to account for the multitude of symptoms and signs that an eating disorder patient may manifest.

Diagnostic Criteria and Description

Adolescent and young adult women account for 90-95% of all anorexia nervosa patients. However, older females, as well as males, in a wide age range also have the disorder. The first research criteria were formulated by Feighner et al. in 1972 and are still widely used. The diagnosis is usually made by fulfilling the criteria in the revised third edition of the *Diagnostic and Statistical Manual* (DSM-IIIR) of the American Psychiatric Association (1987), which include the following:

1. Refusal to maintain body weight over a minimal normal weight for age and height, e.g., weight loss leading to maintenance of body weight 15% below that expected; or failure to make expected weight gain during period of growth, leading to body weight 15% below that expected
2. Intense fear of gaining weight or becoming fat, even though underweight
3. Disturbance in the way in which one's body weight, size, or shape is experienced, e.g., the person claims to "feel fat" even when

emaciated, believes that one area of the body is "too fat" even
when obviously underweight

4. In females, absence of at least three consecutive menstrual cycles
   when otherwise expected to occur (primary or secondary amenorrhea). (A woman is considered to have amenorrhea if her periods occur only following hormone, e.g., estrogen, administration)
   (American Psychiatric Association, 1987, p. 67)

The original Feighner criteria included that at least two of the following
medical manifestations be present: amenorrhea, lanugo, bradycardia,
periods of overactivity, episodes of bulimia, and vomiting (often self-
induced). Based on the more recent DSM-IIIR criteria, there has been a
shift away from diagnosing anorexia nervosa by eliminating possible medical disorders and toward a diagnosis by positive identification on mental
status examination (Anderson, 1983). In a study at Johns Hopkins Hospital, no patient diagnosed as meeting the Feighner criteria for anorexia
nervosa was later found to have an underlying organic explanation
(Anderson, 1977). Increasingly, anorexia nervosa is being seen as a serious
psychosocial disorder. The relentless pursuit of a thin body in spite of
increasingly obvious emaciation is the key phenomenon and must be
present in order to firmly establish the diagnosis.

Bulimic patients have an uncontrollable food craving that leads to gorging, followed by attempts to avoid weight gain through self-induced
vomiting, laxative abuse, and other methods of purging. Bulimia has been
classified as a distinct disorder only since 1980, when it was entered into
the APA's Diagnostic and Statistical Manual of Mental Disorders (DSM-
III), with slight revisions in DSM-IIIR (see Table 1). In addition, a marked
increase in medical complications has occurred as a result of various behaviors practiced by these patients to maintain or reduce body weight
following binging episodes. These include self-induced vomiting, laxative
and enema abuse, and the consumption of diuretics or diet pills. Large
numbers of bulimic patients with potentially life-threatening complications
have required the services of physicians, nurses, clinical dietitians, social
workers, occupational therapists, and psychotherapists for assessment
and management.

The overlap between these two disorders is well demonstrated in a
study by Casper et al. (Casper, Eckert, Halmi, Goldberg, & Davis, 1980).
They found that 47% of their anorectic patients were also bulimic, that
is, they engaged in periodic binge eating. Of these, 57% followed binges
with self-induced vomiting in order to control their weight. Boskind-
Lodahl, as noted earlier in this chapter, has drawn attention to large numbers of bulimic women of normal weight without a history of previous
anorexia nervosa or obesity (Boskind-Lodahl, 1976). At the present time,

Table 1   Diagnostic Criteria for Bulimia Nervosa

---

1. Recurrent episodes of binge eating (rapid consumption of a large amount of food in a discrete period of time).
2. A feeling of lack of control over eating behavior during the eating binges.
3. The person regularly engages in either self-induced vomiting, use of laxatives or diuretics, strict dieting or fasting, or vigorous exercise in order to prevent weight gain.
4. A minimum average of two binge eating episodes a week for at least three months.
5. Persistent overconcern with body shape and weight.

Note. From *Diagnostic and Statistical Manual of Mental Disorders* (3rd ed. rev., pp. 68-69) by the American Psychiatric Association, 1987, Washington, DC. Copyright 1987 by The American Psychiatric Association. Reprinted by permission.

bulimia appears to be a less specific disorder than anorexia nervosa. Further clarification of its diagnostic criterion will no doubt be undertaken in this decade.

The diagnosis of an eating disorder can be made considerably more difficult by the patient's efforts to conceal her weight loss, vomiting, or other purging behavior and its associated symptoms. The anorexic who is exercising excessively to enhance her pursuit of thinness may first present with an overuse syndrome to an orthopedic surgeon or with amenorrhea to her gynecologist. A bulimic of normal weight but with a presenting complaint of dizziness, fainting, or irregular heart rate may require her physician to exhaust the impressive list of disorders that must be included in the differential diagnosis of these complaints.

Covert disorders and chronic wasting diseases, such as an early tumor in the region of the hypothalamus, Addison's disease, inflammatory or malabsorptive bowel disease, and tuberculosis, are always possibilities, as are unusual conditions that include hyperphagia, such as the Kleine-Levin or Kluver-Bucy syndromes. An additional dilemma for the physician is the bulimic diabetic who regularly goes without her insulin as a means of weight control. The list is long and impressive. Unless the health professional includes a detailed psychosocial history in his or her assessment and thinks in terms of a possible eating disorder, the diagnosis will be delayed. With the recent increase in public attention given to these disorders, it is not unusual for parents, school guidance counselors, coaches, school nurses, dance and aerobic exercise instructors, dental hygienists, and even peers to suggest the diagnosis before the girl is seen by her physician.

Medical Assessment

The initial assessment of a patient who may be suffering from an eating disorder should include a general comprehensive history, detailed psychosocial and eating disorder information, physical examination, and appropriate laboratory tests. It is essential that the patient and her family appreciate the equal emphasis being given to both the psychological and organic components of the evaluation. Laboratory procedures such as EEG, skull films, or CAT scan are rarely indicated when the patient is cooperative and the clinical picture is consistent with DSM-IIIR profile for either anorexia nervosa or bulimia. If the history is atypical, if neurological or other signs of underlying organic disease are present, or if in time the illness begins to take an unexpected course, it becomes prudent to assess the patient in more detail. Exhaustive, invasive, and expensive laboratory tests also have a tendency to lead the patient and her family to suspect that something organic must be seriously wrong, if only the doctor were "good enough" to find out what it is. Finally, it is important to make the distinction between complications that develop secondarily to food refusal or purging activities, and those of an unrelated underlying disorder such as diabetes mellitus.

The family with an eating disorder is often a family in crisis. The identified patient may be in a state of denial, or angry and defiant, when first seen. Making her, rather than her parents, the primary historian allows for the development of transference and provides an opportunity for confidentiality. This not only allows the health professional the opportunity to address symbolically the separation of adolescent from parent but is of practical importance, for example, with the bulimic minor who is sexually active and in need of contraception.

Information gathered from the patient's parents or spouse is usually helpful and can be essential due to the frequent denial and manipulative behavior of the patient. In addition, establishing an early therapeutic alliance of all those concerned with the patient's well-being can be useful at a later date, for difficult times lie ahead for the "eating disorders family." For example, the anorexic's family will need to progress well beyond the point at which the patient must remain a "model" child and they a "model" family. Through family therapy, they will need to resolve the misbelief that if only this very frustrating and frightening anorexic behavior would be resolved, everything else would be all right for the patient and her family.

Figure 1 includes basic information on, as well as description of, the patient's eating behavior and significant related history. Figure 2 is primarily a review of family and past medical history and a systems review checksheet. It includes the data necessary for a comprehensive evaluation of the patient's basic health status, as well as potential side effects

Eating Disorders Program

Date _____

Name _____ Age _____ DOB _____

Referring Physician _____

Height _____ %ile _____ Ideal weight (from tables) _____

Weight _____ %ile _____ _____ _____ _____
        Current   Highest (date) Lowest (date)   Desired

History: Specific:

    Food restriction/dieting _____ Caffeine (coffee, tea, cola) _____

    Food-related hoarding _____ Sorbitol (sugar-free gum/candy) _

    Binging _____ Tobacco _____

    Vomiting _____ Alcohol _____

    Laxative use _____ Other drugs _____

    Diuretic use _____ Exercise _____

    Diet pills _____ Ipecac _____

    Enemas _____

    General:

Social
History: Employment:

    Living conditions:

    School:

    Parents' occupations:

    Family conflicts:

    Family finances:

    Sibs:

    Interests:

Figure 1. An initial assessment of an eating disorder patient.

they are prone to experience as a result of the various behavioral components and/or physical states of their condition.

The physical examination of an adolescent female with a suspected eating disorder (see Figure 3) does not include a routine pelvic examination any more often than for most young patients. However, if amenorrhea persists, if the patient is sexually active and in need of contraception, or if a primary gynecological disorder is suspected, a pelvic examination should be done at later date, following appropriate education regarding the procedure.

Laboratory tests are to be selectively ordered, as indicated by the patient's condition. They are generally obtained to determine the extent of

Family
History: Eating disorder _____ Drug abuse _____ ETOH _____ Asthma _____
Allergy _____ ↑BP _____ Heart disease _____ Stroke _____ Obesity _____
DM _____ Thyroid _____ Ulcers _____ Jaundice/liver _____ Kidney _____
Anemia _____ Other blood _____ Migraine HA _____
Seizures/epilepsy _____ Neuro _____ Psych _____ MR _____
Congenital _____ Cancer _____ Affective disorder _____

Past
Medical
History: Previous hospitalizations:

Chronic/recurrent illness:

Medications:

Allergies:

Review
of
Systems: Skin: Dryness _____, rashes/lesions _____, bruising/petechiae _____,
color Δ _____, nail Δ _____, acrocyanosis _____

Hair: Loss _____, texture Δ _____, distribution Δ _____, lanugo _____

Head: Headaches _____, dizziness _____, convulsions _____

Ears: Hearing _____, tinnitus _____, balance _____

Nose: Epistaxis _____, allergies _____, frequent colds _____, smell _____

Eyes: Vision _____, diplopia _____, dryness _____, loss of field _____,
night vision _____

Mouth: Yellowed teeth _____, caries _____, gums _____, tongue _____,
sores _____, dryness _____, "funny tastes" _____, tooth sensitivity _____,
voice change _____

Throat: Sore throat _____, dysphagia _____, parotid swelling _____

Neck: Stiff _____, swollen areas _____, tenderness _____, thyroid _____

Chest: SOB _____, productive cough _____, hemoptysis _____, pain _____

Heart: Palpitations _____, syncope _____

Breasts: Tenderness _____, Δs _____, lumps _____, discharge _____,
atrophy _____

Abdomen: Jaundice _____, hepatitis _____, ulcer _____, pain _____,
hematemesis _____, postprandial discomfort _____, bloating _____,
distension _____, early satiety _____, diarrhea _____, constipation _____,
regurgitation _____

Extremities: Cramps _____, weakness _____, numbness _____, spasm _____,
paresthesias _____, cold intolerance _____, edema _____

Genital: Menarche _____, periods _____, last 2 periods _____, BCP _____,
dyspareunia _____

Urinary: Polydipsia _____, polyuria _____, dysuria _____

Psych: Mood _____, crying _____, appetite _____, energy _____,
↓'d concentration _____, insomnia _____, restless sleep _____,
memory _____, friends _____, depression _____, suicidality _____,
sexuality (dating, interest in opposite sex) _____

Abnormal Findings:

Figure 2. A checklist of family history, medical history, and systems.

Physical
Exam: Supine BP ＿＿ HR ＿＿   Standing BP ＿＿ HR ＿＿

             Respir. Rate ＿＿ Weight ＿＿ Height ＿＿ Temp ＿＿

             Urine: Labstix^R Sp Grav ＿＿ pH ＿＿ Heme ＿＿ Gluc ＿＿
                    Ket ＿＿ Prot ＿＿

             General:

Hair	N	ABN	ND	Lungs	N	ABN	ND
Lanugo	N	ABN	ND	Heart	N	ABN	ND
Skin, nails	N	ABN	ND	Breasts	N	ABN	ND
Head	N	ABN	ND	Abdomen	N	ABN	ND
Ears	N	ABN	ND	Genitals	N	ABN	ND
Eyes	N	ABN	ND	Pelvic/rectal	N	ABN	ND
Field of vision	N	ABN	ND	(if indicated)			
Fundi	N	ABN	ND	Extremities	N	ABN	ND
Nose	N	ABN	ND	Pulses	N	ABN	ND
Mouth	N	ABN	ND	DTRs	N	ABN	ND
Teeth	N	ABN	ND	Sensory	N	ABN	ND
Throat	N	ABN	ND	Coordination	N	ABN	ND
Parotids	N	ABN	ND	Affect	N	ABN	ND
Neck	N	ABN	ND				
Thyroid	N	ABN	ND	Breast - Tanner Stage ＿＿＿			

                                              Genitalia -Tanner Stage ＿＿＿

             Abnormalities:

Assessment:

Laboratory
Tests: CBC ＿＿   Chem Survey ＿＿   UA ＿＿   ECG ＿＿
             Lytes ＿＿   Thryoid ＿＿   Misc: ＿＿＿＿＿＿

Plan:

             Therapy/recommendations:

             ＿＿＿＿＿＿＿＿＿＿＿＿＿＿＿＿＿ M.D. (Resident)
             ＿＿＿＿＿＿＿＿＿＿＿＿＿＿＿＿＿ M.D. (Staff)

Figure 3. A physical examination review sheet.

the sequelae, rather than the presence or absence of an eating disorder. In addition, when various physiological changes are observed, expensive and unnecessary medical investigations are frequently pursued to establish their etiology. If an eating disorder is at fault for the patient's metabolic aberrations, the abnormalities should revert to normal with nutritional rehabilitation and the discontinuation of purging behavior. Such a positive response to medical treatment would thereby eliminate the need for further tests and redirect the patient's attention to the complications being a consequence of her behavior and to the need for change through intensive psychotherapy.

Table 2   Summary of Major Complications Associated With Eating Disorders—Eating and Purge Behavior

Organ System Involved	Calorie Restriction	Binge Eating	Self-Induced Vomiting	Cathartic Abuse	Diuretic/Diet Pill Abuse
Cardiovascular/ pulmonary	Decreased myo- cardial function Heart failure ↓ H.R., ↓ B.P., ↓ C.O. Orthostatis Decreased Lt. vent. mass Arrhythmias during exercise— sudden death Acrocyanosis	Refeeding edema Heart failure, if marginal function	Orthostasis Arrhythmia c̄ ↓ K Adult respiratory distress syndrome Aspiration pneumonia Pneumomediasti- num and subcutaneous emphysema	Cardiomyopathy from emetine (ipecac) Hypokalemic cardiomyopathy Arrhythmia from ↓ K	Arrhythmia from ↓ K Hypertension Cerebral hemorrhage Myocardial injury with phenylpro- panolamine
Endocrine (hypothal-pit. axix)	↓ Metabolic rate 1°, 2° amenorrhea Infertility Breast atrophy Atrophic vaginitis Testicular atrophy Decreased libido				
Skin/hair	Alopecia Lanugo Petechiae Acrocyanosis Hyperpigmentation Hyperkeratosis Brittle nails Cold hands/feet		Calluses	Finger clubbing	
Hematologic	Bone marrow hypoplasia Leukopenia Complement ↓ Thrombocytopenia Anemia				
Gastrointestinal	Constipation Hemorrhoids Hypogeusia Early satiety Postprandial fullness Acute pancreatitis Delayed gastric emptying	Acute gastric dilation or rupture-death Pancreatitis Jejunal dilatation (nonobstruuctive)	Oral cavity trauma Dental enamel erosion c̄ tooth decay Pyorrhea Esophagitis/rupture Parotid hypertrophy Hematemesis Diaphragmatic hernia	Hypokalemic ileus; cathartic colon Mycosal injury— rectal bleeding	
Neurologic	Hypothermia Seizures-low BS Cerebral atrophy- CAT	EEG abnormalities	Seizures 2° to low Na if water loading	Tetany/seizures (↓ Ca, ↑ PO₄) Myenteric plexus injury	Delayed knee jerk Irritability Transient neuro- logical deficit, stroke, seizures
Bone/muscle	Overuse syndromes Osteoporosis/ fracture Muscle weakness Growth retardation		Muscle weakness	Muscle weakness ↓ K Toxic myopathy 2° to emetine	Muscle weakness
Nutritional abnormalities	Anemia Hypercarotenemia Hypervitaminosis A Starvation: ↓ calorie intake, ↓ protein ↑ low density lipoprotein Vitamin deficiency rare	Obesity		↓ Mg ↓ Ca ↑ PO₄ ↓ Absorption of fat soluble vitamins	↓ Mg ↓ K

(Cont.)

Renal/ electrolyte	↓ GFR ↑ BUN: renal Tubular dysfunction ↓ Xylose excretion Diabetes insipidus Nephrolithiasis Lytes usually normal; perhaps low Na and total body K		Metabolic alkalosis: ↓K, ↓ Cl, ↓ HCO_c, ↓H ↓ Na rare	↓ K, ↓ Na Kaliopenic-nephropathy	↓ K ↑ Na ↓ Mg
Edema	Rapid refeeding or rehydration	If starvation background Salt ingestion		May complicate edema Edema with cessation of laxative abuse	
Psychological	Depression Anxiety Suicide				Restlessness, anxiety, agitation, psychosis
		Binge-purge patients may suffer from impulsive behaviors: increased suicide attempts, possibly increased superficial sexual activity, alcohol and other drug abuse, shoplifting. Self-mutilation			

Garfinkel and Garner, and more recently Harris, have published comprehensive reviews of the physical complications resulting from various eating behaviors. Harris has categorized these complications according to the organ system affected or the individual behavioral components or physical states of anorexia nervosa and bulimia (Garfinkel & Garner, 1982; Harris, 1983). Table 2 is an expanded and slightly modified version of his review. These medical complications are secondary to: the starvation process itself; binging behavior; attempts by the patient to control weight artificially by means of self-induced vomiting; and the use of laxatives, diuretics, and anorectic drugs. Bulimic patients are also prone to self-mutilation and suicide attempts. Several young adults in our program carefully concealed burns, deep scratches, and lacerations for fear of discovery and censorship, even while hospitalized and involved in psychotherapy.

Complications are also related to a given patient's general health status; frequency, intensity, and duration of a given behavior(s); growth status; and the quality of care received from the health professionals involved.

Cardiovascular Complications

Cardiovascular complications seen in eating disorders range from mild orthostatic hypotension and bradycardia to severe arrhythmia, cardiac atrophy, intractable failure, and death.

Starvation. The direct effect of starvation on the heart is the reduction of cardiac chamber dimensions and left ventricular mass. Almost all patients have reduced maximum working capacity during exercise, probably due to the marked loss of general muscle mass. These changes have been observed under conditions of protein malnutrition, as well as in anorectics, who usually lose weight by eliminating carbohydrates (Gottdiener, Gross, Henry, Borer, & Ebert, 1978). Although these changes are present in young anorectics to some degree, the adolescent patients appear to have essentially normal cardiac function. Powers reported three cases in which heart failure occurred during treatment of anorexia nervosa (Powers, 1982). One patient had a long history of calorie restriction and was seriously emaciated, another also suffered from poorly controlled diabetes mellitus, and a third consumed large quantities of salty foods so that she might gain weight quickly and leave the hospital. Keys and associates have concluded from their starvation studies that the heart was actually relatively closer to failure in early rehabilitation than it was in the starvation state (Keys, Brozek, Henschel, Mickelson, & Taylor, 1950). They have suggested that the heart, which is able to support the much lower basal metabolic load in late starvation, demonstrates its weakness when the metabolic demand is increased.

Abnormal electrocardiographic (ECG) patterns are present in a majority of anorexic patients studied. The principal findings are (a) sinus bradycardia, (b) extremely low voltage, (c) low or inverted T-waves, (d) A-V block, and (e) several other types of arrhythmias (Silverman, 1974). Of greater significance is the occurrence of arrhythmias during exercise. Gottdiener described one patient who displayed a short run of ventricular tachycardia, and three others with occasional ventricular premature beats, during exercise (Gottdiener et al., 1978). Thurston and Marks found several of their patients to have prolonged QT intervals (Thurston & Marks, 1974). This condition has been associated with sudden death. Many of the ECG abnormalities reported have occurred in the absence of electrolyte imbalance.

Less specific signs and symptoms frequently seen in starvation states that may be associated with compromised cardiac performance include hypotension, bradycardia, anemia, cyanosis, edema, light-headedness, fatigue, and cold intolerance. Bradycardia (defined as a heart rate less than 60 beats/minute) has been reported in up to 87% of cases, and hypotension (defined as a blood pressure less than 90/60 mm Hg) in up to 85% of patients with anorexia nervosa. Brotman and Stern reported the case of a 25-year-old cachectic woman (Brotman & Stern, 1983). Her systolic blood pressure was 88 mm Hg, diastolic was unmeasurable, pulse rate 28 beats/minute, temperature 96.6 F, and respiratory rate 12 breaths/minute. Her arms were cold and swollen, and she had two-plus pitting edema of her legs. Following 14 days of peripheral hyperalimentation, she was vastly improved. The authors postulated that many of her positive clinical findings were a mechanism whereby her body could conserve energy and thereby survive. Treating such a patient with thyroid hormone as a clinical case of hypothyroidism could very well lead to a fatal outcome.

Vomiting, Cathartic, Diuretic, Diet Pill Abuse. Hypokalemia associated with repeated vomiting, laxative, or diuretic misuse increases the risk of arrhythmia. When hypokalemia is present, serial ECGs should be obtained and exercise prohibited. Undoubtedly, many deaths related to purging are secondary to these arrhythmias. In addition, phosphate salts used as laxatives can result in decreased calcium and increased phosphate absorption and ultimately could lead to cardiac arrhythmias.

The repeated or high dose use of the emetic ipecac may cause such cardiac disturbances as conduction defects, dysrhythmia, and a fatal form of cardiomyopathy. Adler et al. recently described a patient who died of ventricular tachycardia under just such conditions (Adler, Walinsky, Krall, & Cho, 1980).

Diet Pills. Appetite suppressants frequently contain phenylpropanolamine, a sympathomimetic amine. This drug has produced significant increases in blood pressure in healthy adults who received one capsule containing 85 mg of phenylpropanolamine. It has also been associated with hypertension and cerebral hemorrhage; hypertension, cardiac arrhythmias, and a seizure; and myocardial injury, with some of these adverse effects resulting in death (Elliott & Whyte, 1981; Horowitz et al., 1980; King, 1979; Pentel, Mikell & Zavoral, 1982; Peterson & Vasquez, 1973).

Pulmonary Complications

Starvation. There have been few reports of pulmonary complications for anorexia nervosa. Several authors have postulated that malnutrition may predispose to spontaneous pneumomediastinum by "thinning" the connective tissue septa of the lungs (Al-Mufty & Bevan, 1977; Donley & Kemple, 1978).

Vomiting. Harris has proposed that the most likely pulmonary hazard of vomiting is aspiration pneumonitis occurring in intoxicated or otherwise debilitated bulimic patients (Harris, 1983).

Cathartics. Lipid pneumonia can result from the aspiration of mineral oil, used for its laxative properties.

Effects on Hypothalamic-Pituitary-Target Organ Axis

Female Reproductive System. Amenorrhea, secondary to starvation, can present as either a primary or secondary condition. It occurs in association with weight loss when the loss is in the range of 10-15% of body weight. The most consistent finding in these patients with amenorrhea is a marked reduction or absence of the pulsatile release of luteinizing hormone (LH) from the anterior pituitary gland (Nillius & Wyde, 1977). The diminished secretion of this gonadotropin accounts for the low ovarian estrogen production. The secretion of the other gonadotropin, follicle-stimulating hormone (FSH), is normal, except in extremely underweight patients. This resembles the gonadosecretory pattern observed in prepubertal girls, whose fat storage is usually well below 17% of body weight.

Although the exact cause for this interruption of menses has not been adequately explained, it would appear to be related to a deficiency of gonadotropin-releasing hormone (GNRH). Evidence for this is as follows: (a) luteinizing hormone (LH) and follicle-stimulating hormone (FSH) can be stimulated from their basally low levels by the exogenous administration of GNRH; (b) the pulsatile administration of GNRH can restore ovulation, which also proves the integrity of the ovary if given the appropriate LH and FSH stimulus; (c) the hypothalamic GNRH deficiency is also supported by the delay in the peak of LH and FSH after GNRH administration; (d) the abnormal response of LH to clomiphene citrate; and (e) the failure to demonstrate positive feedback after estrogen administration (Fears, Glass, & Vigersky, 1983).

Patients with anorexia nervosa usually, but not always, resume menstruation after they have regained weight to more than 90% of average for their age and height. Frisch and McArthur have shown that when patients lose weight, the body sets a point of return to menses at a higher level than their pre-illness weight (Frisch & McArthur, 1974). This is a highly complex issue that involves body composition, psychosocial stresses, exercise status, and the presence or absence of bulimia. There is no evidence to suggest that these patients are not normally fertile after weight restoration and resumption of menses.

Approximately 25% of anorexic women cease menstruation even before they lose weight. It is known that increased endogenous opiates (endorphins) are released within the brain in response to exercise and stress. However, Grossman et al. have shown through naloxone infusion studies that the amenorrhea of patients with anorexia nervosa does not appear to be associated with an increase in opiate tone (Grossman et al., 1982). The pathophysiology of this complication remains unknown.

Low estrogen levels may also occur as a result of a reduction of body fat. Fat cells are involved in the conversion of androstenedione to estrone. Whatever the cause, chronically low estrogen levels may cause breast atrophy and atrophic vaginitis, as well as an increased risk of endometrial carcinoma and osteoporosis. In addition to amenorrhea and infertility, women with masked anorexia nervosa may occasionally present to sexual dysfunction clinics complaining of vaginismus and/or frigidity.

Male Reproductive System. The male with moderate to severe weight loss secondary to anorexia nervosa will develop hypogonadotropic hypogonadism, resulting in low serum testosterone levels. Libido, penile erections, and testicular size may all diminish and return to normal only upon the refeeding of the patient and his return to approximately normal weight (Wesselius & Anderson, 1982).

Growth Hormone. Poor nutritional status is characterized by increased concentrations of growth hormone (GH) and decreased somatomedin levels in some patients. These abnormalities are readily reversed by refeeding. Vigersky has suggested that this elevation is due to chronic hypoglycemia. Its rapid correction by increased calorie intake, rather than weight gain, would appear to support this concept. As with other endocrine changes, further investigation is required (Vigersky & Loriaux, 1977b).

Cortisol. Plasma cortisol levels are increased in anorexia nervosa for two reasons. First, the half-life of cortisol in plasma is increased and its metabolic clearance is delayed. These changes are the result of low triiodothyronine (T_3) seen in states of malnutrition. Secondly, the cortisol production rate is significantly increased as a result of the activation of the hypothalamic-pituitary-adrenal axis and the adrenal gland's unusually sensitive response to stimulation by adrenocorticotropic hormone (ACTH). The mechanism of action of this increased higher center, as well as target organ activity, remains uncertain (Weiner, 1983).

Patients with anorexia nervosa have abnormal dexamethasone suppression tests. When given dexamethasone, their serum cortisol levels are not suppressed. Seriously depressed nonanorexic patients have shown a similar lack of suppression. The fact that patients with anorexia nervosa are frequently depressed has encouraged speculation that there is a relationship between the two conditions. However, clinically depressed, as well as nondepressed, patients with anorexia nervosa have abnormal dexamethasone suppression. This abnormal response can be found in a variety of other unrelated conditions and, therefore, at the present time lacks specificity as a useful diagnostic tool (Fears et al., 1983).

Impact on Pituitary-Thyroid-Target Cell Axis

The thyroid gland continues to produce normal to low normal levels of thyroxin during periods of starvation. The presence of normal thyrotropin

(TSH) levels demonstrates the intactness of pituitary function and suggests that any thyroid changes occurring in anorexia nervosa are not due to primary failure of the thyroid gland itself. Wakeling et al. (1979) have also shown that TSH levels are not related to body weight.

Serum triiodothyronine (T₃) levels are significantly reduced in acute starvation. The decrease in the active form of T₃ is accompanied by a corresponding increase in its inactive reverse form, which is a much less calorigenic hormone. Moshang and Utiger have suggested that the target cells for thyroid hormones have regulatory mechanisms based upon metabolic needs (Moshang & Utiger, 1977). The diminished peripheral deiodination of T₄ to the active form of T₃ seen in starvation states appears to be a physiologic adaptation to conserve calorie stores by diminishing metabolic rate. A similar mechanism may also be present within the pituitary gland (Gardner, Kaplan, Stanley, & Utiger, 1979).

It is important to recognize that the widespread changes in endocrine function that have been reported in patients with anorexia are physiological adaptations to starvation and perhaps to psychological stress. Correction of these abnormalities must be undertaken through nutritional means, rather than hormonal replacement.

Skin Effects

Starvation. A multitude of dermatologic abnormalities can be found in chronic starvation states. The skin is dry, flaky, and irregular (follicular hyperkeratosis). The cheeks and back may be covered with lanugo hair. Petechiae and ecchymoses may be present if the patient is suffering from a starvation-related thrombocytopenia. A yellow pigmentation, especially of the palms and soles, is secondary to the elevation of serum carotene. Whether carotenenemia is due to excess ingestion of carotene-containing food or, more likely, to an acquired defect in its metabolism is not known (Drossman, Ontjes, & Heizer, 1979). The pigmentation gradually returns to normal with weight restoration but may persist for months to years. The skin's coolness and the presence of acrocyanosis are associated with a diminished metabolic rate.

Although vitamin deficiencies are unusual in anorexia nervosa, trace element deficiencies are not. Insufficient zinc intake, for example, may cause the patient's hair to be thin and sparse (Casper, Kirschner, Sandstead, Jacob, & David). Zinc supplementation should be considered in these patients. Skin often has a translucent appearance and the subcutaneous fat is greatly reduced. Occasionally, increased skin pigmentation may suggest Addison's disease to the casual observer.

Vomiting. Self-induced vomiting by inserting the fingers into the mouth or throat can result in the formation of calluses or even ulcerations on the dorsum of the hand from rubbing of the skin against the upper incisors (Russell, 1979).

Hematologic Responses

The major hematologic changes associated with the starvation state of anorexia nervosa include moderate hypochromic anemia, leukopenia, and occasionally thrombocytopenia and a significant depletion of the components and functional activity of complement.

The typical anemia is normochromic in nature. There is no significant hemolysis, and reticulopenia is common. Vitamin B_{12} has been found to be normal, whereas folic acid levels vary from one patient to the next. The use of iron and folic acid supplements must be individualized. The supplements may be of limited value, due to the frequent presence (40-50%) of bone marrow hypoplasia (Mant & Faragher, 1972). The hypoplasia is reversible after several weeks of refeeding. Marked thrombocytopenia accompanied by generalized petechiae and ecchymoses is unusual. Bone marrow hypoplasia is thought to account for this condition.

Peripheral leukocyte counts, as well as absolute neutrophil counts, are depressed in patients with anorexia nervosa. On the other hand, marrow granulocyte reserve has been found to be within normal limits (Warren & Vandewiele, 1973). This is thought to be an explanation for why these patients do not suffer from the serious infections one might expect to see in an emaciated patient. Although historically these patients had been thought to be more susceptible to tuberculosis and staphylococcal skin infections, Bowers and Eckert found no significant differences in infection rates between anorexic and control populations during their prehospitalization and hospitalization periods (Bowers & Eckert, 1978).

Influence on Thermoregulation

Patients with anorexia nervosa frequently feel chilly and prefer to wear warm sweaters when observed on the hospital ward. Loss of subcutaneous fat may account for some of this behavior, but recent studies by Vigersky suggest a more central, perhaps hypothalamic, cause (Vigersky, Loriaux, Andersen, Mecklenburg, & Vaitukaitis, 1976). He and co-workers found that 69% of their anorexic patients, when exposed to acute hypothermia, did not display an initial (paradoxical) rise in core temperature, which in normal controls is caused by peripheral vasoconstriction. In addition, none were observed to shiver. They were able to correlate the severity of this cold intolerance with the degree of weight loss.

Similar weight-correlated abnormalities occur when anorexic patients are exposed to elevated temperatures. They demonstrate an excess rise in core temperature and a delay in vasodilation (Vigersky et al., 1976; Wakeling & Russell, 1970).

Smith et al. reported a young woman with anorexia nervosa who had severe recurrent hypothermia. They discussed the potential roles of thiamine and carbohydrate in the successful thermoregulation of this patient (Smith, Ovesen, Chu, Sackel & Howard, 1983).

Gastrointestinal Effects

Starvation. Individuals who restrict their diet severely may have constipation due to decreased food volume in the gastrointestinal tract or low fiber intake. They may also be clinically hypothyroid, with low normal or depressed T_3. One of the associated symptoms of hypothyroidism is constipation. Decreased appetite, abdominal discomfort, and abdominal distension may all be associated with constipation. Many patients become fixated on maintaining regular daily stooling patterns, even when constipated. Prolonged straining while attempting to defecate may ultimately lead to the development of hemorrhoids and anal fissures.

Acute gastric dilatation after rapid refeeding of malnourished individuals was first noted among prisoners of war released at the end of World War II (Markowski, 1947). Similarly, acute gastric and duodenal dilatation have been noted in patients with anorexia nervosa who are being re-fed as a result of recent extensive weight loss or who overeat voluntarily (Bossingham, 1977; Russell, 1966; Scobie, 1973). Transient non-obstructive jejunal dilatation has also been reported (Haller, Slovis, Baker, Berdon, & Silverman, 1977). Gastric dilatation can result in gastric rupture and death (Evans, 1968; Matikainen, 1979; Saul, Dekker, & Watson, 1981).

An additional factor to consider in regard to gastric complaints is whether patients are on medications that possess anticholinergic side effects. This may contribute to delayed emptying and constipation. Subjective complaints include feelings of satiety or postprandial fullness, even after eating only small portions of food.

Patients with anorexia nervosa have been reported to develop salivary gland enlargement with refeeding. Most likely the enlargement is associated with the vomiting behavior of these persons, either known to the physician or done surreptitiously (Lavender, 1969). The progression of symptoms from the restrictive eating of anorexia to binge eating and vomiting has been frequently observed, and, thus, the association of enlarged salivary glands with the gaining of weight may be due to the addition of vomiting behavior at this point (Andersen, 1983; Levin, Falko, Dixon, Gallup, & Saunders, 1980; Walsh, Croft, & Katz, 1981).

Acute pancreatitis has been found in several malnourished patients with chronic dietary restriction who were suddenly fed large amounts of high-calorie food. Complaints of abdominal pain and elevated amylase levels returned to normal after oral feedings were discontinued. Slow re-introduction of feedings were eventually successful in these patients (Gryboski, Hillemeier, Kocoshis, Anyan, & Seashore, 1980). Webster and colleagues have noted that the pancreas is probably adversely affected by very restrictive eating and malnutrition because it requires a rapid turn-over of protein for enzyme synthesis (Russell, 1966); they have also noted that dietary restriction removes the hormonal and trophic stimulation by gastrointestinal enzymes (Mainz, Black, & Webster, 1973; Webster, Black, Mainz, & Singh, 1977).

The sense of taste has been shown to be decreased in some individuals with restricted nutritional intake, and it is possible that hits hypogeusia exacerbates the eating disorder by making it more difficult for mal-nourished individuals to begin eating voluntarily (Casper et al., 1980). The sense of taste and smell have been related to zinc (Russell, Cox, & Solomons, 1983); two recent studies have each reported success in treating such anorexic patients with zinc supplement (Bryce-Smith & Simpson, 1984; Safai-Kutti & Kutti, 1984). However, in Casper's series of 30 hospitalized anorexics, even though moderately depressed plasma zinc levels were found, these levels did not correlate with taste recognition scores or hypogeusia. This area requires further investigation.

Vomiting.   Self-induced vomiting elicited by sticking fingers or other instruments into the posterior pharynx and eliciting a gag reflex may lead to minor trauma to the posterior pharynx and even to the epiglottis or upper esophagus. Associated bleeding may be reported as hematemesis. Sore throats and/or esophagitis may result from the repeated trauma of self-induced vomiting. Frequent forceful vomiting may eventually lead to hematemesis, especially when the vomiting is induced by the abuse of ipecac. This drug produces vomiting that is more forceful than that associated with stimulation of the gag reflex.

Dental problems may result from repeated vomiting. The tooth enamel is affected by contact with the acid in the stomach secretions present in emesis and also by the increased concentration of oral secretions resulting from dehydration secondary to extensive fluid loss. This material is retained on the surface of the tongue; consequently, the inner surfaces of the teeth that touch the tongue are initially affected. The enamel is eroded, and the teeth appear yellowed; later, numerous caries may result. Some persons require extensive dental repair work, including multiple fillings, root canals, and caps (Hurst, Lacey, & Crisp, 1977). Pyorrhea may also occur for similar reasons. The use of antidepressants with eating disorders patients also results in reduced salivary secretions and can lead to an increased incidence of tooth erosion and caries.

Both the parotid and submaxillary glands may be enlarged in persons who vomit repeatedly. A possible cause of the enlargement may be the repeated intense stimulation of salivation associated with frequent binge eating and vomiting behavior. The enlargement is considered to be sialadenosis, a diffuse, asymptomatic, noninflammatory salivary gland enlargement. Biopsies of the enlarged parotid glands are essentially normal, showing no or only scattered inflammatory cells, no infiltration by adipose tissue, and normal acini, with no filling defects on parotid sialograms and normal minor salivary gland tissue on lip biopsies (Walsh et al., 1981).

Binge Eating. As already discussed, gastric dilatation may occur in previously emaciated individuals who ingest a large quantity of food, but has also been reported in an individual who binge ate but was not emaciated at the time (Mitchell, Pyle & Miner, 1982). At particular risk for gastric dilatation are anorexics who binge occasionally or bulimics with diabetes mellitus whose diabetes has progressed to the stage of causing gastric paresis, with its associated greatly increased gastric emptying time.

Cathartics. Laxative abuse may result in significant diarrhea, with subsequent fluid and electrolyte imbalance. Bulk laxatives (e.g., bran, psyllium) may lead to intestinal obstruction when associated with dehydration and an underlying intestinal narrowing (Po, 1982). In addition, abuse of sodium phosphate-biphosphate laxative products (Phospho-soda) can cause sloughing of the rectal mucosa (Laxatives and cathartics, 1983). Use of anthraquinone laxatives can lead to melanosis coli, which is a change in the mucosal pigmentation. This is reversible if the laxatives are discontinued (Wittoesch, Jackman, & McDonald, 1958). Chronic use of stimulant laxatives can lead to a poorly functioning large intestine or a cathartic colon (Sladen, 1972).

Sorbitol and mannitol, both acting as osmotic agents, may occasionally be used as substitutes for laxatives by persons wishing to purge. The long-term abuse of mineral oil may result in reduced absorption of fat soluble vitamins (Laxatives and cathartics, 1983).

Neurological Results

Starvation. There have been several reports of cerebral atrophy in patients with anorexia nervosa (Cala & Mastaglia, 1980; Euzmann & Lane, 1977; Nussbaum, Sheuker, Marc, & Klein, 1980; Sein, Searson, & Nicol, 1981), with an indication in one patient that this might be reversible with weight gain, though two other patients showed continued abnormalities (Euzmann & Lane, 1977; Sein et al., 1981).

Cathartics. Abuse of anthraquinone cathartics (e.g., senna and cascara sagrada) may result in damage to the neurons of the myenteric plexus. Damage to these neurons has been demonstrated histologically when senna has been administered to mice. Myenteric plexus damage has also been described in a patient with the cathartic syndrome, although after many years of taking purgatives it was impossible to definitely differentiate between damage due solely to purgatives and a pre-existing primary plexus lesion (Smith, 1968).

Phosphate salt laxatives used by persons with impaired renal function can cause hyperphosphatemia and hypocalcemia accompanied by tetany and convulsions.

Diet Pills. Phenylpropanolamine has been associated with transient neurological deficit and nonhypertensive stroke (Johnson, Etter, & Reeves, 1983). It has also been associated with generalized seizures (Howrie & Wolfson, 1983; Mueller, 1983; Peterson & Vasquez, 1973).

Effects on Bone

Chronic anorexia with associated amenorrhea has been shown to be related to osteopenia, with risk factors being related to amenorrhea for 3 years or more, onset of amenorrhea before the age of 13, and delayed pubertal development (Ayers, Gidwani, Schmidt, & Gross, 1984). This osteopenia is thought to be secondary to the low estrogen levels associated with the significantly diminished weight of these patients. Ayers et al. concluded that the osteopenia seen in their young patients (age 13-21) was due to a failure of the normal pubertal apposition of cortical bone, rather than the active bone resorption of postmenopausal osteoporosis. However, the presence of osteoporosis and fractures has been demonstrated in older women with chronic histories of low weight due to anorexia. McAnarney et al. found rib fractures in a 25-year-old female with a 10-year history of anorexia nervosa who had cortical thinning and osteopenia on X rays (McAnarney, Greydanus, Campanella, & Hoekelman, 1983). We have observed a hip fracture in a 36-year-old woman who presented with a 7-year history of anorexia nervosa and amenorrhea. She had decreased bone mineralization and osteopenia, as shown by photon absorptiometry and X rays, respectively.

It has been noted that female anorexics whose disorder began early in adolescence were shorter in height than age- and social-class-matched controls (Crisp, 1969). Lacey et al. have demonstrated delayed skeletal development in patients with anorexia nervosa who were dietary restrictors; they have suggested that bone development ceases whenever the body weight is low enough to result in amenorrhea (Lacey, Crisp, Hart, & Kirkwood, 1979). This is a variable finding, for one of our patients had only a slight delay in bone maturation for age, though experiencing significantly short stature relative to family members. Her adult height has been significantly compromised.

Nutritional Costs

Starvation. It is difficult to demonstrate malnutrition by laboratory tests, even for patients who are obviously emaciated on physical examination, and even when using a test profile such as that proposed by Blackburn (Blackburn, Bistrian, Maini, Schlamm, & Smith, 1977).

In general, in patients who have severely restricted their nutritional intake, total protein and albumin levels remain within normal limits (Halmi & Falk, 1981). Thus, an anorexic with hypoalbuminemia has usually had very severe protein depletion. Ayers et al. performed a nutritional assessment on 14 women (aged 13-21) with anorexia and found no laboratory evidence of protein-calorie malnutrition when they measured total lymphocyte counts, serum transferrin, serum albumin, and delayed hypersensitivity skin testing (Ayers et al., 1984). This nutritional assessment was normal, in spite of all their patients having fulfilled the Feighner et al. criteria for anorexia nervosa (signifying they had lost at least 25% of their body weight) (Feighner et al., 1972).

We have found the creatinine height index to reflect the degree of malnutrition. Since creatinine is a normal waste product of muscle metabolism, the amount of creatine produced reflects the muscle mass of the patient. Creatinine is excreted in the urine; thus, in an emaciated patient with decreased muscle mass, the amount of creatinine excreted would be reduced. In the creatinine height index, the amount of creatinine excreted in 24 hours is compared in a ratio to the expected creatinine excretion for a normal-weight individual of the same height and sex.

Anthropometric measurements, such as triceps skinfolds and middle arm muscle circumference, also parallel the weight gain achieved in hospitalized patients being treated for protein-calorie malnutrition.

Elevated cholesterol levels have been reported in anorexic patients (Crisp, Blendis, & Pawan, 1968; Klinefelter, 1965), with the elevation due to an increase in low-density lipoprotein cholesterol (Mordasini, Klose, & Greten, 1978). This was postulated to be possibly due to delayed metabolism of the low-density lipoprotein cholesterol or to the mobilization of body fat stores. Both high-density lipoprotein and very-low-density lipoprotein cholesterol levels were normal (Mordasini, et al., 1978). Frank hypercholesterolemia was not found by Halmi and Fry (1974). Elevated carotene levels may be related to decreased metabolism of its carrier, beta-lipoprotein, or to a reduced Vitamin A requirement (Pops & Schwabe, 1968), or to increased dietary intake of carotene (Banji & Mattingly, 1981).

Cathartics. As a method of real weight reduction, cathartics are of little benefit, because the absorptive functions of the jejunum and ileum are not disturbed. Even extreme purging producing 4-6 liters of liquid stool decreased calorie absorption by only 12% (Bo-Linn, Santa Ana, Morawski, & Fordtran, 1983).

Renal/Electrolyte Problems

Restriction of fluid intake and/or potassium food sources, in conjunction with vomiting, can result in a severe combination of dehydration and hypokalemic, hypochloremic alkalosis. This, in turn, could lead to cardiac arrhythmias and possible death, among other things.

Starvation.   Renal function studies in patients with anorexia nervosa have demonstrated a decreased glomerular filtration rate and decreased concentrating capacity (Aperia, Broberger, & Fohlin, 1978; Mecklenberg, Loriaux, Thompson, Anderson, & Lipsett, 1974; Vigersky & Loriaux, 1977a). Although there have been differing results in the concentrating response of the kidneys to vasopressin, many anorexic patients, while in a state of starvation, have defects in urinary concentration or dilution, which are suggestive of abnormal secretion of the antidiuretic hormone arginine vasopressin (Aperia et al., 1978; Mecklenberg et al., 1974; Vigersky & Loriaux, 1977a). Gold and co-workers have examined the response of plasma vasopressin to intravenous hypertonic saline in anorexic patients before and after correction of their weight loss (Gold, Kay, Robertson, & Ebert, 1983). All four of their patients had subnormal or erratic responses. Follow-up studies have indicated a gradual correction of their subjects' abnormal levels of plasma and cerebrospinal arginine vasopressin with weight gain. The pathophysiologic consequences of these findings remain to be fully defined. They are important clinically for their role in dehydration, as well as in the water intoxication states sometimes seen in these patients.

Creatinine values are generally normal in anorexics. As expected, BUN values are normal or slightly elevated in dehydration states associated with eating disorders (Halmi & Falk, 1981).

Vomiting.   One of the serious medical dangers associated with eating disorders is that of fluid and electrolyte imbalances. These imbalances are a threat particularly to patients who vomit. Vomiting is associated with a loss of hydrochloric acid and fluid volume from the stomach. The compensation by the body for the resulting dehydration involves kidney mechanisms that result in the retention of sodium ions, but a loss of potassium ions. More specifically, vomiting results in the loss of gastric secretions that contain relatively little potassium, but large numbers of chloride ions. These electrolyte losses plus the loss of hydrogen ions result in metabolic alkalosis. The patient's alkalotic state under these conditions is the result not only of the initial hydrogen ion loss from the stomach but also of ion loss due to renal compensatory mechanisms.

In order to restore volume, sodium ions are reabsorbed in the proximal tubules of the kidney. Because a depletion of negatively charged chloride ions exists due to vomiting, the negatively charged component reabsorbed with positively charged sodium ions has to be bicarbonate. The resorption of bicarbonate with sodium maintains the alkalosis begun with the loss of hydrogen ions from the vomitus. Associated hypokalemia increases the renal threshold for bicarbonate resorption, and higher serum levels of bicarbonate are maintained before renal excretion occurs.

The distal tubules of the kidney respond to dehydration via the renin-angiotensin-aldosterone system. In the distal tubules, under the influence of aldosterone, sodium ions are exchanged for either hydrogen ions or potassium ions, with the potassium ions being preferentially secreted. This results in the major loss of potassium from the body.

With metabolic alkalosis there is a shift of potassium into the cell as hydrogen ions or potassium ions shift out of the cell. This may lead to hypokalemia. It is important to keep in mind that this occurs in the presence of total body potassium depletion, which may be further complicated by diminished dietary intake of potassium. Among other things, the combined effect of potassium depletion contributes to the kidneys' inability to concentrate urine, cardiac arrhythmias, and muscle weakness.

Although the major results of vomiting and the resulting renal compensation are hypokalemic, hypochloremic alkalosis, other renal and electrolyte disturbances can occur. Should a patient present with hyponatremia, one should suspect inappropriately high ADH secretion or excessive water intake (Halmi & Falk, 1981). On the other hand, high normal serum sodium values would reflect a state of dehydration, which is often seen upon admission to the hospital, especially in the case of patients who are restricting fluid intake and are vomiting.

Progressive renal failure has been reported in patients with persistent vomiting (Mira, Stewart, & Abraham, 1984; Russell, 1979). One anorexic patient who vomited had renal tubal vacuolation on autopsy (Wigley, 1960). Kidney stones were reported in a patient who restricted her diet, abused laxatives, and vomited. The chronic dehydration associated with these behaviors could result in an increased risk of stone formation (Silber & Kass, 1984).

Cathartics. Abuse of laxatives may result in the loss of potassium, sodium, and magnesium from the colon (Mira et al., 1984). Chronic abuse of laxatives results in dehydration and excessive sodium losses in the stool, with the resulting hyponatremia leading to a compensatory loss of potassium through the renal renin-angiotensin-aldosterone system, as described above. Among other consequences, there could be abdominal pain due to an adynamic paralytic ileus secondary to the hypokalemia, and a perceived state of constipation, which is due to a clearing of fecal material from the colon by the laxatives (Harris, 1983).

Diuretics. Abuse of diuretics may lead to the loss of potassium and magnesium (Mira et al., 1984).

Diet Pills. Acute renal failure has been reported in patients using phenyl-propanolamine and has been associated with rhabdomyolysis (Bennett, 1979; Duffy, Senekjian, Knight, Gyorkey, & Weinman, 1981).

Psychological Results

Starvation. Transient psychoses have been reported with anorexia nervosa (Grounds, 1982), and many patients are depressed at the time of hospital admission. There is increasing evidence of an association between anorexia nervosa and familial histories of such affective disorders as depression and substance abuse, although this relationship is not predictive (Rivinus et al., 1984).

Vomiting. Many patients with bulimia who purge in various ways have been shown to have evidence of affective disorders (by the dexamethasone suppression test) and to have had family histories of affective disorder (Hudson et al., 1982). This has led to increasing study of the use of antidepressants with these patients.

Binging-Purging. Bulimic patients tend to be more impulsive, to have a higher incidence of substance abuse, to be involved more frequently in legal difficulties such as shoplifting, and to have more suicide gestures or attempts compared to patients who are restrictors (Pyle, Mitchell, & Eckert, 1981). There is also a subset of patients who have episodes of self-mutilation, which are often concealed from their physicians.

Diet Pills. Phenylpropanolamine has been associated with restlessness, irritability, aggressiveness, and sleep disturbances, as well as with psychotic episodes (Dietz, 1981; Norvenius, Widerlov, & Lonnerholm, 1979). Caffeine abuse produces restlessness, agitation, and anxiety, and has also been associated with psychosis (Grounds, 1982; Schaffer & Pauli, 1980, Shaul, Farrell, & Maloney, 1984; Sours, 1983).

References

Adler, A.G., Walinsky, P., Krall, R.A., & Cho, S.Y. (1980). Death resulting from ipecac syrup poisoning. *Journal of the American Medical Association,* **243**, 1927-1928.

Al-Mufty, N.S., & Bevan, D.H. (1977). A case of subcutaneous emphysema, pneumomediastinum and pneumoretroperitoneum associated with functional anorexia. *British Journal of Clinical Practice,* **31**, 160-161.

American Psychiatric Association. (1980). *Diagnostic and statistical manual of mental disorders (DSM-III).* Washington, DC: Author.

American Psychiatric Association. (1987). *Diagnostic and statistical manual of mental disorders* (3rd ed. rev.). Washington, DC: Author.

Andersen, A.E. (1977). Atypical anorexia nervosa. In R.A. Vigersky (Ed.), *Anorexia nervosa* (pp. 11-20). New York: Raven Press.

Andersen, A.E. (1983). Anorexia nervosa and bulimia: A spectrum of eating disorders. *Journal of Adolescent Health Care, 4*, 15-21.

Aperia, A., Broberger, O., & Fohlin, L. (1978). Renal function in anorexia nervosa. *Acta Paediatrica Scandinavica, 67*, 219-224.

Ayers, J.W.T., Gidwani, G.P., Schmidt, I.M.V., & Gross, M. (1984). Osteopenia in hypoestrogenic young women with anorexia nervosa. *Fertility and Sterility, 41*, 224-228.

Bennett, W.M. (1979). Hazards of the appetite suppressant phenylpropanolamine. *Lancet, 2*, 42.

Bhanji, S., & Mattingly, D. (1981). Anorexia nervosa: Some observations on "dieters" and "vomiters," cholesterol and carotene. *British Journal of Psychiatry, 139*, 238-241.

Blackburn, G.L., Bistrian, B.R., Maini, B.S., Schlamm, H.T., & Smith, M.F. (1977). Nutritional and metabolic assessment of the hospitalized patient. *The Journal of Parenteral and Enteral Nutrition, 1*, 11-22.

Bo-Linn, G.W., Santa Ana, C.A., Morawski, S.G., & Fordtran, J.S. (1983). Purging and calorie absorption in bulimic patients and normal women. *Annals of Internal Medicine, 99*, 14-17.

Boskind-Lodahl, M. (1976). Cinderella's step-sisters: A feminist perspective on anorexia nervosa and bulimia signs. *The Journal of Women in Culture and Society, 2*, 342.

Bossingham, D. (1977). Acute gastric dilatation in anorexia nervosa. *British Medical Journal, 2*, 959.

Bowers, T.K., & Eckert, E. (1978). Leukopenia in anorexia nervosa. Lack of increased risk of infection. *Archives of Internal Medicine, 138*, 1520.

Brotman, A.W., & Stern, T.A. (1983). Case report of cardiovascular abnormalities in anorexia nervosa. *American Journal of Psychiatry, 140*, 1227-1228.

Bruch, H. (1973). *Eating disorders: Obesity, anorexia nervosa, and the person within.* New York: Basic Books.

Bryce-Smith, D., & Simpson, R.I.D. (1984). Case of anorexia nervosa responding to zinc sulphate. *Lancet, 2*, 350.

Cala, L.A., & Mastaglia, F.L. (1980). Computerized axial tomography in the detection of brain damage. *Medical Journal of Australia, 2*, 193-198.

Casper, R.C., Eckert, E.D., Halmi, K., Goldberg, S.C., & Davis, J.M. (1980). Bulimia: Its incidence and clinical importance in patients with anorexia nervosa. *Archives in General Psychiatry, 37*, 1030-1040.

Casper, R.C., Kirschner, B., Sandstead, H.H., Jacob, R.A., & Davis, J.M. (1980). An evaluation of trace metals, vitamins, and taste function in anorexia nervosa. *American Journal of Clinical Nutrition, 33*, 1801-1808.

Crisp, A.H. (1969). Some skeletal measurements in patients with primary anorexia nervosa. *Journal of Psychosomatic Research*, **13**, 125-142.

Crisp, A.H., Blendis, L.M., & Pawan, G.L.S. (1968). Aspects of fat metabolism in anorexia nervosa. *Metabolism*, **17**, 1109-1118.

Dietz, A.J., Jr. (1981). Amphetamine-like reactions to phenylpropanolamine. *Journal of the American Medical Association*, **245**, 601-602.

Donley, A.J., & Kemple, T.J. (1978). Spontaneous pneumomediastinum complicating anorexia nervosa. *British Medical Journal*, **2**,1604-1605.

Drossman, D.A., Ontjes, D.A., & Heizer, W.D. (1979). Clinical conference. Anorexia nervosa. *Gastroenterology*, **77**, 1115-1131.

Duffy, W.B., Senekjian, H.O., Knight, T.F., Gyorkey, F., & Weinman, E.J. (1981). Acute renal failure due to phenylpropanolamine. *Southern Medical Journal*, **74**, 1548-1549.

Elliott, C.F., & Whyte, J.C. (1981). Phenylpropanolamine and hypertension. *Medical Journal of Australia*, **1**, 157.

Euzmann, D.R., & Lane, B. (1977). Cranial computed tomography findings in anorexia nervosa. *Journal of Computer Assisted Tomography*, **1**, 410-414.

Evans, D.S. (1968). Acute dilatation and spontaneous rupture of the stomach. *British Journal of Surgery*, **55**, 940-942.

Fears, W.B., Glass, A.R., & Vigersky, R.A. (1983). Role of exercise in the pathogenis of the amenorrhea associated with anorexia nervosa. *Journal of Adolescent Health Care*, **4**, 22-24.

Feighner, J.P., Robins, E., Guze, S.B., Woodruff, R.A., Winokur, G., & Munoz, R. (1972). Diagnostic criteria for use in psychiatric research. *Archives in General Psychiatry*, **26**, 57-63.

Frisch, R.E., & McArthur, J.W. (1974). Menstrual cycles: Fatness as a determinant of minimum weight for height necessary for their maintenance or onset. *Science*, **185**, 949-951.

Gardner, D.F., Kaplan, M.M., Stanley, C.A., & Utiger, R.D. (1979). Effect of triiodothyronine replacement on the metabolic and pituitary responses to starvation. *New England Journal of Medicine*, **300**, 579-584.

Garfinkel, P.E., & Garner, D.M. (1982). *Anorexia nervosa—A multidimensional perspective*. New York: Brunner and Mazel.

Gold, P.W., Kaye, W., Robertson, G.L., & Ebert, M. (1983). Abnormalities in plasma and cerebrospinal-fluid arginine vasopressin in patients with anorexia nervosa. *New England Journal of Medicine*, **308**, 1117-1123.

Gottdiener, J.S., Gross, H.A., Henry, W.L., Borer, J.S., & Ebert, M.H. (1978). Effects of self-induced starvation on cardiac size and function in anorexia nervosa. *Circulation*, **58**, 425-433.

Grossman, A., Moult, P.J., McIntyre, H., Evans, J., Silverstone, T., Rees, L.H., & Besser, G.M. (1982). Opiate mediation of amenorrhea in hyperprolactinaemia and in weight-loss related amenorrhea. *Clinical Endocrinology*, **17**, 379-388.

Grounds, A. (1982). Transient psychoses in anorexia nervosa: A report of 7 cases. *Psychological Medicine*, **12**, 107-113.

Gryboski, J., Hillemeier, C., Kocoshis, S., Anyan, W., & Seashore, J.S. (1980). Refeeding pancreatitis in malnourished children. *Journal of Pediatrics*, **97**, 441-443.

Gull, W.W. (1874). Anorexia nervosa. *Transactions of the Clinical Society* (London), **7**, 22-28.

Gwirtsman, H.E., Roy-Byrne, P., Yager, J., & Gerner, R.H. (1983). Neuroendocrine abnormalities in bulimia. *American Journal of Psychiatry*, **140**, 559-563.

Haller, J.O., Slovis, T.L., Baker, D.H., Berdon, W.E., & Silverman, J.A. (1977). Anorexia nervosa—The paucity of radiologic findings in more than fifty patients. *Pediatric Radiology*, **5**, 145-147.

Halmi, K.A., Brodland, G., & Rigas, C. (1975). A follow-up study of seventy-nine patients with anorexia nervosa: An evaluation of prognostic factors and diagnostic criteria. In R. Writ, G. Winokur, & M. Roff (Eds.), *Life history research in psychopathology* (Vol. 4). Minneapolis: The University of Minnesota Press.

Halmi, K.A., & Falk, J.R. (1981). Common physiological changes in anorexia nervosa. *International Journal of Eating Disorders*, **1**, 16-27.

Halmi, K.A., & Fry, M. (1974). Serum lipids in anorexia nervosa. *Biological Psychiatry*, **8**, 159-167.

Harris, R.T. (1983). Bulimarexia and related serious eating disorders with medical complications. *Annals of Internal Medicine*, **99**, 800-807.

Heinz, E.R., Martinez, J., & Haenggeli, A. (1977). Reversibility of cerebral atrophy in anorexia nervosa and Cushing's syndrome. *Journal of Computer Assisted Tomography*, **1**, 415-418.

Horowitz, J.D., Lang, W.J., Howes, L.G., Fennessy, M.R., Christophidis, N., Rand, M.J., & Louis, W.J. (1980). Hypertensive responses induced by phenylpropanolamine in anorectic and decongestant preparations. *Lancet*, **1**, 60-61.

Howrie, D.L., & Wolfson, J.H. (1983). Pheynylpropanolamine-induced hypertensive seizures. *Journal of Pediatrics*, **102**, 143-145.

Hudson, J.I., Laffer, P.S., & Pope, J.R. (1982). Bulimia related to affective disorder by family history and response to dexamethasone suppression test. *American Journal of Psychiatry*, **139**, 685-687.

Hurst, P.S., Lacey, J.H., & Crisp, A.H. (1977). Teeth, vomiting and diet: A study of the dental characteristics of seventeen anorexia nervosa patients. *Postgraduate Medicine Journal*, **53**, 298-305.

Johnson, D.A., Etter, H.S., & Reeves, D.M. (1983). Stroke and phenylpropanolamine use. *Lancet*, **2**, 970.

Keys, A., Brozek, J., Henschel, A., Mickelsen, O., & Taylor, H.L. (1950). *The biology of human starvation*. Minneapolis: University of Minnesota Press.

King, J. (1979). Hypertension and cerebral haemorrhage after trimolets ingestion. *Medical Journal of Australia, 2*, 258.

Klinefelter, H.F. (1965). Hypercholesterolemia in anorexia nervosa. *Journal of Clinical Endocrinology and Metabolism, 25*, 1520-1521.

Lacey, J.H., Crisp, A.H., Hart, G., & Kirkwood, B.A. (1979). Weight and skeletal maturation—A study of radiological and chronological age in an anorexia nervosa population. *Postgraduate Medicine Journal, 55*, 301-385.

Lasegue, C. (1873). On hysterical anorexia. *Medical Times Gazette, 2*, 265-267.

Lavender, S. (1969). Vomiting and parotid enlargement. *Lancet, 1*, 426.

Laxatives and cathartics. (1983). In *A.M.A. drug evaluations* (5th ed.) (pp. 1265-1309). Philadelphia: W.B. Saunders.

Leibowitz, S.F. (1983). Hypothalamic noradrenergic system: Role in control of appetite and relation to anorexia nervosa. In *Understanding anorexia nervosa and bulimia: Report to the Fourth Ross Conference on Medical Research* (pp. 54-60). Columbus, OH: Ross Laboratories.

Levin, P.A., Falko, J.M., Dixon, K., Gallup, E.M., & Saunders, W. (1980). Benign parotid enlargement in bulimia. *Annals of Internal Medicine, 93*, 827-829.

Mainz, D.L., Black. O., & Webster, P.D. (1973). Hormonal control of pancreatic growth. *Journal of Clinical Investigations, 52*, 2300-2304.

Mant, M.G., & Faragher, B.S. (1972). The haematology of anorexia nervosa. *British Journal of Haematoloty, 23*, 737-749.

Markowski, B. (1947). Acute dilatation of the stomach. *British Medical Journal, 2*, 128-130.

Matikainen, M. (1979). Spontaneous rupture of the stomach. *American Journal of Surgery, 138*, 451-452.

McAnarney, E.R., Greydanus, D.E., Campanella, V.A., & Hoekelman, R.A. (1983). Rib fractures and anorexia nervosa. *Journal of Adolescent Health Care, 4*, 40-43.

Mecklenburg, R.S., Loriaux, D.L., Thompson, R.H., Anderson, A.E., & Lipsett, M.B. (1974). Hypothalamic dysfunction in patients with anorexia nervosa. *Medicine, 53*, 147.

Minuchin, S., Roman, B.L., & Baker, L. (1978). *Psychosomatic families.* Cambridge: Harvard University Press.

Mira, M., Stewart, P.M., & Abraham, S.F. (1984). Hypokalemia and renal impairment in patients with eating disorders. *Medical Journal of Australia, 1*, 290-292.

Mitchell, J.E., Pyle, R.L., & Miner, R.A. (1982). Gastric dilatation as a complication of bulimia. *Psychosomatics, 23*, 96-97.

Mordasini, R., Klose, G., & Greten, H. (1978). Secondary type II hyperlipoproteinemia in patients with anorexia nervosa. *Metabolism, 27*, 71-79.

Moshang, T., Jr., & Utiger, R.D. (1977). Low triiodothyronine euthyroidism in anorexia nervosa. In R.A. Vigersky (Ed.), *Anorexia nervosa* (pp. 263-270). New York: Raven Press.

Mueller, S.M. (1983). Neurologic complications of phenylpropanolamine use. *Neurology*, **33**, 650-652.

Norvenius, G., Widerlov, E., & Lonnerholm, G. (1979). Phenylpropanolamine and mental disturbances. *Lancet*, **2**, 1367-1368.

Nillius, S.J., & Wide, L. (1977). The pituitary reponsiveness to acute and chronic administration of gonadotropin-releasing hormone in acute and recovery stages of anorexia nervosa. In R.A. Vigersky (Ed.), *Anorexia nervosa* (pp. 225-241). New York: Raven Press.

Nussbaum, M., Shenker, I.R., Marc, J., & Klein, M. (1980). Cerebral atrophy in anorexia nervosa. *Journal of Pediatrics*, **96**, 867-869.

Palazzoli, M.S. (1974). *Self starvation.* London: Chaucer.

Pentel, P.R., Mikell, F.L., & Zavoral, J.H. (1982). Myocardial injury after phenylpropanolamine ingestion. *British Heart Journal*, **47**, 51-54.

Peterson, R.E., & Vasquez, L.A. (1973). Phenylpropanolamine-induced arrhythmias. *Journal of the American Medical Association*, **223**, 324-325.

Po, A.L.W. (1982). *Non-prescription drugs.* London: Blackwell Scientific Publications.

Pops, M.A., & Schwabe, A.D. (1968). Hypercarotenemia in anorexia nervosa. *Journal of the American Medical Association*, **205**, 533-534.

Powers, P.S. (1982). Heart failure during treatment of anorexia nervosa. *American Journal of Psychiatry*, **139**, 1167-1170.

Pyle, R.L., Mitchell, J.E., & Eckert, E.D. (1981). Bulimia: A report of 34 cases. *Journal of Clinical Psychiatry*, **42**, 60-64.

Rivinus, T.M., Biederman, J., Herzog, D.B., Kemper, K., Harper, G.P., Harmatz, J.S., & Houseworth, S. (1984). Anorexia nervosa and affective disorders: A controlled family history study. *American Journal Psychiatry*, **141**, 1414-1418.

Russell, G.F.M. (1966). Acute dilatation of the stomach in a patient with anorexia nervosa. *British Journal of Psychiatry*, **112**, 203-207.

Russell, G.F.M. (1979). Bulimia nervosa: An ominous variant of anorexia nervosa. *Psychological Medicine*, **9**, 429-448.

Russell, R.M., Cox, M.E., & Solomons, N. (1983). Zinc and the special senses. *Annals of Internal Medicine*, **99**, 227-239.

Safai-Kutti, S., & Kutti, J. (1984). Zinc and anorexia nervosa. *Annals of Internal Medicine*, **100**, 317-318.

Saul, S.H., Dekker, A., & Watson, C.G. (1981). Acute gastric dilatation with infarction and perforation. *Gut*, **22**, 978-983.

Schaffer, C.B., & Pauli, M.W. (1980). Psychotic reaction caused by proprietary oral diet agents. *American Journal of Psychiatry*, **137**, 1256-1257.

Scobie, B.A. (1973). Acute gastric dilatation and duodenal ileus in anorexia nervosa. *Medical Journal of Australia*, **2**, 932-934.

Sein, P., Searson, S., & Nicol, A.R. (1981). Anorexia nervosa and pseudo-atrophy of the brain. *British Journal of Psychiatry*, **139**, 257-258.

Shaul, P.W., Farrell, M.K., & Maloney, M.J. (1984). Caffeine toxicity as a cause of acute psychosis in anorexia nervosa. *Journal of Pediatrics*, **105**, 493-495.

Silber, T.J., & Kass, E.J. (1984). Anorexia nervosa and nephrolithiasis. *Journal of Adolescent Health Care*, **5**, 50-52.

Silverman, J.A. (1974). Anorexia nervosa: Clinical observations in a successful treatment plan. *Journal of Pediatrics*, **84**, 68-73.

Simmons, M. (1914). Ueber embolische prozesse in der hypophysis. *Archives of Pathology and Anatomy*, **217**, 226-239.

Sladen, G.E. (1972). Effects of chronic purgative abuse. *Proceedings of the Royal Society of Medicine*, **65**, 288-291.

Smith, B. (1968). Effect of irritant purgatives on the myenteric plexus in man and the mouse. *Gut*, **9**, 139-143.

Smith, D.K., Ovesen, L., Chu, R., Sackel, S., & Howard, L. (1983). Hypothermia in a patient with anorexia nervosa. *Metabolism*, **32**, 1151-1154.

Sours, J.A. (1983). Case reports of anorexia nervosa and caffeinism. *American Journal of Psychiatry*, **140**, 235-236.

Thurston, J., & Marks, P. (1974). Electrocardiographic abnormalities in patients with anorexia nervosa. *British Heart Journal*, **36**, 719-723.

Vigersky, R.A., & Loriaux, D.L. (1977a). Anorexia nervosa as a model of hypothalamic dysfunction. In R.A. Vigersky (Ed.), *Anorexia nervosa* (pp. 109-122). New York: Raven Press.

Vigersky, R.A., & Loriaux, D.L. (1977b). The effect of cyproheptadine in anorexia nervosa: A double blind trial. In R.A. Vigersky (Ed.), *Anorexia nervosa* (pp. 349-356). New York: Raven Press.

Vigersky, R.A., Loriaux, D.L., Andersen, A.E., Mecklenburg, R.S., & Vaitukaitis, J.L. (1976). Delayed pituitary hormone response to LRF and TRF in patients with anorexia nervosa and with secondary amenorrhea associated with simple weight loss. *Journal of Clinical Endocrinology and Metabolism*, **43**, 893-900.

Wakeling, A., DeSouza, V.A., Gore, M.B.R., Sabur, M., Kingstone, D., & Boss, A.M.B. (1979). Amenorrhea, body weight and serum hormone concentrations, with particular reference to prolactin and thyroid hormones in anorexia nervosa. *Psychological Medicine*, **9**, 265-272.

Wakeling, A., & Russell, G.F.M. (1970). Disturbances in the regulation of body temperature in anorexia nervosa. *Psychological Medicine*, **1**, 30-39.

Walsh, B.T., Croft, C.B., & Katz, J.L. (1981). Anorexia nervosa and salivary gland enlargement. *International Journal of Psychiatry in Medicine*, 11, 255-261.

Warren, M.P., & VandeWiele, R.L. (1973). Clinical and metabolic features of anorexia nervosa. *American Journal of Obstetrics and Gynecology*, 117, 435-449.

Webster, P.D., Black, O., Mainz, D., & Singh, M. (1977). Pancreatic acinar cell metabolism and function. *Gastroenterology*, 73, 1434-1449.

Weiner, H. (1983). Abiding problems in the psychoendocrinology of anorexia nervosa. In *Understanding anorexia nervosa and bulimia: Report of the Fourth Ross Conference on Medical Research* (pp. 47-53). Columbus, OH: Ross Laboratories.

Wesselius, C.L., & Anderson, G. (1982). A case study of a male with anorexia nervosa and low testosterone levels. *Journal of Clinical Psychiatry*, 43, 428-429.

Wigley, R.D. (1960). Potassium deficiency in anorexia nervosa, with reference to renal tubular vacuolation. *British Medical Journal*, 2, 110-113.

Wittoesch, J.H., Jackman, R.J., & McDonald, J.R. (1958). Melanosis coli: General review and a study of 887 cases. *Diseases of the Colon and Rectum*, 1, 172-180.

Chapter 15

The Multidisciplinary Team Approach to the Treatment of Eating Disorders in Youth

John N. Stephenson
Elizabeth S. Ohlrich
Janet H. McClintock
Sharon W. Foster
Judith A. Reinke
Mary E. Allen
Gordon M. Giles

Anorexia nervosa and bulimia are complex psychophysiological disorders. Although known to physicians for more than 3 centuries, there has been a significant increase in their incidence during the past decade (Garner & Garfinkel, 1978). Although their etiology is more than likely psychiatric, a wide variety of medical complications may occur as a result of self-induced starvation, vomiting, and other behaviors designed to achieve weight loss (Harris, 1983).

These disorders may be severe and potentially life-threatening, with a current mortality rate of 0-5%, and a morbidity rate of 40-50% based on poor psychosocial adjustment and abnormal eating (Hsu, 1980, Wooley & Wooley, 1980). As reviewed by Hsu, the treatment methods are varied, and outcome studies have not been properly designed to assess treatment effects. Less severe cases continue to be followed with some success by individual physicians and psychotherapists. However, in recent years, multidisciplinary teams have been developed in order to better manage the more resistant examples of these psychosomatic disorders.

Referral center treatment programs are frequently divided into several stages of patient care (see Figure 1). Initially, treatment is directed toward stabilizing the patient, as well as identifying and treating immediate medical and psychological complications. The more long-term phase of treatment consists of family, individual, or group psychotherapy, as well as symptom management by medical staff.

Although outpatient care is the predominant form of management, access to an integrated inpatient service is essential for the optimum care

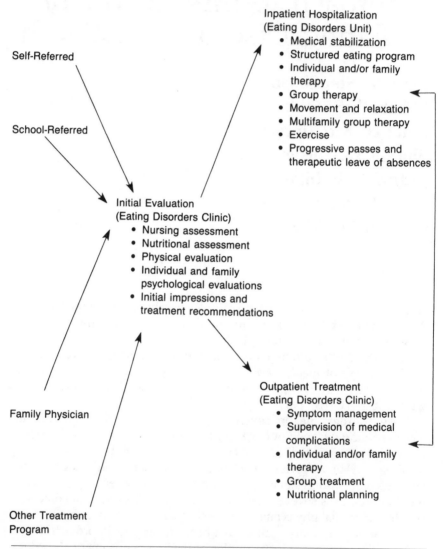

Figure 1. University of Wisconsin Eating Disorders Program.

of many of these patients. Garfinkel, Moldofsky, and Garner (1977a) found that 62% of their patients required hospital admission. Specific indications include breaking the starvation cycle and restoring the patient's nutritional status; interrupting a bulimic's binge-purge cycle and correcting associated medical complications; and utilizing brief admissions for purposes of diagnostic observation, treating complications, transient crises, confronting the patient's denial and the initiation of individual and family psychotherapies (Garfinkel, Moldofsky, & Garner, 1977b).

Adjunctive support groups may be beneficial for the patients and/or their families, such as those facilitated by ANAD (Anorexia Nervosa and Associated Disorders, Highland Park, Illinois), but should not substitute for the individualized treatment program, consisting of symptom management, medical consultations, and individual and/or family psychotherapy. Occasionally, the psychotherapy may be conducted in a group setting.

The Treatment Team

The staffs of most multidisciplinary treatment programs consist of an attending physician, clinical psychologists, consulting psychiatrists, skilled nursing staff—including clinical nurse specialists as well as master's level psychiatric nurses—social workers, clinical dietitians, and occupational therapists. A typical university-based program, with its broader emphasis on research and education as well as patient care, requires even more comprehensive support services.

A multidisciplinary approach to treatment of eating disorders has several goals, which vary according to the orientation and nature of the program:

1. To establish acceptable healthy body weight and medical and nutritional status
2. To decrease and eventually eliminate all unhealthy eating and dieting patterns—especially purging activities
3. To achieve at least enough psychological change within the patient and family to allow for symptom remission without someone else in the family developing problems
4. To enable the family to reach a better level of functioning, so that it can better withstand external and developmental stressors (adolescence, marriage, death), and to allow family members greater emotional closeness without sacrificing the patient's identity.

Initial Evaluation

Patients referred to an eating disorders program, such as the one at the University of Wisconsin Hospital and Clinics, are first introduced to the multidisciplinary team concept when seen for their initial screening outpatient evaluation. By agreement within the team, no patient may be admitted to the program without a complete screening.

This screening includes nursing and nutritional evaluations done by an outpatient nurse and the program's clinical dietitian, respectively. A physician then obtains additional relevant history and systems review from the patient and, when indicated, from the parents. A physical examination, excluding pelvic, is done. Should a pelvic examination be indicated, it is completed at a subsequent, less emotionally charged visit. A brief clinical conference is held, and the information obtained by team members is shared with the clinical psychologist. The psychological evaluation of both the patient and family is then undertaken, following which the participating team members meet to share initial impressions and to devise a treatment plan. Finally, participating team members meet with the patient and her family to discuss the diagnosis and treatment recommendations.

By utilizing various combinations of team members, three to four such evaluations can be accomplished in the course of a half-day clinic. Although this represents a major commitment of the team's resources, the benefits are significant to both the patients and the treatment program. For example, in the course of this assessment process, the concept of multidisciplinary team care can be dynamically presented to the patient and her family. Fewer diagnostic and initial treatment errors are made. Team solidarity is strengthened through this twice weekly exercise, which also serves as an effective model for medical, nursing, and dietetic students, residents, and fellowship trainees assigned to the eating disorders program.

Outpatient Treatment

Patients who have an eating disorder but who are at a level high enough to remain as outpatients are assigned to an outpatient nurse to be seen as frequently as necessary for purposes of symptom management, usually on a weekly basis initially. Whenever possible, this is the same nurse as was involved in the patient's initial screening.

A psychotherapist is located for purposes of individual and/or family therapy. Finding a suitable therapist is the responsibility of the team psychologist involved in the initial psychological evaluation. Group therapy may also be offered via a similar process.

Although most patients have an extraordinary knowledge of caloric values of most foods, they often do not understand, or at least practice, good nutritional habits. A follow-up appointment with the team's clinical dietitian is arranged for purposes of education and monitoring.

Inpatient Hospitalizations

Admitting a patient to an eating disorders unit may occur immediately following the initial evaluation, after a trial of outpatient treatment, or repeatedly during a difficult patient's course of therapy. Decisions to admit are made jointly by the nurse following the patient, the psychotherapist involved, and the physician. For patients known to the program, the decision to admit is often made only after repeated consultations among team members seeking every available alternative. This approach of consultation is not always found in many programs. However, we feel that this philosophy is essential to maintain a treatment team of peers in which the expertise of each discipline is of equal value, rather than having some disciplines subordinate as is the case in more traditional modes of patient care.

While hospitalized, the patient's medical problems are corrected. For the anorexic who has suffered a loss of more than 25% of body weight, this may require a stay of several months for nutritional rehabilitation. The bulimic, on the other hand, may be of normal weight and require a briefer admission to correct fluid and electrolyte imbalance secondary to binging and purging behavior that was out of control. At the time of admission, the patient is briefly interviewed by the clinical dietitian for food preferences. However, the major emphasis is on adequate nutrient intake and "normal eating." Other team members refrain from discussing diet and calories with the patient, except to observe for food intolerance and allergies. Individual and family therapies are intensified but, for purposes of continuity, remain with the outpatient therapists already treating the patient. The patient is also involved in group and multiple family therapy, as well as frequent nursing contacts, centered on underlying issues and symptom management.

If one assumes that the original pathology in anorexia nervosa is a developmental deficit in the capacity for separation-individuation, then the treatment team needs to provide the anorexic patient and her family with certain parenting functions, so that all family members might be helped to achieve a higher level of individuation. As Stern et al. have described, a therapeutic "marriage" between therapists and medical professionals is necessary to provide an adequate "holding environment" for the patient and family (Stern, Whitaker, Hagemann, Anderson, & Bargman, 1981). The hospital eating disorders unit becomes a concrete symbol of the needed holding functions. Under these conditions, the team needs to provide to the family a combination of protective structure, reliability, empathic availability, and support of initiative.

Often the patient who finds herself facing the highly structured nature of the hospital program precipitates a crisis by refusing to eat, becoming suicidal, eloping from the hospital, or engaging in other self-destructive behavior. At such crisis points, the question of who is responsible for intervention—the parents or spouse, the therapist, the hospital staff, the physician, or some combination—often presents a complex clinical dilemma (Stern et al., 1981).

As a result of the dynamics of anorexic families, it is inevitable that the treatment team is drawn into their disturbed interactional pattern. A power struggle between the ward nurses and the patient's parents may occur. The parents may turn to the attending physician when they do not like the advice (or lack of it) that they are receiving from the family therapist; or, since the physician is traditionally viewed as the decision maker of a medical team, parents or patients may vent their anger personally at the physician as their anxieties rise. At such times, even the most disciplined professional members of the treatment team may be tempted to bolt to the relative safety of their own autonomy in order to avoid being blamed for what the patient or parents perceive as the misjudgment and errors of other team members. Careful definition of each member's role in daily decision-making, as well as of the function of the treatment team concept, are essential in avoiding these dilemmas, which would inadvertently cause the team to appear weak and indecisive.

"Splitting" is one of the most common defense mechanisms utilized by anorexic patients. It is a behavior that may seriously complicate treatment. Splitting is used by a patient to decrease her anxiety about positive and negative feelings. The patient's ego is unable to integrate and accept these dichotomous feelings. As a result, these feelings are projected outwardly and split the environment into good and bad parts. On an inpatient unit, the projection of good and bad feelings splits the staff into two groups. Main has described these as "In and Out groups" (Main, 1952). The "In" group feels omnipotent and has rescue fantasies regarding the patient. The "Out" group has the negative side of this projection. Staff membership in either group is not stable and arbitrarily changes. In this process the patient externalizes her internal conflict and in this way often unconsciously manipulates team members to act out the conflict. Splitting is a problem particularly for a multidisciplinary team, in which professional ties are vulnerable to the very nature of the differences between professional disciplines.

The Professional Disciplines

A careful definition of each professional discipline represented on a treatment unit is helpful in understanding further the multidisciplinary team approach to eating disorders patients.

The Role of the Nurse

Nursing, with its 24-hour contact with the inpatients and frequent out-patient symptom monitoring, is an integral component of the multi-disciplinary team. On a day-to-day, hour-to-hour basis, it is often the nurses who make operative the concept of the "holding environment" as described by Adler and Winnicott within the milieu of the inpatient unit (Adler, 1977; Winnicott, 1965). We will discuss in two sections—inpatient nursing and outpatient nursing—the role of nursing in the treatment of patients with eating disorders.

Inpatient Nursing.   Inpatient nursing care can be broken down into three areas of functioning: (a) supervision and monitoring, or the containment of symptomatology: (b) therapeutic interventions; and (c) participation in the multidisciplinary team.

Within the structure of the inpatient program, it is the nursing staff that is directly involved in the disruption of the symptom cycles of starving, binging, and purging with which the patient has become obsessed. The structure of the inpatient unit provides several ways this can be accomplished:

- Daily weights—accurate daily weights are obtained by nursing staff, and the patient is assessed for manipulation of her weight through the ingestion of water, refusal to void, or the use of concealed weighted objects. All staff agree on the method of weighing: in the morning after awakening, in a hospital gown, after voiding. The decision of the nurse doing the weighing is final. If there is a question of water loading, a second weighing an hour or two later may be added. Urine specific gravities may also be obtained at the time of weighing.
- Meal supervision—to assure that the patient is eating the prescribed calorie levels, as well as to intervene in the unusual and abnormal handling of food and rituals.
- Supplementation—the matter-of-fact replacement for uneaten calories with a nutritive supplement.
- After meal supervision—to reduce the opportunity for vomiting, thereby interrupting this pattern of behavior and to facilitate the patient's discussion of her feelings in a more appropriate manner.
- Bathroom supervision—to insure that the patient does not follow through with her urge to vomit, and that surreptitious laxative use becomes known to the staff.
- Restriction of activities and exercise—to disrupt the frantic compulsive exercise patterns such patients have engaged in.

All of the preceding symptom intervention is executed by the nursing staff in an empathic and clear way. The approach is one of benevolent firmness in the "holding environment," which provides security for both the patient and her family. With the symptoms contained, the patient experiences a surfacing of emotions and reactions that have been safely displaced until now by her symptoms. These underlying problems and issues become the focus for nursing one-to-one (1:1) contacts and psychotherapy. Examples can include the following:

- Cognitive and perceptual difficulties—Nursing staff in 1:1 contacts assist and support the patient in her struggle with her changing body image, as well as with her cognitive interpretation of her weight.
- Expression of feelings—Nursing staff provide support and acceptance as the patient struggles with the identification and expression of her full range of affect. Nursing staff encourage the patient to discuss underlying issues in psychotherapy.
- Mirroring—The nursing staff can reflect and mirror the patient's self-initiated feelings back to her as she begins to recognize her feelings, thoughts, and beliefs.
- Assisting the patient with her dichotomous thinking and with the integration of her good and bad aspects into an integrated whole.
- Assisting the patient in reality-testing her world and teaching her about her own body.
- Assisting the patient in setting age-appropriate goals and in fostering independence in her behaviors.

The primary care nurse for the patient also attends family therapy sessions, serving as an alter ego for the patient and as the representative for the multidisciplinary team. The nursing staff provides 24-hour observation of the patient. This includes observing the patient's initial responses to authority and program structure. Additional observations are made of the interactions of the patient with her peers, as well as her interactions within the context of her family, during visiting hours. This information is vital to the multidisciplinary team as it attempts to appropriately respond to the patient's self-initiated inner feelings in the form of program requests to the team. Nursing, within this context, represents the patient and serves as her advocate in gradually reducing program supervision.

This input is essential as the team attempts to respond in an appropriate manner to the patient's progress with a gradual reduction of the limits and supervision of the "holding environment."

Outpatient Nursing. The nursing assessment at the patient's initial screening visit consists of an evaluation of the symptom complex, vital signs, and hydration status. The nurse also reviews with the patient the various components of the clinic visit. As the patient's first contact with the treatment team, the nurse extends a genuine nonjudgmental interest in the patient and her family.

If the diagnosis of an eating disorder is made by the team, a treatment plan is developed that reflects the dual medical and psychological focus of the program. Medical/nursing follow-up, as well as psychotherapy (either individual and/or family therapy), are discussed with the patient and, when appropriate, with her family. Follow-up appointments are scheduled with the nurse prior to the patient's departure from the clinic. Ongoing nursing care for patients with eating disorders represents the establishment of a long-term relationship between the patient and the nurse for purposes of symptom management.

The outpatient nurses assume responsibility for coordination of the patient's care with her psychotherapist. Outpatient nursing care involves the following tasks:

- Symptom monitoring—Nurses monitor weight, electrolytes, blood pressure and pulse, menstruation status, and urine specific gravity, as well as the patient's purging behavior.
- Teaching the patient self-monitoring—Keeping food records that include time, place, and amount of food eaten. The patient is also asked to document her feelings at the time of eating or symptom use.
- Self-reward—The patient is asked to identify activities that are pleasurable to use as alternatives to food, if she is a binge eater.
- Time management and restructuring—Through use of food records, the nurse works with the patient to identify difficult time periods during the day or evening and to assist in restructuring the patient's time to help with symptom control.
- Problem solving—The patient explores with the nurse her solution process, and defines alternate responses and rehearses these.
- Assertiveness—Practicing with the patient, the nurse assists her in appropriately assertive responses.
- Stress management—The patient discusses stressful situations and ways to deal with the situations with the nurse, and learns relaxation techniques, as well as appropriate use of exercise, to decrease stress.
- Contracting—The patient learns how to make appropriate, achievable self-contracts to decrease symptom behavior.
- Cognitive behavior—Rational emotive techniques are used to define the faulty assumptions and perceptions regarding food, weight, and shape.
- Food-related issues—The nurse helps the patient moderate her diet and eating behavior through education, suggestion, and emotional support.

Within the outpatient portion of this "holding environment," each patient is able to work on developing a realistic body image, changing her irrational attitudes toward food, and reducing her anxiety and misperceptions about bodily functions. The outpatient nursing staff, through communication with physicians, therapists, and inpatient staff, coordinates a comprehensive approach to the patient's care. This significantly decreases the patient's ability to continue maladaptive defenses.

The Role of the Psychologist

The unique contributions of the psychologist to the multidisciplinary team are case evaluation, treatment planning, and psychotherapy. In addition, the psychologist is qualified for the larger tasks of program development and evaluation, teaching, and research.

Case Evaluation and Treatment Planning.   Each patient must receive an individualized psychological assessment before being admitted to the program. Development of the concept of how the patient's symptoms serve a psychological function is a crucial way in which the psychologist contributes to the ongoing work of the team. As treatment progresses, it continues to be necessary for the team to have an ongoing understanding of how changes in the patient's symptomatology are reflections of changes in her emotional life. It is a relatively easy matter for helping professionals, out of concern for the potentially dangerous consequences of the anorexic or bulimic patient's behavior, to respond in much the same manner as the patient has experienced in the past from her own family or friends. Arguments can revolve around such issues as being too thin, not eating the right food, exercising excessively, and purging behaviors. Prior to treatment, power struggles about the patient's symptoms were not likely to have been helpful, and most likely led to escalation and exacerbation of the symptoms. The psychologist's objective during the initial screening and subsequent assessments is to develop a hypothesis about the way in which the patient's symptom is an attempted solution to a conflict, usually within the family and/or peer group, that is otherwise seen as nonresolvable.

Psychotherapy.   The role of providing psychotherapy has traditionally been among the most conspicuous of the psychologist's functions. At the University of Wisconsin Eating Disorders Program, psychologists and a psychiatric clinical nurse specialist are the primary providers of individual, family, marital, and group psychotherapy, although psychiatrists, psychologists in private practice, and psychology and psychiatry trainees also provide such services. In other interdisciplinary teams, counselors, social workers, or others may also be among the psychotherapy providers (Hedblom, Hubbard, & Anderson, 1982).

Diverse points of view have been offered with regard to the theoretical and technical approaches most appropriate in working with eating disorders. The most effective psychotherapeutic approach appears to be one that is flexible with respect to specific techniques. It should include attention to interpersonal relationships, object relations, and family systems.

In addition to the variety of techniques used by the therapist to help the patient improve, another major component of psychotherapy is the therapeutic relationship between the therapist and patient. This therapeutic relationship is the cornerstone of psychotherapy. Development of trust is central to this process. The basic technique used to develop this trust is to allow the patient to talk about her problems and feelings. Ruch (1984) has pointed out that when a positive transference is developed, the patient views the psychotherapist in an idealized fashion. The patient's regarding of the psychotherapist as ascendant is often a beneficial and necessary part of the process of psychotherapy. However, Ruch has found that when the therapeutic relationship is not understood by other team members, they may respond with jealousy and irritation to the patient's attributions of positive feelings about the therapist.

In recent years there has been a tendency for other health professionals associated with the multidisciplinary team to become increasingly involved in psychotherapy. It is essential to limit this role only to team members who possess the appropriate education, experience, and credentials; only one team member should act as the patient's individual therapist. If this is not the case, resistant patients may manipulate staff by claiming that they cannot talk openly with their assigned therapist. In addition, if the patient talks with several staff members about significant life events, much of the emotional impact of the disclosure is lost from the therapeutic relationship. Therefore, all members of the team must be aware of the importance of the relationship between the patient and her assigned psychotherapist.

The Role of the Physician

The physician's two major responsibilities are to assess the medical condition of the patient and to communicate findings and discuss treatment plans with other team members.

Outpatient Care.   In addition to determining the patient's general physical status, the initial assessment includes noting the degree of malnutrition present and any complications that may have occurred as a result of the individual's calorie deprivation, purging behavior, or excessive exercise. Although education is a responsibility shared by all team members, the physician plays an important role in the education of the patient and her family regarding her condition and the risk factors of the eating disorder. The physician often assumes the position of the authority figure with both the patient and the family and, thus, is in a strong position to emphasize the medical seriousness of the disorder. From this same position of power, the physician may need to deliver ultimatums when patients are in serious noncompliance with the program.

Symptom management is most cost-effective when done by a highly trained outpatient nursing staff. However, the physician helps to develop treatment goals, establish rate of weight gain and maintenance in patients with protein calorie malnutrition, and is available for consultation about patients who are not doing well and are in need of further evaluation.

Frequently patients who are admitted to the program have been placed on various medications by other physicians who were treating symptoms of the eating disorder, usually before the existence of, and scope of, the eating disorder had been recognized. Medications include, for example, thyroid hormone, potassium supplements, antidepressants, sleeping pills, diuretics, and laxatives. These medications need to be reviewed with the referring physician and patient; frequently, they can be discontinued as the underlying eating disorder is treated. Psychiatric consultation may be helpful regarding antidepressant use.

Inpatient Care.   The physician is responsible for the medical supervision and treatment of inpatients. Each patient should be seen personally on a daily basis to ascertain whether significant medical problems exist. These problems are discussed more specifically in chapter 14. Many somatic complaints are related to the initiation of re-feeding. Such symptoms as bloating, distention, and constipation need to be distinguished from more serious complications, such as acute gastric dilatation. Congestive heart failure has also been reported in association with re-feeding, as has the less severe condition of dependent edema. Other somatic complaints are related to anxiety or depression and consist of vague headaches, abdominal pain, and malaise. A careful history and physical examination, as well as discussion with the nursing staff, usually indicates the etiology. Food allergies and intolerance may also require definition and are areas known for patient manipulation.

Although the physician is the person likely to establish a patient's discharge or maintenance weight, any change in calorie level of the diet should be done in consultation with the program's clinical dietitian. In setting the maintenance or discharge weight and the calorie level, one needs to consider the patient's psychological status, age, height, and sexual maturational level and associated growth rate, as well as degree of exercise. Physical activity programs may need to be added, either in the form of creative movement or true exercise, but, again, these decisions should be done in conjunction with the occupational therapist in charge of this aspect of the program.

Alterations in the treatment plan are discussed primarily in the twice weekly team meetings (half of the patients submit program requests, which are discussed at length at each meeting). If the physician at times other than the team days concludes that the plan must be changed for medical reasons, the reasons for the change must be discussed with the nursing staff and any other appropriate personnel, and agreement must be reached as to the new plan.

The Role of the Clinical Dietitian

Supportive nutrition intervention provides a structure for working with the dietary concerns of the patient as an adjunct to other components of the treatment program. Because such patients tend to be food-focused, the clinical dietitian plays a particularly vital role in separating nutritional from psychological rehabilitation.

The initial dietary assessment is done at the patient's first visit to the outpatient clinic. Follow-up appointments are made if the patient can benefit from further work in menu planning or education. On admission to the inpatient treatment unit, the patient is briefly interviewed for food preferences by the clinical dietitian. Menus are selected by the clinical nutrition staff with consideration of food preferences, but with major emphasis on adequate nutrient intake and "normal" eating. "Special" diet requests by the patient are not appropriate without a medical reason.

The initial diet order is usually 1,200 kcal, no added salt (150-200 m Eq sodium), low fat, and increased fiber. The reason for this caution is to avoid potential iatrogenic complications, such as acute congestive heart failure, re-feeding edema, gastric dilatation, reduced gastric emptying, and constipation. A low-lactose diet may be needed in rare instances of severe malnutrition. This initial low-calorie diet assists the patient in her psychological adaptation to the eating disorders unit. Calories are usually increased in 200-400 kcal increments to the appropriate kcal level necessary to promote weight maintenance if the patient's weight is appropriate for maturational age, sex, and height, to promote weight gains of 0.5-1.5 kg per week if the weight is below the lower limits of that considered to be normal for a given patient, or to achieve weight loss of up to 0.5 kg per week in the case of overweight bulimics. Sodium restrictions are usually removed at the 1,800 kcal level or the fifth day of hospitalization, unless fluid status is a concern.

A second phase of the diet consists of a gradual increase in patient responsibility in nutritional planning, during which the patient is instructed in menu planning and assumes the responsibility of choosing her menus herself. Ultimately, she takes her own tray or chooses her own meal in the hospital cafeteria. Selecting and eating meals while out of the hospital on pass also test the patient's level of symptom control.

From a nutritional perspective, a major goal is to improve weight and nutritional status by means of a balanced dietary plan. Another objective is to "normalize" the unusual eating patterns observed, by instructing on and demonstrating (as in the hospital) a regular meal and snack schedule, appropriate food portioning, and a varied food intake. A final goal is nutrition education of the patient. This includes provision of accurate nutritional facts to the patient, as well as feedback on the patient's erroneous beliefs about food and weight.

In our program the same clinical dietitian sees patients and is available for consultation in both inpatient and outpatient settings. She also attends team meetings and is therefore aware of the clinical progress of each patient.

In summary, the dietitian, in addition to providing reliable nutrition information and individualized plans, provides dietary structure, assistance in setting realistic goals for dietary modifications, and feedback on dietary progress. In addition, the dietitian joins the other members of the team in providing emotional support, reassurance, and empathic understanding of the difficulty experienced by the patient in changing her rigid diet patterns.

The Role of the Occupational Therapist

The occupational therapist (OT) is an expert in rehabilitation, with a special emphasis on the patient's functional ability (Giles, 1985). Although occupational therapy has frequently been underutilized in medically oriented treatment programs for bulimics and anorexics, the situation has begun to change dramatically during the past 5 years. Increasingly, the occupational therapist works in close cooperation with other team members to help these patients achieve psychological, social, and physical competence (Giles & Chng, 1984).

Two major therapeutic approaches are utilized by the occupational therapist in working with eating disorder patients. The first approach is through activities such as movement and expressive art. Although these activities are not directly relevant to the patient's normal life outside the treatment setting, they help to provoke adaptive changes in the way she interacts with, and thinks about, her environment, and thinks about herself as an individual (Giles & Allen, 1985). A second major therapeutic approach emphasizes the practice of skills for independent living. Examples include cooking practice, eating a meal, and clothes shopping, especially after significant weight changes associated with inpatient correction of emaciation (Giles & Chng, 1984).

As the patient becomes more aware of bodily functions, increasingly comfortable with them, and begins to master daily living skills, she is more likely to assume emotional independence (Giles & Allen, 1985). Although these accomplishments may appear obvious, it is often surprising how overinvolved the anorexic's family had become in her basic bodily functions as her disorder progressed (Chng & Giles, 1984).

This approach is a helpful adjunct to the program's heavy emphasis on patient insight through psychotherapy. A psychodynamic approach used in isolation from other intervention strategies may not enable the patient to overcome all of her practical difficulties; thus, the occupational therapist, as well as other team members, emphasizes patient insight in encounters with the patient (Giles & Chng, 1984).

Occupational therapy affords the patient the opportunity not only to talk about social skills but actually to develop social skills and thus integrate her learning in this area. Psychodrama, when used by a trained therapist, can be a particularly effective technique (Giles & Chng, 1984). Working in groups with creative media such as in pottery, weaving, tile making, leather work, and printing allows the patient and staff to work alongside one another in a variety of roles. Often a patient who denies a particular emotion, such as frustration, makes her feelings perfectly clear to herself by the way she handles the clay or the leather work; the presence of skilled staff at such times can help facilitate the patient's recognition of these feelings (Giles, 1985).

The occupational therapist works closely with other members of the team. The nursing staff and occupational therapist work together on many of the aspects of the patient's daily living, and the patient gains insight during such activities. The psychotherapist alerts the occupational therapist as to a given patient's symptom fluctuations and encourages the patient to utilize her activity time to further her overall progress. A typical example is that of a bulimic who after steady progress has a severe setback while out on hospital pass (Giles & Allen, 1985). The occupational therapist's awareness of this event allows for the opportunity to help her reality-test at the next group meeting concerning her ideas about food and weight gain and to help her develop more effective coping strategies.

Individual exercise sessions are of benefit to specific anorexics and bulimic patients (VanDuessen & Allen, 1985). This population as a whole demonstrates difficulty in moderating their general activity level, often doing "too much" or "too little" exercise. Exercise sessions are helpful in teaching those patients what amount of exercise would be appropriate, as well as in providing opportunities for toning, strengthening, and cardiac reconditioning. In some cases, primarily with patients with bulimia, weight reduction may be an additional goal.

Among the more debilitated patients or in those who may experience arrhythmias secondary to potassium depletion, communication between the occupational therapist and physician are essential as the patient's activity level increases (Giles & Allen, 1985).

The Multidisciplinary Team

Multidisciplinary teams grew out of the increasing complexity of the eating disorder patient populations. It has become apparent that no one professional group can handle all, or even most, of the aspects of a given eating disorder patient's needs. Hence, the modern day multidisciplinary team concept has evolved. Which team member is most prominent is dependent to a large degree on the population being served.

Hedblom, Hubbard, and Andersen (1982) have described the Multidisciplinary Treatment Program at the Johns Hopkins Hospital. They have noted that through experience with anorexic patients and their families, members of the team developed treatment practices in areas of their own responsibility that fit together into an overall program of mutual objectives. They found that their roles contained elements that were separate and distinct with regard to function, responsibility, and purpose. Although independent decisions in regard to patient care were made in accord with each component's treatment responsibility, differences and problem solving between disciplines needed to be accomplished on a one-to-one basis, or in small group or large staff meetings. Major changes in treatment plans, however, remained a team responsibility. This, in essence, is the multidisciplinary team.

Disagreements may arise within the team at any given time and are very acceptable as long as the differences of opinion remain team issues. The typical anorexic patient does not benefit from chaos. This can be further complicated by the "splitting" behavior of these patients, as discussed in this chapter. In our program, team meetings are held twice weekly. No single omnipotent staff person is allowed to emerge. Instead, the patient is confronted with the "team decision." Out of the security of benevolent firmness, the eating disorder patient is encouraged to grow.

All members of the multidisciplinary team are involved in educating the general community about eating disorders, providing continuing education to members of their own profession, and teaching and consulting to other members of the team.

Community education can result in earlier recognition of persons who have eating disorders and in increased sensitivity to the psychological aspects of eating disorders. Many educational programs are presented for students at area schools, and workshops are given for staff of local schools. Various combinations of disciplines can be involved in these efforts. The team, especially the psychologists and outpatient nurses directly involved with a particular patient, work with the faculty of schools to plan for the return of patients to school after hospitalization and to provide consultation in regard to patients who begin to regress during outpatient care.

Each discipline is involved in providing to professionals in its own discipline general information on eating disorders, specific information on the approach of their discipline to the management of eating disorder patients, education about the importance of a team approach, and how outside persons may interface with the team. This may occur in workshops or regional conferences on eating disorders or at meetings of the particular disciplines. It may also occur in individual communication with colleagues or referring professionals, such as when the physician discusses a case with a referring physician or when a psychologist refers a patient to a therapist in private practice. The outpatient nurses provide continuity of care by conferring regularly with the therapists of patients that they are following for symptom management. This arrangement may be visualized as an extended version of interdisciplinary team treatment.

Communication and consultation among the team members is crucial to maintain the cohesive approach of the team. The psychologists provide in-service presentations to the nursing staff, especially as new staff are hired, so that the developmental aspects of the disorders and psychological importance of the holding environment are familiar to all staff. The psychologists also regularly meet with individual nursing staff members to discuss particular patients. The physician discusses medical evaluations and diagnosed or suspected complications with other team members, so that they will be aware of potential problems resulting from the complications. Particular program changes for an individual patient are always discussed with the team before being ordered. The clinical nurse specialist serves as the liaison to the inpatient psychiatry service and is involved when patients are suicidal or require court proceedings. The clinical nurse specialist also supervises both inpatient and outpatient nursing staff in regard to their interactions with the patients, treatment plans, and maintaining the holding environment, and works with other team members on program development.

References

Adler, G. (1977). Hospital management of borderline patients and its relation to psychotherapy. In P. Hartocollis (Ed.), *Borderline personality disorders: The concept, the syndrome, the patient.* New York: International Press.

Chng, C.L., & Giles, G.M. (1984). Anorexia nervosa and the family: Etiology and treatment. *Family Perspective,* **18**, 2-9.

Garfinkel, P.E., Moldofsky, H., & Garner, D.M. (1977a). The outcome of anorexia nervosa: Significance of clinical features, body image and behavior modification. In R.A. Vigersky (Ed.), *Anorexia nervosa* (pp. 315-329). New York: Raven Press.

Garfinkel, P.E., Moldofsky, H., & Garner, D.M. (1977b). The role of behavior modification in the treatment of anorexia nervosa. *Journal of Pediatric Psychology, 2,* 113-121.

Garner, D.M., & Garfinkel, P.E. (1978). Sociocultural factors in anorexia nervosa. *Lancet, 2,* 674.

Giles, G.M., & Allen, M.E. (1985). Occupational therapy in the rehabilitation of the patient with anorexia nervosa. *The Occupational Therapy in Mental Health Journal, 6,* 47-66.

Giles, G.M., & Chng, C.L. (1984). Occupational therapy in the treatment of anorexia nervosa: A contractual coping approach. *British Journal of Occupational Therapy, 47,* 138-141.

Giles, G.M. (1985). Anorexia nervosa and bulimia: An activity oriented approach. *American Journal of Occupational Therapy, 39,* 510-517.

Harris, R.T. (1983). Bulimarexia and related serious eating disorders with medical complications. *Annals of Internal Medicine, 99,* 800-807.

Hedblom, J.E., Hubbard, F.A., & Anderson, A.E. (1982). Anorexia nervosa: A multidisciplinary treatment program for patient and family. *Social Work in Health Care, 7,* 67-86.

Hsu, L.K.G. (1980). Outcome of anorexia: A review of the literature (1954-1978). *Archives of General Psychiatry, 37,* 1041-1046.

Main, T.F. (1952). The ailment. *British Journal Medical Psychology, 3,* 129-217.

Ruch, M.D. (1984). The multidisciplinary approach: When too many is too much. *Journal of Psychosocial Nursing, 22,* 18-23.

Stern, S., Whitaker, C.A., Hagemann, N.J., Anderson, R.B., & Bargman, G.J. (1981). Anorexia nervosa: The hospital's role in family treatment. *Family Process, 20,* 395-408.

VanDuessen, J., & Allen, M.E. (1985). Is there perceptual-motor dysfunction in anorexia nervosa? Suggestions for research by therapists. *Physical and Occupational Therapy in Pediatrics, 5,* 51-58.

Winnicott, D.W. (1965). *The maturational process and the facilitating environment: Studies in the theory of emotional development.* New York: International Universities Press.

Wooley, S.C., & Wooley, O.W. (1980). Eating disorders: Obesity and anorexia. In A. Brodsky & R. Hare-Mustin (Eds.), *Women and psychotherapy: An assessment of research and practice* (pp. 133-158). New York: Gilford Press.

Chapter 16

Counseling Techniques: Nutrition Intervention

Judith Reinke

Anorexia nervosa and bulimia are eating disorders characterized by relentless dieting, food preoccupation, and food restrictiveness. In bulimic individuals, periods of uncontrolled eating are followed by self-induced vomiting, laxatives, diuretics, or other methods to rid the body of calories, only to begin again the cycle of restrictive eating and binging. Detailed descriptions of anorexia nervosa and bulimia have been provided elsewhere (Andersen, 1979; 1981; Boskind-White & White, 1983; Bruch, 1973; Garfinkel & Garner, 1982; Mitchell & Pyle, 1982; Russell, 1979).

The symptomatic focus on food, weight, and calories diverts attention from the primary psychological or emotional problems experienced by the person with an eating disorder. The ability to restrict diet and lose weight provides a sense of control and accomplishment. Supportive nutrition intervention, as an adjunct to other components of a treatment program, shows that food and weight concerns are taken seriously. While correcting problems and misperceptions related to food and weight, the patient is simultaneously engaged in other therapies to remedy underlying disturbances and to learn ways to express oneself better than through food and weight.

The extent to which the person with an eating disorder clings to her symptoms often makes it difficult for the practitioner who is concerned with improving the patient's food habits.[1] The dietitian/nutritionist also needs to be aware of the psychological distress the patient is experiencing and to understand the meaning of the patient's reproach, in order to be of help to her.

---

[1]Because the majority of eating disorder patients seen are female, feminine pronouns will be used throughout this chapter. The practitioner involved in nutrition intervention will hereafter be referred to as the dietitian.

An understanding of general nutrition beliefs and eating patterns among patients is necessary before the dietitian can develop a nutritional care strategy.

Nutrition Beliefs

The person with an eating disorder often considers herself to be quite knowledgeable about foods. Her interest may have prompted involvement in formal or informal study of nutrition. However, perceptions and interpretations of nutritional concepts are often distorted by the eating disorder patient.

For example, the patient may be an expert on caloric value of foods but is not able to relate this information to her own caloric requirements. Calories instead provide a rigid structure to use in order to remain in control of eating and to avoid the panic of possible weight gains. If the person consumes a medium-sized apple rather than a small one, she may respond by calculating the additional calories and compensating for these by doing an extra 30 minutes of strenuous exercise.

The prevalent dichotomous reasoning, as has been described by Garner, Garfinkel, and Bemis (1982) is explained as an absolute need for certainty, with the perception that any deviation from complete predictability (e.g., 300 calories/day) results in chaos. Fear of not being able to cope with the consequences of these unpredictable or unstructured events encourages the individual to set up rigid rules, which lead to an idealized and unattainable notion of success. Other examples of this all-or-nothing reasoning are: "If I have one bite of casserole, I have lost all control," and "If I eat more and gain weight, I won't be able to stop eating or gaining."

Persons with eating disorders often attribute magical qualities to particular foods and how these foods effect weight. For instance, the person may think that foods that are "not nutritious" automatically cause weight gain. This is similar to what Garner, Garfinkel, and Bemis (1982) have called superstitious thinking, or believing in a cause-effect relationship between unrelated events. This thinking helps to insulate the individual from information that could change her beliefs, and it is resistant to modulation. Thus, the person who is purging may continue to use laxatives, despite evidence that they are not effective in preventing calorie absorption.

The person with an eating disorder often uses strict interpretation of dietary guidelines to eliminate major food groups from her diet and often has difficulty looking beyond specific foods to the larger general picture of an adequate diet. Basic components of a balanced diet are often overlooked as the individual tries to come up with the "right" selection of nutritous foods.

It is usually difficult for the eating disorder patient to trust nutrition information contrary to her own beliefs. The dietitian needs to understand what the patient believes to be true, and must begin to work with her at her level of understanding. The dietitian should recognize that disturbed thinking among persons with eating disorders is common and applies to other areas besides nutrition.

Eating Patterns

Persons with eating disorders often exhibit unusual eating habits. Many of these patterns may be a result of malnutrition. Some of the behaviors noted in the Minnesota starvation experiment (Keys, Brozek, Henschel, Michelson, & Taylor, 1950) are also frequently seen in patients with anorexia nervosa and are listed below:

- Food preoccupation
- Interest in nutrition and cooking
- Pleasure watching others eat
- High-bulk diet
- Excessive fluids
- Heavy use of spices
- Gum chewing
- Smoking
- Caffeine use
- Slow eating
- Food hoarding
- Increased hunger after eating

The typical diet of a person with anorexia nervosa consists of salads, popcorn, diet soda and/or coffee, and perhaps small amounts of fruits and lean meats. Foods perceived as "fattening," such as red meats, dairy products, and carbohydrates, are often avoided. Although three "meals" per day may be consumed, the total intake is often estimated at only 300-500 calories per day.

Unusual food handling, food hoarding, and other eating rituals may not be initially apparent from the patient's self-report of diet, but they are common among this population. Extremely rigid eating patterns and limited food variety make it easier for the anorexic person to eat, for she will know precisely what her caloric intake will be. This avoids any unpredictability in regard to foods and alleviates fears of weight gain.

The person with anorexia nervosa often reports being most terrified of eating when she is the hungriest or when faced with favorite foods. This is related to her fear of losing control in eating at these times, and she responds by eating less or not at all.

The eating pattern seen in the bulimic person is often as restrictive as in the person with anorexia nervosa, although the bulimic individual is not able to maintain her resolve not to eat. Her dichotomous reasoning suggests there is no in-between, and any "loss of control" results in a food binge.

The typical diet of a bulimic patient starts out "good," i.e., eating nothing or small amounts of "diet" meals. Any diversions from this plan (e.g., eating *anything* or eating something not planned) means she has been "bad" and leads to a full-blown binge, usually consisting of "bad" or "fattening" foods. The binge is often undertaken with the intent to vomit or purge and with the resolve to do better the next day. Calorie intake from binges may range from 1,000-10,000 calories or more, usually in the form of carbohydrates, sweets, dairy products, or snack foods.

The perfectionistic, self-defeating pattern of the bulimic has been reinforced by numerous attempts at strict dieting, including many popular weight-loss programs. As seen in the anorexic patient, the bulimic person has many delusional expectations about the ability of particular foods, in any amount, to contribute to weight changes.

The reader should be aware of research in patterns among "restrained" eaters and to studies of physiological, psychological, and cognitive factors that may contribute to binging behavior (Lowe, 1982; Polivy, Herman, Olmstead, & Jazwinski, 1984). Physiological and psychological deprivation may create the potential for binge-eating, which is then triggered or prevented by cognitions.

Eating patterns of persons with anorexia nervosa or bulimia are influenced by perceptions of what the diet "should" be to achieve weight goals. Many anorexic and bulimic persons are not able to recognize hunger or satiety to guide their eating and thus rely on the self-imposed external structures described above.

The dietitian who understands the reasoning and fears behind eating patterns of eating disorder patients can be more empathetic to their needs and can incorporate this understanding in developing intervention strategies.

Nutrition Intervention

The nutrition component in the treatment of eating disorders can be summarized by four major goals:

1. Achieve and maintain good nutritional status, including correction of hydration and electrolyte imbalances.
2. Improve and maintain an appropriate body weight.
3. Develop stable eating patterns, including regular meals and portion control.
4. Educate the patient on nutrition and related physiological facts.

The dietitian, by developing a clear and consistent nutrition intervention strategy, is able to provide the patient with firm limits and needed structure for dietary progress.

Improving Nutritional Status

Although biochemical parameters of visceral protein and immune function do not demonstrate any severe nutritional abnormalities, anthropometric data and the creatinine-height index frequently indicate depletion of fat and muscle tissue (Kovach, 1982). Fluid and electrolyte disorders may be observed in vomiting patients (Mars, Anderson, & Riggal, 1982) and in those abusing laxatives or diuretics.

Achievement of a positive nitrogen balance and adequate nutritional status are generally accomplished by providing a nutritionally balanced diet and medical management to improve hydration and correct electrolyte imbalances. Rarely is there a need for invasive nasogastric tube feeding or total parenteral nutrition.

Improving Weight

Persons with eating disorders vary from the extremely underweight to those of normal weight or extremely overweight. For the underweight anorexic patient, graduated re-feeding is a primary goal to achieve gradual weight gains to within normal ranges. Huse and Lucas (1983) have provided useful guidelines for developing a refeeding program.

In normal-weight and overweight bulimic persons, stable or improved weight is a lower priority than correction of fluid and electrolyte status, extinction of the binge-purge patterns, and development of more normalized eating habits. Overweight, and even obese, patients who are anxious to achieve weight loss but are out of control with their binge-purge cycles must consider weight loss as secondary to correction of their troublesome eating patterns and associated concerns. Attempts to lose weight usually means a continuation or exacerbation of restrictive all-or-nothing patterns, which tends to keep the restrict-binge-purge cycle in motion without the patient achieving weight loss. Weight loss up to 5 pounds per month is reasonable for persons who are able to develop healthy attitudes about dieting and weight loss.

The question of what makes a reasonable and healthy weight goal often arises. Although it is nearly impossible to come up with *the* best weight for any one patient, there are considerations to keep in mind: (a) the weight should be one that can be easily maintained without continuous dieting; (b) the weight should be stated in a goal range of perhaps 3-4 pounds, rather than as a single weight; and (c) if the patient has irrational fears about a particular weight (often 99 lbs. is the upper limit for patients), she should go over that limit to allow her to overcome her fears.

"Normalized" Eating

Regular and balanced meals, varied food intake, and appropriate food portions are basic objectives for normalized eating.

Irregular meals are a common problem amoung bulimic patients. After skipping breakfast and lunch, the bulimic is likely to binge in the late afternoon or evening. Although she may be afraid of losing control or consuming too many calories, consumption of regular meals is necessary to help break the restrict-binge cycle. Regular meals for the anorexic patient enables more sufficient calorie intake throughout the day.

Portion control and mealtime balance are usually concurrent problems. "Diet" meals consist of a large quantity of high-bulk, low-fat foods and may contain little, if any, protein or dairy foods. Although temporarily filling, these foods do not meet calorie or nutrient needs and do not provide sufficient satiety value. The patient needs to learn how to select an appropriate and balanced meal and snack pattern to meet her calorie and nutrient requirements. Structured guidelines for meals can be extremely useful.

In addition, the person with an eating disorder needs to "normalize" her diet by choosing from a greater variety of foods within her planned pattern. This includes often-avoided carbohydrates, sweets, fats, or dairy products. If the patient is not confronted on the inaccuracies of the attributes she has assigned to these foods, the dietitian may unwittingly collaborate and reinforce her fears that these are bad foods. The patient may be relieved to have permission to eat these foods. The binger suddenly has the "choice" of including taboo foods into her meal plan. Patients usually have difficulty adjusting their thinking to allow themselves to eat from an expanded food supply, but progress is possible when patients are followed in a fairly structured dietary program.

Structure is essential in helping the patient normalize eating patterns, especially until she is able to incorporate better habits and correctly interpret internal signals to regulate food intake. The dietitian must be aware that excessive structure may trigger compulsive tendencies in some patients who may need a more flexible plan.

Educating the Patient

Beginning treatment with explanations of the effects of starvation on the physical and psychological status of the patient, about the food-related behaviors attributed to the starved state, or about possible physiological reasons for food binges do much to assure the patient that she is not a "freak."

It is also important to discuss with the patient some of the unstated misconceptions she may have related to food values and weight, such as her distortion of her own calorie needs, delusions about calories needed to gain or lose weight, and confusion about the difference between body composition and fluid weight changes. The person with an eating disorder needs education in basic nutrition, food group classification, nutrient and caloric needs, and explanations of factors that influence hunger and satiety and/or other basic digestive functions.

The dietitian should recognize the tendency of the eating disorder patient to fragment factual information and to focus on limited aspects, which are distorted to meet her beliefs. The dietitian must be prepared to confront the patient on the discrepancies between her beliefs and actual facts. Since these beliefs are often central to the patient's sense of identity, they are not easily changed. Recognition and feedback on the patient's erroneous thinking can be accomplished without negating her beliefs and undermining her confidence in the dietitian.

Counseling the Eating Disorder Patient

Developing a sense of trust in the counseling relationship is the essential first step in opening communication for accomplishment of mutually agreed-upon goals. The patient may enter the relationship reluctantly, even with hostility and anger, and may be anxious about expectations. The anorexic or bulimic person is often ambivalent about giving up the eating disorder, which may seem to be her primary identity as a person.

Core conditions identified that contribute to the sense of trust include counselor *empathy*, or ability to experience the patient's world as she does; *congruence* or *genuineness*, which is being as one seems to be, consistent over time, dependable, and honest; *positive regard*, or caring; and *unconditionality*, being totally accepting and setting no conditions on caring for the patient (Patterson & Eisenberg, 1981). Respect for the patient's individuality and initiative (when appropriate) also contribute to the relationship. Thus, the dietitian respects and accepts the individual for who she is, is empathic in her understanding of the situation, and acknowledges to the patient the difficulty of the situation, the ambivalence, and the fears that are present.

Occasionally the dietitian encounters a manipulative or uncooperative patient. It is easier for the dietitian to overcome her initial reaction of contempt for this patient if she understands that the patient may be defending her own fear of rejection or abandonment. The dietitian needs to be even more clear in her unconditional positive regard for the patient, and she must remain firm with her objectives.

Obtaining Information

Information must be gathered from each patient in order to assess her nutritional status, as well as her needs for nutrition counseling. A modified dietary questionnaire similar to the one in Figure 1 is helpful in eliciting pertinent information. The patient is usually more willing to talk to

Name _____ Diagnosis _____

Age _____ DOB ___/___/___

Ht. _____ Wt. _____ MAMC _____ % Fat _____

History of eating disorder:

Diet prior to start of eating disorder:

High Wt. _____ When? _____ Low Wt. _____ When? _____ Desired Wt. _____

Methods used to control weight and frequency of use:

Restrict _____ Laxatives _____ Other _____

Binge _____ Diuretics _____ _____

Vomit _____ Diet pills _____ Exercise _____

Food dislikes _____ Preferences, if noted _____

Foods avoided _____ Food cravings _____

Supplements used _____

Typical food intake; describe alternate patterns:

Food frequency:

Milk—	Poultry—	Snacks (non-B)—
Cheese—	Fish—	Gum—
Cottage cheese—	Red meats—	Hot beverages—
Yogurt—	Vegetables—	Cold beverages—
Eggs—	Fruits—	Alcohol—
Peanut butter—	Juices—	
Legumes—	Sweets (non-B)—	

Describe typical binge and when:

Remarks:

Figure 1. An example of a diet questionnaire.

the dietitian when family members or significant others are not present. In some cases, it may be useful to verify the information obtained, if its accuracy is questionable.

Information sought on the development and history of the eating disorder includes initial weight, diets followed (before and after the eating disorder), weight changes, and other methods used to control weight. This information helps to identify the chronicity of poor dieting and rapidity of weight loss. Additional information on diet prior to the start of the eating disorder can help to distinguish specific dietary changes in food preferences and eating patterns that may result directly from the eating disorder, and can be used in assessing long-term nutritional status effecting growth and bone growth.

A 24-hour "typical" food intake report identifies general dietary patterns, regularity of meals and snacks, and specific problem times for the patient. Usually a description of food frequency is needed to complete the picture of likely nutrient intake over the week. Patients are generally cooperative in providing the needed information, but a more thorough report is obtained when specific and pointed questions are asked. Specific questions are also useful to provide direction if the individual engages in lengthy discussions about food.

It is often necessary to ask the patient about food binges, because she may disregard these in her description of a "usual" diet. Most persons appear to be open to discussing the quantities and kinds of foods consumed, but this author is not aware of any studies that confirm or refute the accuracy of patients' reports.

A report of foods avoided and foods craved helps to identify "taboo" foods that need to be incorporated into a normal eating plan. The patient is also able to see the obvious paradox in the similarity of foods reported to be avoided and craved.

Developing a Nutrition Plan

The focus of nutrition intervention and counseling depends on the needs of the client and the treatment setting.

Hospital Dietary Management. Hospitalization is necessary only when the patient is severely nutritionally, medically, or psychologically compromised. The primary initial goals of treatment are refeeding and medical stabilization. The patient is not able to participate in productive nutrition counseling at this time, because she tends to engage in endless discussions about foods. To allow her to do this only reinforces her preoccupation and prevents her from talking about feelings.

The role of the hospital dietitian may be limited initially to a brief introductory meeting with the patient, in which the dietitian attempts to get a clear picture of usual food and nutrient intake, food patterns, problem foods, and a dietary history. This provides data for nutritional assessment and helps to define dietary goals of hospitalization. The dietitian may also obtain information on specific food likes and dislikes, so that menus may be selected for the patient to minimize further obsessions with food.

At this initial phase, dietary goals of hospitalization may be discussed with the patient. For instance, the patient is expected to eat a variety of foods in regular meals and snacks in order to obtain a nutritionally adequate diet. The dietitian can work with the individual to develop a mutually agreeable plan for problem food groups. For instance, other dairy products may be provided to meet calcium needs when milk is not preferred. Another goal may be that although it is understood that the person has difficulty eating foods such as desserts, butter on bread, or dressing on salads, these are expectations of normal eating in the hospital. For many patients, it can be emphasized that the hospital meals and snacks can be used to demonstrate "normal" portions for their needs. The patient can use the structure of the hospital situation to try eating new or avoided foods and to challenge her inaccurate perceptions that certain foods cause her to "blow up." A chart of dietary goals during hospitalization is provided in Table 1.

When the patient has progressed in weight gain or stabilization, is less obsessed with food and calories, demonstrates appropriate eating behavior, and is given more independence in the hospital program, she can take on more responsibility with her food planning.

The patient may now participate in group classes on basic nutrition and meet with the dietitian to receive a food guide from which to plan her

Table 1   Dietary Goals of Hospitalization

To renourish the patient

Three meals and three snacks daily

To increase food variety
  —Nutritionally complete diet
  —"Taboo" foods

Normal use of fats in diet

Meals and snacks to demonstrate "normal" portions and food quantities to meet needs

To challenge erroneous beliefs about magical quality of foods

To educate on individualized food plan

To educate on food planning for specific circumstances

---

hospital menus. She may attend classes discussing vegetarian diets, shopping for food, selecting meals from a cafeteria line, meal preparation ideas, and menu planning for difficult eating situations. As she nears the end of her hospitalization, the patient spends more time off the unit and may require more assistance with nutritional planning and problem solving.

In working with the hospitalized person, the dietitian should realize that the patient lacks confidence and may be anxious as she assumes responsibility for diet. The patient can be reassured by knowing that the dietitian will review all menu selections and provide feedback on these, that there is no "right" or "wrong" diet, and that the patient will feel more comfortable with her menu-planning tasks when she has more experience.

To aid in the transition to outpatient management, in which the patient will be seen less often than when hospitalized, she can develop a preplanned menu for meals outside the hospital and schedule an appointment for follow-up with the dietitian within 1-2 weeks after discharge.

Outpatient Dietary Management. It is often more difficult to coordinate patient care outside the confines of the hospital. However, coordination and communication of patient progress with other key persons involved in the patient's treatment is necessary.

The outpatient nutrition plan should be primarily focused on gradual achievement of weight goals, provision of pertinent nutrition information, development of individualized food plans, assistance in preplanning meals and special events, monitoring of patient progress, and problem solving with the patient as difficult situations arise. Use of behavior modification techniques to help more positively structure the patient's environment (working on behaviors, cues, and consequences) and use of cognitive restructuring to change some of the dichotomous, perfectionistic, or other troublesome thinking are also important. Patients having eating difficulty, new to treatment, or recently discharged from the hospital need closer dietary management than other patients.

Outpatient dietary management is done primarily with individuals, although groups for presentation of basic nutrition material (as in the inpatient groups) may be helpful in generating discussion and cohesiveness. Structured outpatient feeding programs ensure that patients consume nutritious meals daily.

Why Nutrition Counseling?

Nutrition or dietary counseling provides an opportunity for the person with an eating disorder to work on problematic eating patterns without interfering with other therapeutic programs. There are five general components offered by the dietitian:

1. *Reliable nutrition information and education.* The range of information varies from general dietary and nutrition concerns to specific questions on food compositions. Part of the education entails development of a highly individualized food plan and guidelines on how to implement it.

2. *Structure.* The nutrition office provides a physical setting for the patient to come to on a regular basis to review dietary progress and discuss problems or concerns. The patient has a structured food plan, which decreases the amount of decision-making, confusion, and panic involved in food selections. Specific goals can be set for the patient to work on between visits to the dietitian. Food records kept by the patient provide a focus for discussion and allows the patient to more objectively review the weekly progress.

3. *Goal-setting assistance.* The dietitian is able to help the patient set realistic goals that are based on current levels of eating performance and lifestyle. This will result in a greater chance that the patient will experience success and will prevent the patient from being overwhelmed by impossible tasks. When goals are specific (e.g., "I will consume three meals; each will consist of at least one serving from three of the four basic food groups"), the patient knows more precisely which specific behaviors are needed for accomplishment.

4. *Feedback.* The dietitian can provide objective feedback to the patient on her progress and offer direction in how further to proceed. When the patient relates to the dietitian misperceived ideas about nutrition, the dietitian can point out the discrepancies of these concepts and provide more accurate information.

5. *Support and reassurance.* The high-achieving patient often expects a great deal of accomplishment from herself in a short period of time and is disturbed by her inability to meet unrealistic goals. The dietitian, in addition to assisting in goal setting, can help by pointing out the progress overlooked by the patient and can continue to positively reinforce even the smallest changes made. There may be times when the dietitian has little new information to suggest, but she can still offer the patient a great deal of support to continue in her current efforts. Being available when the patient is having difficulty allows her to continue working on the eating problems.

The dietitian can be reassuring by means of the structure she provides, by being firm with the patient, by not allowing the patient to manipulate or violate basis rules or limitations, and by remaining calm and confident when the patient is anxious and panicked.

Summary

The dietitian involved in counseling the eating disorder patient needs to have a clear understanding of the psychological problems and the particular eating difficulties facing the patient, and to have a comprehensive nutrition intervention plan, in order to be most effective in counseling the eating disorder patient. By helping the patient work appropriately on the object of her symptomatic focus (diet), the dietitian can separate this problem from some of the more basic issues to be addressed in psychotherapy.

Numerous nutrition intervention strategies can be planned around the basic goals of improved nutritional status and weight, development of stable and balanced eating patterns, and education on basic and related nutrition concepts. The dietitian needs to develop a sense of trust with the patient for effective counseling to occur and must be empathetic, consistent, genuine, and unconditionally caring, especially with unusually uncooperative or hostile patients.

References

Andersen, A. (1979). Anorexia nervosa: Diagnosis and treatment. *Weekly Psychiatry Update Series, 3*, 1-8.

Andersen, A. (1981). Psychiatry aspects of bulimia. *Directions in Psychiatry,* 1-8.

Boskind-White, M., & White, W. (1983). *Bulimarexia.* New York: W.W. Norton.

Bruch, H. (1973). *Eating disorder: Obesity, anorexia nervosa and the person within.* New York: Basic Books.

Garfinkel, P., & Garner, D. (1982). *Anorexia nervosa: A multidimensional perspective.* New York: Brunner Mazel.

Garner, D., Garfinkel, P., & Bemis, K. (1982). A multidimensional psychotherapy for anorexia nervosa. *International Journal of Eating Disorders, 1*, 3-46.

Huse, D., & Lucas, A. (1983). Dietary treatment of anorexia nervosa. *Journal of the American Dietetic Association, 83*, 687-690.

Keys, A., Brozek, J., Henschel, A., Michelsen, O., & Taylor, H. (1950). *The biology of human starvation.* Minneapolis: University of Minesota Press.

Kovach, K. (1982). The assessment of nutritional status in anorexia nervosa. In M. Gross (Ed.), *Anorexia nervosa.* Lexington: Collamore Press.

Lowe, M. (1982). The role of anticipated deprivation in overeating. *Addictive Behaviors, 7*, 103-112.

Mars, D., Anderson, N., & Riggal, F. (1982). Anorexia nervosa: A disorder with severe acid-base derangements. *Southern Medical Journal,* **75**, 1038-1042.

Mitchell, J., & Pyle, R. (1982). The bulimic syndrome in normal weight individuals: A review. *International Journal of Eating Disorders,* **1**, 61-73.

Patterson, L., & Eisenberg, S. (1981). *The counseling process.* Boston: Houghton Mifflin.

Polivy, J., Herman, C., Olmstead, M. & Jazwinski, C. (1984). Restraint and binge eating. In R. Hawkins, W. Fremouw, & P. Clement (Eds.), *The binge-purge syndrome.* New York: Springer Publishing Co.

Russell, G. (1979). Bulimia nervosa: An ominous variant of anorexia nervosa. *Psychological Medicine,* **9**, 429-448.

Chapter 17

Counseling Techniques: Nonhospitalized Anorexic and Bulimic Individuals

Joan Hornak

In recent years, counselors have had growing numbers of eating-disordered persons knocking at their doors. Unfortunately, many counselors have been inadequately prepared for the overwhelming complexity of treating these clients. Agreement has yet to be reached regarding the most effective treatment modalities, because of the newness of the field. Yet, a variety of counseling strategies have been used successfully. To some extent, the orientation of the counselor can dictate which specific technique might be used. However, a multifaceted, eclectic approach is recommended for treating these multidetermined disorders (Piazza, Piazza, & Rollins, 1980; Russell, 1979).

To be better equipped to work with anorexic and bulimic clients, the counselor must become knowledgeable of treatment techniques discussed in the professional literature. The summary of the literature presented in this chapter is not meant to be original or exhaustive. Rather, it is aimed at familiarizing the reader with a variety of tools used by others who treat nonhospitalized eating-disordered clients. Counseling techniques will be presented for individual treatment of bulimics, individual treatment of anorexics, family treatment, and group treatment of both anorexic and bulimic clients.

Individual Counseling for Bulimic Clients

Initial Session

The major focus of the first counseling session is to gather information about the client's social history and eating patterns. Structured questions best accomplish this and may take written form. This sharing increases counselor knowledge of the client and begins building trust. After some comfort is established in the counseling relationship, it is wise to gather information about eating patterns. This is to determine the extent to which weight, fears, and food interfere with daily functioning. An inventory has been designed by Neuman and Halvorson (1983) for this purpose.

A decision about hospitalization may also be made in the initial contact. Hospitalization for bulimic clients is useful only if the person is severely depressed, ill, or suicidal, or if the client's eating habits are dangerous (Russell, 1979; Fairburn, 1982). It has been found that the bulimic client does well during hospitalization but quickly relapses when the rigid control of the hospital atmosphere is removed (Neuman & Halvorson, 1983).

During the first session, some counselors give the client permission not to stop her binge-purge behaviors yet (Kubistant, 1982; Bauer, 1984). This permission paradoxically relieves pressure and makes the client more receptive to change. It also minimizes the client's perception of the counselor as another parent.

An early session with a bulimic can be centered around educating the client regarding the symptoms, outcomes, and dangers of bulimia (Doane, 1983). Toward this effort, Cauwel's book, *Bulimia: The Binge-Purge Compulsion* (Couwels, 1983), may be especially helpful. Client education may also occur by inviting the client to read a collection of lay and professional articles compiled and placed in a notebook by the counselor. Additional information may be obtained from national eating disorders associations. Such education gives the client an intellectual understanding of what is happening to her. It also shows the client that the counselor shares this cognitive understanding.

It is beneficial to refer the client to a dietitian for further education and weekly weighing. Daily mini-meals may be prescribed through consultation with the dietitian. Regular eating and daily routines are imperative, whereas calorie-counting and weighing more than once weekly should be discouraged. The counselor, dietitian, and client may collectively make some decisions regarding reasonable client activity and weight and therapy goals.

Subsequent Sessions

The addictive quality of bulimia contributes to resistance of treatment among bulimic clients (Casper, Eckert, & Halmi, 1980). These addictive components must be addressed with the client. Specifically, the binge is very gratifying as a reward for hard work, a numbing of bad feelings, or simply as self-nurturing. The vomiting or purge can be reinforcing in that it relieves the guilt of the binge and, for some, is perceived as justly deserved punishment. The client can draw up her own list of the positive, as well as negative, outcomes of her bulimic behavior. The cumulative cost in both time and money are often minimized by bulimics, because they may focus exclusively on isolated incidents (Doane, 1983). Following are additional counseling techniques that have been used with bulimic clients.

- Weight, favorite foods, diets, and eating habits as a child constitute nonthreatening topics for early verbalization in the therapeutic relationship (Kubistant, 1982). However, some bulimic clients use these topics as a ploy to sabotage psychological focus and change (Bauer, 1984).
- It is useful to identify emotional and behavioral substitutes for the binge-purge. Brainstorming alternatives can prepare for this change.
- The counselor can encourage clients to take control of choices. Clients are often surprised to recognize the control they already use as they plan and delay binge-purge behavior. Questions which can lead to control include: Do I truly want food? What specifically do I want? How much? How will I feel if I eat? (Kubistant, 1982). Request clients to delay each binge a designated amount of time (say, 5 minutes) or to schedule it later in the day. Reactions to these experiments can be recorded in a journal.
- Have clients record in journals the details (time, place, companions, feelings, and self-talk) every time they have an urge to binge (Doane, 1983). Help them recognize that they must make a decision about executing the bulimic behavior. This record should reveal trigger situations, people, and times of day; rationalizations; and accompanying emotions. The journal writing, although resisted, can serve to interrupt a binge. Bulimic thoughts can be followed by rational challenge thoughts such as: Is this thought helpful for my recovery? (Neuman & Halvorson, 1983). Challenge thoughts can also be recorded in the journal.
- Desensitization can be applied when antecedent stimulus events are identified (Ferguson, 1976). The counselor can present a guided fantasy containing binge-triggering situations, while the client remains relaxed and creates alternative, nondestructive mental reactions.
- The dietitian might wish to discuss with clients the connection between dieting and eating binges: that dieting insults the hypothalamus, which then demands a binge as a self-survival mechanism (Doane, 1983). Clients should be encouraged to begin eating normal amounts of food at the meal following a binge (Kobistant, 1982). Resumption of normal eating signals an end to the binge-purge-fast-binge cycle. Set point theory can also be explained (Bennett & Gorin, 1982). When clients recognize the role of body heredity in regulating the amount of fat carried, they are less fearful of getting fat.

- Stress management can be taught. To aid this, a self-directed work-book guide by Tubesing (1981) is suggested.
- Bulimics need to deny or minimize their physical messages to per-petuate their illness. To resensitize clients to their body sensations, progressive relaxation can be practiced (Jacobsen, 1964). Positive imagination also can be rehearsed during the relaxed state (Doane, 1983).
- Teach clients to view relapses or slips as positive opportunities to learn new coping skills. Relapse situations must be examined to result in improved coping tools. Negative emotional states and inadequate coping skills usually percipitate relapse (Marlatt & Gordon, 1980). Help clients see how their outrageous expectations of perfect perfor-mance aggravate their difficulties.
- Rephrase exaggerated negative comments in more realistic terms, or request the client to do this.
- Set goals for the number of "free days" (without binge-purge be-havior) per week and per month.
- Clients can read books and attend workshops on assertiveness (Lange & Jakubowski, 1976). Newly acquired assertiveness skills can be ap-plied in resolving issues and unfinished business characteristic of their relationships (Nueman & Halvorson, 1983).
- Workshops in eliminating self-defeating behavior, when available, assist eating-disordered clients in facing their imaginary fears, confronting their excuses, and changing behavior (Cudney, 1975).
- A belief commonly held by eating-disordered clients is that they must behave perfectly to earn the respect of others and to view themselves as competent (Neuman & Halvorson, 1983). These clients must give themselves permission for, and must experience, making mistakes. This becomes easier if the counselor discloses her or her own mis-takes and models normal human error.
- Clients might contribute binge money or pay a weekly fee to a kitty held by the counselor. The money can become a reward for remain-ing abstinent. If money is not a feasible reward, the client can con-struct a list of activities enjoyable to her. Then she can record her daily accomplishments and how she rewards herself by participat-ing in activities from the pleasure list (Doane, 1983).
- The counselor can elicit the support of peers and family members by inviting them to a therapy session. The bulimic can prepare for this session by listing ways significant others can help in her recovery process (Doane, 1983). During and after termination of the therapy process, bulimic clients are strongly encouraged to cultivate and main-tain support systems for themselves.

Individual Counseling for Anorexic Clients

Initial Session

A comparison of bulimia and anorexia (Table 1) provides background information for selecting counseling techniques. Because of some similarities, many of the counseling techniques suggested for bulimics also apply for anorexics. They generally are not repeated; however, some additional strategies are suggested.

Nutritional rehabilitation of the anorexic patient requires attention before underlying psychological issues can be resolved. It is impossible to

Table 1   Comparison of Bulimia and Anorexia

Anorexia	Bulimia
Refusal to maintain recommended minimal weight	Normal or near-normal weight, or even overweight
Afflicts younger age group	Afflicts older age group
Loss of menstrual period	Menstrual period may or may not be lost; irregularities common
Distorted body image common	
The existence of a food-related problem is generally denied	Usually don't have a distorted body image
More self-control	Eating is recognized as being abnormal
Anemia and vitamin deficiencies rare	More impulsivity; alcohol and drug abuse common
Vomiting less pervasive	Anemia and vitamin deficiencies uncommon but not as rare
Eating rituals	Greater incidence of vomiting and other purging behavior
4-25% mortality rate	Generally appear to eat in a normal manner when not binging and when eating in public
	Mortality rate undetermined

Note. From *Anorexia Nervosa and Bulimia*, by P. Neuman and P. Halvorson, 1983, New York: Van Nostrand Reinhold. Copyright by Van Nostrand Reinhold. Reprinted by permission.

do therapy when the client's brain is starving. An important treatment team member is a dietitian who can explain the nutritional needs of the body and the effects of starvation. The dietitian might recommend three to six meals daily and may have the anorexic be presented with more food than is needed at each meal (Doane, 1983). This encourages the client to eat more than she normally would.

A significant goal of the first counseling session with an anorexic person is to initiate a trusting relationship. This task is often resisted because the client views the therapist as an adversary in collusion with her parents (Crisp, 1980). In fact, many anorexic clients enter therapy as the result of outside pressure to change. Interruption of their weight loss is exactly what they fear. The therapist becomes the enemy. To counter these fears, some assurance can be given that the therapist will help monitor the client's weight so that excessive weight will not be allowed (Garner, Garfinkel, & Bemis, 1982).

Relating intimately is often unknown and feared among these low self-esteem, egocentric clients. A sense of identity confusion stems from their perfectionistic, compliant, and occasionally phony behavior (Eckert, 1982). Their identity confusion continues as they adapt their behavior to please their audience and to parrot the opinions of others. They fear discovery of their inconsistency, so they avoid closeness.

Before proceeding with counseling, the counselor should insist that the anorexic client have a physical examination and have had a recent dental exam. Also, some decisions must be made regarding the appropriateness of hospitalization. Some professionals always require hospitalization at the onset of treatment. If the client's weight is 25% below what it should be, hospitalization is necessary. However, if the weight loss is less than 15% of the original body weight, outpatient treatment may be acceptable (Thoma, 1977).

Goals for weight gain can be set, with rewards and privileges contingent upon these goals. A written contract may be established for weight goal attainment and maintenance (Garner, Garfinkel, & Bemis, 1982). Because many anorexics are extremely fearful of weight gain, a reasonable weight gain is 1 pound per week (Doane, 1983). The weight goal should be stated as a 3-5 pound range, so that the client does not become obsessed about a specific number (Neuman & Halvorson, 1983). To avoid a constant hunger state, the client should consume 1,200 or more calories daily (Neuman & Halvorson, 1983). Even the continuation of therapy may be contingent on the client's weight staying above a certain minimum (Garner, Garfinkel, & Bemis, 1982).

Planning for nutritional restoration, initiating meaningful contact, and establishing therapy goals all serve to prepare the client for the counseling task. By this time, hope for recovery should be inspired as counseling continues.

Subsequent Sessions

Following are some counseling strategies that may be useful in subsequent sessions of individual counseling with anorexic clients.

- Frequent weighing can be a time-consuming and frightening compulsion. Panic often occurs at the onset of weight gain, when the client reaches triple digits, and when menses resume (Neuman & Halvorson, 1983). To prevent the potential of daily panic, recommend that the client get rid of her scales at home. Instead, weekly weighing can be supervised by the dietitian with the client's back to the scales (Neuman & Halvorson, 1983). The dietitian can maintain records and contract to report only inappropriate weight to the therapist and client (Doane, 1983).
- Along with the scales, request clients to get rid of their "skinny clothes" (Neuman & Halvorson, 1983). The presence of smaller clothes can be a frightening reminder of change in body size.
- The client should keep a food chart and be involved with the dietitian in weekly meal planning. This involvement gives the client a sense of control over what she eats and forces practice in making choices. Whereas the dietitian maintains the focus on food and physical issues, counseling sessions can be appropriately centered around psychological concerns.
- The client might gain insight by exploring what low body weight means to her and whether her declining weight has brought the social results she desired (Neuman & Halvorson, 1983). Usually the anorexic recognizes with considerable surprise and disappointment that her weight loss has not solved her problems or brought a flood of popularity, as fantasized. In fact, the focus on weight loss is such an all-consuming preoccupation that relationships are avoided.
- The counselor can also help the client examine what purposes the illness might be serving (Crisp, 1980). A client might recognize that her problem diverts attention away from other family (parental) conflicts. She might even perceive a need to remain ill in order to give her parents a united concern. Some anorexics even like the anorexic label and its resulting attention.
- Anorexics experience difficulty in processing external inputs (Eckert, 1982; Thoma, 1977). Mirror images and peer reactions are often distorted. These disturbances in body images must be addressed. Videotaping, pictures, caliper measures, and counselor reaction can provide meaningful feedback (Doane, 1983).
- Videotaping can also be used to portray role playing of assertion and communication skills (Doane, 1983). Special emphasis might be given to the client claiming her individual rights, stating feelings, and resolving conflicts (Neuman & Halvorson, 1983).

- The client may need "corrective experiences" to counteract inadequate or faulty histories (Garner, Garfinkel, & Bemis, 1982). Coping skills may need to be taught, then experienced. For example, the client might initiate an activity historically avoided, ask for what she needs, express anger, or accept praise. Identifying and focusing on these unfamiliar feelings (Bruch, 1973) with the counselor can precede action outside the counseling session.

- Eliminate talk about "fat" from counseling sessions. Substitute the words "becoming healthy" (Doane, 1983). This gives the therapy goal a more acceptable, positive connotation.

- Have clients call a significant other on a regular specified basis to share a crisis or a victory (Garner, Garfinkel, & Bemis, 1982). Because of desiring to please and to appear perfect, it is difficult for these clients to ask for help. Because of feelings of powerlessness, it is hard to reveal successes. Sharing an accomplishment allows for immediate reinforcement and teaches the client that she can get the attention she needs for reasons other than her illness.

- Have clients practice small activities for the sole purpose of pleasure, with no evaluation attached (Bauer, 1984; Doane, 1983). Their rigid, structured campaigns against fat might have eliminated pleasurable experiences from their lives.

- Educate clients regarding laxative abuse. Most calories have already been absorbed by the time food reaches the part of the gastrointestinal track that laxatives affect. Generally, only water weight is lost through laxative use (Neuman, & Halvorson, 1983). A diet high in fiber can bring more healthy and lasting results.

- It is important to continue to identify and reexamine cognitive distortions (faulty thinking and beliefs) regarding the anorexic's daily living (Bruch, 1978). Three areas of distortion that perfectionistic anorexics commonly use have been identified (Burns, 1980). They include overgeneralization about negative events and consequences, dichotomous (all-or-nothing) thinking, and "should" statements that involve excessive criticism when a goal is not obtained. When challenging the anorexic's irrational beliefs, the counselor must first affirm that these thoughts are authentic for the client. With gentle patience and practice, the client's thoughts can more closely approach reality. This can be accomplished by reexamining small aspects of living as they occur (Bruch, 1978). Help the client identify irrational thought patterns, rationally refute them, and replace them with more realistic thoughts (Neuman & Halvorson, 1983).

- Anorexics are often uncomfortable with social eating. The counselor can model normal eating behavior by sharing occasional meals with anorexic clients. This also allows the client to deal directly with feelings she spontaneously has while eating (Doane, 1983).

Because of the fragile identities seen in some anorexic clients, they frequently develop excessive dependency on the opinions of others. Anorexics turn to others for values, personal decisions, and even methods of expressing those "choices" (Doane, 1983). This type of addictive dependency can be perpetuated within their family interactions. When this happens, family counseling is recommended.

Family Counseling for Eating-Disordered Clients

Family therapy has been used more frequently for treating anorexic clients than for bulimics. It is most effective for the younger anorexic who is still living at home (Garner, Garfinkel, & Bemis, 1982). Several authors have described the following interactional patterns that typify families of anorexics: rigidity, overprotectiveness, conflict avoidance, and a mind-reading type of emotional enmeshment (Liebman, Minuchin, & Baker, 1974; Minuchin, Rosman, & Baker, 1970; Schneider, 1981). For counselors who prefer the "systems" model, the goal with families of anorexics is to change dysfunctional communication patterns in order to disrupt the destructive function being served by the client's symptoms (Minuchin, 1974). Another meaningful goal of this work is to generate family support for the client's stronger sense of identity and increased autonomy.

In general, eating-disordered clients are powerless within the family and have limited experience in making choices (Selvini-Palazzoli, 1978). Some of the following strategies suggested by Doane (1983) can facilitate client choices and power.

- Discuss how the eating disorder is affecting each family member and how each enables the behavior to persist. Have each family member recognize his or her limits of control and responsibility.
- Explore the family's pattern of response to the problem. The counselor can have the family enact a typical family problem. Then the counselor and family members can share reactions, observations, role patterns, and alternative responses.
- Suggest that family members give the client responsibility for her eating without teasing or interference. The disorder is aggravated when family members advise and try to control the client's eating.
- Assess the degree to which family members meet the needs of others. Teach family members to take risks in asking for what they need. They can also practice hearing and saying no to a request within the family without feeling personally rejected.
- The counselor can explore and confront abusive or addictive patterns often found in other family members.

- Bauer (1984) has identified two issues that can be addressed and processed during family counseling. One is the "responsible child" role in the family, which is assigned to many eating-disordered clients. Another is the fear of parent abandonment frequently felt by these clients.

When working with the family of a bulimic patient, the counselor can aid the family in setting behavioral rules for the client. For example, the bulimic should be responsible for the expense of her binges. She may be required to eat meals with her family, not binge in the presence of family members, and clean the bathroom after purging (Neuman & Halvorson, 1983).

It is the counselor's decision whether to work with the eating-disordered individual alone, in a group context, or in family counseling. Family therapy can be combined with individual and/or group therapy. Many of the specific techniques described in this chapter for individual and group counseling are also appropriate for family counseling sessions. Research into the efficacy of family therapy for eating-disordered individuals has been limited (Neuman & Halvorson, 1983).

Group Counseling for Anorexic and Bulimic Clients

Group counseling for treating eating-disordered clients is increasing in popularity. Because of the common issues among clients, the group provides an opportunity to share self-help techniques. It also encourages honesty, fosters a less self-centered sensitivity, and alleviates isolation (Neuman & Halvorson, 1983). A disadvantage of group counseling is that some clients learn new anorexic and bulimic behaviors from their peers. They also might avoid change by convincing themselves that group membership in itself proves they are adequately working on their problems (Doane, 1983).

Screening and Parameters

Pregroup screening involves an interview with potential group members to discuss fees, group rules, and composition; to explore the expectations of the potential group member; to disallow inappropriate group members; and to answer questions (Neuman & Halvorson, 1983).

Length, size, and frequency of group sessions may vary. However, less than a 90-minute session weekly would be inadequate to maintain progress. Size can comfortably range from 5 to 12 members. It is strongly preferred that two leaders be available to cofacilitate the group (Doane, 1983). Two leaders can share the responsibility of the group process, support and stimulate creativity in each other, monitor the group progress, and role-play healthy relationships. For the purpose of modeling, it is preferable that at least one of the group leaders be female (Neuman & Halvorson, 1983).

Group Rules

It is recommended that group rules, in written form, be distributed at the onset of the group sessions. Here are some points that can be included in group rules:

Confidentiality. Emphasize that group participants may not identify any other group member or the content of the sessions. Review this rule periodically.

Attendance. If a person misses the group session three times, she will be asked not to return to that group. If a client plans to be absent, she must call someone in the group ahead of the scheduled meeting time. If a decision is made by a group participant to discontinue membership, she must attend a final session to say good-bye (Doane, 1983). This discourages avoidance behavior.

Drugs. Clients under the influence of mood-altering drugs may not participate in group sessions.

Abstinence. Bulimic group members are required to refrain from binge-purge behaviors to retain group membership (Doane, 1983). After three "slips," the client will be asked to leave the group for at least 3 weeks, during which individual counseling can take place. This procedure would also apply to anorexic group members whose weight drops below a predesignated minimum.

Group Goals

Through group therapy, a support network can be created wherein eating-disordered persons learn to reach out to people, rather than to food. In early group sessions, clients can focus on collective goals for the group. Goals which evolved for one group were (Hornak, 1983):

1. to express feelings about anorexic or bulimic behaviors and to minimize self-disgust;
2. to establish trusting, intimate relationships with peers;
3. to express fears regarding discovery and change;
4. to focus on inner impulses;
5. to feel less isolated;
6. to take risks in moving toward greater independence;
7. to explore family dynamics and to recognize behavior causes and choices;
8. to maintain weight and to return to healthy eating patterns.

Techniques

These or similar goals are best pursued through a combination of approaches. Some specific treatment methods are suggested below.

- At the first session, the counselor can provide a list of first names and phone numbers for each group member. Supportive relationships and group cohesiveness can be encouraged by requiring each group member to phone a different group member on a daily basis (Doane, 1983).
- Sessions can begin by having each participant share something positive or report on progress with a homework assignment. Members can also share problems on which they are currently working (Neuman & Halvorson, 1983).
- During the first session, group members can write their personal goals on pieces of paper and seal them in envelopes. Goals can be re-examined at the midpoint of the duration of the group or at the termination session (Corey, Corey, Callanan, & Russell, 1982). This technique allows clients to set a direction and evaluate their progress.
- If the group is open-ended, each new group member can be assigned a sponsor with whom a special sharing can occur (Doane, 1983).
- Because eating-disordered clients typically have difficulty identifying and expressing feelings, have them stay with present emotion by exaggerating it within the group. Feedback and processing with other group members can be invited. Once this technique is learned, clients can practice exaggerating their feelings between sessions and can record their reactions in their journals.
- To strengthen identity, group participants can try out different and more authentic ways of behaving in the group. Specifically, they can practice behaviors that feel more consistent with their beliefs and emotions. After this experimentation, clients can be encouraged to choose ways they want to behave in the future. Practice in decision making can occur in the group setting.
- Nondirective fantasy can encourage group members to better know and share themselves with others. It invites creative expression and indirect exposure. Here are some directions for group members to follow in this experience: "Imagine you are a book. What is your title, style, chapter heading? Which chapters are the hardest to write? Which chapter do you wish to delete? After reading, what do people think?" (Corey et al., 1982).
- Within the group, co-leaders can talk aloud with each other about the group process. They can share what they are observing and experiencing in the group. Their model of sharing feelings and processing within the group both teaches, and gives permission for, group members to do likewise.

- When a group leader makes a mistake, it is important to acknowledge it within the group. Perfectionistic group members need examples for being comfortable with, and learning from, human error. Many eating-disordered persons are dualistic thinkers; they often view themselves as either good or bad. They fear that if they ever "slip" with their eating, they will never get better (Bauer, 1984; Bruch, 1973). Accentuate expressed polarities by having a group member take the two sides and exaggerate the feelings and opinions associated with each. Then, process reactions to this experience within the group. This generates an openness to less extreme positions.
- It is not unusual for anorexic and bulimic persons to have ongoing conflicts with their mothers and to perceive their fathers as emotionally unapproachable (Bauer, 1984). A group member who had difficulty communicating with her parents can select two pretend parents within the group and talk directly with each. The member might begin, "It's hard to talk to you because . . . ," or, "When I try to talk with you, I feel . . ." (Corey et al., 1982).

One therapy group of bulimic students, when viewed as experts in the dynamics of their self-perpetuated disorder, brainstormed some strategies to facilitate their own treatment. Below are their reactions to the question, "How would you advise other bulimics?" (Hornak, 1983).

- Acknowledge that your behavior is destructive and in need of change, and that change is *your* choice.
- Obtain information about bulimia to increase insight into personal behavior.
- Seek professional help, especially group therapy.
- Learn and practice relaxation techniques and find new coping strategies.
- Turn to relationships, rather than food, for nourishment.
- When you know you will have time alone or feel the need for reward or punishment (both are identified functions of binge-purge), substitute a less destructive behavior: jog, relax, nap, binge on low-calorie foods, take a bath.
- Focus on feelings before, during, and after the behavior, in order to share them in therapy.
- Focus in therapy on relationships with parents, and experience the trust and acceptance of group members when expressing intense negative feelings about family.
- Make a deal with yourself to delay gratification (e.g., "If I don't binge today, I can have an ice cream cone tomorrow").
- Set small goals that you can accomplish easily.
- Congratulate yourself for every success.
- Eat with others; eat slowly and talk a lot.

- Drink a lot of water to feel a "good" full.
- Set rigid times to eat, and give yourself permission to eat then.
- Don't wait for someone to cure you.
- A period of self-starvation often leads to a binge, so eat regularly.
- Seek nutrition counseling and try a healthy diet that is supervised by a health care professional.
- Explore your possible ambivalence about giving up these behaviors and your fear of the future without this crutch.
- Do not have junk food available.
- Call a therapy group member when you are tempted to binge-purge.
- Stop distorting feedback about your appearance.
- Through group participation, you will feel less abnormal and incurable.

Identity confusion among eating-disordered clients has been given previous attention in this chapter. In group work, members frequently have difficulty distinguishing between the feelings of the person speaking and their own. To solve this problem, Neuman and Halvorson (1983) have developed an activity called "separating away" for the end of group sessions. In this experience, group members close their eyes and mentally identify their differences from other group members. After focusing on their strengths and individuality, they go through muscle relaxation. At the end, a group member is asked for a positive thought to leave with the group.

Conclusion

The techniques described in this chapter represent a broad range of counseling approaches, including behavior modification, encounter, Gestalt, rational-emotive, and support-group methods. It is important to use a combination of techniques and a team approach if possible. Whatever treatment modality is preferred, the counselor must view and treat each client as a unique individual within the framework of her eating disorder. Caution should be taken against overgeneralizing. It is hoped this chapter will serve as a guide, not as dogma.

Counseling team members must also be cautioned about becoming so involved with the counseling process and techniques that they fail to measure outcomes. One evaluation tool, the Eating Disorders Inventory (EDI), which was developed at the Clarke Institute of Psychiatry and the University of Toronto by David M. Garner, Janet Polivy, and Marian P. Olmsted, helps measure if change has occurred. Another such instrument, the Eating Attitudes Test (EAT) (Garner & Garfinkel, 1979), can be used as pretest and posttest measures. Clients can also record the change in their number of "free days" (days without binge-purge behavior). Some less empirical measures of progress could include maintenance of body weight, change toward the expression of more realistic self-statements, and change in the ability to accurately identify and express feelings (Leclair & Berkowitz, 1983).

Counseling techniques have been the focus of this chapter. Counselors must also be reminded that who they are is more important than the sum total of the counseling techniques they apply. The most difficult task remains with the reader—that of selecting, personalizing, and applying the techniques. May this process lead to further exploration, improved methods, progress, and recovery for eating-disordered persons.

References

Bauer, B.G. (1984). Bulimia: A review of a group treatment program. *Journal of College Student Personnel, 25*(3), 221-227.

Bennett, W., & Gurin, J. (1982). Do diets really work? *Science, 82,* 42-50.

Bruch, H. (1962). Perceptual and conceptual disturbances in anorexia nervosa. *Psychosomatic Medicine, 24*(2), 187-194.

Bruch, H. (1973). *Eating disorders.* New York: Basic Books.

Bruch, H. (1978). *The golden cage: The enigma of anorexia nervosa.* Cambridge, MA: Harvard University Press.

Burns, D. (1980, November). The perfectionist's script for self-defeat. *Psychology Today,* pp. 34-52.

Casper, R.C., Eckert, E.D., & Halmi, K.A. (1980). Bulimia: Its incidence and clinical importance in patients with anorexia nervosa. *Archives of General Psychiatry, 37,* 1030-1035.

Cauwels, T. (1983). *Bulimia: The binge-purge compulsion.* New York: Doubleday.

Corey, G., Corey, M.S., Callanan, P.J., & Russell, J.M. (1982). *Group techniques.* Monterey, CA: Brooks/Cole.

Crisp, A.H. (1980). *Anorexia nervosa: Let me be.* New York: Grune and Stratton.

Cudney, M. (1975). *Eliminating self defeating behavior.* Kalamazoo, MI: Life Giving Enterprises.

Doane, H.M. (1983). *Famine at the feast: A therapist's guide to working with the eating disordered.* Ann Arbor: ERIC/CAPS.

Eckert, E. (1982, October). *Diagnosis and clinical characteristics of anorexia nervosa.* Paper presented at the Eating Disorders Conference, Minneapolis, MN.

Fairburn, C.G. (1982). Binge eating and its management. *British Journal of Psychiatry, 141,* 631-633.

Ferguson, T. (1976). *Habits not diets.* Palo Alto, CA: Bull Publishing.

Garner, D.M., & Garfinkel, P.E. (1979). The eating attitudes test: An index of the symptoms of anorexia nervosa. *Psychological Medicine,* **9,** 273-279.

Garner, D.M., Garfinkel, P.E., & Bemis, K.M. (1982). A multidimensional psychotherapy for anorexia nervosa. *International Journal of Eating Disorders,* **1,** 3-46.

Hornak, N.J. (1983). Group treatment for bulimia: Bulimics anonymous. *Journal of College Student Personnel,* **24**(5), 461-462.

Jacobsen, E. (1964). *Anxiety and tension control.* Philadelphia: T.B. Lippincott.

Klesges, R. (1983). An analysis of body image distortions in a non-patient population. *International Journal of Eating Disorders,* **2**(2), 35-42.

Kubistant, T. (1982). Bulimarexia. *Journal of College Student Personnel,* **23,** 333-339.

Lange, A., & Jakubowski, P. (1976). *Responsible assertive behavior: Cognitive/ behavioral procedures for trainers.* Champaign, IL: Research Press.

Leclair, N., & Berkowitz, L. (1983). Counseling concerns for the individual with bulimia. *The Personnel and Guidance Journal,* **61,** 352-355.

Liebman, R., Minuchin, S., & Baker, L. (1974). An integrated treatment program for anorexia nervosa. *American Journal of Psychiatry,* **131,** 432-436.

Marlatt, G.A., & Gordon, J.R. (1980). Determinants of relapse: implications of the maintenance of behaviors. In P.O. Davidson & S.M. Davidson (Eds.), *Behavioral medicine: Changing health life styles* (pp. 410-450). New York: Brunner Mazel.

Minuchin, S. (1974). *Families and family therapy.* Cambridge, MA: Harvard University Press.

Minuchin, S., Rosman, B.L., & Baker, L. (1979). *Psychosomatic families: Anorexia nervosa in context.* Cambridge, MA: Harvard University Press.

Neuman, P.A., & Halvorson, P.A. (1983). *Anorexia nervosa and bulimia: A handbook for counselors and therapists.* New York: Van Nostrand Reinhold.

Piazza, E., Piazza, N., & Rollins, N. (1980). Anorexia nervosa: Controversial aspects of therapy. *Comprehensive Psychiatry,* **21**(3), 177-189.

Russell, G. (1979). Bulimia nervosa: An ominous variant of anorexia nervosa. *Psychological Medicine,* **9,** 429-448.

Schneider, A.S. (1981). Anorexia nervosa: The "subtle" condition. *Family Therapy,* **8**(1), 49-58.

Selvini-Palazzoli, M. (1978). *Self-starvation: From individual to family therapy in the treatment of anorexia nervosa.* New York: Jason Aronson.

Thoma, H. (1977). On the psychotherapy of patients with anorexia nervosa. *Bulletin of the Menninger Clinic,* **41**(5), 437-452.

Tubesing, D. (1981). *Kicking your stress habits.* New York: New American Library.

Chapter 18

The Effects of Eating Disorders on Families and the Role of Support Groups

M. Joan Mallick

In 1963 Davis wrote a book titled *Passage Through Crisis* about polio victims and their families. Devoid of psychoanalytic interpretations, the book described the behavioral and emotional reactions of families to the diagnosis, treatment, and recovery from polio. This work provided a sensitive description of illness from the perspective of those who live through it every day, namely, the patient and his significant others.

In discussing the implications of his findings, Davis stated the following:

> First, and most obviously, they point to the need for viewing health behavior in a social context much broader than that circumscribed by the consulting room, the clinic, and the hospital. The fact is that a considerable portion of the individual's health and illness experience takes place in locales, and with persons, far removed from the guidance and control of institutionalized medical authority—in the home, at work, with kin, friends, neighbors, and others in the person's routine existence. [Study of the illness from the patient's perspective has furthered] a more realistic appreciation of the patient's situation. (p. 168)

During the past 5 years, a number of personal accounts of the experience of anorexia and bulimia have become available to those suffering from these afflictions (Levenkron, 1978; Liv, 1982; MacLeod, 1982; O'Neill, 1982). These accounts provide sufferers with a sense that their suffering is not singular; they provide the professional with a view of these illnesses that may be different from that provided in the hospital or the psychiatrist's office. However, there are few accounts of the experience of eating disorders told from the point of view of significant others: the parents, siblings, husbands, boyfriends, and girlfriends of the afflicted (hereafter referred to as family members). It is the purpose of this paper to present this perspective.

The information presented here is based on 2 years experience with a support group for families of eating-disordered persons. Assuming the role of participant-observer, this author listened for themes reiterated by families confronted with the crisis, and then the chronicity, of anorexia and bulimia. A core group of approximately six families regularly participated in the group during this 2-year period. This core group provided the author the opportunity not only to verify the important issues facing them in their adjustment to these problems but also to witness their growth and development as a result of their mutual support. Thus, the information represents a wealth of prospectively collected data not available in most other analyses (Garfinkel & Garner, 1982).

The format used in this discussion is similar to that used by Davis (1963) namely, to describe the natural history of the illness experience of the family, including the families' conceptions of the disease and the recovery process, alterations in these conceptions as a result of the hospital and posthospital experiences, and the effects of the child's illness on family functioning. Examples of family reactions and activities are composites of several families utilizing the support groups' services, which include referral and education. In addition to describing family reactions to the illnesses, the role of a family support group in the unfolding of this history will be presented.

The Period of Illness Recognition and Self-Help

Family members experience several difficult periods related to eating disorders. The first occurs when someone in the family begins to suspect that an eating disorder may be present. Recognition may come one of several ways. The first—but, in this author's experience, the least frequent—way an eating disorder can become an acknowledged possibility is that the person with the eating disorder "confesses" the problem to the family. In these cases, the eating-disordered person usually has suffered with the problem for an extensive period of time and recognizes that the illness is controlling her life. Confession to family members becomes a method of easing the burden of carrying the illness by herself. Confessions may occur in dramatic ways, such as tearful admissions as a family watches a television show about eating disorders.

The second way recognition may occur is a slower and subtler sequence. In this instance, family members may observe the deteriorating behavior and physical condition of the eating-disordered member over time and may become concerned that a serious physical condition is causing the problem. Often an eating disorder may be suspected, but the family may hope that the cause is a "less serious" malady, such as an ulcer or another form of indigestion. The first course of action is to seek a medical attention with the family physician. Frequently, the physician consulted is not familiar with eating disorders and focuses attention on ruling out organic causes for the problem. Once these have been ruled out, the physician generally assures the family that there is nothing wrong with the afflicted person. If asked about the possibility of an eating disorder, the practitioner often attributes the problem to a temporary dieting phase common in the life of teenage girls.

In a situation in which an eating disorder truly exists, a family member is confronted with the dilemma of having medical verification that no problem exists but having living proof that a serious situation is at hand. In many instances, he or she begins a desperate search for information about possible causes of the problem, seeking more information about eating disorders. When it becomes apparent that the afflicted person's physical condition and behavior closely match the descriptions given in the literature, the family member, by default, makes the diagnosis of anorexia or bulimia.

The third sequence of events in recognizing eating disorders is played out less consciously than the other two. In this situation, family members may be subconsciously aware that a problem exists but may consciously deny the probability. For instance, a family member may periodically think that another's weight loss is extreme or that her food-related behavior is not normal. However, the conscious response is to accuse oneself of being overly concerned and to go on about the business of everyday life. At some later time, these nagging concerns are not so easily dismissed and, perhaps in conjunction with a media discussion of eating disorders, the undeniable possibility of an eating disorder becomes apparent. Family members who experience this recognition sequence often report that the knowledge "hit us like a ton of bricks."

Often only one family member becomes convinced that an eating disorder is present. In that case, this family member must convince the others that a serious problem exists. Some family members may resist this information, because the possibility that such a serious behavioral problem exists is inconsistent with their belief that theirs is a well-functioning, normal family. Disagreements about the presence or absence of an eating disorder may significantly affect the family by increasing tensions and arguments about a condition which some would rather ignore.

The crisis of this recognition period is characterized by extreme anxiety. Family members who accept the possibility of an eating disorder focus on serious physical effects of the problems. Regardless of how long the condition may have existed in a physically dangerous state before they recognized it, families are convinced that the very next skipped meal, exercise period, or binge-purge cycle will result in death. Family members begin to devote their complete attention and energy to monitoring the problem and searching for ways to resolve it. This anxiety is even greater in families in which not everyone agrees that an eating disorder exists. Those who recognize the problem feel that those who refuse to accept it are wasting precious time in resolving it.

Attempts at Self-Treatment

In a family in which there has not been an admission by the afflicted member, the first difficulty is how to approach her to discuss her problem. Because the eating-disordered person is usually moody, irritable, and withdrawn, the family believes that if they broach the subject of eating disorders with her, not only will they be rebuffed but already strained relationships will be further compromised. Furthermore, they believe that if the affected person is angered by the discussion, the condition will become worse and they will be at fault. Families thus spend a great deal of energy planning how to discuss the subject. They also spend a great deal of energy trying to maintain good relationships with the afflicted person, so that when the plan for discussing the problem is developed, a store of goodwill will already be present.

Despite extreme anxiety about the potential danger of the situation, families often try to resolve the eating disorder without medical assistance. There are several reasons why self-treatment is tried. First, for eating-disordered individuals who have voluntarily discussed the problem with the family, there may be mutual agreement that, because the problem is out in the open, the resources of the entire family can be used more successfully to combat it. The rationale here is that the resources of several concerned people will be more powerful than the resources of only the afflicted person.

Families attempt self-treatment in an attempt to mend strained relationships with the afflicted member. Afflicted persons often do become angry and more withdrawn from the family if the subject of eating disorders is raised. The eating-disordered person may tell the family that there is no problem or that she is sure she will be able to handle it by herself. Family members are then caught in the dilemma of wanting to trust her but not knowing how trustworthy she is. Family members describe themselves as "walking on eggs" with the afflicted one, never knowing whether interactions are going to be harmonious or turbulent. One tactic they use to try to make peace is to allow the eating-disordered individual to prove herself by controlling the situation without medical intervention.

A third reason why families try self-treatment is that they believe that there are simple solutions to the problem. Convinced that the problem is a simple one of eating and weight restoration, they believe that the task is to determine a motivator that will stimulate eating. Perceiving themselves and the afflicted member to be rational individuals, they believe they are as capable as medical personnel of solving the problem.

A fourth reason for self-treatment is that the thought that the problem may indicate an underlying psychiatric problem with the individual and/or the family presents a frightening possibility. Family members see themselves as good parents (mates, friends, etc.). To seek medical attention for a problem that may have psychiatric undercurrents constitutes, in their minds, an admission that they have failed in their attempts to be good parents and friends. Thus, they attempt self-treatment as a method of reinforcing their self-worth.

A fifth reason for self-treatment may be lack of knowledge of, or confidence in, the medical profession. For those who sought the advice of a family doctor and were told not to worry, the prospect of finding adequate medical treatment seems remote. Others do not believe that the problem of eating disorders is widespread enough to warrant specialty treatment centers and despair that such treatment will be readily available to them.

Self-treatment usually encompasses a variety of methods. One component is monitoring of the eating-disordered behavior. Families monitor weight, calorie intake, and exercise programs of the anorexic, and vomiting episodes and laxative use of the bulimic. Monitoring may at first be surreptitious, so as not to upset the individual (who resents the surveillance). If there is no improvement in the condition, monitoring activities may become more obvious, with less emphasis placed on feelings and more on confronting what is perceived as the significant fact of the situation, namely, the failure to gain weight or failure to stop the binge-purge cycles.

Several tactics are used to try to reverse the eating-disordered behaviors. One strategy is to try to reason with the person, pointing out the seriousness, as well as the irrationality, of the condition. Another tactic is to apply negative sanctions against her unless the condition improves. Parents try withholding privileges as diverse as participation in school and family activities, use of the family automobile, and the right to choose a college or to have it paid for by the family. Some husbands have withheld credit card privileges from their wives.

Another tactic is to point out to the person the effect the behavior is having on the family. One family member often points out that another one is "worried to death about you" and that a loving daughter, wife, or girlfriend would be considerate enough of family feelings to abandon such worrisome behavior.

A fourth tactic, often used when others have failed, may be violence. Families have reported physically shaking the afflicted person or throwing household objects in an effort to change behavior. Although some of this violence is precipitated by total frustration with the situation, there is an underlying belief that it may take some action of this magnitude to "shake some sense into the individual."

In the vast majority of cases, any and all of these attempts by families are met with resistance. At best, they result in no improvement in the situation; at worst, they cause the situation to become worse, because the eating-disordered individual strengthens her resolve to control her own life by continuing her weight control efforts. At this point, the family is caught in an ever-accelerating cycle in which parental efforts are met with resistance, which causes increased anxiety, which causes increased efforts, which cause increased resistance, and so on.

Eventually, family energies become focused almost exclusively on the eating-disordered member, often to the point that normal family interactions cease to exist. For instance, spouses may find themselves constantly arguing about the appropriate strategy for dealing with the eating disorder of a child, one spouse advocating leniency, whereas the other advocates stringency. These arguments may become the sole topic of family conversations and may be so time-consuming as to eliminate time for normal family activities. The needs of the other children may be ignored, for their normal concerns with school and extracurricular activities seem less pressing than the serious threats posed by the eating disorder.

Extended family members and neighbors may become involved in the problem, urging the nuclear family to do something about the problem before it is too late. Family frustration with their lack of success thus is mingled with anger at, and resentment of extended family members who, though well-intentioned, seem to appreciate neither the difficulty of the situation nor the fact that every conceivable measure may already have been taken.

Help Outside the Home

It is at a point when self-help measures have failed that many families seek the assistance of self-help groups. Frustrated to the point of desperation, they seek advice from strangers about how to handle the situation. Still convinced that a simple solution to the problem is possible, they seek help from others who, they hope, may have discovered the magic cure that they themselves have missed.

The task of the support group during this period is to help the family accept the futility of their efforts to create a cure within the family setting. Family members must recognize that their monitoring, nagging, and manipulating activities are doing little to resolve the situation. They must accept the fact that the eating disorder is a more complex condition than they can handle on their own. At the same time, they must accept that their efforts were made in good faith and that they are not to blame for the current state of the eating disorder. In short, the family members must realize that they are responsible for neither the development nor the cure of the eating disorder.

This attitude is a difficult one to develop, because family members are usually convinced that the eating disorder would have been much worse in the past or will become much worse in the future if they relax their efforts. In addition, giving responsibility for the condition to the afflicted one seems to be a cold and uncaring strategy, the equivalent of abandoning the person. However, at least one reality supports the notion of giving responsibility for the condition to the afflicted person. That is, legally, anyone over the age of 18 cannot be coerced to seek or accept medical treatment. Thus, for afflicted members who are postadolescent, the right to one's own disease is legally inalienable.

Another task of the support group during the self-help period is to recognize that the purpose of a family support group is not to learn how to resolve the eating disorder, but to help family members cope with a problem without experiencing their own mental or physical deterioration. For a family preoccupied with the eating-disordered member and in a state of high anxiety, this, too, is an absurd notion, for they do not recognize the potential toll that unrelenting worry can have on their own lives.

Often a family attends only one support group meeting, apparently disappointed with the lack of a magic cure and with the seemingly tough attitude they are advised to take with the eating-disordered person. They do not see the value of a group that offers little more than sympathy and understanding. For those who are able to recognize the potential value of this offer, however, the group becomes a strong source of aid during other difficult periods during history of the illness.

The Experience of Treatment, Hospitalization, and Discharge

When the eating-disordered person enters specialized treatment, the acute anxiety of the self-help period subsides and the family experiences a brief period of emotional relief, even euphoria. At this point they are convinced that, having seen the necessity of formal treatment, the major hurdle has been overcome and recovery is merely a matter of time. This honeymoon period is often even more blissful if the member is hospitalized, because the family perceives that the efforts of a team of experts with special curative powers are now available.

The first disillusionment comes when the eating-disordered patient fails to make noticeable progress quickly enough. Progress may be very slow for the hospitalized patient whose physical condition was quite serious upon admission. Restoration of body weight often comes slowly, causing parents to become impatient with the efforts of the ''so-called experts.'' For both hospitalized and nonhospitalized patients, recovery may be delayed because they may not develop the rapport and confidence in their therapists that is necessary for progress. A patient may reject one or more therapists before finding one who inspires confidence. In such situations, family members begin to question the competency of available therapists and begin to believe that no one knows what they're doing.

The family members' disgruntlement is often increased when, while trying to gather information about the components of treatment and the prognosis for recovery, they are told that the content of therapy is privileged communication and that they must trust that progress will eventually be made. The family members become angry at the system and begin to believe that they are being abused, especially because they are generally not informed of the details of therapy on a routine basis. This anger is increased for the family of a hospitalized patient, whose treatment may cost tens of thousands of dollars.

A second emotional trauma often affects parents shortly after therapy has begun. This occurs when the therapist suggests that family therapy may be appropriate, the family's fear of being judged incompetent being thereby inadvertently confirmed. The feeling of incompetence may also be validated if the therapist suggests that family-patient interaction should be reduced or temporarily interrupted.

The dominant emotion during this period is guilt. Relieved of the anxiety that predominated during the recognition period, and threatened by the suggestion of family therapy, family members begin to think about factors that might have contributed to the development of the eating disorder. Parents often obsessively relive earlier years in the afflicted child's childhood, searching for errors in child-rearing practices. A spouse, often encouraged by accusations by the eating-disordered patient, reviews the marital relationship for emotional failures. If family members cannot find any obvious connection between their previous behavior and the development of the eating disorder, they begin to blame themselves for not recognizing the condition sooner. Aided by the wisdom of hindsight, they relive many instances in which the symptoms were so obvious they ''should have been spotted sooner.''

One task of the support group during this period is to help family members to deal with their guilt. Attempts to reduce guilt include having a number of families discuss their differing child-rearing practices, thereby illustrating that no single pattern results in eating disorders; arguing that guilt and blame take precious energy that is best used to deal with the current situation; and advising that families usually have the best interest of the afflicted person in mind and cannot assume blame for actions that were performed with good intentions.

Another task of the support group is to encourage family therapy. Members who have themselves undergone family therapy encourage others to attempt it. They describe what goes on during therapeutic sessions, explaining that therapy sessions are intended not to place blame on either the family or the patient, but rather to discover and resolve ineffective communication patterns that may contribute to the continuation of the disorder. Many admit that they, too, were threatened by, and afraid of, family therapy when it was first suggested to them, but ultimately found it to be helpful. Some even suggest that if the therapist has not already suggested family therapy, the family might initiate it themselves. At the same time, however, support group members advise that if family therapy is not included, the support group can itself act as a source of coping and communicating techniques. General strategies learned during their own family counseling are freely shared with others not in active family therapy.

The Rollercoaster Course of Therapy

For most patients who continue in treatment, improvement in physical condition eventually occurs; as weight is gained or as binge/purge cycles become less frequent, families once again become optimistic. They believe that the eating disorder has been resolved and that the specter of death and the emotional tension that previously existed are things of the past. This optimism, however, often is only a brief respite from the emotional turmoil that resumes when the first of perhaps several relapses occurs.

It is not unusual for eating-disordered patients to regress to pretreatment patterns several times during the course of treatment. Eating disorders are often methods of coping with life stressors, and, therapy notwithstanding, they become convenient coping methods when stressors peak. Thus, weight fluctuations and/or resumption of binge-purge cycles often occur many times during the course of treatment, and the patient experiences alternating periods of improvement and regression. Families are generally still quite emotionally involved in the illness and describe this period as an emotional rollercoaster ride. Their emotional well-being fluctuates with each change in the eating disorder.

The task of the self-help group during this period is threefold. First, group members help one another accept the fact that eating disorders are chronic illnesses. Second, members help each other dissociate their own emotional status from the status of the eating-disordered patient.

Third, they help each other deal with the anger associated with the prolonged illness period.

Family members learn by experience that eating disorders are chronic illnesses. The question in family members' minds is whether after experiencing the anxiety and guilt of previous periods, they have the emotional strength to withstand a prolonged onslaught by the continuing illness. At these times, group members offer themselves as "shoulders to cry on" when the burden seems overwhelming. Older members offer their own survival as evidence that the illness can be tolerated.

Advice on how to survive the prolonged period of illness includes repeating previous advice to "give the illness to the afflicted one and remember that no amount of concern or involvement can force a cure." Family members are also told to "get off the emotional rollercoaster" and to try concentrating on other aspects of their daily lives. Finally, families are told that they have a right to their own personal happiness and a responsibility not to detract from the happiness of nonafflicted family members.

The family is helped to deal with anger in several ways. First, the group accepts the anger as justifiable. Members sympathize with one another regarding the financial burden of the illness, the difficulty they have in communicating their frustration to health care personnel, and the frustration associated with lack of steady progress. Second, whereas in treatment settings family members may be afraid to express their frustration, they are encouraged to do so in the support group. Members advise one another that it is better to express their anger in a sympathetic setting, than someplace where it may provoke unpleasant consequences. Finally, members often vent anger in general discussions of the lack of knowledge about the causes and cures for eating disorders. This generalized venting seems to be an effective method of relieving emotional pressure.

Accepting the Illness

Persons who continue with a support group appear to make a gradual transition over the course of about 2 years. Even persons with an afflicted family member who makes little progress toward recovery are able to develop a quiet (though not happy) acceptance of the situation. They are able to recognize and articulate differences in their attitudes and behaviors toward the illness and the afflicted one. They demonstrate an attitude less focused on themselves and more focused on helping others. Finally, they are able to laugh not only at the bizarre aspects of the illness but also at their previous methods of attempting to deal with it.

Accepting the illness means that energy is free for more productive pursuits. Families often report better relationships with afflicted members, even though the eating disorder may still be in a serious phase. They report a better quality of life for themselves. An indication that support services are no longer necessary is that family members talk of not being interested in discussing eating disorders. They articulate the desire to get on with living, assigning anorexia or bulimia a smaller role in their lives. Recognizing that the support group has played an important role in their coping, they nevertheless express a desire to separate from it and use support group time for more normal pursuits. This reflects a healthy attitude and is perhaps the greatest evidence that a support group has been successful.

Conclusion

Family support groups play an important role in the adjustment to eating disorders. Through the establishment of a caring community, support groups provide a forum through which members can integrate these problems into their lives. In a positive and nonthreatening atmosphere, family members learn that though an eating disorder represents a traumatic episode in their life, such a problem does not need to remain overwhelming.

The Cleveland Anorexia/Bulimia Aid Society has published the following guidelines for families of persons with eating disorders.

Anorexia and bulimia are family problems.

Guilt and blame do not help to cure eating disorders.

The decision to change must be made by the person with the eating disorder—families cannot force a cure.

Parents do the best they can in raising their children.

The afflicted and their families have a right to choose a qualified health care provider.

Helping others helps ourselves.

Families are entitled to a satisfying life outside their role as relatives of an eating-disordered individual.

References

Davis, F. (1963). *Passage through crisis*. Indianapolis: Bobbs-Merrill.

Garfinkel, P.E., & Garner, D.M. (1982). *Anorexia nervosa: A multidimensional approach*. New York: Brunner/Mozel.

Levenkron, S. (1978). *The best little girl in the world*. Chicago, IL: Contemporary Books.

Liu, A. (1982). *Solitaire.* New York: Harper and Row.

MacLeod, S. (1982). *The art of starvation, a story of anorexia and survival.* New York: Schocken Books.

O'Neill, C.B. (1982). *Starving for attention.* New York: Continuum Books.

Part V

Community

Treatment of obesity no longer resides solely in hospitals and clinics. Because obesity is a major epidemic with large profit potential, obesity treatment can now be found in shopping malls, grocery stores, and office buildings. Weight loss programs designed as for-profit businesses are now receiving competition from a new angle. Community-based programs have recently evolved, incorporating exercise, personalized nutrition management, and behavior modification strategies. This section focuses on components of community-based weight loss programs, programs that work, and the role of nutrition counseling.

Chapter 19

Effectiveness of Community Weight Loss Programs

Richard B. Parr

A variety of weight loss programs are offered through various community organizations. Most programs are designed with little concern for that which research has told us about diet, exercise, and behavior modification. Those responsible for these programs are not even aware of more recent information concerning cellularity and metabolic changes associated with weight gain and weight loss. For instance, research by Sjostrom (1980) has indicated that fat cell numbers can increase in adults as a consequence of weight gains. Instead, programs reflect personal or business interests, with more regard for testimonials than for documented practices. Ineffective programs often show weight increases during the treatment phase and, frequently, upon follow-up. It appears that this type of "success" may perpetuate the obesity problem, rather than cure it.

Various weight loss programs available within a community claim success based on their methodology. The advantages of a "community approach" is that specific aspects of a multidisciplinary program can be taught by instructors utilizing their expertise. Lack of coordination, however, results in overlapping, with frequent discrepancies in the effectiveness of treatment modalities. The primary purpose of the "community approach" is to serve persons' needs at a minimal cost. Generally, the instructors volunteer their time for the good of people within the community.

Commercial weight loss clinics have profit as their primary purpose, with weight loss being important for continued generation of business. These programs are often directed by persons who have gone through limited instruction directed at procedures and techniques proposed by the sponsoring organization.

Commercial group programs also have profit as their primary interest. They are generally directed by previous members who are used as models of success within the program. Commercial group programs may or may not use a variety of approaches for obesity intervention.

Hospital-based wellness programs are in their infancy. Weight loss is considered as one of several risk reduction programs offered within the wellness arena. Hospital and clinical institutions have recognized the profit in keeping people healthy, as well as in treating the sick.

Corporations have recently demonstrated an interest in employee programs to enhance wellness and reduce risk for disease. They, too, have realized financial benefits in keeping employees healthy by reducing absenteeism, sick days, and physician visits. The full impact of employee programs is yet to be realized.

Historical Perspective

An evaluation of past weight loss programs gives insight into components that can be incorporated into a successful community program. Disregarding this valuable information and persisting with unsuccessful techniques only provides for future failure.

Stunkard and McLaren-Hume (1959) reviewed 30 years of literature to find that weight loss programs prior to 1960 were primarily dietary restriction with or without anorexic medication. Follow-up of these programs was poor or nonexistent. Weight loss programs in the 1960s and 1970s used a variety of approaches, with behavior modification as the major mode of intervention. The principles of behavior modification, however, were directed almost exclusively to dietary intervention, with little application to exercise. Additionally, these principles have been applied to groups with positive, yet varying, results. Coates and Thoreson (1979) have suggested that better results come with individual prescriptions based on behavioral analysis of each subject. Behavioral approaches to weight loss were reviewed by Stunkard and Penick (1979), who found short-term success attributable to lower attrition rates. Long-term (2 years) success, however, was found to be no better than conventional methods. Stunkard and Penick have suggested several ways to improve long-term weight loss:

1. Increase the typical 10-week program to 16-20 weeks.
2. Increase frequency from once to three to four times per week.
3. Individualize treatment.
4. Use a multifaceted approach, with emphasis on behavior modification.

It is difficult to develop principles of weight loss for community programming because the literature is not conducive to organizing pertinent results. Reported data include numerous variables, such as initial overweight (20-78%), number of subjects (8-165), length of treatment (8-20 weeks), frequency of treatments (one to three sessions per week), and drop-out rates ranging from 0-50%. Stunkard and McLaren-Hume (1959) reported conventional out-patient treatment (diet and medication) drop-out ranging from 25-75%, whereas Stunkard (1978) has shown as little as 10% drop-out when behavior modification is included in the management. Equally confusing is that within these variables, the modes of treatment include a variety of diets, exercise programs, and behavioral techniques, either singularly or in combination.

The effectiveness of weight loss programs have been evaluated by several authors (American College of Sports Medicine, 1983; Curry, Malcolm, Riddle, & Schachte, 1977; Foreyt, Goodrich, & Gatto, 1981; Foreyt et al., 1982; Jeffery, Wing, & Stunkard, 1978; Stunkard, 1978, 1980; Stunkard & McClaren-Hume, 1959; Stunkard & Penick, 1979). Dietary intervention alone results in weight loss of approximately 1 pound per week. When behavior modification is used in combination with diet, weight loss is improved to about 1-1/2 pounds per week. The data become somewhat confusing when exercise is used as the third mode of intervention. Studies show varied weight loss, ranging from an average of 1 to 2 pounds per week. Going by this data, one could question the benefits of exercise, which may, in fact, reduce weight loss, compared to diet and behavior change alone.

The variability in weight loss, however, can be explained adequately when lean body weight, fat weight, and total body weight are considered. Initial status of conditioning and mode of exercise intervention are also important considerations of body composition change with exercise. Exercise increases lean body weight while decreasing body fat. Total scale weight changes reflect the proportion of lean body mass gain to fat loss. Lean tissue weighs more than fat tissue, so it is possible to gain scale weight while losing substantial fat weight, especially for previously sedentary subjects using resistance exercises. Changes in body composition also help explain weight loss plateaus often observed in persons using exercise as a mode of intervention.

Follow-up studies are more discouraging than those showing weight loss during treatment. Foreyt et al. (1981) have indicated that follow-up results are as varied as the weight loss during the treatment phase. Results are contaminated by uncontrolled variables including self-reporting, drop-out rates of 10-90 percent, and intermediary modes of intervention.

Keys to Success

Literature reviews are helpful in gaining insight into the complexity of the problems associated with intervention and management of the overweight person. Additionally, successful approaches can be isolated and implemented within a community program. Personnel, patient selection, realistic goals, and support are components of effective community programs.

- *Personnel.* Personnel must be competent and effective in the various modes of intervention. An otherwise well-conceived program can easily fail under the direction of incompetent leaders. Personnel should be empathetic, knowledgeable, experienced, effective, and interested in working within a community organization.
- *Patient selection.* Patient selection is important to enhance adherence and subsequent success. Most participants in community weight loss programs have tried several other diets or dietary programs and failed. For the most part, participants can screen themselves when given appropriate guidelines for time required, type of program to be used, and the priority that should be given the effort.

  Weight reduction imposes time and behavior change commitments, which frequently create a stressful environment. If there are other major stresses in the person's life, such as marital problems, recent divorce, recent death in the family, or other committed responsibilities, it is likely not a good time to take on the additional stress of weight reduction. Success is improved when the participant determines the best time for weight loss, rather than being coerced by a physician, spouse, or friend.

  A wide variety of approaches to weight reduction is offered within the community setting. Specific information about diet, exercise, and behavior change must be explained; participants' expectations should be thoroughly reviewed. Diets may be rigid, restrictive, or liberal in food choices. Exercise programs may require time commitments and modes of activity that forecast poor adherence. Behavior modification programs also vary, with emphasis placed on techniques that may not fit the personalities of all individuals. Participants must evaluate the specific content and procedures of a community program and determine if it is the right program for them.

  Finally, the participants must commit themselves to weight loss; it must be the number one priority for them. Too often programs include people who have high hopes that at last they have found the answer to ending obesity. It is not uncommon to have members of a community program who openly express that they have tried other options, so they may as well try this. If weight loss is not a high priority in their lives, overweight persons frequently fail.
- *Realistic goals.* Many dieters have exaggerated expectations concerning realistic goals in weight loss. When weight loss goals are not realistic, there is diminished motivation and adherence, and failure is eminent. Goals should be based on the history of obesity, including its onset, family trends, and social interaction. It is important that

the group leader as well as the participant realize that psychological and physiological interactions may impose resistance to treatment. Krotkiewski et al. (1977), for instance, have shown that hypercellularity forms of obesity are more difficult to treat than hypertrophy forms. The determination of attainable goals should be based on scientific evaluation, rather than use of height-weight tables or self-imposed expectations. Use of skinfold measurements or more sophisticated measures of body fatness increases the ability to determine more realistic goals. Realistic goals, however, may be interpreted differently by the group leader who has had experience in these procedures than by participants who think they know themselves well enough to predict success on self-motivation alone. It is important that realistic and attainable goals be thoroughly discussed with participants through consultation and counseling sessions. The importance of consultation is expressed by Bandura (1977), who reported that personal expectations are powerful indicators of success. Discussions should include intermediary and final weight goals, maintenance, and long-term outcomes.

- *Support.* When weight loss is a high priority in a person's life, he or she must openly express this to all concerned and elicit support in adhering to all aspects of intervention. This does not imply that other people have to sacrifice their eating or social patterns, but that they should support the person's weight loss by encouraging adherence. Support should be expected from the spouse, family members, and significant others, including close friends and fellow employees.

The Multidisciplinary Approach

The literature strongly suggests that multifaceted weight loss programs are most successful. Although program leaders tend to favor one mode of intervention over others, it is important to develop a balance of emphasis and instill the importance of all aspects of the program in the participants. It is not a matter of choosing between exercise, diet, and behavior modification, but that these three modes in conjunction with one another offer the greatest benefits. Regardless of the modes of intervention, 80% adherence to a community program results in substantial weight loss for many and allows for the frailties of human nature.

Benefits From Exercise

The role of exercise in weight control has been reviewed by Thompson, Jarvie, and Lahey (1983), who provided treatment guidelines based on these data. It is interesting to note that in a review of behavioral approaches, however, Jeffery and Wing (Jeffery et al., 1978) found that only 6% of weight control studies examined used exercise as a mode of intervention. Behavior modification techniques have been applied primarily to dietary habits, with little application to exercise.

Exercise has been shown to improve the rate of weight loss when it is included as a mode of intervention. Additionally, Stalonas, Johnson and Christ (1978) have shown that results of 1-year follow-up of subjects were improved when exercise was used as a mode of treatment. Moderate exercise has also been shown to reduce calorie intake by reducing appetite (Epstein, Wing, & Thompson, 1978; Thompson et al., 1983). An important principle of exercise is that it counteracts that metabolic decrease associated with caloric restriction (Brownell & Stunkard, 1980). Apfelbaum (1978), Bray, (1969), and Buskirk et al. (1963) have shown 15-30% decreases in metabolic rate accountable to caloric restriction. Bray has indicated a 20% decrease in metabolic rate within 2 weeks that begins 24-48 hours after caloric restriction. Reductions in metabolic rates are often the cause of weight plateaus and can effectively be offset by an appropriate exercise program.

Exercise also reduces stress associated with excessive eating as well as stress related to the trials and tribulations encountered in a weight loss program. When behavior modification techniques are applied to exercise, it becomes apparent that exercise is a good alternative activity to eating.

It is important to prescribe exercise programs appropriate to the population encountered. Overweight and obese persons should use walking as the primary mode of exercise, in order to reduce the occurrence of injury and for overall adherence to the exercise program. Other activities that partially or completely support the body can be used effectively and include cycling, swimming, and cross-country skiing. Intensity and duration of work prescribed must be based on conditioning level and extent of overweight. Bjorntorp (1978) has found increased drop-out rates as degree of obesity increases. Because most obese people are generally sedentary, it is important to phase in the duration of exercise, in order to reduce occurrence of injury and to motivate persons for better adherence.

Components of a Diet

Any diet of reduced calories results in weight loss, if followed over a period of time. The following components often allow greater adherence and provide for long-term weight loss:

- Is nutritionally sound
- Is low in calories
- Is adaptable to individual taste and habits

- Is easy to follow away from home
- Has potential for long-term adherence
- Includes principles of behavior change
- Results in fat loss
- Causes minimal loss of lean tissue, water, and electrolytes

Diets must be nutritionally sound, as determined by criteria exemplified in the Basic Four Food Groups (Daily Food Plan), U.S. Dietary Goals, and Dietary Exchange List (American Diabetic/Diatetic Association). Diets of less than 1,000 calories are difficult to adhere to for long periods of time and jeopardize nutritional content. Community programs should include a minimum of 1,000 calories; 1,200 calorie diets are most likely to show success. Food choices within dietary programs must be varied enough to adapt to individual tastes and habits. Potential for long-term adherence is increased when dietary guidelines are developed for those who eat away from home.

Principles of behavior change must be directed toward the specific dietary regimen given. Techniques for meeting the principles must be varied, so that everyone has the opportunity to meet all the principles related to dietary intervention.

Beyond Diet and Exercise

Principles of behavior modification should be applied to exercise as well as dietary modes of intervention. Techniques typically including awareness and cue elimination should be employed with individualized prescriptions emphasizing self-image, substitute activities, support, health concerns, meals away from home, grocery shopping, the salad bar, and special occasions. Participants must be able to apply principles of behavior change to situations encountered in everyday life. Guidelines for eating away from home are often used without application to principles of behavior change. Use of salad bars and diet plates for weight-conscious people has been highly advertised in recent months, yet caloric intake varies considerably when food choices do not follow behavior guidelines.

Successful Components of Community Weight Loss Programs

Realistic goals developed by the program leader and acceptable to the participant must be based on past history and extent of fitness. Initial weight loss is important for motivation (Silverstone & Solomon, 1965; Stuart, Jensen, & Guire, 1979) and has been shown by Jeffery et al. (1978) to correlate highly with weight loss during the final weeks of treatment.

When programs are individualized, adherence and long-term results are better. The duration of the total intervention program (i.e., a lengthy program) and frequency of meetings have been shown to be instrumental in determining success (Jeffery et al., 1978; Brownell & Stunkard, 1980). Eliciting support from significant others has also been shown to improve weight loss during treatment and as measured at follow-up.

Inactivity and inappropriate eating habits are the two overwhelming contributors to increased weight. Because these lifestyles have been practiced for long periods of time, it is difficult to make abrupt and consistent changes. It is important to phase in the dietary and exercise programs to increase adherence and subsequent success. Exercise can be phased in by 20 minutes of walking per day initially, increased by 20 minutes each day after 2 weeks, and again at 4 weeks. Diets can be phased in by using a strict diet for the first 2 weeks, followed by limited choices for 2 weeks. The final phase of the dietary program can allow for complete choice of food, within the principles initially outlined.

The involvement of a ''cheating'' aspect of dieting can increase adherence and long term success. Cheating implies that the individual can eat a predetermined amount of any food (for example, 300 calories) of their choice, or it may involve a specific day of ''pigging out.'' The cheating aspect allows participants to enjoy food they may have been restricted from and prevents long-term binging.

References

American College of Sports Medicine. (1983). *Position statement: Proper and improper weight programs* (Vol. 15, pp. ix-xiii).

Apfelbaum, M. (1978). Adaptation to changes in caloric intake. *Progress in Food and Nutrition Science, 2*, 543-559.

Apfelbaum, M., Bostsarron, J., & Lacatis, D. (1971). Effects of caloric restriction and excessive caloric intake on energy expenditure. *American Journal of Clinical Nutrition, 24*, 1405-1409.

Bjorntorp, P. (1978). Physical training in the treatment of obesity. *International Journal Obesity, 2*, 149-156.

Brandura, A. (1977). *Social learning theory.* Englewood Cliffs, NJ: Prentice Hall.

Bray, G.A. (1969). Effects of caloric restriction on energy expenditure in obese patients. *Lancet, 2*, 397-398.

Bray, G.A., & Atkinson, R.L. (1978). Factors affecting basal metabolic rate. *Progress in Food and Nutrition Science, 2*, 395-403.

Brownell, K.D., & Stunkard, A.J. (1980). Physical activity in the development and control of obesity. In A.J. Stunkard (Ed.), *Obesity.* Philadelphia: W.B. Saunders.

Buskirk, E.R., Thompson, R.H., Lutwak, L., & Whedon, G.D. (1963). Energy balance of obese patients during weight reduction: Influence of diet restriction and exercise. *Annals of the New York Academy of Science*, **110**, 918-940.

Coates, T.J., & Thoreson, C.E. (1979). Using generalization theory in behavioral observation. *Behavior Therapy*, **9**, 605-613.

Currey, H., Malcolm, R. Riddle, E. & Schachte, M. (1977). Behavioral treatment of obesity: Limitations and results with the chronically obese. *Journal of the American Medical Association*, **237**, 2829-2831.

Durnin, J.V., & Brockway, J.M. (1956). Determination of the total daily energy expenditure in man by direct calorimetry: Assessment of the accuracy of a modern technique. *British Journal of Nutrition*, **14**, 41-53.

Epstein, L.H., Wing, R.R., & Thompson, J.K. (1978). The relationship between exercise intensity, caloric intake, and weight. *Addictive Behavior*, **3**, 185-190.

Foreyt, J. P., Goodrick, G.K., & Gotto, A.M. (1981). Limitations of behavioral treatment of obesity: Review and analysis. *Journal of Behavioral Medicine*, **4**, 159-173.

Foreyt, J.P., Mitchell, R.E., Garner, D.T., Gee, M., Scott, L.W., & Gotto, A.M. (1982). Behavioral treatment of obesity: Results and limitations. *Behavioral Therapy*, **13**, 153-161.

Gwimup G. (1975). Effects of exercise alone on the weight of obese women. *Archives Internal Medicine*, **135**, 676-680.

Jeffery, R.W., Wing, R.R., & Stunkard, A.J. (1978). Behavioral treatment of obesity: The state of the art. *Behavioral Therapy*, **9**, 189-199.

Krotkiewski, M., Sjostrom, L., Bjorntorp, P., Carlgren, G., Garellick, G., & Smith, V. (1977). Adipose tissue cellularity in relation to prognosis for weight reduction. *International Journal of Obesity*, **1**, 395-416.

Schachter, A. (1982, August). Don't sell habit breakers short. *Psychology Today*, pp. 27-33.

Silverstone, J.J., & Solomon, T. (1965). The long-term management of obesity in general practice. *British Journal of Clinical Practice*, **19**, 395-399.

Sjostrom, L. (1980). Fat cells and body weight. In A.J. Stunkard (Ed.), *Obesity*. Philadelphia: W.B. Saunders.

Stalonas, P.M., Johnson, W.G., & Christ, M. (1978). Behavior modification for obesity: The evaluation of exercise, contingency management and program adherence. *Journal of Consulting Clinical Psychology*, **46**, 463-469.

Stuart, B.S., Jensen, J.A., & Guire, K. (1979). Weight loss over time. *Journal of the American Dietetic Association*, **75**, 258-261.

Stuart, R.B. (1967). Behavioral control of overeating. *Behavioral Research and Therapy*, **5**, 357-365.

Stuart, R.B., & Guire, K. (1978). Some correlates of the maintenance of weight loss through behavior modification. *International Journal of Obesity, 2,* 225-235.

Stuart, R.B., & Mitchell, C. (1980). Self-help group in the control of body weight. In A.J.Stunkard (Ed.), *Obesity.* Philadelphia: W.B. Saunders.

Stunkard, A.J., & McLaren-Hume, M. (1959). The results of treatment of obesity. *Archives of Internal Medicine,* 79-85.

Stunkard, A.J. (1978). Behavioral treatment of obesity: The current status. *International Journal of Obesity, 2,* 237-248.

Stunkard, A.J., & Penick, S.B. (1979). Behavior modification in the treatment of obesity: The problem of maintaining weight loss. *Archives of General Psychology, 36,* 801-806.

Stunkard, A.J. (Ed.). (1980). *Obesity.* Philadelphia: W.B. Saunders.

Thompson, J.K., Jarvie, G.J., & Lahey, B.B. (1983). Exercise and obesity: Etiology, physiology, and intervention. *Psychology Bulletin, 91,* 55-79.

Wollersheim, J.P. (1977). Follow-up of behavioral group therapy for obesity. *Behavioral Therapy, 8,* 996-998.

Chapter 20

Community-Based Programs for the Treatment of Obesity

John P. Foreyt
G. Ken Goodrick

The great prevalence of obesity in the United States is due to a combination of sedentary lifestyles and high-fat diets. Both these factors are due in large part to the industrialization of America. A century ago, when most Americans were still farming, the average farmer expended about 1,000 calories per day in physical activity, the equivalent of about 10 miles of jogging. Farmers' wives also had a great deal of physical labor in their chores. Processed foods were rare, and the family spent a much higher percentage of their money on food than is the case today. The prevalence of obesity was about 5%.

Now we are an urban people. A great number of us sit at desks in businesses and corporations. High-fat foods are abundantly available and inexpensive. The 8-hour work days and slow freeway commutes make scheduling significant exercise difficult. Housewives have electric homes. The prevalence of obesity is now about 40%. Thus, changes in social and environmental conditions brought about by industrialization are partially responsible for the dramatic increase in the prevalence of obesity.

Traditional approaches to the treatment of obesity have been disappointing. Clinic- and hospital-based programs, both for individuals and groups, have yielded modest results at best. Because of the limited success of these treatment programs, there has been an exciting movement recently to explore new approaches based in the community to treat obesity. This chapter examines examples of these community-based programs for the treatment of obesity. Intervention conducted at worksites and in schools, through self-help groups, and by large-scale community-wide programs is reviewed.

Worksite Programs

The movement toward corporate involvement in enhancing the health of employees has the potential to reverse the trend toward a fatter America, by creating within the worksite environmental and social conditions conducive to lowerfat eating and to adoption of aerobic exercise habits. Corporations are becoming increasingly interested in helping employees manage their health, not only because of humanitarian goals but also because healthier workers tend to be more productive and less costly (Parkinson & Associates, 1982). Though there are no data showing that obese employees are less productive and use up a disproportionate share of the health care dollar, it is known that the obese generally lead a more sedentary lifestyle, as evidenced by their low level of cardiorespiratory fitness (Rogers, Mahoney, Mahoney, Straw, & Kenigsberg, 1980). Other studies show that the adoption of regular aerobic exercise habits by formerly sedentary employees can reduce absenteeism (Bowne, Russell, Morgan, Optenberg, & Clarke, 1984; Shephard, Cox, & Corey, 1981) and reduce health-care costs (Bowne et al., 1984). Thus, it could be expected that programs that are successful in motivating the obese to lose weight through exercise would be cost-effective. There have been two approaches to worksite weight management programs. One involves the translation of the clinical behavior modification model to the worksite. The other involves making changes in the social and/or environmental conditions at the worksite to motivate all employees to change dietary and exercise habits.

Behavior Modification Groups

There is a vast literature on training groups of obese patients to use behavioral self-management techniques (Wilson & Brownell, 1980). The techniques include keeping food diaries, controlling environmental cues related to eating, setting up a reward system for good behavior, relaxation, and social support. Therapy groups of 10-15 patients meet weekly for 10-20 weeks. Results of such treatment after 1 year show an average weight loss of 10-15 pounds, with a large variability in individual outcomes. It is apparent that the majority of patients do not continue to adhere to the self-treatment recommendations.

There have been only a few controlled studies using behavioral groups at the worksite. Stunkard and Brownell (1980) reported using such groups with 40 obese volunteers. Some comparison groups met at a medical clinic, some at the worksite. Lay therapists (co-workers) were compared to an experienced psychologist for effectiveness. Results showed that attrition was 80% for groups led by the psychologist and 40% for groups led by lay therapists. Lay therapists did slightly better than the psychologist because, perhaps, the workers could identify better with co-workers. Average weight loss was 2.6 pounds at 6-month follow-up.

In a similar study, Brownell, Stunkard, and McKeon (1985) treated 172 garment workers at a worksite. Treatment consisted of 16 weekly group meetings. Forty-two percent of patients dropped out prematurely. The average weight loss was over 6 pounds at 6-month follow-up. It was estimated that $6.36 was spent for each pound lost.

Abrams and Follick (1983) had 133 nurses meet at their worksite for 10 weekly groups. Half the nurses dropped out of treatment prematurely, and only 18% could be evaluated at 6-month follow-up. Thus, high attrition rates appear to be the rule when behavioral weight management groups are done at the worksite.

Drop-out and failure are negative experiences for program therapists and for participants. Why are attrition rates so high, compared to the same treatment in a clinical setting? Several differences in treatment conditions may account for this. For a clinical population, the cost and inconvenience of receiving treatment screen out less motivated individuals. At the worksite, convenience, free treatment, peer pressure from co-workers, and possible perceived corporate pressure may ensure a large attendance of participants who otherwise lack the long-term commitment of clinical patients. Brownell et al. (1985) have suggested that employees might be screened to obtain only those motivated and ready for treatment. Requiring the completion of food diaries and/or the payment of a fee or deposit might help.

Another possible reason for drop-out is either not enough or too much weight loss in the first few weeks of the program. A slow rate of weight loss may not motivate continued participation. A high rate of weight loss may trigger physiological mechanisms that make adherence to diet difficult and relapse likely (Foreyt & Goodrick, 1984). Because employees are at the worksite on weekdays, excessive rate of weight loss could be measured easily and controlled through contingency management strategies.

Environmental and Social Control

An employer can do much to make the worksite conducive to lower fat eating habits and increased exercise. Although there are no data from controlled studies, anecdotal evidence suggests that there is a strong interest among employees in having more healthful, lower calorie foods available, while reducing the availability of high-calorie foods. This has been done by changing the menu of vending machines and company cafeterias. We are now working with a major energy company to help the cafeteria food service develop lower calorie lunch specials that will create adequate employee demand. Nutrition education posters at the worksite reinforce the campaign.

Worksite exercise programs specifically tailored for obese participants should be included. Intensity of individual exercise should be carefully regulated, so that the participant perceives activity as a positive experience (Foreyt & Goodrick, 1984). If such environmental changes in food availability and exercise are made, eventually the prevalence of obesity among the workforce should decline.

Obese persons continually feel stigmatized by normal-weight society (Foreyt & Goodrick, 1982). This usually pressures them to take weight management action periodically. Obviously, this perceived pressure is not effective in ridding most of them of their obesity. Such pressure is experienced as a negative prejudice. A recent, innovative study may have found a way to exert social pressure in a more positive and enjoyable way, utilizing the worksite. Brownell, Cohen, Stunkard, Felix, and Cooley (1984) set up weight control teams in three competing banks as well as teams within one corporation. Employees joined teams by paying a $5.00 membership fee. The money was pooled and given to the winning team. Each member got a self-help treatment manual outlining behavioral self-management methods. Team members were weighed weekly, and team progress was posted prominently.

The spirit of competition this engendered was akin to that found in leisure sports. Employees enjoyed the "game"; morale was boosted. Most significantly, though, attrition from team membership was only 0.5%. Furthermore, the average weight loss at 6 months was over 10 pounds; cost per pound lost was about $2.25. This is the most successful and cost-effective outcome yet achieved.

The potential of similar competitive motivational schemes and other inventive programs needs to be explored. Rate of weight loss should be controlled to no more than 1 pound per week, in order to avoid crash dieting and attrition.

Other Areas for Research at the Worksite

In the Brownell et al. (1984) competitive study, each participant received a self-help treatment manual, given in weekly installments at weigh-in. Thus, self-help materials seem to be as effective as treatment groups under the competitive incentive conditions. Jeffery, Danaher, Killen, Farquhar, and Kinnier (1982) found self-help manuals used in a mail correspondence course to be as effective as groups in terms of end-of-treatment results. Thus, the use of self-help manuals together with incentives may be a practical mode of treatment delivery. One possibility would be to reward weight loss and associated cardiovascular fitness increases according to projected health-care cost savings, so that the incentive programs would theoretically pay for themselves. However, at the current state of the art, the average result in terms of weight loss is not associated with a significant decrease in risk for cardiovascular or other diseases.

In evaluating worksite weight-management programs (Foreyt, Scott, & Gotto, 1980), employees and researchers need to assess cost-effectiveness in terms of costs of personnel used, testing, and time off from work, as well as such benefits as reduced risk, reduced absenteeisms, and improved morale. Attrition may continue to be a problem unless motivation is high due to social pressure or use of rewards. Data on all participants need to be kept on a regular basis, because most regain within 1 year following program implementation. The worksite provides an ideal setting for long-term monitoring, because employees continue to be accessible. Appropriate data to keep include estimated percentage of body fat and cardiorespiratory fitness, which have a more direct relationship to health status than weight. Continued monitoring and retreatment may be possible ways to prevent relapses.

School Programs

Obesity is also a serious problem among the young. There are data suggesting that about 25% of American children are overweight (Forbes, 1975). Eighty percent of obese children grow up to be obese adults (Abraham & Nordsieck, 1960). The odds against obese children losing weight as adults, if they have not done so by the end of adolescence, are about 28 to 1 (Stunkard & Burt, 1967).

Treating obesity in the schools is a logical approach to this problem. Children spend a large part of their lives there, and both changes in eating and physical activity can be taught and monitored.

To date, although the potential is enormous, few studies of the treatment of obesity in the schools have been done. Seltzer and Mayer (1970) reported small, but significant, changes in weight for youngsters who took part in a 5-month treatment program of diet and exercise. Botvin, Cantlon, Carter, and Williams (1979), in a controlled study, found that students who took part in a 10-week diet, exercise, and behavior modification program lost significantly more weight than a matched control group from another school. Other researchers have reported similar results (Collip, 1975, 1980; Lansky & Brownell, 1982; Lansky & Vance, 1983).

Brownell and Kaye (1982) treated 63 obese children, ages 5-12, with a school-based program of nutrition education, physical activity, and behavior modification. Their 10-week program consisted of educating the children and parents, teachers, the physical education instructor, food service personnel, school administrators, and the nurse's aide. Ninety-five percent of the children in the treatment program lost weight, compared to only 21% of an obese control group that did not receive the program. The experimental children had a 15.4% decrease in their percentage of overweight and lost an average of 9.7 pounds.

Foster, Wadden, and Brownell (1985) reported results of a program conducted in grades 2 through 5 of a Catholic school in Philadelphia. The treatment was particularly innovative, for the program was conducted primarily by older children trained as peer counselors. The treatment program included training in physical activity, nutrition, and behavior modification; a special exercise class; lunch box checks to monitor food selection; and rewards for both weight loss and food selection. Results indicated that the obese children lost weight and decreased their degree of obesity during the program, compared with obese children in a control school, who gained weight. Children in the experimental group also showed significant improvement in food selection and had significantly greater improvements in self-concept. The changes in weight, food selection, and self-concept were only partially maintained by the time of an 18-week follow-up. The authors concluded that their peer-based treatment program is a feasible one, but different approaches are probably necessary for long-term maintenance of the changes.

Overall, the studies conducted in the schools to date have been modestly encouraging. The use of normal-weight peer counselors, as reported by Foster, Wadden, and Brownell (1985), appear particularly promising. The use of buddy systems and peer support have been reported in other areas, with positive results, and should be applicable to obese children. Training teachers and parents in behavioral strategies also appears logical. Unfortunately, far too few studies have been conducted in schools to date to conclude that these approaches are of benefit to obese children over the long term. However, the school is potentially such a strong source of support that its use in the treatment of obesity appears as one of the most promising trends in the field.

Self-Help Groups and Community-Wide Programs

Self-Help Groups

Self-help groups had their beginning in nineteenth-century England (Stuart, 1977). One of the first and best known of the American programs is Alcoholics Anonymous, and some current self-help programs are patterned after it. One of the more popular self-help groups for obesity is TOPS (Take Off Pounds Sensibly), an organization founded in 1984, with over 300,000 members in 12,000 chapters (Stuart, 1977). Although self-help is potentially an important treatment approach, Levitz and Stunkard (1974) have reported on the high attrition rate of TOPS groups, a finding that appears universal among self-help organizations for weight reduction. Weight Watchers, founded in 1963, has more than a half million members throughout the world (Stuart, 1977). Although the program is undoubtedly helpful for many individuals, attrition is also a serious problem here. Volkmar, Stunkard, Woolston, and Bailey (1981) reported that by week 12, 70% of the members of the club they studied had dropped out.

Self-help groups are a major movement in our country. They have an enormous potential to help persons change behavior. However, strategies to assist self-help groups with behavioral change and reduction in attrition are needed if their potential is to be realized.

Community-Wide Programs

Several large-scale community programs have attempted to change health-related behaviors (Stunkard, 1980). Two of the best known ones are the Stanford Three Community Study and The North Karelia Project. The Stanford Three Community Study (Farquhar, Stern, Maccoby, & Russell, 1976; Farquhar et al., 1977) tried to reduce cardiovascular risk factors of the citizens of two small towns in California. Its primary intervention consisted of an intensive media campaign involving television, radio, and newspapers. Results were encouraging, with a reported decreased risk of coronary disease of 17% by the end of the 2-year study. The researchers are now conducting an even larger five-city study in an attempt to replicate and extend their findings.

The North Karelia Project (Puska et al., 1978) was another large-scale community program that attempted to reduce cardiovascular risk factors. This Finnish study had as its aims the reduction of smoking, of elevated serum cholesterol, and of high blood pressure. Because Finland has the highest rate of coronary heart disease in the world, attempts to reduce cardiovascular risks are particularly important there. Many efforts were made at the community level over the five-year study. Community campaigns were held to educate the citizens, relying on the media, similar to Stanford's approach. The involvement and cooperation of such groups as the dairy industry and sausage companies were attempted, and changes in milk, butterfat, and high-fat meats were made.

Preliminary results indicated that the prevalence of myocardial infarction decreased by 21% and strokes by 31%. There was a 20% decline in all cardiovascular disease over the length of the study. Results clearly suggested that community-wide programs like this one could reduce unhealthy behaviors. Although obesity was not addressed directly in either this project or the Stanford Three Community Study, as dietary behaviors improve, obesity should also be reduced.

Conclusion

Community-based programs for the treatment of many disorders are increasing in number. These programs are particularly relevant to the control and treatment of obesity because the development of obesity is in large part a result of how we choose to live. The implementation and evaluation of community-based programs are complex tasks requiring ingenuity and cooperation from many disciplines at many levels. The examples cited in this chapter give reason for optimism. It is hoped that these innovative approaches to the treatment of obesity are just the beginning of more controlled investigations. The future of research in this area is especially promising.

Acknowledgment

The writing of this chapter was supported by USPH 5 RO1 AM30921-02/02.

References

Abraham, S., & Nordsieck, M. (1960). Relationship of excess weight in children and adults. *Public Health Reports, 75,* 263-273.

Abrams, D.B., & Follick, M.J. (1983). Behavioral weight loss intervention at the work site: Feasibility and maintenance. *Journal of Consulting and Clinical Psychology, 51,* 223-226.

Botvin, G.J., Cantlon, A., Carter, B.J., & Williams, C.L. (1979). Reducing adolescent obesity through a school health program. *Journal of Pediatrics, 95,* 1060-1062.

Bowne, D.W., Russell, M.L., Morgan, J.L., Optenberg, S.A., & Clarke, A.E. (1984). Reduced disability and health care costs in an industrial fitness program. *Journal of Occupational Medicine, 26,* 807-816.

Brownell, K.D., Cohen, R.Y., Stunkard, A.J., Felix, M.R.J., & Cooley, N.B. (1984). Weight loss competitions at the work site: Effects on weight, morale, and cost-effectiveness. *American Journal of Public Health, 74,* 1283-1285.

Brownell, K.D., & Kaye, F.S. (1982). A school-based behavior modification, nutrition education and physical activity program for obese children. *American Journal of Clinical Nutrition, 35,* 277-283.

Brownell, K.D., Stunkard, A.J., & McKeon, P.E. (1985). Weight reduction of the work site: A promise partially fulfilled. *American Journal of Psychiatry*, **141**, 47-51.

Collip, P.J. (1975). An obesity program in public schools. *Pediatric Annals*, **4**, 276-282.

Collip, P.J. (Ed.). (1980). *Childhood obesity* (2nd ed.). Littleton, MA: PSG Publishing.

Farquhar, J.W., Maccoby, N.M., Wood, P.D., et al. (1977). Community education for cardiovascular health. *Lancet*, **1**, 1192-1195.

Forbes, G.B. (1975). Prevalence of obesity in childhood. In G.A. Bray (Ed.), *Obesity in perspective* (DHEW Publication No. [NIH] 75-708). Washington, DC: U.S. Government Printing Office.

Foreyt, J.P., & Goodrick, G.K. (1982). Gender and obesity. In I.A-Issa (Ed.), *Gender and psychopathology* (pp. 337-355). New York: Academic Press.

Foreyt, J.P., & Goodrick, G.K. (1984). Health maintenance: Exercise and nutrition. In E.A. Blechman (Ed.), *Behavior modification with women* (pp. 221-244). New York: Guilford Press.

Foreyt, J.P., Scott, L.W., & Gotto, A.M. (1980). Weight control and nutrition education programs in occupational settings. *Public Health Reports*, **95**, 127-136.

Foster, G.D., Wadden, T.A., & Brownell, K.D. (1985). Peer-led program for the treatment and prevention of obesity in the schools. *Journal of Consulting and Clinical Psychology*, **53**, 538-540.

Jeffery, R.W., Danaher, B.G., Killen, J., Farquhar, J.W., & Kinnier, R. (1982). Self-administered programs for health behavior change: Smoking cessation and weight reduction by mail. *Addictive Behaviors*, **7**, 57-63.

Lansky, D., & Brownell, K.D. (1982). Comparison of school-based treatments for adolescent obesity. *Journal of School Health*, **52**, 384-387.

Lansky, D., & Vance, M.A. (1983). School-based intervention for adolescent obesity: Analysis of treatment, randomly selected control, and self-selected control subjects. *Journal of Consulting and Clinical Psychology*, **51**, 147-148.

Levitz, L., & Stunkard, A.J. (1974). A therapeutic coalition for obesity: Behavior modification and patient self-help. *American Journal of Psychiatry*, **131**, 423-427.

Parkinson, R.S., & Associates (Eds.) (1982). *Managing health promotion in the workplace: Guidelines for implementation and evaluation*. Palo Alto, CA: Mayfield.

Puska, P., Virtamo, J., Tuomilehto, J., et al. (1978). Cardiovascular risk factor changes in a three-year follow-up of a cohort in connection with a community programme (the North Karelia Project). *Acta Medica Scandanavica*, **204**, 381-388.

Rogers, T., Mahoney, M.J., Mahoney, B.K., Straw, M.K., & Kenigsberg, M.J. (1980). Clinical assessment of obesity: An empirical evaluation of diverse techniques. *Behavioral Assessment*, **2**, 161-181.

Seltzer, C.C., & Mayer, J. (1970). An effective weight control program in a public school system. *American Journal of Public Health*, **60**, 679-689.

Shephard, R.J., Cox, M., & Corey, P. (1981). Fitness program participation: Its effect on worker performance. *Journal of Occupational Medicine*, **23**, 359-363.

Stern, M.P., Farquhar, J.W., Maccoby, N., & Russell, S.H. (1976). Results of a two-year health education campaign on dietary behavior. *Circulation*, **54**, 826-833.

Stuart, R.B. (1977). Self-help group approach to self-management. In R.B. Stuart (Ed.), *Behavioral self-management: Strategies, techniques and outcome* (pp. 278-305). New York: Brunner/Mazel.

Stunkard, A.J. (1980). The social environment and the control of obesity. In A.J. Stunkard (Ed.), *Obesity* (pp. 438-462). Philadelphia: W.B. Saunders.

Stunkard, A.J., & Brownell, K.D. (1980). Work site treatment for obesity. *American Journal of Psychiatry*, **137**, 252-253.

Stunkard, A.J., & Burt, V. (1967). Obesity and the body image: II. Age at onset of disturbances in the body image. *American Journal Psychiatry*, **123**, 1443-1447.

Volkmar, F.R., Stunkard, A.J., Woolston, J., & Bailey, R.A. (1981). High attrition rates in commercial weight reduction programs. *Archives International Medicine*, **141**, 426-428.

Wilson, G.T., & Brownell, K.D. (1980). Behavior therapy for obesity: An evaluation of treatment outcome. *Advances in Behaviour Research and Therapy*, **3**, 49-86.

Chapter 21

Nutrition Counseling Skills

Ann C. Grandjean

Nutrition counseling brings together a counselor and a client, with their individual backgrounds of experiences, beliefs, and biases. The client enters counseling with a history of success or failure, domination or submission, acceptance or rejection, and with a positive or negative self-image. The client may enter the relationship with a hostile attitude toward the counselor or may see the counselor as an advocate. The counselor enters the relationship with a history of successes or failures, negative or positive experiences in counseling, and possibly preformed expectations regarding the client. These experiences, beliefs, and biases carried into the counseling setting influence the outcome.

The success rate in weight reduction attempts is disheartening. If the criteria for success or "cure" of obesity is reduction to ideal weight and maintenance of that ideal weight for 5 years, a person is more likely to recover from almost any form of cancer than from obesity (Bray, 1976; Brownell, 1982). Stunkard, a leading researcher and practitioner in the area of obesity, said, "Most obese persons will not enter treatment for obesity. Of those who enter treatment, most will not lose weight, and of those who lose weight, most will regain it" (Stunkard, 1958).

Indeed, the success rate for the treatment of obesity is poor. Why is the success rate so low? Is obesity such a difficult problem? Is it a disease or disorder that is resistant to treatment? Is its etiology multivariant, whereas its treatment is monodimensional? Does part of the problem lie in the counseling?

Etiology and Treatment

The field of obesity is long on diagnosis and research into etiology but short on effective treatments. Numerous etiologies of obesity have been proposed:

- Inability to monitor internal satiety signals (Drewnowski, 1983)
- Brown fat (Sullivan, Nauss-Karol, & Cheng, 1983)

- Fat cell number/size (Hirsch & Knittle, 1970)
- Heredity (Mayer, 1980)
- Environment (Mayer, 1980)
- Metabolism (Keys, Brovek, Henschel, & Mickelson, 1950)
- Set point (Keesey, 1980)

To address these causes, various treatments have been developed or utilized, including diet, exercise, chemicals, surgery, behavior therapy, and cognitive restructuring. Although numerous treatment modalities are available, this author believes that insufficient attention has been given to matching the client with the treatment(s) and the client with the counselor. Some clients respond better to a very structured approach, whereas others need more flexibility. The same is true of counselors. It also appears that some clients respond best when the counselor assumes an authoritarian position, as opposed to the role of a facilitator. Selling and Ferraro (1945) have made the following suggestions for diet and nutrition counseling:

1. Know the client's personality
2. Know the client's psychological surroundings
3. Eliminate emotional tension
4. Assist the client in knowing his or her own limitations
5. Arrange the diet so that it has the effect of encouraging the client
6. Allow for occasional cheating

These recommendations are valid today and set the stage for matching the client and treatment.

Successful Counseling

Nutrition counseling is both an art and a science. There are various skills the counselor needs in order to be successful (Snetselaar, 1983). Communications skills are fundamental to successful counseling. Margaret Ohlson in 1968 made recommendations for successful counseling. In a subsequent publication for dietitians, she stated that "mutual liking and respect are important for a free discussion. The dietitian must create an atmosphere within which the patient responds freely. This is only possible when she has learned to listen, as well as talk" (1973). Listening to what the client feels is as valuable as listening to what he or she says.

Verbal communication is a cornerstone in nutrition counseling. The question "What do you eat for breakfast?" may elicit a different response than the question "Tell me about a normal morning for you." Likewise, use of the words "should" and "should not" may cause a much different response or reaction than a more flexible approach.

Nonverbal communication often delivers a stronger message than verbal communication. If verbal and nonverbal communication are not synchronized, the result is a mixed message. For example, frowning while saying, "Oh, how nice" can confuse the client. Nonverbal behaviors include eye contact or lack of it, smiling, head shaking, leaning forward or away from the client, gesturing, and looks such as surprise, frowning, or dismay. The successful counselor is tuned in to nonverbal communication on the part of both the client and the counselor.

Assessment

One of the basic rules of education is to "start where the learner is." Essential for determining this starting point is assessment. Assessment provides the information necessary for proper matching of client and intervention modality. An effective counselor realizes that assessment is the foundation for everything that follows in counseling. The basis of assessment is to determine what and how much the client is eating as well as numerous factors influencing those choices (Snetselaar, 1983).

In some situations, body image may be a component of assessment. Body image is the mental picture of one's own body and how one feels about it, as well as what one thinks others see and feel about his or her body. Body image perception varies widely among obese people and can even fluctuate greatly in the same person (Bruch, 1973; Stunkard, 1976). Some previously obese patients, even after significant weight reduction, continue to "see" themselves as large (Bruch, 1973). Body image disturbances do not occur in emotionally healthy obese people, and body image disparagement in obese persons occurs most frequently among those who have been obese since childhood (Stunkard, 1976; Stunkard, 1980b). Various methods can be used to assess body image perception. However, the most common methods utilize body-distorting mirrors or an anomorphic lens apparatus that distorts a photographic image of the patient (Drewnowski, 1983).

Overweight clients may not have a genuine desire to lose weight (Snetselaar, 1983). They may be in the counseling session at the insistence of their spouse, friend, parent, or physician. On the other hand, the client may have a genuine desire to lose weight, but that desire is not shared by others close to the client. Determining these influencing factors, if they exist, is part of the assessment process. Voluntary cooperation of the client is necessary for success. Support from those close to the client is valuable.

To ensure that the counselor and client have the same goal in mind, a goal weight can be established. In determining a goal weight, the counselor and client need to consider the ideal weight as determined by the counselor, the ideal weight as determined by the client, and the client's "desired" weight. Another factor to consider may be the ideal weight as determined by the client's spouse, parents, or children. It is not uncommon to find significant differences in the perceived best weight. It is sometimes more appropriate to have the goal be "pounds of weight lost," rather than a target weight. This can be set in increments, thus establishing short-term goals.

A dieting history can provide valuable information. Knowing which methods the client has used in previous attempts at weight reduction and how the client thinks or feels about these methods can be helpful in selecting the appropriate intervention. Examples of useful information include

- weight history (weight as child, weight at age 20, etc.);
- number of times weight loss has been attempted;
- methods tried;
- number of successes, failures, regressions;
- which method(s) resulted in weight loss, weight gain, no change;
- what the client likes and dislikes about various methods; and
- why the client thinks and feels various methods worked or failed.

Dietary intake data may be helpful. The value of such data is contingent on the individual client and the accuracy of the data. Information on types and amount of foods eaten and methods of preparation can be useful in identifying potential problem areas in the diet. The same information can also be useful in designing a diet, if one is to be used.

Environmental data such as socioeconomic status, food availability, food storage and preparation facilities, and the client's ability to prepare food should be considered during the assessment phase. It is also important to assess the behavioral aspects of eating. Information concerning eating patterns, food-related thoughts, and food-related cues is often enlightening. One method of collecting such data is a food diary (see Figure 1).

Physical inactivity is associated with obesity and is an important factor in a weight reduction program (Brownell & Stunkard, 1980). Therefore, obtaining information on physical activity is important. Determining the client's current habits can be useful, but of more value is determining the client's potential for physical activity.

Treatment

Despite all the developments in the treatment of obesity, it is still true that the only way to lose body fat is by establishing a negative energy balance, and reducing caloric intake is still the primary means of producing this negative balance (Stunkard, 1980a). Numerous techniques have been developed to help clients achieve a negative caloric balance. Identifying the most appropriate method(s) for each client is one of the counselor's challenges. Several treatment modalities can be used in the

Day of week _____   Name _____

Time	Minutes spent eating	M/S	H	Body position	Activity while eating	Location of eating	Food	Quantity	How prepared	Eating with whom	Feeling while eating

M/S: Meal or snack

H: Degree of hunger (0 = none, 3 = maximum)

Body position: 1 = walking, 2 = standing, 3 = sitting, 4 = lying down

Figure 1. Food diary. *Note.* From *Learning to Eat* by J.M. Ferguson, 1975, Palo Alto, CA: Bull Publishing. Copyright 1975 by Bull Publishing. Adapted by permission.

management of obesity, including diet and exercise, surgery, psychotherapy, self-help groups, and pharmacological agents. Individualization of treatment is the key (Stunkard, 1980a).

Evaluation

Evaluation is essential to determine effectiveness. The ultimate evaluation in the treatment of obesity is weight loss. However, it may not be appropriate to use weight loss as the only indicator of change. Evaluation may include assessing changes in the client's behavior as well as the counselor's effectiveness (Snetselaar, 1983). If the objectives have not been achieved, counseling returns to the assessment stage. In weight control, evaluation necessitates long-term follow-up if true success is to be determined.

References

Bray, G.A. (1976). *The obese patient*. Philadelphia: W.B. Saunders.

Brownell, D.K. (1983). Obesity: Behavioral treatments for a serious, prevalent, and refractory disorder. In R. K. Goodstein (Ed.), *Eating and weight disorders: Advances in treatment and research* (pp. 41-71). New York: Springer.

Brownell, K.D., & Stunkard, A.J. (1980). Physical activity in the development and control of obesity. In A.J. Stunkard (Ed.), *Obesity* (pp. 300-324). Philadelphia: W.B. Saunders.

Bruch, A. (1973). *Eating disorders*. New York: Basic Books.

Drewnowski, A. (1983). Cognitive structures in obesity and dieting. In M.R.C. Greenwood (Ed.), *Obesity* (pp. 87-101). New York: Churchill Livingstone.

Ferguson, J.M. (1975). *Learning to eat*. Palo Alto, CA: Bull Publishing.

Hirsch, J., & Knittle, J. (1970). Cellularity of obese and nonobese human adipose tissue. *Federation Proceedings, 29*(4), 1516-1521.

Keesey, R.E. (1980). A set-point analysis of the regulation of body weight. In A.J. Stunkard (Ed.), *Obesity*, (pp. 144-165). Philadelphia: W.B. Saunders.

Keys, A., Brozek, J., Henschel, A., Mickelsen, O., & Taylor, H.L. (1950). *The biology of human starvation*. Minneapolis: University of Minnesota Press.

Mayer, J. (1980). Obesity. In R.S. Goodhart & M.E. Shils (Eds.), *Modern nutrition in health and disease* (6th ed., pp. 721-740). Philadelphia: Lea & Febiger.

Ohlson, M.A. (1968). Suggestions for research to strengthen learning by patients. *Journal of the American Dietetic Association, 52*, 401-404.

Ohlson, M.A. (1973). The philosophy of dietary counseling. *Journal of the American Dietetic Association, 63*, 13-14.

Selling, L.S., & Ferraro, M.A. (1945). *The psychology of diet and nutrition.* New York: Norton & Company.

Snetselaar, L.G. (1983). *Nutrition counseling skills.* Rockville, MD: Aspen.

Stunkard, A.J. (1958). The management of obesity. *New York Journal of Medicine, 58*, 79-87.

Stunkard, A.J. (1976). *The pain of obesity.* Palo Alto, CA: Bull Publishing.

Stunkard, A.J. (1980a). Introduction and overview. In A.J. Stunkard (Ed.), *Obesity* (pp. 1-24). Philadelphia: W.B. Saunders.

Stunkard, A.J. (1980b). Psychoanalysis and psychotherapy. In A.J. Stunkard (Ed.), *Obesity* (pp. 355-368). Philadelphia: W.B. Saunders.

Sullivan, A.C., Nauss-Karol, C., & Cheng, L. (1983). Pharmacological treatment, II. In M.R.C. Greenwood (Ed.), *Obesity* (pp. 139-158). New York: Churchill Livingstone.